THE
NEW
COVENANT

THE
NEW
COVENANT

THE DRAMATIC STORY BEHIND THE FAITH
ONCE FOR ALL DELIVERED TO THE SAINTS

◆BOB EMERY◆

Unless otherwise noted, all Scripture quotations in this book are taken from the New American Standard Bible, © Copyright The Lockman Foundation 1960, 1962, 1963, 1968, 1971, 1972, 1973, 1975, 1977. Used by permission.

In some instances where the NASB used the word "earth," the author substituted the word "land" which is an equally accurate translation from the Greek. For example, in Revelation 1:7, the NASB reads, "all the tribes of the earth." Here, the author preferred to have it read, "all the tribes of the land." Where the NASB originally capitalized deity pronouns such as "He" and "Him," the pronouns have been lowercased to keep the style of this book consistent.

Quotations from Josephus come from *The Complete Works of Flavius Josephus,* published by Kregel Publications, P.O. Box 2607, Grand Rapids, MI 49501. Used by permission.

Illustrations by Tim Irvin
Tirvin4@triad.rr.com
Cover Design: Sarah O'Neal
Eve Custom Artwork
se_oneal@yahoo.com

Published by:
BenchPress Publishing
P.O. Box 5846
Charlottesville, VA 22905
Website: www.BobEmeryBooks.com

ISBN: 978-0-9669747-5-1
Printed in the USA
ISBN eBook: 978-0-9669747-4-4

DEDICATION

*To all of my Jewish and Gentile brothers and sisters in Christ;
those who, from every tribe, tongue, and nation, have been
chosen and called out from this world to be the people of God,
his holy nation, the Church, the bride of Christ, and who
have become partakers, through his marvelous grace, of the
New Covenant.*

TABLE OF CONTENTS

ÎNTRODUCTION

The Messenger is the first book in the trilogy entitled *The New Covenant.* This volume covers the time period from Christ's spiritual battle in the garden of Gethsemane to his victorious ascension from the Mount of Olives at Bethany. The story takes place in Jerusalem and unfolds through a dialogue between the apostle John and Titus, a young Gentile apostle trained by Paul. Paul had just returned to Jerusalem for the last time, with Titus and some other young Christian workers, before his arrest and deportation to Rome. In this portrayal, Paul asks the Beloved Apostle to spend a day with Titus and describe to him the details of the events surrounding our Lord's trial, crucifixion, burial, resurrection, and ascension, as well as to point out some of the special features of Jerusalem, the temple, the priesthood, the sacrifices, and the festivals and explain their relevance for those who follow Christ.

When I began working on this book, I had two main goals. First, to retell this wonderful story, combining the information we have in the gospels and other parts of the New Testament with additional historical facts, descriptions of the temple and other significant locations in Jerusalem, and research done by scholars to give the reader a more vivid understanding of where and how these events took place. The second was to draw out spiritual lessons from the story that we, as believers, can benefit from today. But I was to find out that there was a third reason for writing this book, one that did not become clear to me until years later.

The original manuscript was completed in 2003, but lay dormant for nine years. During that time, I published two other books. The first was *Called to Rebuild,* a commentary on the remnant books of the Bible—Ezra and Nehemiah, along with Haggai, Zechariah, and Malachi, with applications for the church today. The second was *His Desire Is for Me,* a thirty-day devotional and commentary on the Song of Songs.

Upon completion of *His Desire Is for Me,* I began searching for a new writing project. During that time period, from 2005 to 2012, my work has taken me to Israel and the Middle East several times a year. I have begun to feel quite at home in Israel and have developed relationships with many of the Lord's servants and ministry leaders there, both on Palestinian and Messianic sides. I have also become intimately acquainted with some of the issues and conflicts between the two groups—both political and theological. At the root and the core of the theological differences, one topic continues to rise to the surface as the key issue, just like cream rises to the top in a bottle of milk. That issue is a proper understanding of the New Covenant. Or, put another way, since the cross of Christ, is there only one covenant between God and his people, or are there two? Is the Old Covenant God made with Israel still in effect? Or has it been nullified and replaced by the New Covenant, which embraces all of God's people regardless of race, bloodline, or ethnicity?

These are weighty theological questions, and they have a tremendous impact on how we approach and understand the Scriptures. They affect our views of evangelism and eschatology (end-times theology). And for those living in "the Land," they affect how believers—from both Jewish and Palestinian backgrounds—view one another, and ultimately how the practical outworking of the unity of the body of Christ plays out in Israel— and from there, at least to some extent, around the world. (Beyond this, there are political implications that will not be addressed in this book.)

With this as a backdrop, I returned to this manuscript (originally entitled *From the Garden to Glory)* and began to look at it through new eyes. Some years ago (in 1998) I published my first book, entitled *An Evening in Ephesus, with John the son of Zebedee.* It was a dramatic commentary on the book of Revelation as told by the apostle John. The setting was John's return to Ephesus from the Island of Patmos. Ephesus was one of the original seven churches of Asia to receive his letter containing the revelation of Jesus Christ prior to John's return from exile. In my fictional presentation, questions arise about the letter and what it meant. Not all are clear on the symbolism John used. So there, in a house church meeting, John unpacks and explains the letter contain the revelation, pulling back the curtain of the symbolic language and explaining its mysteries.

An Evening in Ephesus was self-published. I did hardly anything to promote it. It sold less than three thousand copies, and people heard of it only by word of mouth or through a scanty website that I put up. But now, having looked at *From the Garden to Glory* once again, a new thought emerged: Why not make it part of a trilogy? Why not three books, with a common thread, each singling out different time periods from the first-century church and tracing the theme of how the New Covenant was established? *The Messenger* would be the first, documenting the circumstances around Christ's death on the cross, his resurrection, and his ascension, which established the New Covenant. The second would be *The Message,* which traces that covenant as it was understood and took root in the minds of the apostles and first-century believers, the conflicts that arose because of it, and how the document containing the twenty-seven books that we now hold in our hands and call the New Testament (the New Covenant) actually came into being. Finally, the third book, *The Marriage: The Final Revelation (An Evening in Ephesus* revised), is John's own commentary on the book of Revelation. This is the capstone of the series. In it, we will look at the final book in the New Testament, which brings the full unveiling of the New Covenant to a close.

All three books in this trilogy center around the apostle John, the "beloved disciple." A great deal has been written about the apostle Paul, his writings, and the prominent role he played in the first-century church. Much less has been written about John, and the spotlight rarely seems to fall on him and the role he played. From reading the New Testament, it seems that John's influence was much more behind the scenes and less prominent than that of Peter, Paul, or even Jesus's brother James. He appears in the gospels as the beloved disciple, but then does not reappear for nearly forty years, at which time we are left with his contributions to the Scriptures. He wrote the last of the gospels, the last of the epistles, and the final book in the Bible, the book of Revelation.

John was a giant of a man. Although the full force of his life's impact seems to have had a delayed fuse, he remains among the most influential figures in all of Christian history. It is no wonder that he will ever be one of the glorious foundation stones of the heavenly city, the New Jerusalem.

Bob Emery
Charlottesville, Virginia

PART I

THE MESSENGER:
FROM THE GARDEN TO GLORY

CONTENTS: THE MESSENGER

"Behold, I am going to send my messenger, and he will clear the way before me. And the LORD, whom you seek, will suddenly come to His temple; and the messenger of the covenant, in whom you delight, behold, he is coming,' says the LORD of hosts."

Malachi 3:1

PROLOGUE

A.D. 58

"Son of Thunder, how are you, my brother? I must say that it only gets better seeing you every day since we have arrived." Paul strode up to me with a grin and embraced me. Releasing me from his strong embrace, Paul stepped back and motioned to the young man behind him. "This is Titus. You remember him, do you not?"

"I am not doing badly for a man beginning to feel his age," I said with a smile. "It is good to see you as well. And most certainly I remember Titus. He is the young man from Antioch, Syria. He came with you and Barnabas to Jerusalem nine years ago for the council meeting that convened over the gospel you were preaching to the Gentiles. How quickly the time has passed!" Titus appeared not to have aged much. He was in his early thirties, a handsome man with black hair, a well-groomed beard, and a loose-fitting bleached white tunic with a brown belt.

"It has indeed. Titus came with me from Ephesus to deliver the collection we have raised from among the Gentile churches for the suffering Jewish Christians here and in the rest of Judea. We wanted to arrive in time for the harvest feast of Pentecost so that we could share this harvest with you."

As Paul had testified at our gatherings over the past few nights, for the better part of three years he had been busily involved with a church-planting school in Ephesus, training eight young men who represented different Gentile churches in Galatia, Macedonia, and Achaia. Using Ephesus as a base, Titus and the others had been hard at work planting churches throughout Asia. They had done a commendable job! This Titus, he was a special young man.

"It is quite a tale you and your companions have related to us about the incredible things God has done among the Gentiles. Praise God! Have you experienced any trouble from our zealous Jewish brothers, who have not yet seen the light about Jesus, the Messiah, since you have arrived? Do their leaders know you are here?"

"No, not yet," said Paul. "I did get some suspicious looks in the temple with those four men you, James, and the other elders suggested I take with me to go through our purification rituals. But we made it in and out of the temple area with no incident. So far, so good." Paul looked reflective for a moment, and there was something about his tone—did he expect trouble? If he did, he said nothing about it. Instead, he continued to talk about the reason he and Titus had come.

"Throughout the Gentile churches, people have been laying aside some of their money on the first of every week to send to their Jewish brothers and sisters here in Jerusalem and Judea. We know that times have been hard for you and that there are a lot of needs. Not only are Titus and these young men with me church planters, but they are also delegates from their respective churches, entrusted to accompany me and help deliver this gift. My ardent hope has been that by this gesture, the Christians here will take a more favorable view of those who have believed from among the Gentiles. I know it is difficult for Jews like you and me, who stem from a race once chosen by God to bear his light to the world, to be on the receiving end of such a love offering. But I hope this will help soften some hearts here."

"Yes," I said. "Word is spreading about the generous collection you all brought with you. People are talking about it throughout the city. I am grateful, Paul—not only for the gift, but also for your passion to see the barriers torn down that separate God's people."

Paul nodded in humble agreement. "I have a favor to ask of you, John. There are some matters I need to attend to here in the city. Tomorrow I plan to go again to the temple to bring some of the alms we've collected and present them as an offering. But today I want to see my sister and her son, whom I have not seen for years. Our brother Titus has been looking forward to this visit to Jerusalem for a long time. He is excited to be here, and especially to be here at the time of Pentecost. He has wanted for some time to talk with you and some of the other brothers and sisters who actually walked with Jesus and knew him in the flesh. In fact, that is about all he talked about on the ship from Asia to here! I was hoping you might have some time to spend with him. Show him around; talk with him about your own experience with the Lord."

I could not help but agree when I saw the glow and anticipation on Titus's face. Paul was not exaggerating the young man's eagerness! "Certainly, Paul," I said. "I would consider it a privilege to spend time with this young disciple. It is the very least I can do, considering the effort he has expended in helping to carry those heavy sacks of coins all the way to Jerusalem! I have tomorrow free."

"Good," said Paul. "I hope that you will share with him as much as you can—especially about our Lord's final days in Jerusalem, his crucifixion, resurrection, and ascension. There are so many symbols here, all part of our traditions and history as Jews, that our Gentile friends know little about. Titus has heard me speak of Christ as the reality and fulfillment of all the sacrifices. When he preaches, he can describe the temple and the duties of the priests, though he has never seen those duties performed. He understands the spiritual significance of the burnt offering, the sin offering, and many other things. But I would like for him to see, with his own eyes, where these things take place—now, while the temple still stands. It is becoming clearer to me all the time that we are living in the last days of the Old Covenant."

A mix of sadness and hope crossed his weathered face. "Soon, the fulfillment of all that Jesus said on the Mount of Olives about the destruction of the temple and the city of Jerusalem will be realized. Then these symbols, these pictures, will no longer be around."

"Do not worry, Paul," I said, as my own anticipation of taking this young man under my wing and personally instructing him mounted. "I will give him a tour that he will not soon forget. After all, I was one who leaned on Jesus's breast and was drawn close to his very heart. With God's help, I will do my best to impart some of that heart to this young apostle."

"That is all I could ask," said Paul.

"Titus," I said, "pack a little food for a noon meal tomorrow, and bring it along with you. Meet me in the morning at the third hour in the garden of Gethsemane. That is where we will begin."

CHAPTER 1

THE GARDEN

I arose early and ate a light breakfast of dried fish, goat cheese, and bread and then made my way to the garden. I wanted to arrive well before Titus, for this was a quiet, peaceful place—one of my favorite places to awaken the dawn with my prayers, a place drenched with memories and significance.

It was a beautiful morning—warm, with a slight breeze and clear skies. Sparrows could be heard chirping from the grove of olive trees. Pairs of robins chased one another playfully in their springtime mating rituals.

At last I saw Titus approaching. My eyes caught his form just as he was veering from the heavily trodden road ascending the Mount of Olives from Jerusalem onto the narrower, less worn path leading into the garden. There was a bounce and eagerness in his gait, and he was right on time. I called out to him, "Good morning, Titus!" and motioned for him to come join me. "I am glad you were able to find your way here without any problem."

Taking a shortcut to me, he left the path and passed between two large, bushy olive trees, their graceful green and silver leaves, dark and narrow, mingling where two branches were growing slightly into one another. Ducking and pushing a larger branch aside with his forearm, he emerged just a few feet from where I was standing.

"Hello, John," he said with an avid grin. "Paul's directions were easy to follow. So this is the garden of Gethsemane!" His tone changed to one of awe as his eyes slowly moved around the garden, and he breathed in its beauty and the tranquility hovering over it. Clearly he knew something about what had transpired here not so many years ago.

"Yes," I said. I pointed to a patch of green grass on the gently sloping hill where we could sit down. "They call this the oil press garden, named for that oil press over there." I pointed to the ancient press that had been there as long as I could remember. The sun was shining off it, bathing it in morning.

"As you can see, this is a peaceful setting, more an orchard than a garden. Most of the trees are olive trees, but there are a few other varieties. Jesus brought us here frequently to teach and share with us. Though our last time with him here was not a pleasant one, I often feel drawn back to this place."

Titus nodded and began to open his mouth as though he might ask a question about that last time here with Jesus, but I was not quite ready yet to be the teacher. "Tell me, Titus, how is our brother Paul doing?" I asked.

"He has not really shared his emotions with us," Titus said, "although we have observed an unusual intensity about him. He has been warned everywhere, over and over again, that it might not be wise for him to come to Jerusalem. Even before boarding the ship at Tyre for Jerusalem, we had a prayer meeting on the beach with some of the disciples there with whom we had stayed for seven days, including the wives and children. They prayed for all of us, but especially for Paul. Some admonished him; others tried cautiously to dissuade him from coming. But he would not listen. While we were in Caesarea, the prophet Agabus came down from Judea to see Paul. Upon seeing him, Agabus took Paul's belt from around his waist, bound his own feet and hands with it, and said, 'This is what the Holy Spirit says: "In this way the Jews at Jerusalem will bind the man who owns this belt and deliver him into the hands of the Gentiles."' At that point we all, including Philip, his virgin daughters, and all the local believers, began begging him not to go up to Jerusalem. But it was no use. Paul was resolute."

Titus's face was full of emotion—admiration most of all. "None of us know what will be his fate. But in his heart of hearts, I think Paul really hopes for the opportunity to preach the good news to Nero Caesar himself. He has sometimes spoken to us about his conversion—how on the road to Damascus Jesus spoke to him and said that Paul would bear his name to kings. That has not yet happened, so I think Paul believes that his time has not yet come."

"Paul is indeed an extraordinary fellow," I said. "A chosen vessel, certainly. One day I hope his wish will be fulfilled. Meanwhile, we will have to keep our brother uplifted in prayer, that he be kept safe and that God's will be done." I paused and took in the sight of the olive trees again. Now was the time to teach.

"I have many questions for you about what is happening among the Gentile churches and about your experience of Christ, but those questions will have to wait. My assignment this morning is to show you around Jerusalem. I thought this would be as good a place as any to start. I am ready if you are."

"I am ready, John," Titus said. I grinned—the young man had barely been holding his readiness back. "I am guessing that you brought me here to tell me what it was like the night Jesus was arrested."

"Excellent intuition," I said. "So yes, let us begin with what happened on the night of our Lord's arrest. We had just finished our last supper together in the large, furnished, second-story guest room at a house of the Essenes.[1] Jesus had many important things to tell us that night. He knew his departure was imminent. He told us that we would be scattered and that we were about to weep and lament, but that our sorrow would be turned to joy. Our hearts were heavy because of his words, but we were living in a state of denial. We did not want to believe that what he was saying was true."

For a brief moment, as I spoke, I recalled the heaviness of that evening—the confusion and denial.

"After we sang one final hymn together, he led us down from the upper room. It was about eight o'clock. We quickly passed through the narrow streets of the city and across the double-tiered bridge spanning the Kidron Valley to the Mount of Olives—to this place where we are sitting now.

"When we entered the garden, Jesus told the other eight disciples to wait by the entrance. He took Peter, my brother James, and me a little further and asked us to remain there and to keep watch with him. He was intensely burdened. He went ahead several steps by himself, then collapsed to the ground. He began crying out, in loud cries, to the Father. He was in the vortex of the most intense—no, ferocious—spiritual conflict of his life. It was over a cup."

"What was the cup?" asked Titus.

"It was the cup of the Father's will," I responded. "Think of it! Did drinking the cup of his Father's will require him going to the cross? Or was it possible that at this last hour, the cup might pass from him? That was his battle. Here in this garden, our Lord, who was always filled with the Spirit, like a ripe olive that is full of oil was pressed and crushed this final time so that the Spirit could flow out from him to bring Life and healing to all mankind—true Life, *zoe* life. The cup he had to drink involved taking upon himself the sins of the entire world and being separated from his Father, with whom he had enjoyed constant, uninterrupted fellowship from all eternity."

"What did you do while you were watching?" asked Titus, hushed.

"Truthfully?" I responded. "I am ashamed to say it, but we fell asleep."

"What?" said Titus, astonished. He shook his head a little—clearly that was not what he had expected.

"You heard me correctly," I said. "We fell asleep. It was not the first time I have fallen asleep at a major event. It happened on the mount where our Lord was transfigured also. As you may have discovered already for yourself, as I had to, though our spirits are willing to do the will of God, our flesh is still very weak.

"An hour passed before he returned to wake us. While we slept, he had fought. The spiritual conflict that raged over that cup was more intense and violent than any street brawl you could imagine. Leaving us again, he returned to do battle. Then he came back to rouse us again, that we might fight too and stand with him. But we were not able. Arousing us for yet a third time, his hair matted with sweat, his forehead and cheeks streaked with sweat and the blood from the vessels in his face that had ruptured during his agonizing struggle, his peace and calm had returned. In the presence of God, his Father, in spiritual realms he had gained the victory. He had embraced the cup the Father was asking him to drink—the cup of humiliation, pain, abandonment, wrath, and death—and he would drink it all with dignity. Such a matchless example of how to embrace and accept the crosses God gives us to bear! I have never seen anything like it."

I paused for a moment, dwelling on the memories. "At about eleven o'clock we got up and returned with him to the garden's entrance. There we found the other eight disciples also asleep. Jesus awakened them. As we gathered for the last time, we looked back in the direction of the city and saw, at a distance, a mob coming toward us, carrying torches and lanterns. Eleven of the twelve of us standing there were petrified!

"A full moon was out. We saw in its light a young boy racing ahead of them. When he reached us he bent over gasping, trying to catch his breath. It was John Mark, the nephew of Barnabas and son of Mary. He was up late and getting ready for bed when he heard a commotion outside his window—the guards passing by Mary's house after not finding us in the upper room at the Essene monastery. John Mark saw Judas Iscariot with them and overheard them say they were going to the garden to look for Jesus and arrest him. With no time to waste, he bolted out the door and ran ahead of the mob, hoping to warn us.

"Why the soldiers carried the torches and lanterns, I am not sure. Maybe they thought Jesus would run or hide and that they might have to look for him among the trees. Because it was the Passover season, tens of thousands of visitors had flooded the city. The Roman authorities were on high alert to maintain order. Tensions were high. Jewish Zealots were trying to incite the people against Rome. Any political uprising would need to be swiftly dealt with. The charge against Jesus was that he claimed to be a king. Any threat to Caesar's authority could not be tolerated."

Titus nodded. The Gentile world was no stranger to political tensions, though few places in the Roman Empire could rival Palestine in that regard!

"When they arrived at the garden, Judas stepped forward from the mob, which consisted of a cohort of about six hundred Roman soldiers and a number of the temple guards along with some of the chief priests and Pharisees. He walked directly up to Jesus and began showering him with kisses. This was the prearranged signal for the authorities to identify Jesus.

Though Peter was scared, I have to give him credit for his courage. He was ready for a fight. The odds were not good. We were outnumbered sixty to one. Peter pulled out a sword, which he had concealed under his upper garment, and took a swing at Malchus, the servant of the high priest. He wanted to split his head open like a melon—but we were fishermen, not warriors. He barely missed his mark and ended up only lopping off Malchus's ear.

"Jesus intervened and touched the bloody side of Malchus's head, and his ear was instantaneously restored. He told Peter to put away his sword. I have never forgotten the sense of things happening all around us . . . as though legions of angels stood anxiously poised in unseen realms, awaiting the command to intervene. But the command never came. Jesus knew that he had to drink the Father's cup.

"The soldiers and guards seized him and hauled him away. The eleven of us fled in fear. John Mark, dressed in his sleeping clothes, was not so fortunate in getting away. Two men grabbed at him. Trying frantically to escape, he broke loose and streaked for home naked, leaving his garment in their hands. Once we felt that we were out of danger, Peter and I slowly but cautiously followed at a distance to see where they were taking Jesus."

"John Mark told me some of this story, but not in so much detail—especially the part about him running home naked!" said Titus. "I met him in Jerusalem when I was here the first time. He traveled back to Antioch with us after we had come for the council of elders and you all sent us on our way with your blessing, endorsing the gospel that Paul and Barnabas were preaching among the Gentiles."

I remembered that meeting well. "John Mark is a good brother," I said, "although I understand he did have some troubles on the journey which resulted in a conflict with Paul, causing him to return early from Paul and Barnabas's church-planting trip to Galatia. Mary, his mother, has opened her house to the church for years for us to use as a meeting place. Following Peter's arrest, it was there that we were praying for his release. Peter showed up, shocking everyone, after an angel led him out of prison. Amazing, is it not, how we can pray for something and then marvel when God actually answers? Peter is the one who led John Mark to Christ."

I placed my hands on my knees and raised my eyes up the slope of the Mount of Olives. "Well, Titus, there is much more to tell. But I think we should leave here now and move farther up the mountain to another special place. We will have a much better view of the city. From there, I would like to give you an orientation to Jerusalem and the temple. Then I will tell you about the trial."

CHAPTER 2

JERUSALEM, THE TEMPLE, AND THE SACRIFICES

"Behold, Jerusalem!" I said, spreading out both arms to introduce Titus to this scene, hallowed to all Jews. We both stood motionless, beholding the spectacular panorama of the city before us—the temple right in front of us, with its snow-white marble and glittering gold; the lower city to the left, with its narrow streets, marketplaces, shops, and bazaars. Behind the temple was the upper city, with its palaces, expensive homes, and spacious gardens. And butted up against the temple on the right and to the north stood the intimidating Roman Fortress of Antonia, the size of a small city in itself.

"This is the city over which our Lord wept!" I said as I extended my arm and my fingers panned the city from one end to the other.

"Historically," I told Titus, "when the Israelites first entered the land of Canaan under Joshua's leadership, Jerusalem was called Jebus and was inhabited by a people called the Jebusites. Joshua never conquered them. It was not until King David took the city hundreds of years later that it came under Jewish control. Jerusalem was—and remains—a strategic city. It is nestled between the ancient lands where the tribes of Benjamin and Judah settled, and it is a city with its own water source, the spring of Gihon. The ancient City of David, where he captured the Jebusite citadel of Millo, has long since disappeared and been rebuilt and is now the priests' quarter, or the Ophel."

The streets below us were packed with foot traffic and travelers riding donkeys, horses, and camels, as well as shoppers and merchants pulling carts and carrying heavily laden baskets. The noise and bustle of the city rose all the way up the slope.

"There are about seven million Jews scattered throughout the Roman Empire, which accounts for about seven percent of the population of the world. A little over one percent—about 100,000—makes Jerusalem their home.[2] During the Passover week, however, the city swells by an additional 250,000 pilgrims."

I pointed across the valley below to the front of the temple. "That rather sharp drop-off you see in front of the temple and the fortress is the western bank of the Kidron Valley, or as we sometimes call it, the Valley of Jehoshapat." A two-tiered bridge spanned the narrow valley, with seven arches on each level. "That is known as the Bridge of the Red Heifer.[3] It leads to the road called the Descent of the Mount of Olives,[4] which will take us up to the summit of the mountain. The road continues on the other side to the city of Bethany, and from there, on to Jericho. The Kidron Valley is a dry ditch for most of the year, but when we get rain during the winter months, the runoff waters cause a river to flow through it. Eventually those waters empty into the Dead Sea, about twenty miles away. That is the lowest spot on the earth—a quarter-mile below the level of the sea."

Beyond the Kidron to the left, just outside the southern wall of the city, smoke was rising. "That smoke comes from the constantly burning fires of the city dump. The place is called Gehenna. In the Jewish mind, Gehenna so pictures what hell must be like that the word has become synonymous with hell. Jesus taught often about the reality of such a place.

"Five miles further south is the city of Bethlehem, the birthplace of two great kings. David was born there, and it is where he was anointed by Samuel to be the king of Israel. Bethlehem means 'the House of Bread.' It was also the birthplace of the Son of David." I smiled as I remembered the story. "In the fields surrounding Bethlehem were the temple flocks, tended by the shepherds. It was there, one night that an angel and the host of heaven appeared to them announcing the birth of a Savior and Messiah. They ran to the village and found Jesus inside a stable. Other lambs destined for sacrifice surrounded him. Not only was he born the Lamb of God, but he was placed in a food trough, a symbol that he had come as the heavenly food—the Bread of Life—to satisfy the spiritual hunger of a starving world."

"We see the temple before us," said Titus eagerly. "Obviously, it is the centerpiece of the city. Can you tell me about its history?"

This was a story I knew well and was anxious to tell. The temple was central to so much of my heritage and my faith, and to the faith of this young Gentile as well—though he might not fully realize it yet.

"From up here on the mountain we are looking west," I began. "The temple you see in front of you is not the original temple. It is actually the third one. King David conceived the plan for the first temple over a thousand years ago, though his son Solomon built it. David went to great lengths to draw up the plans, collect all the materials, and finance its construction. Through the spoils of war, he amassed one hundred thousand talents of gold and a million talents of silver in the national treasury for its construction, not to mention the timber, the stones, and bronze and iron beyond weight. In addition, he added another three thousand talents of gold and seven thousand talents of silver from his own personal treasury.[5]

"After the Babylonians came and destroyed Solomon's temple, a remnant of Jews led by Zerubbabel returned from Babylon seventy years later to rebuild it. This second temple was completed about five hundred years ago. Though it was a third larger, in no way did it compare to the beauty and splendor of Solomon's original temple. It is recorded in the book of Ezra that some of the old men who had been alive to see the first temple actually wept when the foundation of Zerubbabel's temple was laid.

"Herod the Great built the third temple that we are looking at now. At the Passover celebration about twenty years before our Lord was born, Herod announced his grand intention to restore and rebuild the second temple. It took another few years to train one thousand priests and Levites to work as masons and carpenters before the work actually began. Ten thousand additional skilled workmen were hired and a thousand wagons employed to transport the large stones from the quarry to the building site. My own father spoke to me often of the spectacle as the temple was built. This temple was the crown jewel of all Herod's achievements.

"The four walls surrounding the temple are each six hundred feet in length, enclosing it within a perfect square. The visible wall supporting the platform where it is built rises an average height of about 450 feet above the Kidron Valley, with foundations that are sunk into the ground another 150 feet in depth. The highest point of the temple, the southeastern corner, towers 600 feet over the Kidron. That is the pinnacle of the temple, where Satan took Jesus and tempted him, saying, 'If you are the Son of God, throw yourself down from here and God will command his angels concerning you.' But Jesus put Satan in his place by quoting a passage from Deuteronomy which says, 'You shall not put the Lord your God to the test.'"

"That story has always encouraged me," Titus said, eyeing the high point.

I continued. "The temple is built over the only living spring in the area, the Gihon, which provides the water supply for all the activities associated with the temple service. Private citizens and the rest of the city are supplied by water from cisterns and pools that collect rainwater, and by the elaborate aqueduct system that you can see some of the workers working on even now.

"Though it has been a work in progress for years, this temple is a work in vain. I am confident it will soon be destroyed as our Lord predicted—probably by the Romans. Just two days before his crucifixion, in this very place, Peter,

---

1   The amount David gave for the temple from the money accumulated from spoils of war and his own personal treasury, amounted to approximately $234 billion in today's dollars.

James, Andrew, and I listened as Jesus prophesied about the destruction of Jerusalem and the temple. He said that within one generation—forty years—not one stone of the temple would be left upon another, and the city would be destroyed beyond recognition. That prophecy was made twenty-eight years ago. When it will actually happen, I do not know. But one thing is for certain: we are living in the last days, and Jesus promised that some of us who were alive when he spoke those words would live long enough to see these things come to pass."

"I understand that the temple must be destroyed," Titus said, his eyes still drinking in the sight of it, "but it is a sad thing. Its design is marvelous—so intricate and beautiful."

I nodded. "All three temples were patterned after the tabernacle built by Moses in the wilderness. But that tabernacle was also a pattern, or replica, of something else. When God brought Moses up the mountain in the Sinai Desert, he opened the heavens for him and gave him a revelation of something resembling a building—something outside of time and space, eternal in the heavens. God then told Moses to build a tabernacle on earth and to make it look like what he had seen in the heavens."

I smiled, wondering over my own words. The immensity of it never ceased to move me. "Moses saw from a distance what was from the beginning: the one whom we heard, saw, touched, and lived with—the Word of Life. I think you might know who I am talking about."

"Yes, I do," said Titus with a smile. "You are speaking about the Lord Jesus Christ."

I nodded. "On that mountain, God showed Moses the true tabernacle in the heavens and the priesthood that serves that tabernacle.[6] When our Lord Jesus stepped down out of heaven and came to earth, for thirty-three years the glory of God was housed in the tent of his physical body. Unlike the temple—though much like the tabernacle that Moses built—Jesus was not glorious in his outward appearance. When looking at Moses's tabernacle from the outside, one could see only the white curtains that represented righteousness, surrounding a small structure that was covered in badger skins. Similarly, when looking at Christ, one could observe his righteous behavior, but beyond that, his appearance was completely ordinary. Yet on the inside, he contained the glory of God like no other. And we beheld that glory."

"An amazing symbol," Titus said.

"That is only the beginning of the symbolism," I answered. "The tabernacle in the wilderness was portable. It moved around from place to place. But it was only temporary. Later, when Israel settled in this land, God put in David's heart the desire to build a more permanent place for God to reside—the temple. As we take a closer look at the temple and consider some of its features, we will talk more about the spiritual significance these things have for us today—all of us."

"I am here to learn, John," Titus said. "Hold nothing back!"

I smiled at the eagerness of my student. "I will begin by describing the farthest point of the temple and then move toward us," I said. "The westernmost part of the temple was designed to be the place where God dwelt. Facing east, toward where we stand, the Lord could look out from the Holy of Holies into the Holy Place, then into the outer court—where the sacrifices were made—and all the way out to the outer sanctuary located up here on the Mount of Olives, so he could see everything that transpired in the temple. Symbolically, everything done in the temple was to be done in his presence."

"You speak of an outer sanctuary here on the Mount of Olives," said Titus quizzically. "Of what do you speak?"

"We will come to that later," I said. "But first, I will describe the temple before us." I pointed to the imposing structure at the far end of the temple platform.

"The structure that you see there, with the four huge columns in the front and the large red curtain in front of its doors, houses the Holy of Holies and the Holy Place. That is the curtain I saw torn in two when Jesus died. The women who stood with me at the foot of the tree where he was crucified saw it as well, as did the Roman centurion in attendance that day. It was a startling, breathtaking spectacle, even in the midst of our grief, to see that curtain—eighty-two feet high, twenty-four feet wide, and four feet thick— ripped completely in two.[7]

"The Holy of Holies is farthest from us and is shaped as a perfect cube, thirty feet long, thirty feet wide, and thirty feet high. In the tabernacle and Solomon's temple, the Holy of Holies housed the ark of the covenant, the mercy seat, and the cherubim."

"What do you mean?" interrupted Titus. "Are they no longer there?"

"That is correct," I said. "The place where the mercy seat once stood is occupied by nothing more than a large stone called the foundation stone. That is where the high priest sprinkles the blood on the Day of Atonement. The original ark, along with the tablets, Aaron's rod that budded, and the jar of hidden manna, was raided by Nebuchadnezzar when the first temple was destroyed, and to this day they all are lost somewhere, covered over by the sands of time.

"Separating the Holy of Holies from the Holy Place, which is a room sixty feet long from east to west and thirty feet wide, is a wooden partition. Over the door to the Holy of Holies in the center of that partition hangs the veil, which is beautifully embroidered with cherubim.

"Immediately outside the veil, in the Holy Place, is the altar of incense. Incense burns there day and night on a small altar made of acacia wood and overlaid with gold, filling the room with the scents of its precious spices—a sacred perfume designed by God himself. Against the southern wall, to our left, is the golden lampstand. On the northern side of the room, opposite the lampstand, is the table with the sacred bread."

A beautifully paved court stretched out before the holy structure. I directed Titus's gaze toward it. "As the priests come out through those large doors and the curtain, they enter the outer court, more formally known as the court of the priests. If you look up, above the doorway, you can see the golden, decorative image of a great vine with clusters of grapes hanging from it, as tall as a man.

"There in the court of the priests, to our left, is the fifteen-foot-wide brass basin filled with water. In Solomon's temple the basin was supported by the figures of twelve bronze oxen, facing outward; now, it is upheld by the figures of twelve huge lions. That is where the priests wash their hands and feet so as to be made clean before entering the Holy Place."

Everything we had seen was rich with significance, but few things more than the object I pointed out next—a massive stone altar with horns on its four corners. "To the left of center, in the same court, you can see the altar of burnt offerings. That stone altar is close to fifty feet square and rises to a height of fifteen feet off the ground. The walkway around it is for the priests. They always walk to their right. The inclined ramp you see leading up to the altar and the walkway stretches out about fifty feet and is half as wide. A mound of salt is always kept by the altar to accompany each sacrifice. Those horns rising up at the corners are about eighteen inches high. Each is hollow and houses a silver funnel. That is where the priests pour out the drink offerings of water and wine at the Feast of Tabernacles. I will have more to say about that later."

"What happens to all the blood from the sacrifices?" asked Titus.

"When the priests kill the sacrifices, they catch the blood in certain designated vessels. A portion is poured out at the corners of the altar. The rest is poured at the base of the altar. A drainage system carries this away where it empties into the Kidron Valley. " I answered.

"And what about all the ashes and remains from the sacrifices?"

original tabernacle and temple showed us that he is the one who judges in righteousness, but with grace and mercy. And finally, the ark, with its tablets, Aaron's rod that budded, and the hidden manna, shows us that he is the one who imparts to us the divine nature through his resurrected life, though it is hidden from the world."

Beaming, Titus offered his hearty amen. "Well said, John. You are a shining example of what I have to look forward to becoming, with more wisdom that comes from revelation—and age!"

CHAPTER 3

THE TRIAL

We stood up and stretched. I pulled out a goatskin full of water and handed it to Titus. He lifted it in the air and drank from its cool stream before handing it back for me to do the same. Refreshed, we both sat down under the olive trees once again, and I picked up the trail of my story.

"After they arrested Jesus, they whisked him away from the garden, led him back across the bridge spanning the Kidron, and brought him into the temple area. They stopped at the dividing wall because the Roman soldiers were not allowed to proceed any further. From there, the temple guards took him to the residence of Annas, the deputy high priest. By then, it was a little after midnight.

"During the time of the Passover, Caiaphas, the high priest, and his deputy, Annas, would leave their homes in the wealthy district of the upper city and stay in a private residence especially for the high priest located on the temple grounds. That private residence is located in one of the chambers surrounding the sanctuary and is called the Counselor's Chamber. Both men stayed in different sections of the same chamber and shared a common courtyard.

"As the fortress looking down on the temple makes clear, Rome is the supreme power over Jerusalem. Rome delegates its authority to governors. Pontius Pilate, for one, worked with local leaders to maintain the peace, and the local governor is actually the one to appoint the high priests. One would think they serve in that position because of their godliness and bloodline, but actually their appointment is political and based more on their cooperation and ability to work with Roman authorities.

"It was necessary for Caiaphas to have Annas there as a backup in case something went wrong and he was not able to carry out his duties in the celebration of the Passover. Annas was actually Caiaphas's father-in-law and the patriarch among the high priests. He had begun to serve as high priest forty years ago, and five of his sons had since succeeded him. This year it was Caiaphas who occupied that high office. After a preliminary examination by Annas, Jesus was handed over to Caiaphas for more questioning.

"Caiaphas hastily summoned all the members of the Sanhedrin for an emergency meeting. Messengers were sent out to round up all seventy of them. The full council is made up of seventy-one members, a third coming from the ranks of the Pharisees, a third from the Sadducees, and a third from the elders. Many of the Pharisees are scribes—experts in the law. The Sadducees are priests, and the elders come from prominent families around Jerusalem. Two officers, including the high priest, preside over this body.

"Over the course of the next few hours, they arrived at Caiaphas's house as the questioning continued." My spirit darkened as I spoke, remembering the injustice of that night. "We were there—Peter and I, watching from the shadows. They tried desperately to obtain false testimony against Jesus because they were intent on putting him to death. But even though some came forward with fabricated stories, they could not get their stories straight. Jesus remained silent, watching the circus. He did not complain, murmur, or threaten. He summoned all of his attention and focused it inwardly upon his spirit, where he beheld his Father. If his Father said nothing, he would say nothing. Regally he stood before his accusers, savoring, as a taste of good wine, another sip from the cup of his Father's will.

"The tension mounted. Frustrated, Caiaphas finally stepped forward from among the others and commanded Jesus, 'I demand, in the name of the living God, that you tell us whether you are the Christ, the Son of God.' This was the most solemn oath known to Hebrews and required a truthful answer."

I had never forgotten what I heard that night, and my voice fell to a hush as I told the story. "'I am,' answered Jesus. 'And you shall see the Son of Man sitting at the right hand of power, and coming with the clouds of heaven.'

"Caiaphas knew exactly what Jesus was referring to. He was quoting from Daniel, who had prophesied about the Messiah who was to come: 'And behold, with the clouds of heaven one like a Son of Man was coming, and he came up to the Ancient of Days and was presented before him. And to him was given dominion, glory, and a kingdom, that all the peoples, nations, and men of every language might serve him. His dominion is an everlasting dominion which will not pass away; and his kingdom is one which will not be destroyed.'

"The high priest lost control of himself. 'Blasphemy!' he shouted, tearing his robes. No one took notice at the time, but for Caiaphas to do such a thing legally disqualified him from being high priest. In Leviticus, Moses recorded that it was forbidden for the high priest to uncover his head or tear his robes, lest he die. That office would have to be forfeited to another. In the eyes of God, Jesus, who did not blaspheme but told the truth, assumed that vacant office. Three days later he ascended to the Ancient of Days to become the high priest forever over the household of God.

"But of course, that night the council was blinded to the truth. 'Why do we need other witnesses? You have all heard his blasphemy. What is your verdict?' yelled the high priest, the veins popping out in his neck."

I shuddered at the memory. "'Guilty!' they shouted. 'He must die.'

"This broke all the rules that normally governed the Sanhedrin. Typically, after a case is heard, the younger judges with less seniority vote first so their elders will not unduly influence them. The last to vote are the eldest among the council. This time, the high priest spontaneously rushed straight to judgment, and in the heat of the moment, he brought all the rest of the council along with him. They laid their hands on Jesus and began to spit on him and beat him.

"I had cautiously followed the crowd and caught up with them by the time they reached the courtyard of the Counselor's Chamber. I was an acquaintance of Caiaphas, so I was allowed into the courtyard, and I remained there while Jesus was taken inside and questioned by Annas. Later, I saw Peter standing by the gate, and I asked the woman watching it to let him in also. She did. While we were standing around the charcoal fire they had made to keep warm, a servant girl recognized Peter. Three times he was accused of being one of Jesus's followers. Three times he denied it. With the third denial the cock crowed, just as Jesus had predicted. Horrified at what he had done, Peter dashed from the courtyard, crying bitterly."

I hung my head. "It was Peter's greatest shame, yet through it Jesus showed us not only how weak we all are, but also how great his forgiveness is. In the fear and confusion of that night, it was a marvel we did not all fall as Peter did.

"They continued to beat Jesus, and then they blindfolded him and began mocking him. Finally they adjourned this meeting, planning to reconvene at daybreak in the Hall of Polished Stones, where the Sanhedrin officially conducted business.

"The Hall of Polished Stones is only a few dozen paces from the Counselor's Chamber. Its location east of the Holy of Holies was to symbolically show that all judgments rendered there were made in the presence of God. The Sanhedrin is the highest Jewish court in the land. The law requires that trials involving capital offenses be conducted in the Hall of Polished Stones, and only during daylight hours. The council reassembled that morning, but only sixty-nine of the seventy-one were present. Two men stayed home in protest.[10] One was a secret disciple of Jesus, a wealthy man named Joseph, from Arimathea. He is the one who courageously stepped forward to ask Pilate for the body of Jesus after his crucifixion and provided him with a tomb for burial. The other was Nicodemus.

"After all the council members were seated, Caiaphas entered the room. He took his place in the center of the long, semicircular bench, which reached halfway around the wall. On either side of him were seated the other members of the council. A secretary was present to record every word on a scroll of papyrus. Jesus stood alone in the center of the room.

"The council then went through the formality of officially casting their votes. The verdict was guilty as charged of blasphemy. Not having power to execute criminals, the Sanhedrin still needed to get permission from the Roman authority to carry out the execution. So they bound Jesus and sent him to the governor, Pontius Pilate. By now, it was about 6:30 on Friday morning."

Titus interrupted. "The Hall of Polished Stones—was that the same place they later tried Stephen before stoning him to death?"

"No," I said. "Remember I told you that hall was damaged beyond repair by the earthquake that occurred at the moment of Jesus's death. Following that, the Sanhedrin moved their official place of meeting to the Trading Center,[11] which is also located in the temple area. That is where Stephen was tried. It seems that God took notice. The judgment made against Jesus was the last one they would ever make from that place.

"Pilate was staying at the castle in the Fortress of Antonia that night. During the Passover season the governor stays in the fortress, though his personal residence is in the upper city. It was expedient for him to be nearer to his troops, who were controlling the crowds. Sometime during the night, his wife, Procula, who was staying at their usual residence, was awakened by a terrible nightmare about Jesus. She penned an urgent message warning her husband not to have anything to do with 'that righteous man' and sent it to him by way of a servant."

"I know that I am getting ahead of your story, but whatever happened to Pilate?" asked Titus.

"Pilate was recalled to Rome six years after the crucifixion, after serving as governor of Judea for ten years. There are uncorroborated stories that he became so troubled over his role in sentencing Jesus that he committed suicide. But we do not know that for sure. One thing we do know, however, is that his wife, Procula, eventually became a believer and follower of the Lord.[12]

"When Jesus was taken to Pilate, he did not actually go through a Roman trial. In fact, he did not even stand trial for the crime he was convicted of by the Sanhedrin, which was blasphemy! The members of the Sanhedrin knew they needed political charges if Pilate was to convict him, so they accused him of treason. Pilate questioned Jesus and asked if he was, indeed, king of the Jews. His answer was a simple, 'Yes.' He went on to explain that he was not an earthly king and that his kingdom was not of this world. Pilate hardly knew what to make of it, but he was under tremendous pressure to keep Palestine under control, and the Sanhedrin was bent on manipulating him.

"The Jews would not enter the Roman fortress, especially the day before the Passover, because they did not want to become defiled. So Pilate came out from the castle and addressed the crowd that had gathered, which consisted mostly of the chief priests, members of the Sanhedrin, temple guards, and some early morning worshipers. This was not the same crowd that had joyfully received him, waving palm branches and shouting 'Hosanna' in his triumphant entry into Jerusalem just five days earlier. Pilate told them that he had found nothing wrong with Jesus and that he was guilty of no crime. He was about to go back inside the fortress when a loud voice from the crowd caught his attention: 'He causes riots everywhere he goes, all over Judea, from Galilee to Jerusalem.'

"Pilate turned and looked back. 'So he is a Galilean, is he?' The crowd answered, 'Yes.'

"Pilate knew that Herod Antipas had come to Jerusalem to be here for the festival. He also knew that Galilee was under his jurisdiction. Pilate thought he could get off the hook by passing Jesus on to Herod, who could take responsibility for any decision. After all, Herod was much more familiar with Jewish religious law than Pilate was. So to Herod Jesus was sent.

"Herod Antipas was one of the sons of Herod the Great, who commissioned the temple to be built. Herod the Great was still king at the time of Jesus's birth; it was he who ordered all the babies in and around Bethlehem who could possibly have been the Christ child to be killed. His son Antipas ruled over Galilee as well as the lands east of the Dead Sea.

"Herod Antipas already had the blood of one prophet on his hands— Jesus's cousin, John the Baptizer. But he had wanted to meet Jesus for some time. He had heard about the miracles Jesus performed in Galilee and thought maybe he could get Jesus to perform one for him.

"Jesus had wept over John. Now he stood before the one who had ordered John's head severed from his body with a sword and delivered on a platter to his wife, Herodias, whom John had condemned for her adulterous marriage with Herod. Formerly she had been the wife of Herod's half-brother, Philip.

"Herod asked Jesus question after question, but Jesus refused to answer.

Finally his questions turned to ridicule. Getting nowhere, he turned Jesus over to his troops, who mocked him and dressed him in a white robe like those worn by candidates for a political office. Then they returned him to Pilate.

"Since most of the accusations against Jesus occurred here in Jerusalem, and this was Pilate's domain, Herod decided to decline the responsibility for killing another prophet. He probably had other reasons for not wanting to be the judge of Jesus. His chief steward, Chuza, and his adviser, Manaen, had become followers of Jesus, and many of his Galilean subjects were as well. Better for him to sit this one out and turn Jesus back over to Pilate.

"So Pilate brought Jesus out in front of the growing crowd and announced that neither he nor Herod could find this man guilty of anything worthy of death. He told them he would have Jesus flogged and then released.

"It was the governor's custom to release one prisoner each year during the Passover celebration. Pilate thought he could get Jesus off by offering the people a choice of releasing either him or a notorious criminal named Barabbas. The chief priest and Jewish leaders began inciting the raucous crowd until they shouted out in unison, 'Kill Jesus. Release Barabbas!'"

"Who was this character Barabbas?" Titus asked. "It makes no sense to me that they would have asked to have him released. The only explanation I can think of is that this was part of the sovereign plan of God."

"To show you just how right you are, I will tell you the story behind Barabbas," I answered.

"To some, Barabbas was a revolutionary hero. To others, he was nothing more than a run-of-the-mill, no-good dead-ender. He was in prison for a murder he had committed during an insurrection against the government in Jerusalem. But there was one fascinating thing about him. That was his name.

"You see, his full name was Jesus Barabbas. Barabbas means 'Son of the Father.' So his name literally meant, 'Jesus, Son of the Father!' You spoke earlier about the different sacrifices and how they were pictures to help us understand Christ. As you will see with Barabbas, God was still in the business of painting pictures to help us understand his plan right up until the end.

"The Day of Atonement is a very special day for us Jews. It is the only day each year when the high priest is allowed to go inside the Holy of Holies to sprinkle blood before the presence of God to cover over the sins of the people. On that day, two identical goats are brought to the temple. In appearance, there is no difference between the goats at all. The high priest draws two lots from an urn, called the *calpi,* located close to the wall nearest the Fortress of

Antonia on the eastern side of the court of the priests. The lots are identical, except that the inscription on one reads, 'For Jehovah'; the other reads, 'la-Azazel,' meaning 'For the Evil One.' The high priest holds a lot over the head of each goat. The goat that draws the lot 'For Jehovah' will be killed. It is sacrificed on the altar, its blood is sprinkled in the Holy of Holies, and its carcass is taken to an outer altar, farther up on the Mount of Olives—which I will show you in just a few minutes—and burned to ashes.

"The goat that draws the lot 'la-Azazel' is turned to face the people. The high priest then lays his hands on the head of this goat and prays over it, placing on it all the sins of the people for the entire past year. Then he faces the people and solemnly pronounces, 'You shall be cleansed!'

"This goat, known as the scapegoat, is then led out through Solomon's Porch and the East Gate, across the bridge to the Mount of Olives. There it is handed over to a stranger, a non-Israelite, and led away into the wilderness. It is taken down the Hinnom Valley about three miles away to a place called Beth Chaduda, where it is allowed to go free.[13] In later years the priests have adopted the practice of pushing it over a cliff to ensure its immediate death.

"That wilderness area is a desolate place. The only things that can survive there are scorpions and snakes. Occasionally a wild goat or gazelle can be sighted, and at night the only sounds are the eerie howls of jackals or hyenas. It is near the place where Christ was led by the Spirit of God to defeat Satan during his forty days of temptation. Only a few miles from Beth Chaduda, however, is that part of the Promised Land that flows with milk and honey and abounds in fullness, a reminder that there is only a short distance separating paradise and the place of absolute devastation."

"Incredible!" exclaimed Titus. "Barabbas and Jesus outwardly had the same names and titles. Jesus was pictured in both parts of this sacrifice. On one hand he was the one who bore all our sins and carried them away. On the other, he was the pure and righteous one whose blood was shed to cover our sins!"

"Exactly correct! And when the people turned Jesus over to Pilate, that fulfilled the illustration that the scapegoat would be turned over to a Gentile, who was given the authority to take it away to death. Our God knew exactly what he was doing and planned everything down to the last detail. So the people picked Barabbas and let him go free. The real 'Son of the Father' would be executed.

"Pilate argued with them, 'If I release Barabbas, what should I do with this man?'

"They all shouted, 'Crucify him! Crucify him!'

"For a third time Pilate insisted that he found no reason to sentence Jesus to death. The crowd responded with louder shouts: 'Away with him, away with him, crucify him!'

"Pilate heard the distinct voice of one person in the crowd who shouted out, 'We have a law, and by that law he ought to die because he made himself out to be the Son of God!'[14] Now Pilate was more afraid than ever.

"Someone else shouted, 'If you release this man, you are no friend of Caesar. Anyone who declares himself a king is a rebel against Caesar.'

"By now, Pilate probably thought to himself, *If I do not have him put to death, the Sanhedrin may very well report to Rome that I did not put to death one who was competing for the throne of Tiberius Caesar. That could mean my removal from office, punishment, exile, or death.* He was in a difficult place.

"Once again he asked the crowd, 'Shall I crucify your king?'

"They shouted back, 'We have no king but Caesar!'

"Pilate sent an attendant into the fortress to bring out a basin of water. He washed his hands in front of the crowd and said, 'I am innocent of this man's blood. The responsibility for his death is yours.'

"The people yelled back, 'We will take that responsibility. His blood shall be on us and on our children!'

"So Pilate sentenced Jesus to death, as they demanded. He released Barabbas and ordered Jesus to be flogged."

I winced as I recalled the scene. "The Roman soldiers seized him and stripped him of his clothes. They tied his hands and tethered him to a stake in front of the fortress. Then they administered the brutal whipping with a small whip made of braided leather thongs, studded with sharp pieces of bone, spikes, and rock that ripped into the flesh on his shoulders, back, chest, and the back of his legs. Flesh and muscle were ripped away from his bones, and later, as he hung on the tree, the prophecies of David from the Twenty-Second Psalm were fulfilled when he uttered: "I can count all my bones. They look; they stare at me."

"The soldiers hastily draped his clothes over his bloody body and dragged him back into the fortress. There they played a spiteful game with him that is known as the King's Game.[15] The soldiers take a condemned criminal and use him as a token in a game, moving him around to different stations that are etched in the stone floor of the fortress. At each station, some new cruelty is inflicted.

"They called out the entire battalion, stripped him once again, and put a purple robe on him. One soldier ripped off several branches from a thorn bush growing inside the fortress courtyard. He wove them together into a thorny crown and drove it into Jesus's head. They moved him to a different station, and another soldier placed a stick in his hand as a scepter. They mocked him and bowed down to him. When they finished with that, they took turns pounding him with their fists and hitting him on the head with the stick. It took real cowards to do that to one who had already gone through a previous beating and then been nearly whipped to death! When they finally tired of mocking and beating him, they removed the purple robe and dressed him in his own clothes. Then they led him out to be crucified."

"Whenever I have heard that story told," moaned Titus, "I am left speechless. What God was willing to allow his Son to go through to pay the price for you and me!"

"Yes, Titus," I said. "But we have not even come to the crucifixion yet. The real suffering was still ahead of him." I stood and shook the dust from my clothes. The sun was growing stronger overhead, and the sounds from the city were increasing in volume as the day continued. "Let us walk a little farther up the mountain. I will take you to the scene where the central event in all of history took place. We can talk along the way."

"Yes," Titus responded, as he rose and we strode along up the hill together. "I wish to see that place. One thing you did not mention in your story was what became of Judas. I know that after he betrayed the Lord for thirty pieces of silver, he hung himself."

The mention of my one-time brother pained me as it always did. "Yes, what happened to Judas was a tragedy. For thirty pieces of silver—the cost to purchase a common slave or an ordinary suit of clothes—Judas sold his soul."

I shook my head. "Judas was the only one among us not from Galilee. He was not a fisherman or a farmer or someone with an ordinary profession like Peter or me. He came from priestly stock, from the line of Aaron. Judas actually had the credentials of a priest.

"Ironically, Judas reclined next to Jesus, on the left—the place of honor—at the Last Supper. I was on the other side of our Lord, and the three of us all dipped out of the same bowl. Jesus actually broke bread, dipped it in the sauce, and offered it to Judas, knowing full well that Judas intended to betray him.

"After the Sanhedrin sentenced Jesus to death, Judas became terrified and filled with remorse. He returned to the area by the sanctuary, where he found some of the leading priests and council members. He tried to give the money back, but they brushed him off. 'That is your problem,' they said.

"Frantic by now, he entered into the Holy Place, where only priests are allowed to go, and cast the coins on the marble floor. Then he went out and hanged himself.

"The thirty pieces of silver became known as blood money because it had been used to pay for a murder. The priests could not accept it or put that kind of money into the temple treasury, so they used it to buy the potter's field over in the area where the Kidron and Hinnom Valleys intersect, and they turned it into a cemetery for foreigners. To this day, that field is still called the Field of Blood.

"But there is even more symbolism here, Titus. Another 'picture,' as you call it. Judas, a priest, 'sprinkled' the blood money in the Holy Place inside the temple. Though Jesus was actually killed up here on the Mount of Olives, that blood money represented his blood being sprinkled in the Holy Place. On the Day of Atonement, the high priest not only goes into the Holy of Holies to sprinkle the blood of the sacrifice before God, but he also sprinkles that blood in the Holy Place, and on all the holy things, including the table, the incense altar, the curtain—everything!"

"Incredible!" said Titus. "And as our high priest, Jesus ascended into heaven—into the real Holy of Holies into the presence of his Father, taking that blood with him. When the Father sees that blood covering us, he sees us as completely forgiven."

"Yes," I said. "And to draw even more from that illustration, on that special Day of Atonement, the high priest has to take five complete baths and wash another ten times. On that day alone he sheds his normal costume of priestly garments and wears only pure white. This illustrates the righteousness that is required to approach God and come into his presence. When Christ ascended to the Father as our high priest, he came into his presence in perfect holiness and righteousness. Not only does the Father see our sins forgiven, but also, when he sees his holy and righteous Son, he sees us in him. Now, when we stand before God, covered by the blood of Christ, we are not only forgiven, but we are as holy and righteous as the Son himself!"

CHAPTER 4

THE MOUNTAIN OF GOD

We continued our trek further up the mountain on the well-worn, winding road known as the Descent of the Mount of Olives. No more than ten minutes had passed when I brought the two of us to a halt.

"I want to stop here," I said to Titus as I put my left arm on his shoulder and turned him slightly to face back toward the city. With my right arm pointing back at the temple, I continued, "Imagine a straight line from where you stand to the center of the temple. Think of that as the radius of a circle. From here to there is about three thousand feet in distance. Now, with your mind's eye, imagine a circle with the temple as its center, and that radius extending in every direction all around the city. That radius represents the boundary of what we call 'the camp.'[16] Everything inside of that radius is considered inside the camp. Everything outside is outside the camp. The walls surrounding Jerusalem are not the boundary of the camp, but the circumference of that circle is.

"This distance has been key to determining the boundary of the camp of Israel since the time of Moses. Up here on the Mount of Olives, that radius extends to just about the point at which we are now standing. Now, ask me why this is important."

"All right, John, why is this important?" mused Titus, playing along with my game.

"It is important because just outside of this three-thousand-foot boundary is where the third altar of the temple stands. It is right over there." I shifted my pointing finger to a place not far away, a spot where the untrained eye would recognize no significant distinguishing features. "The first altar, coming forward from the Holy of Holies, is the incense altar. The next is the brazen altar. But up here on the Mount of Olives is the third altar, called the *miphkad* altar.[17] It is just outside the camp and is the place where the red heifer is sacrificed."[18]

"Paul said that he really wanted you to tell me about this," Titus said with excitement.

"The red heifer sacrifice is one of the least understood of all the sacrifices outlined by Moses in the Torah. There is a degree of inexplicability and mystery to it that makes it difficult for even Jews to understand. But for the follower of Christ, it illustrates one of the most precious and glorious aspects of what our Lord's death on the cross accomplished for us. The Day of Atonement gives us half the picture. The sacrifice of the red heifer completes it.

"A pure red heifer is very rare. It must be a young female cow between two and four years old, with red-colored hair and without any white or black hairs on its hide. It can never have been under a yoke or mounted by a bullock. From the time of Moses until now, there have been only seven or nine—I am not sure—red heifers sacrificed in the history of our nation. Moses sacrificed the first. Ezra offered another. The remaining heifers—five or seven, depending on the right count—have been offered over the past five hundred years. That is about one red heifer sacrifice in every century!

"The animal is selected in the temple area and then led out through the East Gate, across the bridge spanning the Kidron Valley that bears its name—the Bridge of the Red Heifer—to the miphkad altar, that outer altar located outside the camp. There it is killed.

"The miphkad altar is not made of brass, like the brazen altar at the temple. This altar is a stack of wood consisting of cedar, pine, and fig. It is stacked in rectangular fashion, but with the side facing west—back toward the temple—left open. As I said earlier, this was so that God, who faced east, could have a full view of everything pertaining to the temple, its service, and the sacrifices. The priest leads the animal into this corral-shaped altar and faces back toward the temple. He kills the animal by slitting its throat with one swish of the sharp knife in his right hand. He cups his hand under the throat of the bleeding animal, catching its blood. Then, dipping his finger in that blood seven times, he sprinkles it toward the Holy of Holies as an offering to God.

"From this vantage point on the Mount of Olives, the high priest can easily see over the eastern wall directly into the sanctuary. The eastern wall was constructed slightly lower than the other walls specifically for this purpose.[19]

"After sprinkling the blood, the priest moves outside the corral and ties together a bundle of cedar wood, hyssop, and scarlet wool. Setting fire to the altar, he throws the bundle on top of the carcass of the red heifer and watches as it all goes up in smoke. Once everything has been consumed and the fire goes out, the ashes are collected and divided into three parts to be stored for future use. One part is kept at the temple, another is kept here on the Mount of Olives, and the third part is disseminated among the priesthood serving outside of Jerusalem in other parts of Israel."

"I remember Paul saying something about how the priests mixed the ashes with pure spring water and used it for some purification rituals. But honestly, that must have been one of those days when Paul went on for a long time, and I might have dozed off a little bit. Tell me why those ashes were so significant?"

I nodded. "Ashes represent the final form of all living things. These ashes symbolize the finished work of Christ on the cross. The ashes from the red heifer are mixed, as needed, with water that issues from a living spring. If an Israelite sins, he can come to a priest who mixes a small portion of ashes with water in a large jar and sprinkles it upon the unclean person to purify him and make him clean again. Then that person can once again enter the temple. On the Day of Atonement, the sacrifice is offered for all the sins the people have committed, looking backwards, for the past year. But beginning right after the Day of Atonement, people start accumulating sins once again. How can they be clean and enter the temple after that? The red heifer sacrifice, therefore, was for the needs the Lord's people would have in the future."

"I think I understand, John," said Titus, "but what is the practical application? Please be just a little more specific."

"When you originally repented of your sins and came to Christ, asking him for forgiveness, how many of your sins did he forgive?" I asked.

"All of them," Titus responded.

"You have answered correctly." I said. "But now, after you have been a believer for over a decade—what happens now if you sin?"

"I confess my sins, and I know that I am forgiven," Titus responded quickly.

"But what of the sins you might commit in the future? Tomorrow, next week, next month, next year, five years from now? Have they already been forgiven or not?" I asked him.

"When you state it in this way, I must say yes—I believe that he has already forgiven those sins as well."

"He most certainly has!" I said emphatically. "Jesus's death on the cross was once and for all. He bore the punishment for all our past sins, present sins, and future sins in his body on that tree. He will never have to come back to die for any more sins again. His blood washed them all away. We can come to our great high priest and have the Holy Spirit apply the finished work of Christ to our lives. His death was once for all time, for all of our sins, and he will never have to come back to die all over again for sins that may be committed in the future."

"Praise the Lord!" said Titus. "That makes it pretty clear that there is nothing we can do to earn our salvation or forgiveness. He has already done it all for us. We just need to believe, accept it, and walk in it."

"This is the gospel message boiled down to its very essence," I said. "And it was pictured here in the red heifer sacrifice hundreds of years before Jesus came."

Titus looked to the ground and held his face in his hand, concentrating intently on what he had just learned. "What did the cedar wood, hyssop, and scarlet wool thrown on the fire, have to do with the sacrifice?" he asked as he looked back up at me.

"In the Book of the Kings it says that, 'Solomon spoke three thousand proverbs and wrote one thousand and five songs. He spoke of the trees, from the cedar that is in Lebanon even to the hyssop that grows on the wall; he spoke also of animals and birds and creeping things and fish.' The cedar and the hyssop speak of the whole world—everything from alpha to omega. In the book of Isaiah the Lord said, 'Come now, let us reason together, though your sins are as scarlet, they will be white as snow; though they are red like crimson, they will be like wool.'

"So the scarlet represents our sin. Combined with the cedar and the hyssop, this is a picture that the sins of the whole world were placed on Christ: big sins, small sins, medium-sized sins, yesterday's sins, today's sins, tomorrow's sins. More than any other picture, the red heifer sacrifice shows us that what he did on the cross was perfect and complete. It is sufficient for all our needs for all our lifetimes."

Titus responded, "So all the other sacrifices take place at the altar in the temple, but the red heifer sacrifice is required to take place outside the camp. Is that why, in order to fulfill this picture, the Lord had to be crucified up here?"

I acknowledged that this was true.

"But I thought Paul said that Jesus was crucified at a place called the skull. I don't see any outcropping of rocks or anything that resembles a skull around here," said Titus.

"No, there is nothing like that up here on the mountain," I said. "Jesus was crucified at Golgotha, which means 'the place of the skull.' But in Hebrew the word *golgolet,* which translates into *golgotha* in the Greek, can also mean 'head.' *Miphkad* means 'numbering place.' This area around the miphkad altar is where official censuses are taken. It has to be outside the camp in order to include those people who, for whatever reason, are unclean. It is also the place where heads were traditionally counted when the army assembled to go out to war. Before battles, the army would exit the city by crossing the

Bridge of the Red Heifer and come to this open area on the Mount of Olives. Their heads were counted before they went out and again after they came back to see how many losses were inflicted. So Golgotha is the place of the heads, and this is the place on the mountain where our Lord was crucified."

As Titus's head turned, scanning the mostly bare mountainside, all of a sudden it came to a stop. Pointing to a place not far away, he asked, "I see a place in the distance where there looks to be a mound of ashes. Is that the miphkad altar?"

"No," I said, "but it is very close to it. That is *Beth ha-Deshen*, which means 'House of Ashes.' It is the place where all the ashes from the sacrifices made in the temple are taken.[20] It forms somewhat of a natural drainage system where the rains wash the ashes down the mountain into the Kidron Valley. From there, the waters carry them further south to fertilize the gardens that provide food for the priests. The ashes from the red heifer kept here on the mountain are stored at Bethphage, the village for the priests who serve at the outer sanctuary.

"Bethphage is a walled village a short distance east of here, just over the crest of the Mount of Olives on its western slope. It is not far up the road. I hope that we will be able to visit there today, but we may run out of time. Maybe on another day you can make this trek again and see Bethphage, and just beyond it, the village of Bethany.

"Bethphage is the place where we ran ahead to secure a donkey for Jesus to ride into the city when he was on his way from Bethany to Jerusalem. The people waved palm branches and cast their outer garments on the Descent of the Mount of Olives in a way reserved only for royalty. They shouted, 'Hosanna, (which means, save us)! Blessed is he who comes in the name of the Lord, even the King of Israel!'"

I smiled at the memory of that glorious day. "They were looking for a king. They were calling out to him to save them from the Romans, not to save them from their sins. But this did fulfill the prophecy of Zechariah which said, 'Rejoice greatly, O daughter of Zion. Shout in triumph, O daughter of Jerusalem! Behold, your king is coming to you; he is just and endowed with salvation, humble, and mounted on a donkey, even on a colt, the foal of a donkey.'

"In addition, those familiar with the Scriptures would also be reminded of a scene from the story in 1 Kings where David called for the anointing of Solomon, his son. Solomon rode on David's mule down this very path to the Gihon Spring. There, Zadok the priest and Nathan the prophet anointed him as king over Israel. Christ's riding on the mule suggested that he too belonged to the lineage of David and Solomon, and as the Son of David, had the legal right to be king."

"Even more prophecies about the Messiah fulfilled. How could the Jews have missed it?" Titus asked, shaking his head.

"The Jews were looking for a Messiah," I told him, "but you must understand what that meant to them. The Messiah, or the Anointed One, they were looking for was the one on whom the Spirit of God would rest. And not only that, but as the prophet Joel said, he would be the one who would pour out that Spirit on all of God's people.

"During the former days, before the New Covenant was enacted through the shedding of Christ's own blood, God's supernatural power and anointing would come upon specific individuals to fulfill specific tasks. Through this anointing, people could exercise superhuman strength, as in the case of Samson, or could speak with authority on behalf of God. In other cases the anointing upon an individual could enhance a person's creative abilities, giving them...wisdom, understanding, and knowledge, as was the case with the craftsmen who made artistic designs for the tabernacle of Moses. In any case, the Spirit's coming upon people was temporary, not permanent, and only experienced by a few.

"Seeing and hearing of the few throughout history who were the recipients of this temporary, supernatural anointing—an anointing which could be withdrawn—caused our people to look forward to the day when God would send one on whom the fullness of the Spirit would rest. This one would, in turn, pour out that Spirit upon all flesh. In that day they hoped to see a universal experience and access to the Spirit of God that extended beyond the few—the prophets, priests, and kings—so that all would have access to the divine presence. Teachers would no longer be needed in Israel, but God would write his laws in their hearts based on his Spirit indwelling each one.

"In hindsight, this has certainly been true, but our people were so convinced in their understanding that this Anointed One, who was to be full of the Spirit and who would pour out of that Spirit, would be a political leader who would deliver them from the oppression of Rome. They failed to recognize that in order for him to impart the Spirit, he first needed to fulfill the role of the Suffering Servant foretold by Isaiah, resulting in his humiliation and death on the cross. This fact, the majority of Jews have still not come to accept."

"Amazing!" breathed Titus.

"Yes, it is," I said as Titus reached under his tunic for a small satchel, pulled out a small crust of bread, and tore off a bite. "Now, I would like to tell you more about Bethphage, for though it is small, it is a very interesting place. Bethphage is the only place outside the camp that is considered by the Sanhedrin to be an official part of the city of Jerusalem. Not only does a small contingent of priests live there, but it is also the place where all the census and genealogical records are kept. If one needs to be able to prove his priestly lineage in order to enter the temple, this is where he will come to find the records."

"If all the genealogical records are kept there, then this would also be the place to check to see if one claiming to be the Messiah was of the royal bloodline of King David, right?" asked Titus.

"Yes," I said, smiling at his perceptiveness.

Titus continued, "Earlier you described how Jesus predicted that days of vengeance were coming to Jerusalem within this generation and that this city would be left desolate. If that is true, then not only the temple but also the city and this place of records will likely be destroyed, correct?"

"That also is true, Titus," I said. "That is what we are expecting. But Jesus did say that when we see armies surrounding the city we must flee, so there is still some time remaining to us."

Titus continued with his train of thought. "If Jerusalem is completely destroyed as you say, and if that includes this place of records, how would the Jews ever be able to identify the Messiah if someone was to come along later and make that claim?"

"The records would be lost, and such verification would be impossible," I said. "There would be no way to confirm the credentials of anyone making the claim to messiahship. I have known our Lord well enough to know his attention to detail. Destroying those records has undoubtedly figured into his plan. But it is a good point you raise, Titus.

"There are a few other things about this place that I would like to share with you. First, the name Bethphage means 'House of Unripened Figs.' Have you heard the story of Jesus cursing the fig tree?"

"No," he replied.

"That happened right near Bethphage as well," I said. "Five days before his crucifixion, the day he was hailed with hosannas, we returned from the temple and spent the night in Bethany. We left early the next morning to make the two-mile trip down the Descent of the Mount of Olives to the temple once again. On the way, Jesus saw a fig tree just off to the side of the road near the walls of Bethphage. It was covered with leaves, which was strange because the fruit normally appears soon after the leaves do; yet there were no figs on it. It was not even the season for figs yet. But Jesus, fixating on that tree, cursed it. The next day we passed by it again and saw that it had completely withered.

"When he first cursed that fig tree, we were perplexed. We did not really understand why he had done it. But following this, Jesus took us to the temple again and began to teach in the colonnade surrounding the court of the Gentiles. On that occasion he confronted the chief priests and elders, saying, 'Therefore I say to you, the kingdom of God shall be taken from you and given to a nation producing the fruit of it.' Then we made the connection: Israel was that barren fig tree. Like Adam and Eve, who used the leaves of the fig tree to clothe their nakedness, Israel has clothed herself with all the outward beauty of religion in order to hide her nakedness. Jesus sent an unmistakable message to the nation of Israel that he was through dealing with a nation that did not bear fruit.

"As I have thought about that event over the years, I have come to some further conclusions about its significance. I think there is also a deeper, spiritual lesson to be learned from the fig tree. It reminds me of one of the earliest stories recorded in the book of Genesis, one that took place in the garden of Eden."

"You have piqued my interest," Titus said. "Please tell me."

"You remember the story of Adam and Eve's disobedience in the garden and how they fell by eating from the Tree of the Knowledge of Good and Evil?" I asked.

"Yes," said Titus. "I am quite familiar with the story."

I proceeded to tell him that the only tree referred to by its species in that story is the fig tree. The couple must have been very near to the fig tree after they became aware of their sin and nakedness, because they took leaves from its branches and sewed them together to hide their shame. For this reason, in Jewish lore, the fig tree has always been associated with the Tree of the Knowledge of Good and Evil.

"When Jesus cursed that tree, through which sin and death first came into the world, he was foreshadowing that through his obedience, he was about to release creation from the curse of the fall. Through one man's disobedience, sin and death entered into this world. But through one man's obedience, God's original purpose for the whole human race would be restored, and we would be made alive. The second Adam was not going to repeat the mistake of the first!"

I returned to the story of Bethpage.

"In addition to the Hall of Polished Stones," I continued, "the Sanhedrin had a second official meeting place in Bethphage.[21] People who are unclean, and lepers who have to stand before the council to be judged, are barred from the temple area. So they needed a place outside the camp where they could convene for such trials and for special situations. Among those special situations was the sentencing and excommunicating of rebellious leaders. Since Jesus was respected by many as a rabbi, or teacher, and was accused of blasphemy and practicing magic, they considered him to be a religious leader who was leading people astray. Therefore, his official sentencing was required to be conducted at Bethphage. So it was there, outside that camp, that Jesus was judged and excommunicated from the house of Israel. From the Sanhedrin's point of view, Jesus died as a Gentile and not a Jew."

"Remarkable!" said Titus, shaking his head in near disbelief. "This mountain has been the scene not only for things of historical significance, but of rich symbolism as well."

"Oh yes! But there is so much more," I said. "This is the mountain where Jesus spent most of his time when he was in the vicinity of Jerusalem. Though he would teach in the temple during the day, we always spent the night somewhere on the Mount of Olives. Often we would stay in Bethany at the home of Mary, Martha, and Lazarus. Unlike Jerusalem, that was the place where he felt at home and enjoyed being with his friends. That was the place where Mary poured oil on his feet and wiped it with her hair. That was the place where he was worshiped.

"Jesus actually spent more time teaching at different locations on the Mount of Olives than he did in the temple. You will find it interesting that the Jews have another name for the Mount of Olives: in Hebrew, it is also called 'the Mount of the Anointing.' Translated into Greek, that means 'the Mountain of the Christ.' The Mount of Olives is the place where he made his home, where he loved to teach and be with his friends, where he performed miracles, and where he was crucified, buried, resurrected, and ascended. Truly, this is *his* mountain.

CHAPTER 5
THE CRUCIFIXION

The sun had risen higher in the sky, turning the palm-sized layers of flint stone and flakes beneath our feet hot as we surveyed the place where the cross once stood. Golgotha was barren now, nothing about its landscape hinting at the astounding event that had taken place here. "Now I will tell you about the crucifixion," I said, as we found a spot to sit down.

"It was a little past eight o'clock on that Friday morning twenty-eight years ago.[22] Pilate ordered six hundred of his soldiers to go before Jesus and the other two criminals, commanding them to line the road leading to the place of execution. Worshipers were already beginning to stream down the mountain toward the temple with their lambs to have them slaughtered for the Passover Feast that night, and they needed to control the crowds. Close to twenty thousand lambs met their fate that day.

"Fighting their way upstream against the hoard of people moving in their direction were two condemned criminals, the real Passover lamb, the four soldiers that surrounded each prisoner, the chief priests and members of the Sanhedrin, and a growing number of onlookers, including women who were mourning and weeping. Jesus was never out of my sight, as I, too, fought the crowd, following close behind. The centurion in charge of the execution led the procession. They followed the same course as was taken when a red heifer was led to slaughter, crossing the bridge bearing that name and moving up the Descent of the Mount of Olives to Golgotha.

"Each of the three men sentenced to die was required to carry his own *patibulum,* or crossbeam, to which he would be nailed. Each patibulum was made of cypress wood and was about six feet long, five inches thick, and ten inches high, weighing about forty pounds. Shouldering the beam on his fresh wounds, Jesus staggered forward up the hill."

Titus interrupted. "One of our close friends in Antioch, Syria—Simeon, the black man from the city of Cyrene on the coast of North Africa—told me this part of the story. He and his wife and their sons, Rufus and Alexander, migrated to Antioch after the persecution broke out in Jerusalem. Though Paul was responsible for starting that persecution, he became close friends with the family, even living at their house. Simeon's wife is like a mother to him."

"Simeon is a dear brother," I said. "He was among the spectators standing along the road when Jesus stumbled and fell, sprawling on the ground before him. One of the guards ordered Simeon to pick up Jesus's patibulum and carry it the rest of the way for him."

Speaking of Simeon reminded me of still more symbolism that had played out that day. "I am getting a little ahead of myself, but after Jesus had been raised from the dead three days later, he appeared to the eleven of us apostles and those who were with us. At first we were frightened and thought we were seeing a spirit. Then he showed us his hands and his feet and let us touch him. As it began to sink in that it really was him, we were overcome with joy and amazement. He casually asked for a piece of fish to eat. Then he sat down with us, opened the Scriptures, and spoke to us about all that had been written about him in the law of Moses and the prophets and the psalms.

"He told of one portion of the Scriptures concerning Abraham. I am sure you have heard the story from Paul, but perhaps not with all of its symbolism explained. God told Abraham to offer Isaac on one of the mountains in the mountain range called Moriah. That includes the Mount of Olives and the rest of the prominent higher places around Jerusalem.

"Abraham was around 130 years old. His son Isaac was in his thirties— probably about the same age as Jesus. When Isaac realized that he was going to be the sacrifice, he was old enough, big enough, and strong enough to protest and even put up a fight to resist his father, but he did not. As a picture of Christ, he was willingly bound and placed on the wood to be killed and offered to God. And as an added detail in the story, Isaac even carried the wood upon which he would be sacrificed. Like bursts of light going off in our heads, Jesus opened our eyes to see that these things that happened nearly two thousand years before were a foreshadowing of how he would bear his own wood and willingly offer himself up to his Father."

I shook my head in amazement once again. "When sentencing someone to die by means of crucifixion, it is the Roman practice to have them executed as near as possible to the scene of their crimes. If that cannot be determined or is not possible, the next best place for them to be crucified is near the place where they are arrested.

"Since Jesus was accused of blasphemy—claiming to be God—and of treason, a reasonable place to choose for his execution would be the area around Golgotha. After all, this was the general vicinity where the people had hailed him as king when he came down the mountain on the donkey. This is where they cried out, 'Blessed is he who comes in the name of the Lord, even the king of Israel!' And since he was arrested in the garden of

"The tomb was a subterranean cave, carved out of limestone rock. It had two chambers—a larger, square entry room for use as a mourning chamber where people could gather, and a smaller, rectangular place cut out of the wall, where the body was laid. Joseph and Nicodemus dislodged a large, heavy stone that was perched in an elevated position in front of the entryway, and it rolled down the slight incline and came to rest, sealing the cave.

"Throughout Jerusalem that night there were those who joyfully celebrated the Passover Feast; others who were more subdued, and while they ate, pondered the day's events; and those of us who had no stomach for the meal at all. We were confused, lost, and brokenhearted."

"John, would it be possible for me to see the tomb where Jesus was buried?" Titus asked.

"Certainly. I had planned to take you there. It is very close by—right over there," I said, pointing to a garden surrounded by a grove of myrtle and cypress trees. "Let us go visit our tomb."

"Our tomb?" inquired Titus, with a quizzical look.

"Yes, *our* tomb," I repeated emphatically. "It was not only Jesus's tomb, but the tomb in which the entire fallen human race was buried. Come, let us go."

CHAPTER 6
THE RESURRECTION

We walked a short distance to the entrance of the tomb. As we approached, Titus asked, "Did Joseph of Arimathea not use this, after all, for his own tomb?"

"No," I answered. "Considering the rather unusual circumstances, he thought it best to purchase another grotto in which to rest his bones. Since that time, we have been using this cave as a place to meet. Let us go inside."

Titus went first, ducking into the darkness. He nearly tripped on a young man seated near the entrance.

"Oh, excuse me! I didn't mean to interrupt," he said, embarrassed to find others already inside the cave sitting and kneeling on the ground in prayer.

"Do not be embarrassed," I said. "For you have done nothing wrong. This is a prayer meeting. This place is constantly used as a place for the saints to gather. Greetings, brothers!" I said to the small band of worshipers. "I want to introduce you to my new friend, Titus. His hometown is Antioch in Syria. He is one of the Gentile workers Paul has been working with in Ephesus. He is a good brother. Maybe I can persuade him into returning and speaking to you some afternoon. Inwardly, he is really a Jew at heart, just like us! You would be amazed and greatly encouraged by his knowledge of the Lord and his grasp of spiritual things."

The half-dozen or so gathered looked up at Titus and me with a welcoming smile.

"We would love to join you now to pray and fellowship, but we still have many things to talk about, and it is beginning to get late. Titus just wanted to see the tomb. We will take our leave now and find a place outside to eat our lunch and continue our discussion. Pray for this brother, and do not forget him. I believe that he is one whom God will use in a mighty way."

They tried to prevail upon us to stay, but we declined. Exiting the cave, we looked around for a place to sit down and eat.

"If I were a piece of boiled fish, where would I want to be eaten?" joked Titus. "I think that flat rock and stump along the path look to be as inviting a place as any." The shade of a cypress tree beckoned us to the site.

"They do indeed," I commented. "And it just so happens that the place you have chosen would have given us front-row seats for a legendary footrace that passed by here some years ago. I will tell you about it in a few minutes."

After taking a few bites from the fish in his hand, Titus said, "As you described the crucifixion, John, your words painted such a vivid picture for me that it almost seems as if I were there myself. Who can fathom the depth of the love of God—that he was willing to allow his Son to suffer so much for our redemption?"

"You can say that ultimate love and ultimate evil intersected on that tree," I replied. "The Son of God came from heaven to earth to do moral battle with Satan and all his evil forces. For three days, the results seemed uncertain. But on the third day, love triumphed."

"I am also astonished," Titus said, "at how God orchestrated all those events and how so many prophecies, made hundreds of years before, were fulfilled down to the last detail. They could never have happened by chance. The earthquake, the stones splitting open, and especially the tearing of that curtain in the temple must have given people the idea that something truly ominous had just occurred!"

"We were too overcome with grief to grasp the significance of those events at the time," I said. "But later, after the Lord had risen and appeared to us, our eyes were opened. It was as if the glory hidden behind the veil inside the temple burst into our souls, filling, as it were, the whole temple with his glory."

"When I have heard the story told by Paul and others, I always thought it was the inner veil that hung between the Holy of Holies and the Holy Place that was torn in two."

"And that is true," I replied. "It was. But for a priest to get to the Holy of Holies, he must go through that outer curtain as well. It needed to be rent apart also. That was something the centurion and the rest of us were able to observe from up here on the mountain.

"There was a profound lesson that Jesus wanted to teach us by the tearing of the curtain. In the Genesis story of the fall of Adam and Eve, you will remember that God sent our first parents out of the garden and stationed two cherubim, with flaming swords, in front of the Tree of Life to keep them from coming back to eat of that tree in their fallen condition. The next place we read about the cherubim is in Exodus, where God gave Moses instructions to construct all the furniture in the tabernacle. We read that God told him to make a curtain of finely twined linen to hang at the entrance to the Holy of Holies, separating it from the Holy Place. And embroidered into the fabric of that curtain were pictures of those cherubim."

Titus was listening intently; the dried fish lay forgotten in his hand.

unblemished lamb and kill it at twilight. Then they were to take the blood of the lamb and apply it to the doorposts of their houses. They were to roast the lamb without breaking any of its bones. They did this by placing the lamb on two wooden spits, one extending the length of its body and the other horizontal, curiously resembling the shape of a cross. Then they ate the lamb in haste while they were leaving Egypt so that it would give them strength for their journey.

"The blood on the doorposts protected the children of Israel from the death angel that God released in Egypt to slay the firstborn of every home. When the angel saw the blood on the doorposts, he would pass over that home and no harm would come to those inside. So the blood of that lamb was for their protection and deliverance. The meat of the lamb was for their nourishment and strength.

"In the book of Exodus, Moses refers to Egypt as the 'house of slavery.' This was not the place God had in mind for his people to live. God had a better place for them: the land of Canaan, a place of freedom and fullness."

"You know our history well," I said with a smile.

"In our Christian experience, before we each met the Lord, we were all in slavery in one form or another—it does not matter if we were Roman citizens, freemen, or slaves. Some are enslaved to their own ambitions, or to strong drink, money, immoral lives, or the pleasures of this world. Satan, represented by Pharaoh, wants to keep us in that place of bondage. But God wants to deliver us.

"Just as God sent Moses to the Jews so long ago, he sent Jesus to us. They applied the blood to their doorposts. We apply the blood of Christ to our lives. His death resulted in our passing from death into life. When God sees the blood of Jesus covering us, we are delivered from the judgment we deserve.

"But there is more to the story. God wanted to take the children of Israel from Egypt—the house of slavery—through the wilderness to the Promised Land, which he wanted to give them for an inheritance. As believers, our inheritance is Christ, not some physical land. God wants to give all of us—whether Jew or Gentile, slave or free—Christ, and he wants us to know him in his fullness—the height, depth, length, and breadth of him. In order for us to do that, he needs to deliver us from whatever slavery we were in. The journey for us is from the bondage of our flesh, our Egypt, through the wilderness of our souls to dwell in our spirits, where we find our inheritance, Christ himself.

"The blood on the doorposts is the starting point. We apply the blood to our lives, and we pass from death to life. But then the people ate the roasted lamb. This corresponds to us enjoying Christ as our salvation. The joy of the Lord gives us the strength to take the first steps in leaving Egypt and getting out of Satan's kingdom."

I clapped enthusiastically. "Good for you, Titus!"

"But that is not all. After eating the roasted lamb, the people set forth, leaving Egypt, and came to the edge of the Red Sea. They turned to see the Egyptian soldiers in their chariots coming after them to take them back to Egypt. The people were trapped and needed another miracle. They needed God to show up for them again.

"God instructed Moses to extend his staff over the Red Sea. The waters parted, and the people walked across on dry land. When the Egyptians tried to follow, the waters covered over them, and they were all destroyed.

"The people's experience of going through the waters of the Red Sea corresponds to baptism. For us, baptism represents our decision to leave the world behind and step out by faith to follow the Lord. It is the point where we are willing to say to the Lord, 'We are leaving Egypt behind and never going back.'

"Once they got out into that wilderness, there was more things the Lord wanted to show them about himself. He wanted to teach them to rely on him as their daily bread coming down from heaven, so he sent them the manna, even as he wants us to know him as our daily bread. Though the salvation experience is wonderful, the picture we see from the Passover is that this is only the starting point of the Christian life."

"You have been taught well, Titus," I said, proud of this young man. "You clearly understand the difference between the pictures and the reality. The Passover, indeed, marked the starting point of the Hebrew nation. You might say that it is our annual birthday celebration. Moses even gave us a different way to number our calendar months, beginning with Nisan, to emphasize the fact that this was a new beginning for us. In the same way, when we come to Christ, we have a new beginning. Old things have passed away. All things have become new."

"I feel like I have been spouting off once again," said Titus. "I need to learn from you. What else can you teach me about lessons you have learned from the Passover?"

I mused his question over. "You have covered many of the basic lessons already. But God is in the business of constantly showing us new things. Many times he shows us something and then years later brings us back to the same thing and shows it to us again. But by this time we have had much more experience and can appreciate the same thing even more, because we have an even greater perspective.

"There is a little-studied detail from the Passover that I think reveals to us another divine principle. About three million people left Egypt with Moses. I would estimate that probably between 150,000 and 300,000 lambs were slaughtered that night.

"When Jews eat the Passover meal, it is usually in small companies of ten to twenty people. Here in Jerusalem, after the Lord brought in such a bountiful harvest—with three thousand people being saved on the day of Pentecost, and then later, five thousand men at one time, not counting women and children—the church swelled in size very rapidly. Within a few years, there were well over twenty thousand believers in the church. We continued to meet in Solomon's Porch in the temple for as long as we possibly could. We were thankful for that because it was a great place to teach the multitudes. But the real meetings of the church, where brothers and sisters could intimately share what Christ was doing in their daily lives and build deep relationships with one another, happened in homes. Gazelles live in the mountains. Fish live in the sea. The Jews meet in the temple and in their synagogues. The pagans meet in their temples and at their shrines. But the church meets in homes. That is our natural habitat.

"Christ promised us that things would be different after the Holy Spirit came. But until that actually happened, we had no way of comprehending what he meant. He had talked about the church, but we had no idea of what it was really supposed to look like. If you had asked us, before Pentecost, what our understanding of the church was, we would probably have said something like, 'The church must be being with Christ, having him as our center, being in his presence, fellowshipping and interacting with him and one another. That has been our experience. So that must be what church is.'

"With twenty thousand people meeting in homes throughout the city, the church in Jerusalem met in a minimum of four hundred homes. We did not plan it that way. It just happened. But when we understood that Christ was no longer physically present with us but was now present in Spirit, we saw that the new believers needed to learn to know him together just as we had—in informal settings, in homes, around meals, along the roads, on the side of mountains, by the sea. This is just like the Passover, which was not intended to be regularly observed in some large coliseum or temple, but in the intimacy of small groups and in homes.

"After the death of Stephen, when persecution came to the church through the hand of Saul, those big meetings in the temple came to an abrupt halt. So they lasted only a few years. When Christians fled the city and settled in the other cities of Judea, they just continued doing what they had learned to do in Jerusalem. They kept meeting together in homes, sharing Christ together, and taking their meals together with joy and gladness of heart, as they had done before."

"We Gentile believers also meet in homes," said Titus. "But I would love to know how closely our meetings correspond to yours. What did your meetings actually look like in those early days?"

"Would you like me to describe a church meeting before Pentecost or after Pentecost?" I asked.

"What?" responded a bewildered Titus. "I thought the church was born on the day of Pentecost when Peter preached the gospel and three thousand got saved!"

"That is true," I said. "But what we experienced before Pentecost, when the Lord was training us, was actually the church in its embryonic form. That is where we learned what the church was, and that is what we wanted to pass on to others."

"Very well!" said Titus, leaning back as if for a long story. "Tell me about a pre-Pentecost church meeting."

There are so many examples to choose from, I thought. *Where should I begin?*

Finally, I said, "I think I will tell you about a meeting in the city of Capernaum, on the western shore of the Sea of Galilee. But first, I need to give you a little background.

"The day before, we had been in the Gentile region of the Gerasenes, where Jesus healed a demoniac. He had gone there to get away from the crowds and get some rest. This demoniac was possessed by a legion of demons. Jesus cast them out of him and sent them into a herd of pigs, and the man was restored to his right mind. We crossed back over the sea in a boat and came ashore about a mile from Capernaum. A large crowd of people was waiting for Jesus there."

I closed my eyes and pictured the color and noise of the crowd on that shore—several thousand people, flooding the city and the countryside, all clamoring for Jesus's attention. Had there ever been a prophet with such power to draw people to himself?

"One man in the crowd was a synagogue official named Jairus. He had a twelve-year-old daughter who was sick to the point of death. He made his way to the front of the crowd and earnestly pleaded for Jesus to come to his home and lay his hands on the little girl so that she would get well and live. So Jesus and the rest of us headed off for the man's home.

"On the way, a woman who had suffered from a severe bleeding problem for twelve years knifed her way through the crowd and reached out to touch the fringe of Jesus's outer garment. He was wearing a *tallit*, a prayer shawl with fringes and a blue tassel on each of the four corners, which our rabbis and teachers of the law commonly wear."

I smiled and shook my head, remembering the image of that woman when Jesus called her out of the crowd. "For her to touch the fringe of Jesus's tallit was a violation of the law, for it was forbidden for anyone who was not a family member to touch the tallit of another. But this woman was desperate, having spent everything she had trying to get well. She was instantaneously healed. Jesus felt power go out of him, and he called upon the woman to identify herself. Rather than chastising her for breaking the law, Jesus called her 'daughter.' This woman's faith made Jesus look upon her as part of his family. Being ceremonially unclean as she had been for twelve years, instead of making Jesus unclean by touching him, she was purified as his incredible cleanness surged back into her!

"As he spoke to her and told her that her faith had made her well, messengers from Jairus's house pulled Jairus aside and told him that his daughter had died and that Jesus was no longer needed.

"Jesus overheard them and said to Jairus, 'Do not be afraid any longer, only believe.'

"He commanded the crowds not to follow him. He summoned Peter, James, and me, along with Jairus, and we went on to the man's home.

"When we arrived, we found a great commotion inside. Everyone was grief stricken. The family, relatives, and friends were weeping and wailing loudly. A few of them had already begun playing a funeral song on their flutes. Then Jesus took charge. 'Why all the commotion, and why is everyone crying? The child has not died. She is just asleep.'

"Their sobbing quickly turned to hysterical laughing, anger, and ridicule. They must have thought, *Is this man crazy? We all know she is dead!*

"Then Jesus told them to leave the house. He took Jairus and his wife, along with the three of us disciples, into the bedroom where the child lay on a mat. Taking her limp hand in his, Jesus said to her, 'Little girl, I say to you, get up!' Immediately she opened her eyes, got up, and began to walk around the room."

I stopped. Titus looked confused. "Are you still with me, Titus?"

"I have gone nowhere, John. I am just trying to figure out what this has to do with a church meeting."

"Precisely what I am about to tell you," I said, grinning. "Now you will hear about the church meeting we had that night!

"That evening we returned with the rest of the disciples to the home of some friends we knew in the city. It was a large home, and our hosts graciously prepared a large meal for us. We sat down, and the women began serving the food. Peter could not contain his excitement any longer. He blurted out, 'You would not believe what happened today in the house of Jairus! Jesus raised a little girl from the dead!' Then he began to tell the story, picking up from where Jesus, the three of us, and Jairus had departed together for Jairus's home.

"'And when he took her hand and she got up and started to walk, the rest of us in the room nearly lost our minds!' he said. 'The mother and father were blubbering uncontrollably for joy. John and James and I were momentarily stunned, but then we spontaneously erupted in weeping and laughter along with the rest of them. The mother embraced her daughter, kissing her over and over again and holding her tight. Jairus just looked into the face of Jesus, convulsing, unable to speak, but with an expression on his face that said, 'How could I ever thank you enough?'"

"Now you have me crying too!" said Titus, thoroughly engaged in the story.

"Tears of joy are not uncommon when you are around Jesus!" I said.

"Before Peter could finish, James interrupted and said, 'After everyone calmed down we spent some precious moments there with the family. Jairus threw his arms around Jesus's neck and embraced him, repeating the words, "Thank you, thank you." When he was finished, his wife surprised us all and unabashedly did the same. Jesus talked with them for a while. He smiled at the young girl, motioned her to come to him, and gave her a long hug. I will never forget her face as she rested her head calmly on Jesus's chest. We prayed for the family and for their daughter. Finally we left the room, passed through the living room, and opened the front door.'

"Andrew, who was eating this story up and hanging on every word, exclaimed, 'What did all the people outside say when they saw the little girl alive?'

"Then it was my turn. I told them how we went out in front of the house and how all the relatives and friends who saw the little girl walking out, holding on to her mother's dress, reacted. Some cried; some dropped their flutes to the ground in amazement; some raised their eyes toward heaven and their arms in the sky and shouted, 'Glory to God!' They all kept looking at one another in astonishment.

"Interestingly, Jairus's name means 'the Enlightened One.' His face was lit up like a candle. The light was certainly blazing in his house that day!

"Then one of the other disciples—I don't remember who—brought up what had happened earlier that day, when Jesus healed the woman who touched his garments. After we thoroughly relived and rehashed that, we started to recall the miracle the day before with the demoniac, and so it went long into the night. As we ate and fellowshipped together over what Jesus had done, there was a lot of laughter and praise, along with occasional songs which seemed appropriate for the occasion."

"What an amazing night it must have been!" exclaimed Titus.

"That was church as we knew it," I said. "And that is what it was like being together with Jesus for those three-and-a-half years."

"I am not sure if I am ready to hear about another meeting—the after-Pentecost variety," said Titus. "It will take me a while just to digest this last one. But since I did ask, and I am keenly interested, please tell me what those meetings in homes were like in the early years of the church in Jerusalem."

I had told Titus that our time with Jesus before Pentecost was our experience of the church in its embryonic form. After the baby was born, so to speak—at Pentecost and beyond—for a while we were in over our heads. We didn't know what to do. We were just following the leading of the Spirit as best we could, and the result was "church."

"The church in Jerusalem was born with a life of its own. The living, risen, exalted Christ was moving in and through his people. Most of what happened could not have been planned or anticipated. The church just grew organically. Pilgrims visiting the city wanted to stay. Peter had the boldness to tell them to sell all they had and remain. A few years before, all of us had left everything. He was not asking them to do anything we had not already done ourselves.

"People began selling their belongings to help meet one another's needs. They piled into houses where believers lived or rented apartments that were available. The shortage of space combined with the numbers of people meant that every home was packed from wall to wall. At night, bodies occupied every available space on every floor. The church was born into a wild, chaotic, out-of-control, and glorious environment.

"I remember one meeting in the home of Mary, Barnabas's sister. Her home was always packed out, with at least twenty-five to thirty people, and I frequently dropped by to participate in those meetings. Barnabas was staying there, along with his family, John Mark, other cousins and relatives, out-of-town guests, and a number of newcomers who had just become a part of the church.

"As the day began, one by one people rolled off their mats and found a place to get cleaned up and dressed. After breakfast they went in different directions. Barnabas, along with John Mark and some others, usually headed off for Solomon's Porch. The other apostles and I had been going there every day to meet the crowds and teach them about Jesus. Some of the people stayed at home to help straighten up and prepare meals. Others went out to the market to buy food. Still others had to work. Some were out looking for work.

"In the evenings they all straggled in at different times. It did not take long before everyone felt like family. In different parts of the house, small clusters of brothers and sisters exchanged casual conversation. When supper was served, everyone gathered in the living room and took his or her place on the floor for the evening meal.

"After someone gave thanks for the food, it was Barnabas who opened with something like, 'You would not believe what Peter was talking about at Solomon's Porch today!' After he related some of the stories Peter and the rest of us had told about being with Jesus, John Mark interrupted, adding his part to the story. Then someone else piled on with what he had heard and seen. Others, who were not at Solomon's Porch, asked questions. There was always a lot of laughter. Things were very informal. Each person felt free to participate.

"After all the sharing about what had happened in the temple had ended, one of the women introduced a friend she had met at the market that day. This friend had just recently received the Lord. She had been invited to come and give her testimony and meet some of her new family. She was introduced and shared about how she met Jesus. When she finished, several of the brothers and sisters spontaneously responded with, 'Amen,' 'How wonderful, Sister!' 'Hallelujah!' And they encouraged her in the Lord. Mary suggested that we all pray for her and for her family.

"About that time, the door opened and another brother burst inside with a big smile on his face. 'I found a job!' he shouted. He took his place on the floor in front of a plate and began sharing how the Lord had led him to the foreman in charge of a building project in the upper city. The man had given him work and said that he could come back because there would be much more to do in the days ahead. When he finished, everyone praised God. 'God answers prayer!' John Mark shouted. Someone else suggested an appropriate song of praise, which we all sang heartily together. Then, as in all our meetings, different brothers and sisters took the opportunity to talk about fresh miracles, prophetic revelations, and new insights from the Scriptures that they had seen.

"When that ended, one of the sisters said, 'I need to share something with everybody. My little girl has been running a high fever. I am very concerned about her. Could you all please pray for my baby?'

"Without delay, every heart in the room turned to God, and the baby and her mother were lifted up to the Lord in prayer. Some of us got up from our places and laid hands on the child. Someone else asked if there were any other needs we should pray for. A few responded. More prayer. Sometime during this particular gathering, we broke bread and passed a cup of wine around the room—symbols of the living Christ who shed his blood for us, made us one body, and gave us the Life we now shared together."

I smiled at the memory—of that meeting and of so many others like it. The warmth, love, and enthusiasm of those early days had carried me through many a hard time since.

"Those meetings were characterized by their informality, freedom, sincerity, and personal interaction. There were many heartfelt testimonies and personal stories about people's encounters with the Lord. We sang from the psalms, and many brothers and sisters began composing their own spiritual songs. There was much prayer, praise, and glorious worship. Everything was centered on Jesus Christ. There was really no difference between the first meeting I described to you and this one. The only difference was that in the first, Jesus was present in body. In the second, he was equally present, only in Spirit."

Titus responded by telling me that in Antioch they had known the same experience. They had never known anything but meeting in homes. Paul, Barnabas, Simeon, and other respected brothers and sisters who lived in Antioch were all able to minister the Lord from house to house. The Syrian church received a variety of teaching from a number of different personalities. But they also experienced the diversity of hearing all the brothers and sisters contribute in the meetings, some with a psalm, some with a hymn, a testimony, a teaching, a prayer, a prophetic word, and so on. According to Titus, this was true of all of Paul's churches and the churches they had planted throughout Asia. I marveled as he spoke. I knew from my own experience how beautiful it was to see the different expressions of what God was doing in individual lives and to watch them express the Lord through the unique personalities God had given them. This could not happen in a crowd like the ones where we assembled at Solomon's Porch. That was a different kind of meeting altogether.

"When Paul was training us brothers in Ephesus," Titus said, "he rented a space in the school of Tyrannus to hold those meetings. School was conducted there in the mornings, but in the afternoons the building was free. Paul worked in the mornings in the marketplace, mending tents and repairing other leather products. But in the afternoons he would arrive at the school to teach Timothy, Gaius, Sopater, Aristarchus, Secundus, Tychicus, Trophimus, and me, along with anyone else who showed up. Paul's intentions for those meetings were to teach and equip us, similar, I suppose, to what you brothers were doing with the crowds at Solomon's Porch. But our training meetings did not interrupt anything the church in Ephesus was doing. They continued to meet together in homes throughout the city."

"From all that Paul and you have said," I told Titus, "it seems that Ephesus has become a ministry center and the strategic city from which many churches have been planted in the Gentile world—much as Jerusalem was the place God initially used to reach Jews all over the Roman Empire."

"It is true, John," said Titus. "I can remember Paul's excitement as the two of us set out for Ephesus together from Antioch, Syria, on his third missionary journey. Along the way we stopped in Derbe to pick up Gaius, and then in Lystra to pick up Timothy. Paul had sent word ahead to Sopater from Berea and to Aristarchus and Secundus from Thessalonica to meet us in Ephesus. Tychicus and Trophimus, from Asia, joined us there also. Paul talked with me for hours about what he planned to do there. He wanted to teach us and then send us out with one another to get practical experience at planting churches. Ephesus was the perfect location to establish a training base to equip workers to take the gospel throughout Asia and Europe. It is the forth largest city in the entire Roman Empire, with a population approaching 300,000—surpassed only by Rome, Alexandria, and Antioch, Syria. It has a beautiful port, with people coming and going all the time along the trade routes to Asia in the east, and it is the jumping-off point into Europe on the north."

I sat in reflection for several minutes, imagining the city Titus described and recalling what I had learned from Paul about the work there. I could feel the Lord implanting something in me as I mused, and I lifted a silent prayer.

"You have planted a seed in my heart, Titus," I said. "One day, if the Lord wills, I must visit Ephesus and the churches the Lord has raised up in Asia through you brothers."

"You would be more than welcome!" he replied. "The brothers and sisters there would be beside themselves with joy if you should ever decide to visit them. We hold you original apostles in very high esteem."

I nodded to acknowledge the honor he gave me, but I knew that God was every bit as much at work in these newer converts as in those of us who had been first. "I can see God's hand in purifying his church through the work he is raising up among the Gentiles. You are more open to new things than the Jews. In many of the meetings now throughout Judea, our people spend too much time debating different points of the law and trying to instigate rituals that suck the life right out of the meetings. This is primarily because a good number of Pharisees have come to Christ, and they are beginning to bring their legalism into the church. It is a constant battle here. You Gentiles do not have as much religion flowing through your veins as do we Jews! You are experiencing a freedom that is frightening to most Jews—they do not know how to handle it. But as we step back and consider that the gospel with which we have been entrusted must be preached to the whole world, it seems as if the work God is doing among the Gentiles is now central to what he is doing in these days."

"I know, John," Titus responded, "believe me. We are seeing the gospel go to places it has never gone before. But we have also seen this resistance and stubbornness from the Jews throughout Galatia, Macedonia, Achaia, and Asia. It is the Jewish religious leaders who have been the main source of persecution against the church. Paul has nearly two hundred stripes on his back to prove it. But even if the main thrust of God's work now is to establish a witness among all nations in the Gentile world, we are acutely aware that it is no reason for us to become proud. It is a work of God's unmerited favor."

"Amen, Titus. Wise words indeed! Now tell me, what would you like to hear about next?"

"I would like for you to continue your story, John. I want to hear what happened after Christ was taken from the tree."

"Very well," I said. "But first, let us find another place to sit. We have lost the shade from the cypress." Titus jumped up first, extended his hand to me, and hoisted me to my feet. We moved around a bit, stretched, and then relocated under the boughs of a large myrtle tree just opposite the cypress. We leaned our backs against its trunk, stretched out our legs in the grass, and continued.

"The priests and the Pharisees were very fidgety about leaving Jesus's body unattended in that grave. It was common knowledge among them that he had said after three days he would be raised from the dead. So they sent a delegation to Pilate, asking him to send some soldiers to seal the tomb and guard it until the third day. Pilate was still aggravated with them for forcing him into the position of having to give Jesus over to be crucified, so he told them that their own temple guards would need to secure it as best as they could. So at the end of the Sabbath, after sundown, they sent their own guards to seal the tomb and stand watch.

"Following the Sabbath, early on Sunday morning, Mary Magdalene, Mary the mother of James, my mother Salome, and Joanna brought the spices they had prepared to anoint Jesus's body to the tomb. In this climate, bodily decay begins quite rapidly, and the aromatic spices help to cover the stench. Joanna was the wife of Herod Antipas's chief steward, Chuza. She was well connected politically and a woman of considerable means. She, along with Susanna and other women from Galilee, contributed heavily out of her private funds to help support Jesus and the rest of us as we traveled throughout the land.

"They left the city while it was still dark, and by the time they arrived at the tomb, the sun had just risen. On the way, as they were discussing among themselves who might be there to help them roll the heavy stone away from the entrance, a severe earthquake shook the ground beneath them.

"When they arrived, to their surprise, the stone was already rolled away. The guards were nowhere to be found. The women went inside, but the body was not there. They were perplexed. Then, on their right, an angel suddenly appeared. His appearance was like lightning, and his garments were white as snow. Then another angel appeared. The women were terrified. They buried their faces in their hands and fell to the ground.

"One of the angels said to them, 'Why do you seek the living one among the dead? He is not here; he has risen. Remember how he spoke to you while he was still in Galilee, saying that the Son of Man must be delivered into the hands of sinful men, and be crucified, and the third day rise again. Go tell his disciples and Peter, that he is going before you into Galilee and that you will see him there.'

"They left the tomb and hurried back to report these things to all the rest of us. When they entered the room where we were staying, they found all of us still weeping and mourning. Peter was the worst. He had denied his Lord and was in the pit of despair.

"'We just came from the tomb. Jesus's body is no longer there! Two angels appeared to us and told us that he has risen from the dead!' Mary exclaimed.

"At first it sounded like nonsense, and no one was willing to believe it. But then Mary said, 'The angels told us to come back here and tell you. And Peter, they mentioned you by name. They said to be sure to tell Peter. Tell Peter that he is risen!'

"Peter's lips were still quivering and his eyes swollen and red from all the tears he had shed. Just moments before the women entered that room, Peter had been inconsolable—a totally crushed and broken man. For several moments he tried to comprehend the words he had just heard. Suddenly, from some deep place within, hope sprang up in him once again. He leaped to his feet and dashed out the door. I followed in hot pursuit.

"Peter and I racing for that tomb must have been quite a scene—arms flailing in the air, tears streaking down our faces. To this day I have never let Peter forget that I got there first!"

"So this is the famous footrace that you alluded to earlier, right?" Titus interrupted.

"Indeed!" I responded hastily, wanting to get back to my story.

"When we arrived I stopped to look inside, but Peter flew right by me. We saw the grave clothes and the facecloth that had covered Jesus's head neatly folded in the place where his body had lain. After looking around, we returned to where everyone was staying. Though we had seen with our own eyes that his body was not there, we still did not understand the Scriptures. But all that changed in just a few hours when Jesus appeared.

"Trailing behind us, Mary Magdalene had returned to the tomb also. By the time she arrived, we were gone. Though she had heard from the angel, she was still weeping. She looked inside once again and saw the two angels once more. 'Woman, why are you weeping?' they asked. She said to them, 'Because they have taken away my Lord, and I do not know where they have laid him.'

"As she turned to leave the tomb, she saw a man she thought to be the gardener. He asked her, as well, why she was crying. Brushing by him she said, 'Sir, if you have carried him away, tell me where you have laid him, and I will take him away.'"

"But the first time she saw the angels they told her that he had risen. Why did she still think the gardener might have taken his body somewhere?" Titus inquired.

"I cannot answer that, Titus." I said. "We can all be a little slow to believe. But this does illustrate one thing: it takes Jesus to reveal Jesus. Unless he reveals himself to us, we remain in the dark.

"Though Jesus was the one talking to her, through those blurry eyes she still had not recognized him. But then he spoke her name: 'Mary!'

"She spun around. Only one person spoke her name like that. She recognized his voice. 'Teacher!' she exclaimed. Breaking with all Jewish custom, she threw her arms around him and clung tightly to him.

"'Stop clinging to me,' Jesus said. 'I have not yet ascended to the Father; but go to my brothers and say to them, "I ascend to my Father and your Father, and my God and your God."' During that brief appearance to Mary, he was just moments, maybe seconds, away from appearing before his Father and presenting himself and being accepted as the perfect sacrifice for the sins of all humanity. That was also the first time he had ever called us brothers.

"For the fourth time that morning, Mary hastily made the trip between the tomb and where we were all staying. Bursting through the door she said, 'I have seen the Lord!'"

"So Mary Magdalene was the first one to see the risen Christ?" Titus asked.

"Yes. Jesus honored her by giving her a place in history as the first evangelist to ever proclaim the good news of the risen Savior!"

"John, I have another question," Titus said. "We all know that Jesus said he would rise again on the third day, but if he was crucified on Friday, and placed in the tomb Friday evening, how does that add up to even two full days if he rose Sunday morning? What am I missing here?"

"It is the way we Jews number days," I responded. "Any part of a day counts as a full day. Jesus was crucified on Friday. That is one day. Then there was the Sabbath. That makes two. Then he rose on Sunday morning. That accounts for three days."

Titus nodded, but I wasn't finished. "Three days following the Passover also marks another special day for the Jews. It is the celebration of Firstfruits. That Sunday morning, just before sunrise, a priest leaves the temple to examine a nearby field that has recently been planted. His mission is to retrieve a small stalk of grain, which will represent the firstfruits of the coming grain harvest. Then he brings it back to the temple, waves it before God at the altar, and asks for God's blessing for a bountiful harvest. That morning, just about the time the priest reached down to pull that little sprout from the ground, a violent tremor shook the earth beneath him—the same earthquake that Mary and the women felt. That little stalk the priest harvested was not the only thing that came out of the earth that day!"

"Jesus Christ, the Firstfruit! He fulfilled that picture too!"[25] Titus said in anticipation.

"Yes," I said. "Jesus came out of that tomb. Some things he took with him into the grave did not come out with him: all of our sins, sin itself, Satan, the world, the rulers and principalities, the flesh, the old creation, the law, and death. Those things remained buried. But something else also came up out of the grave that day. That something was the church—his bride—his new creation. That includes you and me, Titus. We are part of that bride. We came out with him because we were in him when he arose!"

"Oh, I love to be reminded of that," said Titus. "He died, so we died. He rose, so we rose. He sat down in heavenly places at the right hand of the Father, far above all rulers and authorities and every name that is named, and we sat down with him. Hallelujah!"

Titus's face seemed to shine, and I drank in the presence of the Lord as we sat and worshiped together. "I cannot tell you what it will be like when we all have to stand before God and give an account. But as for me, I can only imagine that when I am summoned into his presence and he asks me, 'John, on what basis do you think that you have a right to enter this holy place, where only absolute perfection can dwell? Are you without sin? Has absolutely every deed you have ever done, every word you have ever spoken, and every thought you have ever thought been righteous and holy? It must be so, because nothing short of holiness can enter this place. How do you plead?', my only hope will be to respond something like this: 'My merciful God and Savior, I thank you from the depths of my being that you sent your Son Jesus to come to this earth. I thank you that he lived such a perfect life. Everything he ever did, everything he ever said, everything he ever thought was completely righteous and holy in your sight in every way. I thank you that he not only came to die for my sins on that tree and to bear the judgment that I deserved, but that he also came to be my substitute, and that you see me in him. In your eyes, his history became my history. Therefore, everything I have ever done, everything I have ever said, everything I have ever thought has been completely righteous and holy. On that basis alone, I have the right to enter in.'"

"Amen!" roared Titus. "Pity the poor soul who enters into the presence of God thinking his own good deeds will merit his entrance into heaven."

I nodded, my heart burdened again for the Jewish people who had not yet turned to their Messiah. But my story was not finished. "So the Firstfruit was raised from the dead, went into the presence of his Father, and received a glorified body. When we go into the presence of the Lord, there will be a body waiting for us as well, one that he has prepared. It will be a spiritual body, just like his. The only difference will be that ours will be without the wounds in the hands, the feet, and the side. Those trophies will be borne for all eternity by the Lamb of God who died for the sins of the world."

Titus breathed another "Praise God," and I continued to unfold the symbolism of that new day. "In exactly seven weeks the same priest returns again to the field to harvest some of that ripened crop. Would you believe, that day marked our next great celebration, the Harvest Feast, or the Feast of the Fiftieth Day, which in Greek you call Pentecost?"

"I must tell you, John," said Titus, "I am flabbergasted by all the pictures in the Scriptures and in creation that teach us something about Christ. Paul's teaching to us has been that Christ is the spiritual reality behind all things."

His voice gained intensity as he launched into sharing his own revelation.

"Before this world was ever created, God and Christ existed in perfect harmony and fellowship. But God had a purpose that motivated him to create. He created the heavens and hung the stars, the moon, and the sun. He made the earth with all the plants that contained seeds and reproduced after their own kind. He created the different species of animals that reproduced after their kind. And then he formed the man and the woman, and they reproduced after their kind.

"Jesus said that unless a grain of wheat falls into the earth and dies, it remains alone, but if it is allowed to die, it will come up out of the earth and bear much fruit. He used a physical example out of this creation to teach us something about himself.

"He was the creator. Seeds were his idea. God laced these pictures into the creation to help us understand something about his Son. God knew that Christ would die and be buried, that he would rise again, and that he would bear much fruit. Every seed there has ever been in this creation is only a picture of the *real* seed that existed before the creation! And just like the picture seeds, the *real* seed has the power to reproduce himself. Once he is planted in us, it is his purpose to reproduce himself in us and conform us perfectly to the image of Christ. So it would be accurate to say, John, that before the creation there was not only God, and Christ, but there was a seed! And that seed was Christ!"

"Yes, my dear brother," I said, delighted by this rich, spiritual conversation. "And there was also a lamb, and bread, and water, and much more. All of these earthly shadows are just reminders of some aspect of what Jesus Christ is for us."

"I cannot tell you, John, how many times I have begun my day with a piece of bread and some water and looked at them, and then spontaneously said something to God like, 'Dear God, I thank you that this bread and water that I am about to eat and drink are not real. I thank you that they are only pictures to remind me that Jesus Christ is my real food to eat and my real water to drink.'"

"I do the same," I said. "It has become my habit to praise God not only for my daily bread, but for the one it represents."

"We talked earlier about God's purpose in leading his people out of Egypt, through the wilderness and into the land of Canaan, and how he gave them the land as their inheritance," said Titus. "They started out by experiencing his provision of a lamb, then bread from heaven, then water from a rock. Eventually they got to the land of Canaan, and there they found a land of fullness. It was a land with milk and honey, pomegranates, olive oil, minerals, iron—everything they would ever need. In the Scriptures, the land of Canaan gives us probably the most complete picture of Christ. He is everything we will ever need."

"That is true," I said. "But we also know that when the children of Israel got to the land, they found enemies there. God had given them the land, but it was their job to possess it. They took the land, not all at once, but little by little. This is our experience. When Christ came into us to live, we received all of him. We do not experience that all at once, but little by little we begin to take possession of him as he reveals more and more of himself to us. We move forward from knowing him just as the Lamb, or as our Savior, to knowing him as our daily bread for strength and as our spiritual refreshment to quench our thirst. He plants his Life in us as a tiny seed, and then that Life begins to grow. One day, when we leave this place of sojourn, I am confident that we will enter a realm where we know him as our All in all."

"What an incredible inheritance and hope!" was Titus's response. "So, John, Mary Magdalene was the first one to see him. When did he appear to the rest of you?"

"It was that Sunday night.[26] The day had been quite full. Jesus had risen from the dead. He had appeared to Mary and the women. Then he appeared to two of our brothers who, after hearing Mary's report and the testimony of Peter and me after we had been to the tomb, left for Emmaus, a small town seven miles from here. While they were traveling on the road, Jesus joined them. They were talking about all the things that had just taken place, but their eyes were prevented from recognizing him. Jesus asked them, as if he did not know, what these things were that they were talking about. They stopped in their tracks and looked very sad—though they had heard the testimonies, they were still confused and unsure of what was happening.

"'Are you the only one visiting Jerusalem and unaware of the things which have happened here in these days?' asked one of the brothers.

"Jesus returned their question with a question. 'What things?' he asked.

"Then they started spilling out the story of all that had happened. When they finally stopped for air, Jesus said to them, 'O foolish men and slow of heart to believe in all that the prophets have spoken! Was it not necessary for the Christ to suffer these things and to enter into his glory?' Then he began to open the Scriptures to them and show them things about himself—how he had to suffer and die. They begged him to stay with them longer, for they had reached their destination, and it was getting late. He did.

"As they sat down to eat, Jesus took a small loaf of bread and asked God to bless it. Then he broke it and gave it to them. In that moment they recognized him, and in that same moment he disappeared. They wasted no time hurrying back to the place they knew we were staying.

"When they arrived, they pounded on the door. It was locked because we were afraid it might be the Jewish leaders and some of the temple guards. We were expecting that they might come for us at any minute. We let our brothers in and bolted the door behind them.

"They were so excited they could hardly stand it. They began to relate the story in all its detail. They tried to convince us, using the Scriptures that Jesus had explained to them, that he was the Christ and that it was necessary for him to suffer and die as he had. But we were still skeptics. Then suddenly, out of nowhere, he appeared in our midst.

"He did not knock. He did not come through any door or window. But suddenly there he was! Our eyebrows hit our hairlines. We were both shocked and afraid. We thought we were seeing a ghost!

"Jesus said to us, 'Why did you not believe the women or these brothers? Why are you afraid? Why do you doubt? Look at my hands. Look at my feet. You can see that it is really me. Touch me. I am not a ghost. Ghosts do not have bodies.'

"Then he spread out his hands and held his open palms and pierced wrists before us. He lifted his feet to show the holes where the spikes had fastened him to that tree. Then he showed us his side. A hush filled the room.

"Then he said, 'Peace be with you.' And with that, his head slowly turned around the room as he looked at each of us and breathed the Holy Spirit into us.

"We stood there stunned, but filled with joy and awe. He asked us if we had anything he could eat. We gave him a piece of boiled fish—just about like that one you inhaled for lunch. We stood around, watching in wonder, as he ate."

"Why did he do that? Why did he stop for a lunch break at such an epic moment?" Titus begged to know.

"I cannot tell you," I said. I laughed. "Maybe it was because he was hungry. Or maybe it was just to show us how natural and normal it would still be to know him in a new way. The times we had around meals together were among those we enjoyed the most when we were with him. Or it could have been to plant the seeds in our minds of an even deeper spiritual principle. At the end of the last supper we shared with him before Gethsemane, he prayed that we would understand that he would be in us, we would be in him, and we would all be in the Father. He had just breathed his Life into us. He was the great fisherman, and we were the fish he had caught. It could have been that he was demonstrating that like these fish, he had taken us into himself. He in us, and we in him."

"Why is it such a strange concept for the human mind to grasp—that God enjoys eating with man?" Titus asked. "The religious nature in us would imagine that if God ever did step out of his realm into ours to reveal himself, he would arrive with all the pomp and ceremony of a great worldly king and say something like, 'Here I am. I am your God and king. You are my subjects. Bow down and grovel in the dust and worship me.'

"But Jesus is not like that. He was born in a feeding trough, in a simple stable, making a humble entry into this world. By coming in such a way, he began by revealing himself to his creation, lying there in the manger, as food, and later as the Lamb of the Passover to be eaten, and as bread and water that are alive. As Paul has taught us, his birth also happened to coincide with the Jewish celebration of the Day of Trumpets. Though they did not know the significance of what they were celebrating that day, heaven knew—the angels knew—that the trumpets were announcing the arrival of the King of all kings who was born into the world on that day."

I smiled as I listened—Titus was forgetting himself and taking over again. But I joyed to hear him speak, and I did not interrupt.

"His first appearance to you apostles, after his resurrection, reminds me of when God summoned Moses and the elders of Israel into his presence on the mountain in the wilderness. I am sure they were probably shaking in their sandals and did not know what to expect. But when they did go up to where he was, the Scripture says that they ate and drank with God. When they were far away from him, at the base of the mountain, they were terrified of him. But when they drew near, they discovered an intimate God who wanted to eat and drink with them.[27]

"People are just that way. The farther they are from God, the more they misunderstand him and think that he is someone up there in the sky with a big club in his hands, just waiting to punish them and take them out. How wrong that concept is!"

"So true," I said.

"After he ate some fish with you, what happened next?" asked Titus.

"Then he began to open our minds to understand the Scriptures," I said. "He started in the books of Moses and then went through the prophets and the psalms. It all became so clear. He is at the very center of all the Old Covenant Scriptures. They all speak about him."

"Going through all of those books would take days—or even weeks. There was so much to say and explain!" said Titus.

"Yes," I affirmed. "There was. He did not stay long on that occasion—as long as we would have liked. But the opening of the Scriptures did not stop when he left. As a matter of fact, it had just begun.

"He had told us that it was necessary that he go away so that he could send us the Helper, who would be with us forever. Naturally, he was speaking about his Spirit. When he was with us in the flesh, he said that this Helper was abiding with us and would be in us. Then he said that he would not leave us as orphans, but that he would come to us. He also said that the Holy Spirit would teach us all things and bring to our remembrance all that he had said to us. Once he came to live in us, he immediately began showing each of us things about himself and recalling to our minds things that he had said. His teaching and the unfolding of the riches in the Scriptures about himself had only begun.

"Before departing from us after that first appearance, he told us all to go to Galilee and that he would meet us there. We were all from there originally, so he was sending us home. Thomas, the only one of us eleven apostles who was not present, missed out on that appearance. We tried to convince him, but finally gave up. 'Unless I see in his hands the imprint of the nails, and put my finger into the place of the nails, and put my hand into his side, I will not believe!' he said. Eight days later, in Galilee, Jesus gave him that opportunity when he appeared to us again."

"I have heard that story," said Titus. "I assume it was a most sacred moment for Thomas when Jesus did appear to him."

"Yes, and not only for him, but for all of us," I said. "Jesus invited Thomas to put his finger in the nail wounds and his hand in the place where the spear had pierced his side. Thomas cautiously did. Then, sinking low to the ground in front of Jesus, with no more doubt, he struck a high note in the annals of worship as he breathed the words, 'My Lord and my God!'"

"So from Jerusalem you went to Galilee?" Titus asked. "It was probably good that Jesus sent you there to get out of Jerusalem until things cooled down a bit. Besides having the joy of seeing him alive, I assume you were relieved that you did not have to deal with the religious leaders and the temple guards who had fresh blood on their hands."

"In his wisdom," I reflected, "Jesus did call us away to meet with him again in Galilee while we were all still getting used to this new experience of having the Holy Spirit live inside of us. There were far fewer distractions there."

"Whatever happened to those guards who were supposed to be guarding the tomb? When Mary and the women got there, they apparently were nowhere to be found."

"When the earthquake came and the stone rolled away from the tomb, those guards were scared out of their wits. I am sure they ran from there as fast as their legs could carry them. They did report in to the leading priests and told them what had happened. The religious leaders convened a meeting to decide what to do. Unfortunately, what they chose to do was lie. They paid the soldiers off so they would tell people that Jesus's disciples had come during the night while they were sleeping and stolen the body. The guards took the money and held to their story. It circulated quickly among the Jews, and it is still the cover-up they hold to this day."

I stood and stretched my legs once more. "I think it is time to move on once again, Titus. Shall we walk some more? So far on this mountain, I have shown you the garden of Gethsemane as well as the places where Jesus was crucified, where he was buried, where he arose, and where he first appeared. Now, let us go further up the mountain—and I will show you where he ascended."

CHAPTER 7

GLORY

We trudged up the hill on the stony road until we reached the crest of the mountain. Below us was a full view of the eastern slope of the Mount of Olives and the road bearing its name. Our eyes soaked in the panorama, including the Bridge of the Red Heifer arching the Kidron Valley and leading to the temple, the whole city of Jerusalem, and the mountains in the background. To our backs, about a quarter of a mile farther up the road to Jericho, was Bethany. Between where we stood and Bethany was the walled village called Bethphage. A warm breeze blew in our faces.

"Can you feel the breeze up here on the mountain, Titus?" I asked.

"I most certainly can. It is blowing into my face," he responded.

"Very observant, my young apostle!" I said with a smile. "Which direction is it coming from?"

"Since we are looking in a westerly direction at the temple, and the wind is blowing in our faces, I would have to say that it is coming from the west!"

"Brilliant, Titus! Brilliant!" I said. "Turn around now, and look toward Bethany. As I told you, Bethany was the place where the Lord felt most at home. He was among friends there. It was where Mary, Martha, and Lazarus lived. It was also the place where Simon the Leper made his home. These were all people destined to an insignificant place in history, with no rank and no hope for fame. But then they met Jesus and became the friends of God. Bethany was also the last site where we saw Jesus before he ascended to the Father.

"Our Lord, and the rest of us, always felt welcome in Bethany. What a contrast to Jerusalem! Though followers of Christ hung on his every word as he taught in the temple, Jerusalem is the religious capital of Israel and is distinguished by its formality, legalism, and caste of religious professionals. It is a place where people can get lost in a crowd and only know God from a distance. In Jerusalem, we knew little more than confrontation. It was there where Jesus overturned the moneychangers' tables; faced opposition from the Pharisees, the Sanhedrin, and the elders; and on several occasions was almost stoned. Jesus always felt more comfortable among the sinners and those who knew they needed a Savior, as opposed to the self-righteous."

I sat down on a low, serpentine stone wall, conveniently in the shade. "Bethany was different," I continued. "After a challenging day in Jerusalem, Jesus could go to Bethany and relax and be among friends. It was a place of informality and intimacy, a place where he could come at any time to eat, fellowship, be adored, and served. Bethany represents what the church should be today.

"But besides all of that, Bethany also has another distinction. Its name means 'the City of Misery.' You see, a leper colony is there. People believe that leprosy is spread by the wind. That is why the lepers stay in a place downwind of the city, outside the camp. If they are found outside of the boundaries designated for them, they could receive forty lashes.

"Jewish rabbis have their own laws about how close they can get to lepers. If the wind is not blowing, they can get within six feet. If the wind is blowing, they are not supposed to get within 150 feet downwind of them. But praise the Lord, Jesus was not like those rabbis! He ate with the lepers, touched them, and showed them genuine love and compassion."

"He is no stranger to those who call misery their home," Titus quickly added.

With the rooftops of Bethany clearly within our vision, I motioned for Titus to come sit down beside me. "I would like to talk with you about the next events that took place—Jesus's ascension and his enthronement. But in order to set the table for that discussion, I need to give you some more background. I need to tell you about another feast."

Titus shook his head from side to side. "There's something about feasts and God that seem to go together," he responded.

"There are three main feasts that all Jewish males are required to attend each year. They are the Passover, the Harvest Feast, and the Feast of Tabernacles. We have already discussed the significance of the Passover. The Harvest Feast, or Feast of Weeks, which we all call Pentecost, is celebrated fifty days after the Passover. You recall that at the time of Firstfruits, the priest goes out into the field to bring back a tiny sprout to the temple in anticipation of the harvest? Now, at the Harvest Feast, he returns to the same field early in the morning and gazes upon a whole field ready to be reaped. He cuts enough stalks of grain to form two bundles. Then he returns to the temple, separates the grain from the stalks, grinds the grain into flour, adds water and yeast, and forms two lumps of dough. He tosses the dough into an oven and waits for it to bake.

"When it has finished baking, he removes the hot loaves. A ritual follows that morning in which the priest takes those loaves to the altar and offers them in thanksgiving to God for a bountiful harvest. This is the pinnacle of the Harvest Festival. That, as you might put it, is the picture.

"After his resurrection, Jesus appeared on several occasions in Galilee and spoke to us very plainly about the kingdom of God. Then he told us we needed to return to Jerusalem. Once we were back here, he appeared to us again. The last time we saw him, he led us out as far as Bethany. He commanded us not to leave Jerusalem until what the Father had promised had come to us. He reminded us of John the Baptist's teaching: John had come to baptize with water, but Jesus had come to baptize with the Holy Spirit. Jesus told us that would happen in just a few days. He said that we would receive power when the Holy Spirit clothed us, and that we would be his witnesses in Jerusalem, in all of Judea and Samaria, and even to the ends of the earth.

"When he finished those words, a cloud appeared above us in the sky. I can only assume it must have been the same or a similar cloud that led and protected the children of Israel on their exodus through the wilderness. Jesus spread out his arms in a priestly fashion and pronounced a final blessing upon us. Then he ascended into that cloud, was engulfed by it, and vanished into another dimension. He came into this world in a miraculous way—being born of a virgin—and left in an equally miraculous way—disappearing into thin air.

"Astonished once again, we returned to Jerusalem to the upper room where we were staying. Imagine this: Peter and me and James, Andrew, Philip, Thomas, Bartholomew, Matthew, James the son of Alphaeus, Simon the Zealot, Judas the son of James, Mary the mother of Jesus, Mary wife of Clopas and James's mother, Mary Magdalene, Salome, Joanna, Susanna, and about a hundred others—in all, about 120 people—living together in that upper room. What a practical lesson that proved to be for the events that would take place in a few days!

"We knew Jesus had ascended to the Father, but we still had questions. He had spoken to us about the coming kingdom in which he would reign, but when could we expect that? He had told us that absolute authority had been given to him in heaven and on earth and that we should make disciples out of all nations. But how were we supposed to do that? And he had informed us that he would be taking his seat on the throne of heaven to be coronated by his Father as King of kings and Lord of lords. But how would we actually know that had happened? We were all of one mind. We had to devote ourselves to prayer and seek his face.

"That brings us to Sunday morning, the day of Pentecost.[28] Caiaphas, the high priest, had gone out into the field early that morning and harvested two bundles of grain. By about 8:30 he was back in the temple waving two loaves of bread as a meal offering to God. Following that, all the Jewish males danced for joy in the courts of the temple and sang the *Hallel*, lines taken from Psalms 113–118.

"About that same hour, we were in the upper room. God had taken 120 seeds that had been crushed and made one together, added the water of the Spirit to them, combined that with the yeast of a resurrection, and made us into a single loaf. We were worshiping and offering ourselves to God. Suddenly a loud noise, like a violent, rushing wind, descended from heaven, and the Holy Spirit fell on us. Tongues of fire rested upon our heads. We began to speak in other languages as the Spirit gave us ability. As they danced and sang the Hallel in the temple, a heavenly joy erupted in that upper room.

"We poured outside into the street below. Multitudes who were just returning from the temple started gathering to investigate the noise—Jews who had come from all over the world for the feast. There were Parthians and Medes and Elamites, and residents of Mesopotamia, Judea, and Cappadocia, Pontus and Asia, Phrygia and Pamphylia, Egypt and districts of Libya around Cyrene, and visitors from Rome, both Jews and proselytes as well. We began proclaiming to them, in their own languages, the mighty deeds that God had done—how he had sent Jesus to die for our sins and then raised him from the dead on the third day. They were amazed because they could tell we were all Galileans, yet they were hearing our message in their own tongues. They clamored among themselves, asking each other, 'What does this mean?' Some mockers and skeptics wrote us off as all being drunk with sweet wine. But it was too early in the morning for that.

"Then Peter stepped forward from among us, emboldened and empowered by the Holy Spirit, and proclaimed a message that lasted only about fifteen minutes but that cut like a blade into the hearts of the crowd gathered around us. 'Men of Israel, listen to these words: Jesus the Nazarene, a man attested to you by God with miracles and wonders and signs which God performed through him in your midst, just as you yourselves know— this man, delivered up by the predetermined plan and foreknowledge of God, you nailed to a cross by the hands of godless men and put to death. But God raised him up again . . .'

"Their consciences were pierced. The Holy Spirit was convicting people right and left. They began crying out, 'Brothers, what must we do to be saved?'"

I smiled as I recalled the passion with which we all preached and baptized that day. Truly, we were changed men—not the fearful doubters who had hidden away after the crucifixion! "Probably one of the greatest proofs of his ascension was how he changed our lives and gave us such boldness and authority when he poured his Spirit out. And I assume you know the rest of the story."

"Yes, I do," responded Titus, as an eager student correctly answering a question from an admired teacher. "I wish I had been there! About three thousand souls repented, were baptized, and were brought into the kingdom that day."

"That is right, partly," I explained. "That is what happened on earth. But this is what was happening in the heavens—"

"John, I hate to interrupt and be a stickler for details," Titus cut in apologetically, "but I thought you said two loaves came out of that oven. You say that one of those loaves represented the 120, but what about the other? Is that important?"

"It certainly is," I said, appreciating his astute attention to my every word. "I will get to that part of the story in a few minutes. But before I do that, I must tell you what was happening in heaven. To look only at what happened on earth is to miss the most important part of the story.

"There are many ways to approach this, but I will begin with a prophecy from Psalm 2. God said to our Lord, 'You are my Son, today I have begotten you. Ask of me, and I will surely give the nations as your inheritance and the very ends of the earth as your possession.'

"The Father had promised Jesus that if he asked for the nations, he would give them to him as his inheritance. When Jesus ascended into the heavens, he received four things from his Father: a throne, a kingdom, an inheritance, and the ends of the earth as his possession. With angelic hosts as witnesses, there was a coronation. God anointed and crowned Jesus as the King of kings and Lord of lords.

"Psalm 45, speaking of Christ, says, 'Your throne, O God, is forever and ever; a scepter of uprightness is the scepter of your kingdom. You have loved righteousness, and hated wickedness; therefore God, your God, has anointed you with the oil of joy above your companions.'

"Anointing a person's head with oil is a most solemn and significant event. Priests are anointed when they assume their office, and occasionally prophets as well. Anointing is also the God-ordained ceremony to be performed at the inauguration of a king.

"Jesus had returned to the glory that he had known with the Father from eternity and sat down upon his throne, having completed the work of redemption. As we were praying in that upper room, the Father in heaven was anointing the Son and installing him as Lord and King of the entire universe.

"Psalm 133 is so rich. It says, 'Behold, how good and how pleasant it is for brothers and sisters to dwell together in unity! It is like the precious oil upon the head, coming down upon the beard, even Aaron's beard, coming down to the edge of his robe.' As the anointing oil was poured upon the head of Christ, our heavenly king and high priest, it flowed down upon the beard and to the very edges of his garments.

"I sometimes think that the 120 of us there at Pentecost must have been the beard. We were the first ones to be covered with that precious oil after it was poured out upon his head, but before it flowed down to cover the rest of the body. His kingdom had touched down in Jerusalem, and as you are witness, Jesus is now receiving the nations as his inheritance and extending his kingdom to the ends of the earth."

"How exactly does what John the Baptist said fit into all of this? Is the baptism of the Holy Spirit the same as the coming of the kingdom?" Titus inquired as he tried to fit all the pieces of this mosaic together in his mind.

"Allow me to digress," I said, "but then get back to answering your question. I will tell you a little about John. His story is quite remarkable. Then we will look at what he said.

"John and Jesus were cousins. John grew up in the wilderness. His parents had taken him to the desert, where he was hidden and raised by the Essenes following Herod's order to kill all the infant children around the time of Jesus's birth. After Jesus's return from Egypt with Mary and Joseph, they raised him in Nazareth, a small village of no more than about two hundred people. So the two cousins knew each other hardly at all while growing up.

"Sometime while he was out there all alone in the wilderness, God spoke to John just as he had spoken to Moses in the burning bush. This is what he said: 'He upon whom you see the Spirit descending and remaining upon him, this is the one who baptizes in the Holy Spirit.'

"John had been commissioned by God to go around the land baptizing people in water. Upon one of those people, the Holy Spirit would descend. By this sign God would reveal the Messiah to John.

"Imagine John preaching a gospel of repentance from sin and thousands of people coming to him. He would take one after the other into the Jordan River and immerse them in water. *Is this the one?* He must have thought. Dunk. Splash. No. *Is this the one?* Not this one either. Then he saw many of the Pharisees and Sadducees coming to him for baptism. He called them a brood of vipers, for he was certain that the Spirit would not be descending on any of them!

"People wanted to know about John. Who was he? He continually responded by saying, 'I am not the Christ. As for me, I baptize you in water; but one is coming who is mightier than I, and I am not fit to untie the thong of his sandals; he will baptize you with the Holy Spirit and with fire. His winnowing fork is in his hand to thoroughly clear his threshing floor, and to gather the wheat into his barn; but he will burn up the chaff with unquenchable fire.'

"One day Jesus arrived at the Jordan from Galilee and came to John, asking to be baptized by him. At first John protested, saying, 'I need to be baptized by you, and yet you come to me?'

"Jesus said, 'Permit it at this time, for in this way it is fitting for us to fulfill all righteousness.' Jesus did not need to be baptized for repentance, because he had nothing to repent of. But this was the beginning of Jesus's public ministry. He had decided to begin his ministry by being baptized as a symbol to the Father that he was ready to commit himself to the work of redemption and offer himself as the sacrificial lamb to die, be buried, and rise again to take away the sins of the world. John consented, and Jesus was baptized.

"Immediately after he came up out of the water, the heavens opened and the Spirit of God descended as a dove and rested on him. A voice came out of heaven saying, 'This is my beloved Son, in whom I am well pleased.'

"With this, John knew that his work was accomplished. This was the one who had come to baptize in the Holy Spirit and with fire.

"It is interesting that John's message was not, primarily, that he had been sent to identify the one who was to come and die for the sins of the world. Make no mistake, after he recognized that Jesus was the one God had chosen, he did tell people that Jesus was the Lamb of God who would take away the sins of the world. But far more prominent in John's message was the fact that God had told him that Jesus's primary reason for coming was to baptize people in the Holy Spirit—and fire.

"To understand what it means to be baptized in the Holy Spirit and fire, we must consider what John said right after that. He said, 'His winnowing fork is in his hand, and he will thoroughly clear his threshing floor; and he will gather his wheat into the barn, but he will burn up the chaff in unquenchable fire.'

"On the day of Pentecost, the Holy Spirit came upon twelve men, then a hundred and twenty, then three thousand. We were plunged into and enveloped by the Holy Spirit. That day the church was born, and God immersed 3,120 people into the body of Christ. He was beginning to gather his wheat into the barn. That was the real significance of the Harvest Feast on the day of Pentecost."

"Paul and Barnabas have taught us that on the Last Day all the nations will be gathered before him, and he will separate them from one another as the shepherd separates the sheep from the goats," Titus said. "He will put the sheep on his right, and the goats on the left. Then the King will say to those on his right, 'Come, you who are blessed of my Father, inherit the kingdom prepared for you from the foundation of the world.' The he will say to those on his left, 'Depart from me, accursed ones, into the eternal fire which has been prepared for the devil and his angels.' That final judgment—is that the baptism in fire?"

"You are an excellent student, Titus!" I responded. "Consider what happens when a thresher separates the grain with a winnowing fork. He thrusts the fork into the grain, then throws the grain up into the air. The husks are separated from the grain, and the wind blows the husks away. The grains fall to the ground and are saved. The wheat is gathered into the barn, but all the husks that are left are burned up with fire. In very simple terms, God sent Jesus to build the church—the baptism of the Holy Spirit, gathering those who are saved into the body of Christ—and to baptize with fire, or judge the world.

"And now I think would be the appropriate time to answer the question you asked earlier, because it is all so related."

"I am sorry, John," said Titus, appearing a bit confused. "I forget. What question was that? I have had more than a few today!"

"The one about the two loaves," I replied. "Do you remember? You asked me why I said that on the day of Pentecost the Lord made us into one loaf, when in the picture that took place in the temple, the priest waved two loaves as an offering before the Lord."

"Oh, yes. Now I remember." The look of confusion drained from his face. "What did that other loaf represent?"

"All those who believed on the day of Pentecost were Jews," I said. "They were clothed with the Holy Spirit, plunged into Christ, and made a part of his body. Any Jew who subsequently believed in the Lord in the days and years following also became part of his body. There is not a new 'baptism of the Holy Spirit' each time a new person believes. From Pentecost forward, all Jews who believed qualified as members of his body based on what happened that day. Jesus gave Peter the keys to the kingdom, and on that day he opened the door for the Jews.

"To learn about that other loaf, I will have to tell you about another event that happened a few years later in the seacoast city of Caesarea, seventy miles from here. A centurion named Cornelius, from the Italian cohort, lived and served there. Cornelius was a God-fearing man. He gave much money to the poor and prayed regularly. One day as he prayed, an angel of the Lord appeared to him and said, 'Dispatch some men to Joppa to find a man named Simon, who is also called Peter. He is staying with a certain tanner named Simon, whose house is by the sea.'

"Peter had been traveling around throughout Judea, Galilee, and Samaria. He was visiting some of the saints in Lydda, and while he was there, he healed a man named Aeneas, who had been bedridden and paralyzed for eight years. As a result, the whole city of Lydda, and the nearby city of Sharon, turned to the Lord.

"Lydda is near Joppa. Some disciples from Joppa heard that Peter was in Lydda and begged him to come to them because a precious sister named Tabitha had taken sick and died. She was renowned in the area for her charitable deeds and kindness. Peter went with them and entered the upper room where her body lay. He knelt over her and prayed. Then he gazed intently at the body and said, 'Tabitha, arise!' She did just that. Word of it spread throughout the area, and many more believed. Things were glorious.

"While Peter was in Joppa, however, things were not all that glorious for him. Yes, the Lord had used him to raise Tabitha from the dead. But the Lord was also dealing with Peter. I do not need to tell you how prejudiced our people are toward the Gentiles. Our laws strictly regulate what we are and are not supposed to do in our interaction with them. Jews are not supposed to eat with Gentiles or even go into their houses. Gentiles are looked upon as dogs."

"Not exactly a very loving attitude," Titus responded quickly.

"You are right, Titus. That kind of pride certainly does not please God. From before the foundations of the world, his plan was to call people from all nations to himself. He called us Jews first and gave us laws that separated us from the Gentiles, but we were also meant to be a light for them, have humble hearts knowing that it was not because of anything special about us that he chose us, but just because he loved us. But our people did not keep a humble heart. Instead, they became proud. And that is the culture in which we have been raised. That is where our minds and attitudes were when Jesus first called us, so obviously there was much his Spirit needed to do in our hearts to transform us to make us more like him."

"I accept your apology, on behalf of your entire race, for all the snobbery and ill-treatment that every Gentile who has ever breathed has received from the hand of the Jews," Titus said, his eyes sparkling mischievously in a brief moment of triumph.

"Very well," I said in response, "and I accept yours, also, for all the suppression and ill-treatment we Jews have received at the hand of those Gentile Romans here and throughout the empire."

"Apology granted," he returned. "That leaves neither Jew nor Gentile anything to be proud about, does it?"

"Correct," I said, "and that is precisely the point Jesus was about to make to Peter. As I said, while Peter was in Joppa, a Roman port, God was dealing with him. Of all places, he ended up staying in the home of Simon the Tanner. Jesus wanted to do something in Joppa, and he wanted to use Peter to do it. So he arranged the circumstances. Jews do not normally like to go to Joppa, because among the major industries there is the one with which Simon was involved—working with the skins of dead animals. To us, that is an unclean profession. Plus, the place reeks with the smell of dead animal carcasses. So here was Peter, staying in the home of Simon—at best, an uncomfortable situation. Unless the Lord had arranged these special circumstances, Peter probably would never have gone there on his own.

"At about noon, Peter went up onto Simon's housetop to pray. The smell of the food being prepared below was a welcome reprieve from the stench of dead animal carcasses wafting in the air. Peter became hungry. Suddenly, he fell into a trance. The Lord showed him a vision. Peter saw a white sheet descending from heaven, lowered by its four corners to the ground. In it were all kinds of four-footed animals, crawling creatures, and birds—creatures that were unclean according to Jewish law. A voice came to him saying, 'Get up, Peter, kill and eat!'

"Peter responded, 'By no means, Lord, for I have never eaten anything unholy and unclean.'"

Titus raised his eyebrows. "That strikes me as quite unusual, John: Peter using those three words in the same sentence—'Certainly not, Lord.' How can he be our Lord when we are telling him what to do?"

"It was a mistake the Lord graciously overlooked," I said. "But then the voice came to him a second time and said, 'What God has cleansed, no longer consider unholy.'

"Three times the Lord reasoned with Peter in this way. Then the vision went away.

"Peter was perplexed. But about this time two of Cornelius's servants and a soldier he had sent appeared at the gate of Simon's home. 'Is there a Simon Peter staying here?' they called out.

"Peter heard the voice below. At the same time he heard a voice from above saying, 'Three men are looking for you. Get up, go downstairs, and with naked faith, accompany them without misgivings, for I have sent them myself.'

"Peter hurried downstairs and introduced himself. 'I am Simon Peter. Why have you come?' They explained that Cornelius had been directed by a holy angel to send for Peter to come to his house and give them a message from God. Reluctantly, Peter invited these Gentiles into the house and gave them lodging. The walls of Peter's bigotry were showing cracks and beginning to crumble.

"The next morning Peter, the three men, and some of the brothers and sisters from Joppa headed out for Caesarea. Cornelius had been waiting for them and had called together his relatives and close friends. When Peter arrived and entered the house, Cornelius met him and fell at his feet and worshiped him."

Titus chuckled. "Done like a true Roman."

"'Stand up!' Peter said, grabbing Cornelius under the arms and helping him up. 'I am just a man like you.'

"Then Peter humbly confessed what God had shown him: that he, a Jew, should not call any person unholy or unclean. Then he asked Cornelius why he had sent for him. Cornelius recounted the story and told Peter that all the people present in that room stood before God and Peter to hear what Peter had been commanded by the Lord to say to them.

"Peter began, 'I most certainly understand now that God is not one to show partiality, but in every nation the man who fears him and does what is right is welcome to him.' Then he gave them the simple gospel message about Jesus and how he had been put to death but raised again on the third day, and that he was the one appointed by God to judge the living and the dead. 'Of him all the prophets bear witness that through his name everyone who believes in him receives forgiveness of sins.'

"With that, unexpectedly, the Holy Spirit fell upon all those who were listening to the message! Peter and the Jews with him were amazed because the gift of the Holy Spirit had been poured out upon the Gentiles also. These joyful new believers suddenly began speaking in other languages and exalting God.

"Peter had seen and experienced this before. 'Surely no one can refuse the water for these to be baptized who have received the Holy Spirit just as we did, can he?' he exclaimed. Then he ordered them to be baptized in the name of Jesus Christ. Afterward, he stayed with them for a few days.

"Word quickly got back to Jerusalem ahead of Peter that Gentiles were receiving the Word of God. When he returned, a lot of us took issue with him. 'You went to uncircumcised men and ate with them?' we asked. I am not proud of my own position then, but this is often the way it is with the Lord. If you continue on with him, sometimes he will lead you, as he did with Peter, to places that other people just cannot accept or understand at first. You must walk alone. This can sometimes become a suffering that the Lord asks us to bear.

"Then Peter calmed us all down and told us the whole story of what had happened. He got to the point in the account when he said, 'And as I began to speak, the Holy Spirit fell upon them just as he did upon us at the beginning. And I remembered the word of the Lord, how he used to say, "John baptized with water, but you will be baptized with the Holy Spirit." Therefore, if God gave to them the same gift as he gave to us also after believing in the Lord Jesus Christ, who was I that I could stand in God's way?'

"Peter was clear that the same baptism in the Holy Spirit that had happened on the day of Pentecost had happened at Cornelius's house as well. The real significance was not so much that they spoke in other languages, but that the Gentiles were immersed into the body of Christ just as the Jews had been.

"When one steps back to look at these two events—what happened on the day of Pentecost and what happened at Cornelius's house—from the perspective of history, it is fascinating to compare them to what happened at the Tower of Babel. At that time, the whole earth used the same language. Fallen man started to build a city with a tower that would reach into heaven. This was human effort and the essence of man-made religion—men doing something in their own strength and hoping to please God by their own works.

"But God was not pleased. He acknowledged that they were one people. There was a unity among them, but its source was fallen human life. God even acknowledged that nothing they purposed to do would be impossible for them. But if it came from human strength, it was corrupt. So God confused their language so they could not understand one another's speech. The building came to an abrupt stop.

"At Babel, God confused mankind's language, and the people were divided. But at Pentecost and again at the house of Cornelius, when they were baptized in the Holy Spirit they were united by being able to speak in the same languages. God gave this miraculous sign, not only to practically communicate the gospel message, but also to show that by his Holy Spirit he would bring all the nations of the world together in one body through the power of his own indestructible life. This is the New Covenant message.

"As for Peter, he had been deeply prejudiced, as we all were. He not only had a heart problem, he had a theology problem. It took a revelation from God to slay that in Peter. Jesus had wanted to go to Cornelius, but he wanted Peter to take the message. Before he could go to the Gentiles, he needed to do a work in Peter's heart. Our Lord could have been very practical and sent Philip, the evangelist, who already lived right there in Caesarea, but Peter was the one he chose to go. After all, Jesus had given the keys of the kingdom to him. At Pentecost, he opened the door to the Jews. There in Caesarea, he would be the one to open the door for the Gentiles as well.

"So there were two installments to the baptism of the Holy Spirit that John the Baptizer foretold: the first to the Jews, the second to the Gentiles. That was the significance of the second loaf. Baptizing those Gentiles in the house of Cornelius opened the way for all Gentiles thereafter to be made part of the body of Christ."

"Thank you, Lord," said Titus, raising his eyes toward heaven. "Had it not been for that, John, you and I would not be having this conversation today!"

Titus nodded as he thought more about my words. "This is the same message that Paul ministers among the Gentile churches. Less than a year ago, while Paul was in Ephesus, he sent a letter to the church in Corinth addressing many of their questions and problems. Then he sent me there to see how they had received his letter. Prejudice was alive and well in Corinth also. The church was divided. People were taking sides, aligning themselves with particular personalities they favored and separating themselves into different groups. Paul emphatically told them in his letter that by one Spirit we all have been baptized into one body: whether Jews or Greeks, slaves or free, we were all made to drink of one Spirit. Christ is not divided."

"That is true. He is not divided. The age of God working with and speaking to only one nation has come to a close. The time of the Old Covenant is past. Now all who believe in Jesus and accept him as their Lord become a part of God's one Holy Nation—no matter who they are. The only remaining thing to happen to bring down the final curtain on the Old Covenant age will be the destruction of Jerusalem and the temple, as our Lord predicted."

"The prophet Daniel had something to say about that, did he not?" asked Titus.

"He had much to say about it," I replied. "We are told in Daniel that his book was sealed up until the end times of the Old Covenant. But now, since the Messiah about whom he prophesied has come and died on the tree to put away sin, Daniel's visions have been clearly revealed and his book has been opened."

"Are you speaking about the vision of the seventy sevens in the book bearing Daniel's name?" Titus asked. "I have long wished to better understand this."

"Indeed I am. It all began when God spoke to Daniel while the people were in captivity in Babylon," I recounted. "God said to Daniel, 'Seventy sevens have been decreed for your people and your holy city, to finish the transgression, to make an end of sin, to make atonement for iniquity, to bring in everlasting righteousness, to seal up vision and prophecy, and to anoint the most holy.'

"The seventy sevens could have referred to any increment of time—seven days, seven weeks, seven months, or seven years. In this case it referred to years. These seventy increments of seven years were divided into three groups—one group of forty-nine years (seven increments), another of 454 years (sixty-two increments), and one final group of seven years. The duration of this prophecy covered a 490-year period.

"God told Daniel that from the issuing of a decree to restore and rebuild Jerusalem until Messiah the Prince, there would be 49 years and 454 years, or 483 years. The 49 years referred to the time from the issuing of the decree for those Jews who returned from Babylon to finish rebuilding Jerusalem's temple to its actual completion. That decree to rebuild and restore Jerusalem was not the one issued by Cyrus 538 years before Christ, but the one decreed by Ezra in 457, during the seventh year of the reign of King Artaxerxes of Persia, who ruled from 454 to 424. From its completion until Messiah the Prince was another 454 years. That entire 483-year period culminated at the time Jesus was baptized and began his ministry at age thirty. This was the coming of the Messiah that Daniel had spoken of.

"Daniel said that during the seven years following the 483 years, the Messiah would be cut off. During that time he would make a firm covenant with the many, and in the middle of those seven years, he would put a stop to sacrifice and grain offering. Jesus's public ministry lasted three-and-one-half years, and with his death on the tree, the need for further sacrifices and offerings came to an end. The remaining three-and-one-half years in that period concluded around the time the gospel first went to the Gentiles at the house of Cornelius. Symbolically, that was the time the second loaf came out of the oven. So, as were all the other prophecies concerning Christ in the Scriptures, Daniel's prophecy was precisely fulfilled as well."

"I find it interesting that the 490 years also ended right around the time of Paul's conversion, did they not?" Titus said. "Jesus appeared to him on the road to Damascus and appointed him to bring the gospel to the Gentiles. That was a sovereign, defining moment on the part of God."

"Yes, I suppose you are right," I agreed. "You could look at it that way as well."

"So that is why those magi from Babylon were searching the sky for a sign of a coming king around the time of Jesus's birth," Titus said. "They must have figured that if a Messiah were to reveal himself, he would be a grown man. So they did some back-calculating and took that bright star in the sky as a pronouncement from heaven of the birth of this king who was to come. Daniel made his prophecies while in Babylon. The prophecy he made about the Jews being in captivity there for seventy years had come true. The one he made about the time remaining before the temple would be completed and Jerusalem restored came true. They must have been keeping record over the years, because if he had been right before, then most likely he would be right again on an even bigger prophecy about a coming Messiah."

These disciples of Paul show a remarkable understanding and aptitude for spiritual things and a knowledge of Christ from the Scriptures, I thought.

I responded to Titus's last comment: "The only thing about those 490 prophetic years that still remains a mystery is Daniel's reference to the 'desolations,' and to the city and the sanctuary being destroyed. That has not yet come about. But the prophecy did say that in those last seven years, the desolations would be determined. We interpret that to mean that the determination was made when Jesus prophesied from the Mount of Olives over Jerusalem and the temple and predicted their destruction within one generation. And of course, that prophecy was given within that last prophetic seven-year period. We fully expect to see the last remaining part of this solemn prophecy come to pass as well, but exactly when, we do not know."

I grew silent for a moment as we stared out at the city of Jerusalem. "We only know it will be soon."

CHAPTER 8
THE FINAL FEAST

The sun had grown hot, but we were sheltered under the branches of a tree, and I still had much to say. "How are you holding up, Titus?" I asked. "Am I wearing you out, or can you still take a little more?"

"I have waited years for an opportunity like this! Do not stop now. What else can you tell me?"

"I have spoken to you about the significance of two of our three required feasts that draw our people from all parts of Judea and the Mediterranean world to Jerusalem. As believers, we can see that the Passover and the Harvest Feast each convey a different aspect of spiritual reality. But there is yet a third feast that reveals even more to us about Christ and about God's purpose. That is the Feast of Tabernacles.

"I have physically attended all three feasts throughout my life. Spiritually, however, I have only attended the first two. The last one is something we all still wait to celebrate.

"The Feast of Tabernacles takes place around the end of September or the beginning of October and is the most joyous of all the feasts. The Passover, as you recall, was celebrated six months earlier. By that time in the fall, all the crops have been harvested and stored, and all the fruit has been gathered as well. Grapes have been made into wine; olives, which ripen from August to September, have been stored or pressed into oil; raisins have been dried. By this time all the people of Israel have finished their work, and they await the latter rains that will prepare the land for the next new cycle of planting and harvest.

"The Feast of Tabernacles lasts seven days and is celebrated at the height of our seventh month. It begins five days after the Day of Atonement. Unlike the other feast days, the Day of Atonement is a day of fasting. Israelites fast to humble themselves for the sins they have committed the previous year. After the atoning sacrifice, all of Israel is considered clean. If there is ever any time of year when the people feel free and at rest, it is at this time. Their sins have all been covered for the prior year, and they have been restored to right relationship with their God.

"With the Day of Atonement behind, the majority of the sacrifices during this festival are free-will offerings and peace offerings. This is not a time to focus on sin; rather, it is a time to celebrate with thanksgiving and gratitude. The atmosphere of a joyous, protracted party characterizes the event.

"At special occasions like this, people's hearts are merry and feeling generous, and this spills over on the poor. The poor, the debtors, the homeless, the strangers, and the outcasts are all made to feel welcome and given a place at the table.

"This feast is also called by another name: the Feast of Booths. For seven days the people are scattered all about Jerusalem and on the surrounding hills, living in temporary shelters they make from palm and willow branches. Those huts can be seen everywhere within a Sabbath day's walk from the temple—all through the city, lining the streets, filling the squares, and dotting the fields, gardens, vineyards, orchards, and hills. These booths must be made from living branches, not dead wood. They become the people's homes for the week—where they live, eat, sleep, pray, meditate, and rest.

"The symbolism for the Jew is twofold. First, in looking back, it is a reminder of the booths, or tents, our forefathers lived in during their wilderness journey, and of God's faithfulness in ultimately leading them to the Promised Land. But it also holds an element of future expectation. This is seen in the third name by which the feast is called: the Feast of Ingathering. This celebration anticipates a great and final harvest whereby all Israel and all nations will be gathered together unto the Lord.

"Over the course of this week, seventy bullocks, fourteen rams, and ninety-eight lambs are sacrificed at the altar. Our people have been taught that the seventy bullocks correspond to the number representing all the nations of the world.

"But there is still more to this celebration. On the last day of the feast, the climax focuses on the ritual performed by a priest. This priest goes out of the temple with a golden pitcher to draw water from the pool of Siloam. That is located to the southeast of the temple, where the Kidron and the Tyropoeon Valleys intersect. The pool is fed by the sweet waters of the living spring called Gihon, over which the temple is built.

"After fetching the water, when the priest reenters the temple by way of the Water Gate—which derives its name specifically from this ceremony—the trumpets blast. A second priest carrying a pitcher of wine joins him. Together they ascend the sloping ramp leading to the altar. There at the altar, they offer a drink offering to the Lord. The wine is poured into the silver basin located in one of the horns of the altar. The water from the pool of Siloam is poured into another. The priest reads a portion of Scripture from Isaiah 12:

'Therefore with joy shall you draw water out of the wells of salvation.' He ends with, 'Cry out and shout, you inhabitant of Zion: for great is the Holy One of Israel in your midst.'

"The water is a reminder of when Moses struck the rock in the wilderness, producing water for the people. It also points to the future in anticipation of God's promise in Ezekiel and Zechariah that someday waters will flow out from the temple and Jerusalem, becoming waters of life and healing. Music plays, the Hallel is sung, the shofars sound. The people joyfully wave their palm and willow branches in the air. Now, Titus, guess what happens next."

"I have no idea." Titus responded. "It sounds to me like you are describing the peak of the event. I would say after that the celebration is pretty much over, and people leave to go home."

"You are right, my friend," I said. "That is the usual sequence of events. But not when Jesus attended the feast the year before his crucifixion. That was a special year. At the very moment when all the people were waving their branches in the air, during a moment of silence after the flutes had played, the psalms were sung, and the trumpets sounded, Jesus bellowed from the crowd in a voice heard by all, 'If anyone is thirsty, let him come to me and drink! He who believes in me, as the Scripture said, from his innermost being will flow rivers of living water!'

"He was speaking about the Spirit, which had not yet come because he had not yet been glorified. That day, Jesus announced that he was the reality of all that the physical temple, along with all of its services, stood for. Everything the temple signified would finally and forever be replaced by the one standing in their midst.

"What a showstopper that was! The crowd was stunned. They were divided. Some were saying, 'This is the Christ!' Others at least recognized what he said as being prophetic. Still others were perplexed and started speculating about whom this person was. Nothing like this had ever happened before. Even the temple guards, who are supposed to keep order at these celebrations, were so shocked and spellbound that they did not know what to do. But no one dared lay a hand on him.

"I believe, my brother, that your spirit has already grasped the symbolism here. Christ came as the fulfillment of this feast, just as he was the fulfillment of the Passover, the firstfruits offering, Pentecost, and the Day of Atonement. The water and the wine poured out as a drink offering to God by the priest pictured the Life and the joy in the Spirit that we would partake of once Christ became a Life-giving Spirit.

"As if that was not excitement enough for one feast, Jesus returned the following evening for a repeat performance. That took place at the candelabra-lighting ceremony. Within the temple, in the court of the women, four great candelabras are erected for this special occasion. Young men climb up on ladders that lean against these tall candelabras, which are filled with oil, and light them with a torch. The light from these blazing lamps lights up not only the whole temple, but all of Jerusalem. With this as a backdrop, at the height of the event, Jesus once again proclaimed in a loud voice for everyone to hear, 'I am the light of the world; he who follows me will not walk in the darkness, but will have the light of life.'

"He was more than just a light to the Jews. He is the light of the world. I marvel at the symbolism we see in this, the last of the great feasts. Christ is the reality of this festival as well. There is something of his Spirit that we can know and experience now, yet there is so much more of him. Christ is our Life and he is our joy, but we are only getting a foretaste of that now.

"The tents are a picture also. More than two thousand years ago God instructed our forefathers to construct those booths as a picture to help us understand that his purpose is for us to live in Christ! Christ is our booth in whom we live and move and have our being. One day, however, when all of the redeemed will have set aside these earthly tents in which we live, in that day we will find ourselves gathered together in the blazing light of his presence with all the saints. It will be a day in which we drink from the river of the water of life, and do it with great joy. That is when we will celebrate the fullness of this feast—when we eat and drink of him together at that great Feast of Tabernacles—the final ingathering that awaits us in the heavenly places, when time shall be no more."

CONCLUSION

It was beginning to get late. It was time that I return my young friend to Paul and the others.

"I have thoroughly enjoyed this time, John," said Titus. "I cannot tell you what it has meant to me to hear some of these stories from the lips of one who was actually there and who stood in the very places where these incredible events took place. It has been such a help to me. I will never forget this."

Feeling that it had been an equally good investment of time for me, I told Titus to take what he had learned and pass these things along to faithful men who would also be able to teach others. Motioning to Jerusalem below, I took a step back and encouraged Titus to take the lead in following the road back to the city.

As we were about to start our descent, he hesitated. "Wait, John," he said. "Before we leave, I have just two more questions."

More questions, I thought to myself. *This is truly an inquisitive young man.* "Ask away," I said.

"I have had a request on my mind ever since you began sharing with me early this morning. I hope you will consider doing this for the sake of brothers and sisters like me and for all who will hear the gospel, even after you and Peter and Paul and all the others who were witnesses to these things have departed. As I have traveled with Paul and the others throughout the Gentile world, I have come across people who have heard many tales and fables about the Lord. There are even those who claim that their teaching has come directly from your lips or from some of the other apostles. Though there may be a grain of truth in what they say, still, their teachings do not ring true. I would like to ask if you would consider putting these things you have been sharing with me into writing for all the children of the faith to learn and benefit from."

I was quite surprised by my own reaction. "Oh, Titus!" I said. "There are so many things that Jesus did! If they were written in detail, I suppose that even the world itself would not contain the books that would be written. We have been so busy serving the Lord here and around Judea that we have simply not had time to give ourselves to this task. But as you have seen, the empire the Romans rule over is expansive, and there are many who have not heard the pure gospel and the story of our Lord from the hearts and lips of those who were closest to him.

"You are not the first to make this request. It is something that Peter and I have discussed at length, but so far, the timing has just not been right. Besides, I have to admit that there is even more to the gospel than Peter and I have been given. Clearly, our Lord singled out Paul for the specific task of bringing the gospel to the Gentiles, and he has given our brother some special revelation, as we have heard and seen in some of the letters that have come from his hand.

"We have not yet discussed this with Paul, but I think that because of his special revelations, he would have something very valuable to contribute to such a body of writing if it were to be put together. This is food for serious thought. I will bring it up again with Peter. Truly, there is a body of sacred writings inspired by the prophets of old that point to the things that have come. In a veiled way they tell the story of Christ, only in picture form. In themselves, however, they still only make up the record of the Old Covenant. It makes sense that one day we, as believers and participants in the New Covenant, would have a body of writings of our own. This is something that I feel strongly is important and, by the grace of God, will be accomplished. Thank you for sharing your desire for it with me. And now, what about your second question?"

"I have been wondering, John," said Titus, somewhat sheepishly, "why did Paul call you the *Son of Thunder?*"

That struck me as funny. I threw my head back, laughing out loud. "That was the nickname that Jesus gave my brother James and me," I told him.

"Why that name?" he persisted.

"You are aware," I said, "that our Lord gave Simon the name *Stone.* He has proved to be just that. As for the names given us, some think it was because of our tempers and dispositions. Granted, James and I have had our boisterous moments, so that may be part of it. But I am hopeful that there was another reason."

"And what might that be?" Titus asked.

"In the Hebrew language, the word *thunder* means 'the voice of God.'"

"So that means you are the voice of God?" he inquired.

I responded, "No, Titus, if anything, just the *son* of the voice of God. As with Peter, I would like to think our Lord had some more noble reason in mind for giving us such names. It may have something to do with a special purpose he, as yet, has for me to be his voice and his spokesman. Your first question, therefore, may be more than just a question for me to consider." I smiled. "It may be prophetic.

"Now, I am guessing that Paul is expecting you back soon, and he might have plans for you and your companions this evening. It has been a pleasure spending time with you, my young apostle and newfound friend! May the Lord bless you as you continue to proclaim his name and raise up churches throughout the Gentile world."

"The pleasure has been all mine, Son of Thunder," Titus said as he reached out and grasped my hand. "May the Lord continue to use you as his voice and his spokesperson until in every place the gospel is proclaimed and all those whom he has chosen have become partakers of the New Covenant message!"

"Until the day we meet again," I responded, as I pulled Titus to myself and gave him one strong and final embrace, "or until we are gathered together with those from all nations to celebrate the *real* Feast of Tabernacles. I wish you a warm farewell!"

PART II

THE MESSAGE

INTRODUCTION

As its title indicates, this section of the trilogy focuses on the *message* of the New Covenant: how it evolved, how it came to be understood by the first-century apostles and the church, and how the collection of books contained in the New Testament (or, translated another way, the New Covenant) that we read today were selected.

If you were to ask the average Christian who has some Bible knowledge how the New Testament canon was selected, the common answer would most likely be that it was determined sometime in the second, third, or fourth century by some church council that made the final determination of which first-century writings were divinely inspired and should be included in the New Testament Scriptures. The record shows, however, that this is not true.

F.F. Bruce, a recognized biblical scholar whose work *New Testament Documents: Are They Reliable?* is considered a classic in the discipline of Christian apologetics, wrote, "What is particularly important to notice is that the New Testament canon was not demarcated by the arbitrary decree of any Church Council. When at last a Church Council—the Synod of Hippo [Carthage] in A.D. 397—listed the twenty-seven books of the New Testament, it did not confer upon them any authority which they did not already possess, but simply recorded their previously established authority."[29]

A similar note is struck by John Urquhart in his work *The Bible, Its Structure and Purpose,* where he writes, "The striking fact that the early councils had nothing whatever to do with forming the Canon of the New Testament, has been so emphasized by a number of writers that one is astonished that it is not more widely known."[30]

The fact is that the New Testament books did not become authoritative because they survived the scrutiny of some third or fourth-century church fathers and were formally included in a canonical list. Even though in A.D. 367 Athanasius did declare what he considered to be the canonical text—the very New Testament we have today—his declaration was not the origin of the original New Testament canon of Scripture. No. These books were authoritative because *since the first century they had been regarded as such*—as divinely inspired and as having apostolic authority.

In reading the New Testament itself—especially 2 Peter—it should be noted that the apostles Peter and John were the ones who officially canonized the New Testament books. *They* were the only two remaining of the original apostles at the time Peter wrote 2 Peter (James, John's brother, had already been killed) who had heard the utterance from on high at the transfiguration where God the Father pronounced, "This is my beloved Son with whom I am well pleased" (2 Peter 1:17–18). *They* were the ones whose prophetic word was more valid according to 2 Peter 1:19. *They* were the ones whose prophecies were not made by an act of human will but by the inspiration of the Holy Spirit—2 Peter 1:20–21—resulting in Scripture. And *they* were the ones sanctioning Paul's writings as "Scripture"—placing them on par with inspired Old Testament writings according to 2 Peter 3:15–16.

Working on the basis of that premise, this book in *The New Covenant* trilogy will not only delve into the content or the message of the New Covenant, but it will also attempt to piece together in this fictional account a plausible sequence of events in the formation of the Scriptures, the people involved, and the collaboration that took place among the major apostles—Peter, John, and Paul—prior to A.D. 70 that ultimately led to the book we know today as the New Testament.

CONTENTS: THE MESSEGE

"Behold, days are coming," declares the LORD, *"when I will make a new covenant with the house of Israel and with the house of Judah."*

Jeremiah 31:31

PROLOGUE

A.D. 66

You have asked a rather innocent question: how did the New Covenant come into being? The simple answer is that there has never been a time when the New Covenant has not been in existence, for it began in God, in a covenant agreement between the God the Father and God the Son, long before time—before this world was ever created. The outworking of that covenant, in time and among those of us who have received the Word of Life, is another matter. That is a story filled with danger, intrigue, mystery, suffering, tears, heroism, and glory. And it is a story I am now uniquely qualified to tell. For you see, as of only a few short months ago, I am the last remaining of the original apostles.

I am still recovering from the grief of hearing that our dear brothers Peter and Paul suffered violent executions at the hand of Nero Caesar earlier this year. Timothy and John Mark were fortunate to escape from the city of Rome with their own lives, but they came straight to me in Ephesus with a report from our two brothers. It may have been the last message either of them were able to communicate before their deaths. Along with that report, Timothy and John Mark also brought with them the scrolls, the parchments, and the bindings that had occupied the work of Peter and Paul up until the very end.

It has been thirty-six years since the death and resurrection of our Lord Jesus Christ and the coming of his kingdom. But even now, the full story of the New Covenant and what it means for God's people has not been completely told. Even I do not know how it will end. But this one thing I do know: I know that he who began this work, according to his marvelous foreknowledge and plan, will complete it. And when he completes it, it will be perfect, just as he is perfect.

I wish to begin this story with a tribute to a predecessor, a giant of a man with remarkable accomplishments and stature in the history of the Jewish people. That man was Ezra. Not only was he involved in the rebuilding of the temple in Jerusalem after the Babylonian captivity and the author of the book bearing his name, but he is also credited with writing 1 and 2 Chronicles, portions of Nehemiah, and the book of Esther. On top of all this, perhaps Ezra's greatest accomplishment was collecting all the books contained in the Old Covenant—the Pentateuch, the histories and prophetic books, and the poetry books and the psalms, and putting them all together in one book. What a task! What an accomplishment!

I feel a special affinity with this man. For like Ezra, I too have been assigned a task. That task is to complete what was begun by Peter, Paul, James, myself, and other eyewitnesses to the life of our Lord and to his resurrection. My charge is to put together a book that will embody God's highest revelation to man: the revelation of the New Covenant. The work that Ezra finished, though a foundational and significant part of God's revelation to humankind, was only a foreshadowing of something far greater which was yet to come, something that would make the Old Covenant writings that he compiled pale in comparison to the glory that has now been revealed to us. These were things predicted by the prophets Ezekiel, Jeremiah, and other prophets of old, things which all the Old Covenant prophets longed to see, for they perished without having received what was promised. For this work, I have been called. And for this, the Lord has been preparing me for these last forty years. As one who owes everything to my beloved Lord and Savior, as one who is not worthy of such a calling, I have embraced this commission as a sacred honor and trust bestowed upon me through his boundless wisdom and infinite grace.

With this brief introduction, I lift my pen now to share with you the message—the story of the covenant that has changed all our lives. For as our dear brother Paul so profoundly stated under the guidance and inspiration of the Holy Spirit in one of his letters that have become part of holy writ: "All things belong to you, and you belong to Christ; and Christ belongs to God."

I will begin my story at a time approximately seven years ago when our brother Paul was in prison in Caesarea. For the past year he had been awaiting a hearing following his arrest in Jerusalem on trumped-up charges by the Jews. Only two weeks before his arrival in Caesarea (under the heavy military escort of 472 Roman soldiers—two centurions, two hundred soldiers, seventy horsemen, and two hundred spearmen), he had set foot in Jerusalem after the culmination of a long ship ride and a three-year missionary journey in Asia.

Accompanying him was his band of apprentices—eight Gentile church planters whom he had been training for two years, using as his base the school of Tyrannus in Ephesus. These young apostles and traveling companions included Titus, from Antioch in Syria; Timothy, from Lystra in Galatia; Gaius, from Derbe in Galatia; Aristarchus and Secundus, from Thessalonica in Macedonia; Sopater, from Berea in southern Macedonia; and Tychicus and Trophimus, from Ephesus. They had come with Paul as delegates from their respective churches with a love offering—a collection of money from churches in the Gentile world that Paul had raised up—for the poor believers in the church in Jerusalem. Rounding out the number in this troupe to ten was a physician named Luke who, like his nephew Titus, was from Antioch. Luke had joined Paul toward the end of this third journey, giving himself to serve the Lord alongside Paul and tend to his medical needs.

By the time Paul was a year into his imprisonment, the others who had come with him to Jerusalem had returned to their homes or been dispersed abroad to other places in the Roman Empire where they continued to preach the gospel and plant churches. Only Luke and Aristarchus remained with Paul in Caesarea. Paul ended up spending another year there in prison before appealing to have his case heard before Caesar and being sent off to Rome, chained to a Roman centurion by the name of Julius. Luke and Aristarchus accompanied him on that journey.

Paul spent another two years under house arrest in Rome. Before he was released, he authored some of the highest and deepest pieces of Christian literature ever penned.

Back in Jerusalem, while Paul was still in Caesarea, for some time I had been contemplating writing him a letter. But I kept putting it off. The truth is, I was somewhat intimidated by Paul—perhaps even a little afraid of him. I could not match his wits, and the gospel that he preached was so radical and uncompromising.

I had never spent much time with Paul. I had only been with him on three occasions. But his history is fascinating and significant to us all, and every time our paths crossed, it was a milestone in the story of the New Covenant. In the beginning, the church in Jerusalem lived in fear of Paul. Then known as Saul, he led the first great persecution against the church—especially after the death of Stephen. The persecution became so dreadful that all of the followers of Christ except us apostles abandoned the city and migrated to settle in other cities in Judea. Some went as far as Damascus and Antioch, Syria. But God used this event to multiply the number of churches in the world from one to close to one hundred nearly overnight!

Paul was filled with passion for the law and a zeal for our ancestral traditions. A Pharisee trained up by Gamaliel, one of the great Jewish rabbis, Paul's knowledge and zealotry were unmatched. Coming from that background, Paul had a most incredible conversion experience. He saw the Lord in a blaze of light while on the Damascus Road and heard the Lord speak to him, telling him how much he would suffer and how he would be used among the Gentiles. This took place approximately four years after the day of Pentecost, the day on which the church in Jerusalem was born.

Following his conversion experience, he virtually disappeared from sight. We learned later that he went away to Arabia and then returned once more to Damascus. We in Jerusalem heard that he was preaching the faith that he had once tried to destroy, but we had no contact with him. We could only praise God for the stories we were hearing.

After his conversion, he did not make the annual pilgrimages here to attend the feasts, as did other Jews throughout the empire. It was probably three years before he returned to Jerusalem. On that visit he spent fifteen days becoming acquainted with Peter. But he met none other of the apostles at that time, save James, our Lord's half-brother, who had come to hold a prominent position of leadership in the Jerusalem church. I was away ministering to other churches in Judea and never saw him on that visit.

It was about eleven years later that I first met him. He appeared suddenly one day with Barnabas and a Gentile disciple named Titus. Prior to his coming, a prophet from our midst, named Agabus, visited the church in Antioch and prophesied about a coming famine throughout the entire world that would be very severe. The church in Antioch raised a collection and sent Paul, along with Barnabas and Titus, to deliver the relief gift to the brothers and sisters dwelling in Judea.

Paul did not want to call attention to himself, attend any meetings, or circulate among the believers here. Besides delivering the gift, his sole purpose seemed to be to meet with James and Peter and me so that he might submit the gospel he was preaching among the Gentiles to us, and in doing so, confirm that the gospel he had been given and the one we were preaching were the same.

Upon hearing his presentation and the message that God had given to him, we found no fault. At the time, he even asked us if we thought it was necessary for Titus to be circumcised. It was a curious but relevant question, because many among us, who adhered closely to the law, felt that it was imperative that a Gentile convert be circumcised, or he could not be saved. In the end, we decided that Titus did not need to be circumcised, and we sent them on their way with the right hand of fellowship. We concluded that Paul had been entrusted with the gospel to the uncircumcised, just as Peter was to the circumcised. That was twenty years ago.

Later that year, the Holy Spirit spoke to Paul and Barnabas in a prayer meeting in Antioch, commissioning them to a work he had called them to. They took John Mark, Barnabas's nephew, with them to assist and help with their baggage, but after a shipwreck going from Cyprus to the region of

Galatia, he'd had enough and returned to Jerusalem. Paul and Barnabus were gone for two years.

It was not long after his return from Galatia that Paul had a public confrontation with Peter, who was visiting Paul's home church of Antioch, Syria. Prior to the coming of certain men sent by James, Peter would freely eat with the Gentiles, living as a Gentile among them. But when these men—former Pharisees who had converted to Christ and were zealous for the law—came, Peter started distancing himself from the Gentiles and would no longer eat with them. Paul was away at the time, but when he returned to attend one of the church's love feasts and saw Peter and Barnabas, along with all the Jewish brothers, sitting together and avoiding eating with the Gentiles, he was furious. He rebuked Peter publicly and to his face. This resulted in a great debate. It was finally decided that Paul, Barnabas, and some others should come down to Jerusalem to meet with the apostles and the elders here to settle this matter once and for all.

That led to my second meeting with Paul seventeen years ago, when he presented his case to the council in Jerusalem. After much debate, it was Peter who stood up and testified that God makes no distinction between Jews and Gentiles and that Jews are saved through the grace of the Lord Jesus in the same way as the Gentiles. Repeating almost verbatim the rebuke Paul had leveled at him in public, Peter added that we Jews could be guilty for putting God to the test by placing upon the Gentiles' necks a yoke that neither our fathers nor we had been able to bear. James then stood up and bore witness to Peter's words, concluding the debate by determining that we Jews should make no more trouble for the Gentiles who were turning to God by requiring them to keep various points of the law. It was determined that a letter should be written to this effect and sent with Paul and the others to the church in Antioch.

My third and final meeting with Paul took place during his last visit to Jerusalem when he arrived with his apostolic team and a second love offering, only two weeks before his arrest and deportation to Caesarea.

When I think of Paul, what most stands out to me is this: Paul was a man like a double-edged sword. With one edge he brought much blessing, but with the other, he stirred up a lot of trouble!

It was for that reason that I agonized over writing that letter. I was conflicted within because I did not know where this all might lead—whether there would be some way that we could work together or if I would just be stirring up a nest of hornets.

But this I can say now, looking back: it is a good thing for us to face our fears. It was good that I chose not to allow fear to rule over me and cause me to shrink back from following the inner urgings of the Holy Spirit. For that letter, along with the letter Paul sent to me in return, would set in motion a plan, orchestrated by the sovereign hand of God, that would forever change the course of human history.

I believe that we are in the final stage of seeing the full, ripened fruit of that letter reaped. The result will be a legacy: a body of writings, a spiritual library that will be left behind for all future generations. These writings will clearly reveal the eternal covenant that has been, is, and will be the foundation upon which all of God's relationship with man is based. It is a covenant of grace—pure grace—that originated in the heart of God, is fulfilled through the power of God, and has as its purpose to bring us into our full inheritance, which is oneness with God. This covenant of which I speak *is* the New Covenant.

—John, the Elder, and the disciple whom Jesus loved

CHAPTER 1

THE LETTER

A.D. 59

"We have heard nothing in recent days from Philip about the condition of our brother Paul or whether he has received a trial date," I said to Simon Peter and his wife one spring afternoon as we broke bread beneath the branches of a blooming almond tree outside their home. The evangelist Philip dwelt in Caesarea, where Paul had been imprisoned for some time.

"You are right," responded Peter between bites of bread dipped in fresh olive oil. "It has been about a year now that he has been cooped up in a prison cell in Caesarea waiting for Felix to make up his mind what to do about the charges brought against him. I wish there was something we could do to speed up the process. The wheels of justice certainly seem to be turning slowly."

I dipped a piece of bread in the same plate of oil and raised it to my mouth, leisurely chewing and swallowing the morsel as I reflected, waiting for the right moment to reveal the purpose of my visit.

"I have been thinking about Paul a great deal lately," I said. "In fact, I have had a burden as of late to write to him about the discussions that you and I and James have been having. I started the letter and then stopped, several times. But now I have finally finished it. I brought it with me, and I would like for you to read it."

"Certainly I will read it, John. But why did you feel compelled to write to Paul about this?"

I frowned. "I am not sure. But the thought kept coming back to me over and over again. I finally determined it to be the prompting of the Holy Spirit, so I sought to be obedient. I do not have to tell you, Peter, that we are but a couple of simple, uneducated fishermen. We have learned so much from the Lord and have received much revelation from him. He has opened the Scriptures to us and revealed himself to us in all the books of Moses, the prophets, and the psalms. But when I consider what we are about to do, I persuaded that we must solicit Paul's input. Consider his training. He was educated by the renowned Gamaliel, one of the greatest teachers in the history of Israel . . ."

"Yes, I remember Gamaliel," Peter interrupted. "We are in debt to that man for our very lives, for he interceded on our behalf before the council when we were brought before them and charged to preach the gospel no more."

"Yes, I remember it well," I said. "And I also remember walking away from the council, but not before being flogged! I thought to consult with Paul not only because of his education, but because of his mastery of the Scriptures, the extraordinary way the Lord appeared to him, his revelations, and the sway he holds among believers in the Gentile world. I think his input into what we are considering would be valuable."

Peter leaned back. "I can see why you would want to approach him about this matter. Let me see the letter."

I reached for a satchel that lay on the floor at my feet, unrolled the scroll, and slid it over on the table in front of Peter.

"Please read it out loud," I said, fixing my eyes on my trusted friend. His wife did the same.

He cleared his throat. Then, in his deep, strong, husky voice, he slowly began to read:

To our beloved brother Paul:
Greetings in the precious name of our Lord Jesus Christ.

We continue to be concerned and to pray for you and your predicament in Caesarea as you await your trial. It has been nearly a year since your arrest in Jerusalem. Kindly inform us of your condition when you have opportunity, and let us know if there is anything we can do to be of help to you.

I write this letter to share something with you to which I have given much thought—going back to the days just before your arrest in Jerusalem. I have shared these things with Peter and James, the half-brother of our Lord, and we are of one mind concerning this. You may recall leaving your young coworker, Titus, with me one day, asking me to escort him around Jerusalem. It was a memorable day for both of us as I explained to him all that happened during the last week of our Lord's life on earth and his subsequent death, resurrection, and ascension. Though in age I am Titus's elder, he also became my instructor.

My time with Titus left a deep impression with me. Never before had I known the depth of a Gentile's knowledge of our Lord Jesus or the understanding a Gentile believer could have of the spiritual realities behind all of the laws, rituals, and practices that we have inherited as Jews. There was no doubting his knowledge that these were only pictures and types of things yet to come, fulfilled in the person and the work of the Christ. It is becoming clearer to me all the time that God does not have one plan of salvation for the Jews and another for the Gentiles. Both must come to fully embrace the spiritual realities of the unseen Christ who lives, in Spirit, within the hearts of all who believe.

With that in mind, beloved brother, I have suggested to Peter and James that we, as eyewitnesses to that life which was before time with the Father, was God and is God, and was manifested to us, have an obligation—not only to the Jews, but to all Gentiles as well—to accurately document the life and teachings of our Lord Jesus in writing. For there will continue to be others who come to faith in nations far away who will never have heard a firsthand account such as only we can provide. When you add to this the fact that already much distortion, speculation, and myth surrounding the Christ has begun to enter into the churches and corrupt the pure message we received, we feel a growing burden of the necessity of such a project.

We are now only in the early stages of implementing this endeavor. Peter has begun to work with John Mark to compose an account of the life and teachings of our Lord. (John Mark makes an excellent amanuensis!) Matthew, the Galilean tax collector and one of the twelve, has volunteered to provide another perspective, written primarily for the Jews, which will portray Christ as God's sovereign, eternal, and promised king—the Son of David, whose throne will never end and in whom all of the nations of the earth will be blessed.

With your knowledge of the law and the Scriptures, and the special calling of God on your life to take the gospel to the Gentiles, we thought you should know what we are planning. We want to solicit your input and any advice you might wish to give us as to the content and scope of what we are about to do.

Peace be with you, as well as a speedy deliverance from your bonds.

We await your response.

The brothers and sisters in Jerusalem send their greetings,

John

When Peter finished the letter, he gazed off into the distance, musing for what seemed like several minutes. Finally he spoke.

"You have done well. John Mark and I have discussed this and are ready to begin. I have confidence in what Matthew can do as well. But where I think Paul could be of great assistance to us in helping to craft a document for Jew and Gentile alike is in his ability to clearly lay out the relationship between the Old Covenant that God made with our forefathers and the New Covenant, which our Lord established through the shedding of his blood. This would expand the scope of the project considerably."

"So are you in agreement to send the letter?"

"Most certainly," said Peter. "Have you shared it with James?"

"Not yet," I replied. "But I plan to."

"If he is of one mind with us, then I say, by all means send it, John," Peter said. Confidence gleamed in his eyes. "Let us commit this matter into God's hands and then wait for an answer from Paul."

CHAPTER 2
PAUL'S RESPONSE

A.D. 59

The Mediterranean port of Caesarea is the capital of Judea, the seat of the Roman government in this part of the world, and headquarters for the Roman legions. It is also the official residence of the Roman governor.

The population of the city is half Jewish and half Gentile, which reflects the ethnicity of the church there. Paul was being held in the Roman praetorium, a large complex located between the city's seaside amphitheater and the hippodrome, which seats twenty thousand people. The deep harbor there, built by Herod the Great, makes Caesarea one of the finest ports in the entire eastern Mediterranean.

The day following my discussion with Peter, I showed the letter to James. Though he was not as quick to agree as Peter, nonetheless, it was not difficult to gain his approval to send the letter. Within two days I found a trustworthy brother from the church in Jerusalem who was planning to go with his family to Caesarea, and from there, to board a ship headed for Alexandria. He had been converted at Pentecost and had plans to visit relatives whom he had not seen in almost twenty years. From Jerusalem to Caesarea is about a three-day journey by foot. I gave him instructions to deliver the letter to Philip, who would bring it to Paul on his next visit to the prison.

About a month passed. Then, early one afternoon, I received a knock on my door. I opened to find a Roman soldier sent by Cornelius, at Phillip's request. He carried a leather pouch with a strap hanging from his shoulder. In it were several scrolls. He introduced himself as Marcus, and I invited him inside.

Removing the pouch from his shoulder, he handed it to me. "I have been sent by Cornelius to deliver these to you. They were given to him by Paul."

"A thousand thanks!" I responded. "I was expecting to hear from Paul, but this is much more than I anticipated! Please, upon your return, thank Cornelius and greet him and his household, as well as Philip, his daughters, and the rest of the church there."

Marcus politely agreed to do so and then departed. I closed the door behind him, alone with the scrolls. Should I open them now? Or should I gather Peter and James and open them when we were all together? The latter option seemed the better one, so I left immediately for the home of Simon Peter.

On the way, I stopped by to pick up James. By the time we arrived at Peter's home, it was early evening.

"What brings the two of you here?" Peter inquired as he invited us inside.

"We have received our answer from Paul," I said with a gleeful smile. My sense of excitement had been building, and by now I felt like a young child who had just received a present. I removed the pouch from my shoulder and spilled the scrolls on Peter's table.

The room was dimly lit, so Peter retrieved a small oil lamp and a candle, lit them, and placed them on either side of the table.

"Sit down," he said, motioning to two feeble wooden chairs. "This is a delightful surprise! Let us see what our brother has sent us."

I picked up the first one. This scroll was different from the others—it was smaller, its contents shorter. I suspected it would introduce the rest. I untied the strap, unrolled it, and scanned it quickly. The others leaned toward me, their eyes fixed on me and upon the scroll, wide with expectation.

"This is the letter we were waiting for. It is addressed to the three of us. I shall read it." I cleared my throat.

> Dear John, Peter, and James,
> Greetings!
> Blessed be God for his sovereignty, his timing, his magnificent purpose, and the witness of his Holy Spirit!
> I rejoiced greatly, even to the point of tears, when I received your letter, for I was encouraged beyond words. What I am about to share with you will, I am sure, bring your hearts joy as well.
> You would have had no way to know, but the burden you shared with me is a burden I have been carrying as well. For some time now I have had a strong desire to see an account of the life and teachings of our Lord Jesus put in writing—primarily for the sake of the Gentiles. It was not less than six months ago that I shared this burden with Luke, who is with me here, and asked him if he would help with this undertaking. He is a brilliant man, quite articulate, and given to detail. Gladly, he agreed.
> From the time we arrived in Caesarea, Philip, the evangelist, and his family, including his four prophetess daughters, have almost adopted him. He has already questioned Philip in great detail, as well as Cornelius, and has been to our Lord's hometown

of Nazareth and to Galilee conducting interviews. Next, he was planning to go up to Jerusalem to speak with the three of you, as well as the other apostles and eyewitnesses, including Mary, the mother of our Lord, who I trust still lives with the family of John. So the research into this project has already begun! Can we not see the mighty hand of God at work? What wisdom in having a variety of witnesses, as well as diverse points of view, represented in this undertaking!

But there is more I must tell.

My dear brothers, as Luke and I have discussed, the story of the Christ must not end with his resurrection, and his teachings must not be enshrined only in that which he said and did before he ascended on high. That was only the beginning of what Jesus began to do and teach. But now, he lives on! He is continuing his mighty acts and teaching through the members of his body as the living and abiding Word of God continues to multiply throughout all the nations and throughout the whole world!

Luke's account will go further. He will also trace the history of how the church in Jerusalem was born and then spread to Judea, Samaria, and finally throughout the Gentile world. For part of that story, he will need your help! I want to see events like the outpouring of the Holy Spirit upon the Gentiles, which took place in the house of Cornelius, included. Though he has heard from Cornelius, still, he needs Peter's firsthand account as well. Luke's historical and chronological account will document how the New Covenant—the eternal and now the only covenant between God and man—has been fully established among a new race of people: Jew and Gentile alike who believe, his church, his body, his holy nation, his bride.

As the Old Covenant has its foundational books in the Pentateuch, followed by the twelve historical books beginning with Joshua and ending with Esther, so too, the record of the New Covenant will need its foundational books. The foundational books will tell of the life and the teachings of Christ. The historical book will describe the birth and development of the church, spanning its inception in Jerusalem to its spread throughout the empire. I am certain that this is the burden of the Lord.

So I will work with Luke, and I would ask the three of you to work together as well—compiling the sacred and holy truths that

God has committed to you. And then, at some future date (if I ever get out of this cell) we shall meet together, and by the grace of God, leave behind for future generations a written version of the New Covenant. It should be something like its Old Covenant counterpart, which cannot change and will not be added to but which will endure until the full manifestation of his glorious kingdom in the new heavens and new earth, when time and this old creation will cease to exist.

Regarding my circumstances, I have been granted relative freedom in my bonds. I am able to receive guests and am in good company, having with me, besides Luke—when he is here— Aristarchus, the Macedonian from Thessalonica, who has been tending to my needs. I also receive frequent visits from the church here in Caesarea.

Please pray for Felix, the governor, who has earthly jurisdiction over my release. On numerous occasions he has summoned me, and we have talked at great length about the Lord, but he still has a great fear of the Jews and continues to hope that some bribe will come from me to secure my release, a bribe that I am unwilling to give.

As for the other scrolls that I have sent along, they are copies of letters that I have written to some of the Gentile churches. I have copied them especially for you while passing time in my temporary quarters here in Caesarea. Our brother Luke has kept me amply supplied with chimney soot, papyrus, and reeds to complete the task, which has taken the better part of this past month. I have also included some notes as to when and for what reason the letters were written. I hope you will find them useful.

One final thing. You asked me if there was anything you could do to help me in my situation. There is one thing. If you have favor with any high-ranking Roman official here in Caesarea, could you please inquire of him and ask if he could use his influence to have me transferred to a cell with a view of the sea?

Your brother in bonds for the sake of Christ,

Paul

After finishing the letter, I slowly rolled up the scroll, gently placing it back on the table. We gaped at one another in silence.

Peter slowly shook his head from side to side, and then in a whisper, uttered but one word: "Amazing!"

"Amazing, indeed! Praise God!" responded James.

We shared our initial reactions to Paul's letter and chuckled at his humor, but our conversation did not last long. Sensing that we were left with almost too much to think about and digest, I brought the evening to a rather abrupt close. "I think we need some time to reflect upon what we have just read. I suggest we go no further tonight. Let us meet again tomorrow morning and devote the entire day—or as much time as is needed—to looking at these other writings Paul has sent to us."

They both agreed.

Rising from the table, we embraced each other and said our good-byes. We had no idea, especially Peter and me, how much these two letters—mine and now Paul's—would influence and shape our destiny.

CHAPTER 3
THE OTHER SCROLLS

A.D. 59

We had agreed to meet, once again, at Peter's home at the third hour. I arrived early, ahead of James. On the table where we had sat together the night before was a wicker basket containing the first letter along with the remaining six scrolls. We heard a knock on the door. Punctual as usual, it was James. Peter called out for him to come inside. James entered. In his right hand he was carrying a scroll of his own.

We wasted no time in sitting down together at the table. We began with prayer, each of us bowing his head and offering our time together to the Lord to be used and blessed by him.

I opened our conversation by suggesting that we each take two of the scrolls, open them, and get a general idea of their contents. The others agreed.

We each reached into the basket to get "our" scrolls. Then we took about fifteen minutes sizing up to whom they had been written and what they had to say.

I had picked a letter to the church in Thessalonica and another to the church in Corinth. James had chosen another letter addressed to the Thessalonians and one to "the beloved of God in Rome." Peter's lot turned out to be another Corinthian letter as well as one written to the churches of Galatia.

"I would venture a guess that you hold the plum, Peter. That letter to the Galatians, more than any other piece of writing, has single-handedly upset the entire world," I said.

"Yes," replied Peter, studying the writing in his hand. "This was the first letter Paul ever penned—perhaps even the first notable piece of Christian literature ever written. Paul certainly did not save his most potent wine for last. He served it up right at the beginning!"

James raised up the scroll he had brought with him, making sure we all saw it. "I suggest we go over the Galatian letter first," said James. "I have a special interest in that letter above all others. And it relates to this, which I have brought with me."

Seeing that he had piqued our interest, he continued, "You recall that not long after the council we held in Jerusalem with Paul, Barnabas, and Titus,

I wrote a letter to the twelve tribes of Israel that are disbursed abroad. Word had leaked out about the conclusions we came to in that gathering, and some were led to believe that we had rejected the law of Moses completely. Others were confused from hearing about this very letter from Paul, believing him to be saying that good works are of no value at all and that only believing in God is important. This faulty notion has even led to loose living on the part of some of our Jewish brethren. My letter was written not long after Paul's, but was addressed to a completely different audience. I am keenly interested in comparing the two to see if there are contradictions or irreconcilable differences. But we can save the comparison for later."

So the letter to the Galatians was our starting point. And a fitting starting point it turned out to be! After we huddled together and read through it in its entirety, Peter was the first to react.

"Brothers, what we are looking at here, as Paul has stated, is not a message from man or that originated with man, but a revelation that has come from God. Like a marksman trained for the kill, Paul takes dead aim at the question of how a person attains right standing with God and then continues in that right standing, and his arrow strikes right at the heart."

He shook his shaggy head. "I cannot read this letter without being personally convicted. As those whose responsibility it is to shepherd the flock, I must raise the question to you: have we become soft? Have we compromised? Have we strayed from the message that Christ alone is sufficient for salvation? Have we not opposed vigorously enough the message adhered to by a good number of priests and converts to Christ who are zealous for the law, that it takes something else, besides Christ—whether it be circumcision or observing the feasts, holidays, dietary regulations, or other aspects of the law—to ensure our right relationship with God?"

He let the question hang in the air for a few minutes before continuing. "I will be the first to admit that the fear of men is, perhaps, my greatest weakness. As you well know, I boasted to the Lord that I would never deny him, and then within hours of his pending crucifixion, I denied him three times before the cock crowed. And again in Antioch, I compromised the truth when, out of fear, I yielded to the pressures of the party of the circumcision and received Paul's public rebuke.

"I ask you to remember how we began. Remember how, at first, we were filled with the Holy Spirit and how fearlessly we stood before the rulers, the elders, the scribes, Annas, Caiaphas, and John and Alexander, all of whom were of high priestly descent, when they commanded us not to speak and teach in Jesus's name? Recall our words and our boldness of spirit when we said, 'Whether it is right in the sight of God to give heed to you rather than God, you be the judge; for we cannot stop speaking what we have seen and heard.' And remember Stephen, and how fearlessly he too proclaimed the message of Christ in the face of opposition. Look at the price he paid!"

Peter fastened his eyes first on James and then on me and said, "Are we guilty, in any way, of compromising? Of toning down the white-hot message of Christ, such as Paul presents here in this letter? Have we become conciliatory, not bold enough to correct those who are in error? And if so, is it because of the fear of men?"

No one spoke. We all sat silently, with our heads bowed. In a strange way, I had been right to fear contacting Paul—for as he always did, he was stirring us up again. Finally, I broke the silence.

"The background preceding this letter only makes it stronger. Remember, there were those who had come to Christ from the party of the circumcision here in Jerusalem who were not happy at all with the decision we made at the council and to which the Holy Spirit bore witness. They went to Antioch to spy out the liberty in Christ being experienced by Jew and Gentile alike. They were greatly offended when Paul publicly opposed you to your face, Peter. As a result, a group of them, knowing about the gospel Paul preached in Galatia and the new churches he had raised up in Antioch, Iconium, Lystra, and Derbe, set out to visit those churches and discredit Paul and distort his message. The so-called 'good news' they preached sought to destroy the foundation which Paul had laid and add additional requirements from the law for those new believers to follow, such as circumcision."

I reached for the scroll, and placed it directly in front of Peter. "Paul's reaction was nothing short of a declaration of war! Look here at what he wrote," I said, pointing to the very line: 'But even if we, or an angel from heaven, should preach to you a gospel contrary to what we have preached to you, he is to be accursed.' This was something over which Paul was prepared to fight to the death and take no prisoners. Never before have I heard such a holy hatred for the legalism preached by these Judaizers, these false workers, these 'dogs,' these enemies of the cross, as Paul calls them. He even goes on to say that he wishes that those who wield the knife to circumcise others would go even further with themselves and cut off their own genitals! This is harsh language. These are strong, uncompromising words!"

"Yes, these are strong words," interrupted James. "But is Paul being too extreme in his pronouncements? After all, is it so bad, for instance, that believing Jews from all over the empire come three times a year, along with those who do not recognize Jesus as Messiah, to celebrate the feasts?

Can we not see all the pictures of Christ embedded in these celebrations and appreciate them, even though others do not? And cannot we still show solidarity with our Jewish brethren and even use these times as opportunities to share Christ with them?"

Peter chimed in, "Most certainly that is one point of view, James. But where does it end? The Galatians turned back to what Paul referred to as the elemental things, to which they had become enslaved once more. Read again what he wrote: 'You observe days and months and seasons and years.' In fact, what he was saying was that they were now observing Sabbaths, monthly celebrations, the annual feasts, and the sacred years. You can almost feel the horror of that thought dripping from his pen when he wrote, 'I fear for you!'

"It was people from our midst—the Judaizers—who taught them these things, not Christ! Can we not see the pictures of Christ in the sacrifices that are being made at the temple each day as well? But does that mean we are to continue offering those sacrifices when he has offered himself, once and for all, and now there is clearly no more need of any sacrifices? Would we not be crucifying the Lord afresh if we were to go back to the temple and blend in with the rest of the Jews and offer sacrifices in blood? Would that message communicate that our Lord had died in vain? Where is the line to be drawn?"

I added, "In another of these letters, written to the Corinthians, Paul argues that Christ *is* our Passover. He is the reality of what the Passover Feast symbolized. With the reality here, is there still a reason to celebrate the picture, let alone impose such celebrations on the Gentiles?"

"But our Lord, he celebrated the Passover!" protested James.

"Yes," Peter shot back. "But our Lord celebrated the Passover as one living under the law and the only one who completely fulfilled the law. Does that mean that he intended for the Passover, or for that matter, the Feast of Firstfruits, or the Harvest Feast, or Purim, to continue as rituals that he wants us to observe now, when he is the fulfillment of them all? Or the bread and the wine—the only two ordinances besides baptism that he left behind for us to symbolize the New Covenant—are they not enough?

"In this letter, Paul writes of two distinct covenants. One proceeds from Mount Sinai, represented by Hagar, the law that results in slavery. The other proceeds from another realm—from the Jerusalem above— represented by Sarah, who bore Isaac, the child of promise. This covenant represents a life lived by the Spirit leading to freedom. Then what does he say? 'Cast out the bondwoman and her son, for the son of the bondwoman shall not be an heir with the son of the free woman. So then, brothers and sisters, we are not children of a bondwoman, but of the free woman.'"

James pushed back his chair and in an instant, rose to his feet, directly challenging this line of argument. Clearly agitated, in an angry voice he responded, "Are you, Peter, along with Paul, suggesting that we throw out the law altogether? That it is of absolutely no value?"

Peter, mirroring James, stood as well and then reached over, placing both hands on James's shoulders and applied a gentle, downward pressure. As both men sank back down into their seats, he said, "Calm down, my brother. Sit back down. Listen, now, as I take Paul's side on this for a moment."

With both men now back in their chairs, Peter continued, "Paul rightly points out that God initiated a covenant with Abraham 430 years before the law came through Moses. Abraham became an heir to that promise and was reckoned by God to be righteous by believing—not by observing the law, for the law was not yet given.

"Paul also makes three undeniable points. First, that the purpose of the law was not to save or justify anyone. It was given to show us our sinfulness, for no man is capable of abiding by all things that are written in the law. For if we should fail in even one point, as Paul says, we fall under a curse.

"Second, the law was given to keep us in protective custody until faith in Christ came. Sinful people need a set of laws to live by or they will destroy themselves.

"And finally, the law has become our tutor to lead us to Christ. Paul compares the law to the slave tutors who act on behalf of Roman children from ages six to fourteen, accompanying them to school to make sure they learn from the schoolmaster. That is precisely what the law does. It leads us to see our need to be justified by faith in Christ. He goes on to say that now that faith has come, we are no longer under a tutor. In other words, the Old Covenant was given to show us our need for a New Covenant!"

Peter spread out his hands as though beseeching us to see what he saw. "Chains of gold or chains of rusty iron are still chains. They still hold people in bondage, even though one has a more attractive appearance than the other. I think the reason Paul, and the Holy Spirit, for that matter, deals so severely with legalism is that it is so wily, so subtle. It may not seem so bad, but as Paul said, it became a trap for believers in Galatia—as if they had come under the spell of a witch! Even Barnabas was carried away by it. Even *I* was carried away by it. We are all susceptible.

"Legalism, with its message of the necessity of Christ plus something else in order to make us righteous before God, results in an outward appearance of religion but strikes at the very foundation of the message Christ delivered to us. At the heart of the New Covenant is the truth that our emphasis should not be on outward behavior, but on knowing him—on knowing the indwelling Spirit of Christ. What was it that changed us, and continues to change us? Is it not knowing Christ? It is seeing him! For as Paul so clearly states, if we walk by the Spirit, we will not carry out the desires of the flesh. It is when we attempt to conform to rules, observe rituals, and focus on laws that we may have an outward appearance of righteousness, but we are confusing the source of righteousness with the fruit of righteousness.

"So then, our message should be that righteousness is purely a result of the grace of God, and that by grace we are justified through faith. The outworking of that righteousness comes through knowing Christ alone and allowing him to live in us and manifest his own righteousness. That, and that alone, will produce righteousness pleasing to God. For as Paul boldly proclaims, 'I have been crucified with Christ, and it is no longer I who live, but Christ lives in me; and the life which I now live in the flesh I live by the faith of the Son of God, who loved me and gave himself up for me. I do not nullify the grace of God, for if righteousness comes through the law, then Christ died needlessly.'"

A calm suddenly filled the room. James crossed his arms and sat quietly, mulling over Peter's words. I felt it was my turn to speak.

"Let me make an observation, my brothers, for I think this dialogue has been most helpful in shining light on what, perhaps, is a much bigger issue. When at first we discussed the idea of formulating some writings—whether by Peter, or by Matthew—about the Lord's life and teachings, we were all in agreement. Then we heard from our brother Paul. He also wants to include the written history of the birth of the church and its spread throughout the world. We thought this was a good idea as well. Then he sent us these letters." I smiled wryly. "And they are as explosive as ever, and as necessary for us.

"Now I am beginning to see the need for yet another piece to this document that we are talking about putting together. In order to tell the complete story of Christ, his life, his teachings, and the New Covenant which he inaugurated, do we not need to include letters like this as well?"

I tapped the Galatian scroll. "If this is a message, as Paul claims, that came to him directly from God, then should we not include this letter in the Holy Scriptures which we are compiling?

"In fact, when you consider the Jewish sacred writings, are they not recognized to have different divisions consisting of the law, the historical books, and the prophets, being the basic foundational books, and then the holy writings, or the psalms? And all of these were divinely inspired.

Should we not, then, include in our own testament, books that are not only foundational and historic, but ones that are prophetic, doctrinal, and holy in that they reveal Christ and the wisdom and inspiration critical to understanding this faith that we have received? Is the Old Covenant book not a pattern that we can look to in compiling a book of our own, which records and explains the very things the Old Covenant Scriptures foretold?"

I slowly rolled up the scroll in my hands. "I suggest that we make no hasty decisions, but that we think about these things overnight and then come back together again tomorrow. We will then hear from James and look at his letter in light of what we have just read and discussed."

CHAPTER 4

THE LETTER FROM JAMES

A.D. 59

We reconvened at the same time and the same place around Peter's table the following morning.

"Today is your day in court," Peter jested as James rolled out his scroll in front of us.

James flashed a quick smile in return. Because of his keen resemblance to the Lord Jesus, for an instant I caught a glimpse on his face of the same smile as that of the Master we had grown to know and love. My eyes momentarily filled with tears, although the others did not notice, as I was filled with nostalgia and the longing to see him again.

James opened our talk. "We left off our discussion yesterday by looking at a passage in Paul's writing where he stated, 'It is no longer I who live, but Christ lives in me.' Brothers, I am certain we all agree that this must be the heart of our message. We lived with Christ in the flesh—I from my birth—and knew him according to the flesh. But after his death on the cross and resurrection, he appeared to you brothers in the upper room and breathed upon you, and you received the Holy Spirit. Jesus was, therefore, no longer as one outside of you, but at that moment, he took up residence inside of you by the Spirit. From then on, with the exception of the forty days in which he appeared to you—and specifically to me, in his resurrected body, when I saw the light of who he really was—now all who by faith come to know him, know him by means of his indwelling Spirit.

"So our message—the good news which is the heart of the New Covenant—is this: 'Christ in you.' He came with a Life from another realm—a divine, eternal Life that he shared with the Father before time began—and that is the Life we have received. That is the Life we have been called to live by and share together. But the question for me is, what is real faith? There are those who say they believe in God, but have no evidence in their lives to prove it. Even the demons believe in God, but they tremble in terror. My letter was written, specifically, to address this point."

"Your point is well taken, James," said Peter. "In our discussion yesterday about Paul's view of the law, and of salvation through God's unmerited favor alone and not by our works, it was clear that Paul was taking dead aim against an outward form of religion, not against holy living. Of all the things that provoked our Lord to anger the most, was it not the outward displays of religion and the hypocrisy of the Pharisees? Though in pretense they appeared religious, yet did he not call them 'whitewashed tombs'? Certainly they believed in God, but what kind of faith did they exhibit? For that reason I think it would be quite instructive to compare what you wrote with this letter from Paul."

"First of all," answered James, "like Paul, I point out that if a person is to keep the whole law, but stumble in one point of it, he has become guilty of all. And we all stumble, so we all desperately need some other means by which to find acceptance with God.

"But faith by itself, without actions, is merely a dead, stinking corpse. Real faith produces good works, as Paul also pointed out. He spoke of the fruit of the Spirit being love, joy, peace, patience, kindness, goodness, faithfulness, gentleness, and self-control, against which there is no law. In other words, there is no law by which a man can be told to have joy that will result in his having joy. Joy is the fruit of living by the Life of our Lord, in the spirit. In the same way, there is no law that can insist a person be kind, because kindness that is merely human at its source can lead to showing preference between those who are rich and those who are poor—as I pointed out in my letter. Godly kindness does not discriminate. God's kindness extends to the rich and the poor equally. Paul clearly states that living by the Spirit will produce the fruit of both good character and good works. I used illustrations in the lives of real people to demonstrate these very truths. For example, Abraham offering Isaac, or Rahab, the harlot, receiving the spies sent out by Joshua and protecting them."

"Yes, James, this is all true," said Peter. "But what about the high standards you set for human behavior in this letter? Are they not just another form of law—a stricter one? For instance, you say, 'Consider it all joy, my brethren, when you encounter various trials.' Do you mean consider it *all* joy? What if there is only one drop of sadness? Does not God keep our tears in a bottle and take note of our wanderings, as David said in the psalms? Or if I happen to have just the slightest doubt when I ask God for wisdom, does that mean that he will not answer me at all? Or if the poor man fails at any time to glory in his high position as a son of God, or the rich man fails at any time to see that his riches mean nothing and that like the flower, he will pass away—are you saying these are all standards that men and women should be expected to live by?"

"And what about taming the tongue?" I added. "Though the human race has been able to tame the wild animals, there is a wild animal in our mouths that you say no one can tame. This reminds me of our Lord's Sermon on the Mount, where he quoted the ancients and said, 'You have heard it said that "You shall not commit murder," but I say, whoever says, "You fool!" to his brother, shall be guilty enough to be damned in hell. Or everyone who looks at a woman with lust for her has already committed adultery with her in his heart.' Humanly, not only what the Lord said, but what you say, is impossible to live up to!"

"Precisely the point I was making," said James. "With man, living up to the standards of divine Life is impossible! But with God, all things are possible. That is why I said that the man who endures under trial is happy indeed, for once he has been approved, he will receive the crown of *Life* that the Lord has promised to those who love him. In humility, if we receive the implanted Word by listening for the Lord's voice, then he will empower us with his very own Life to do what he commands. Such high standards of behavior should drive us all to our knees and to the Savior, in order to receive the grace to live the life that God has intended for us to live.

"In relation to the rich and the poor, we might also ask ourselves the question, what is prosperity? We know how the world defines prosperity—material success, health, and the accumulation of things. But what about our Lord, who never committed a sin? He lived a perfect life. And in the economy of God, he was the most prosperous man who ever lived. What did he have at the end of it all? A cloak and suffering on the cross. How distorted our idea of prosperity is! Life may not seem fair from our human standpoint, but there is mystery with God. Our treasures belong to another realm. His plan is good, and we are loved."

"In relation to the tongue, let me jump in," I responded. "No man can tame the tongue, but remember what the psalmist said: 'Set a guard, O Lord, over my mouth.' The taming of the tongue, indeed, requires a work of pure grace—and that from the Lord."

"If a person's so-called 'faith' is really nothing more than a demonic faith," James continued, "it will result in a life that is characterized by jealousy, selfish ambition, worldliness, arrogant boasting, disorder, and every evil thing. I have seen it in the midst of our Jerusalem church, much to my sorrow. If it is a real faith, it will permeate every part of a man or woman's life—their social relationships, their speech, their handling of money, their attitude toward temptation, and their concern for the most vulnerable among us."

"Brothers," I said, "this discussion has been rich, and we could continue. But I am now clearer than ever before of the task ahead of us. We have been called to put together a body of writings beyond just the life and teachings of the Lord Jesus—one which fully unveils the many splendors of the New Covenant. People need to understand what this covenant means for them, and they need to have it in writing. The two letters we have read and discussed these past two days have both been inspired by divine revelation. Yet they are different. They provide different views of the same truth. They provide key building blocks in explaining this faith that has been delivered to us. Do either of you disagree with what I have said so far?"

"No, John, I am in full agreement," said Peter.

"I too am of the same opinion," answered James.

"Then let me make an announcement to you, to the angels, and to our Lord himself," I said. "On this day, as we embark to tell, in complete detail, the story of our Lord, his life, his teachings, and the advent of the New Covenant, we have begun—not with his biography, but with these two letters. These two letters are the first inductees into the holy library of Scriptures that we have been commissioned from on high to compile. These two letters are the first pieces of a document that shall henceforth be known as *The New Testament.*"

CHAPTER 5
A VISIT FROM LUKE

A.D. 59

A few days later I had the good fortune of welcoming a delightful visitor to my door. It was Dr. Luke. He had arrived on horseback from Caesarea, packing some personal items, a leather bag containing scrolls and parchments, and another bag with his medical supplies and instruments. I welcomed him into my home and introduced him to my wife and to Mary, the mother of Jesus, whom I have cared for since our Lord's crucifixion and who has become like a mother to me.

He stayed with us for three days before we could find a more permanent residence for him during his time in Jerusalem, for he planned to be there for about three months conducting interviews.

While he stayed with us, we enjoyed long hours talking and discussing the life of our Lord and our experiences with him. He also told us stories about his travels with Paul and how different the expression of the church in the Gentile world was compared to that of the Jewish churches in Judea. Luke had a particular affinity for Mary, and a good deal of his time was spent with her, as the two of them would often go on long walks together and talk for hours on end.

As a physician, Luke was one who was used to treating all kinds of diseases and working among the poor. He was a man of great compassion. He had no reservations about going anywhere to treat the sick, regardless of their race, religion, status—whether freeman or slave—or occupation. He told me that often he would find himself in the most miserable, insect-and disease-infested homes of the poorest of the poor, treating their wretched diseases. But he counted it a joy because he often found them to be the most receptive to the gospel message. Luke's empathy for the poor had gained him a reputation as one with a heart for the lowly, and the more I got to know him, the more I knew that our Lord's own compassion for the poor, the lost sheep, and the downtrodden of this world would shine brightly through Luke's writings.

On the last evening of his stay, as we were sitting around talking after supper, Luke asked me how it was that Mary had come to live with me and my family. I told him that I was the only one of the original twelve apostles who witnessed the Lord's crucifixion, along with Mary, her sister (also named Mary), Mary Magdalene, Salome, and some other women. When Jesus saw his mother standing next to me at the foot of the tree on which he hung, he said to Mary, "Woman, behold, your son." After that, he said to me, "Behold, your mother." From that time until now she had been living with us in our home.

Luke explained to me that Paul also had a godly woman in his life whom he referred to as his mother. She was the wife of Simeon of Cyrene, the black man from North Africa who had carried our Lord's cross. She was also the mother of Alexander and Rufus. Paul had stayed with their family during the years he made Antioch, Syria, his home and served the Lord in the church there.

"How are Simeon and his family?" I asked Luke. "We knew them well while they were here but have not seen them for years. Simeon was one who gave his life to Christ on the day of Pentecost, along with three thousand others who believed."

"Simeon has gone on to be with the Lord," Luke said. "But he became a powerful prophet and teacher while he lived in Antioch, and he was present in the prayer meeting when the Holy Spirit spoke to Paul and Barnabas and set them apart for the apostolic work he had called them to among the Gentiles. Subsequently, at Paul's urgings, Simeon's wife and sons moved to Rome to become part of the church there."

Luke then began fumbling through his bag until he found a parchment with some notes on it. "Mary, do you mind if I ask you some more questions tonight?" he said. "Bear with me as I take notes."

"Not at all," said Mary. "In fact, I will fetch a loaf of bread, and we can share in a cup of wine together as we celebrate the remembrance of him."

"An excellent idea!" I said. "Stay seated, Mary." I got up from the table to retrieve some bread, a skin of wine, and a cup.

After I filled the large cup, Luke began. "Tell me, Mary, some more details about the birth of our Lord."

"We will be up late into the night if I tell that story," Mary responded with a sigh. "I think I would like to begin by telling you what qualified me to be chosen as the mother of our Lord."

While they talked, we all took turns sharing from the cup. Mary's story was long, but always worth the hearing. "My father, Eli, was the fortieth in a line of descendants from King David. Later, if you would like, I will write for you all their names. In order to fulfill the prophecy of Isaiah and of the other prophets, the Christ had to be a descendent from our father David. For Isaiah said, 'A child will be born to us, a son will be given to us; and the government will rest on his shoulders, and his name will be called Wonderful Counselor, Mighty God, Eternal Father, Prince of Peace. There will be no end to the increase of his government or of peace, on the throne of David and over his kingdom, to establish it and to uphold it with justice and righteousness from then on and forevermore. The zeal of the Lord of hosts will accomplish this.' So it was according to God's predetermined plan and the Lord's doing that this high honor was bestowed upon me.

"You have heard how the angel Gabriel appeared to me. I was only about fourteen at the time and a virgin, betrothed to Joseph. The angel told me that I had found favor with God and that I would conceive and bear a son and call his name Jesus, and that he would be great—that he would be called the Son of the Most High. He told me that the Lord God would give him the throne of his father David and that he would reign over the house of Jacob forever, and that his kingdom would have no end. He said that the Holy Spirit would come upon me, and this child would be called the Son of God.

"It was all so overwhelming, but what could I do but surrender? The same angel Gabriel who appeared to me also appeared to Elizabeth and her husband, Zachariah, and promised them a son who would go before Jesus in the spirit and power of Elijah."

Mary proceeded to tell Luke the story of how the angel had appeared to Zachariah while he was serving in the temple, and how he was struck dumb for his unbelief until the things that the angel had spoken had come to pass. And she spoke of how her cousin Elizabeth, who was advanced in age, had conceived a son and was in her sixth month already before Mary became impregnated with the divine seed.

"So I visited Elizabeth and stayed with her for three months," Mary said. "When I first entered her house and greeted her, Elizabeth's baby leaped in her womb, and she was filled with the Holy Spirit. Then she cried out with a loud voice, 'Blessed are you among women, and blessed is the fruit of your womb. And how has it happened to me that the mother of my Lord would come to me? For behold, when the sound of your greeting reached my ears, the baby leaped in my womb for joy!'"

Luke was listening intently, recording every word.

"Following that," Mary continued, "the Lord gave me a magnificent song that filled my heart, which I sang to Elizabeth at that time."

"Will you sing us that song, Mary?" Luke pleaded. "I would love to hear it coming from your lips."

"I have sung it to him—to our Lord and to my Christ—times without number, but each time, I cannot do it without a flow of tears," Mary said, hesitating.

"Go ahead, Mary, sing your song." I urged her.

So Mary, looking heavenward, elbows at her side with her hands spread out, palms up, breathed deeply and then began to sing, "My soul exalts the Lord, and my spirit has rejoiced in God my Savior. For he has had regard for the humble state of his bond slave . . ."

When she had finished, we were all facedown on the table with our heads in our hands, weeping uncontrollably along with her, worshiping and exalting our God in his holy presence.

Luke, continuing to sob, tried to speak. "What a night this has been for me! To share in the bread and the wine with the family of John and with Mary, the mother of our Lord! And to partake of this blessed fellowship together! Surely, what we have heard and experienced this night will be recorded in the book."

Composing himself, Luke then spoke directly to Mary.

"Mary, in the account of our Lord's life that I intend to assemble, this story will be first. For not only must it be told, but in a symbolic way, your life exemplifies what the church is intended to be. For you were merely a humble and lowly bondservant, but one for whom God had a plan and who was visited by the Holy Spirit. Then, the Holy Spirit, with your permission, formed Christ inside of you, without any help from man. And finally, in the fullness of time, you gave Christ to the world. This is God's work, from beginning to end. And this is his work in the church as well."

"Thank you," Mary said, wiping away her tears. "Indeed, he has exalted the humble, and he is to be exalted. He fills the hungry with every good thing."

"It is late, and we all should retire," I said. "What are your plans for the morrow, Luke?"

"I thank you for your hospitality these past three days, John. My new hosts with whom you arranged for me to stay have a guest room prepared and said that I could come and go as I please. But let me ask you, Mary, whom do you suggest that I see tomorrow?"

Mary thought for a moment, and then her face brightened with a smile of wisdom and joy. "Since you have heard the story tonight of how our Lord visited two humble and obscure women, I suggest that you hear the story of two other women whom Jesus spent time with and loved. I think tomorrow would be a good day for a journey to the city of Bethany. It is only two miles away, just on the other side of the mount called Olivet. There live the two sisters, Mary and Martha, whose brother, Lazarus, Jesus raised from the dead. Why don't you go to them and have them tell you their story?"

"An excellent idea," Luke said. "I shall leave early in the morning, so do not count on me for breakfast." He stood, gathering his things. "I want to thank you all for the most marvelous fellowship. I do not know when I will see you again, but I hope that it will be soon."

With that, we all retired for the night. Though Peter would see Luke intermittently over the next few months, it would be eleven months before I heard from him again, and that, in a hastily written letter from Caesarea.

CHAPTER 6
PROPHETIC LETTERS

A.D. 59

Shortly after Luke left my home, James informed Peter and me that he was planning a trip to the north to visit some of the churches and believers in his hometown of Nazareth, in Cana, and in some of the other small cities rimming the Sea of Galilee. He said that he would be gone for a month—perhaps two—and would not be able to deliberate with us over Paul's letters in the near, foreseeable future. But he took Matthew, also called Levi, with him so that the two of them could have some time to collaborate on the details of Matthew's version of our Lord's biography. Peter and I continued to meet in his home to go over Paul's letters to the Thessalonians, the Corinthians, and the Romans.

"I am growing more and more excited," I told Peter one day, "for in my mind's eye, I am beginning to see this collection of letters and writings that we have talked about coming together into one volume. It is marvelous to think that the world will one day have an official set of scrolls, ratified by us apostles, which will contain so many spiritual riches. May the Lord give us wisdom in what to include and what to leave out!"

"In whatever the Lord leads us to select, John, I believe that we should hold this criteria before us: there should be at least one theme contained in each book that not only supplements and supports all the other writings, but that has its own unique contribution. As light can be divided into the seven colors of the rainbow, so this collection should be one that lifts up the Light of the World and reveals the spectrum of his truth in all of its resplendent colors."

Several scrolls lay open before us, and Peter skimmed them as he spoke. "Of the letters we have before us, I would like to discuss a common thread in three of them—the two shortest, written to the Thessalonians, and the longest, written to the Romans. Though there are many other themes developed in each of these books—especially Romans, which I suspect could turn out to be the most magnificent treatise on the gospel ever written—Paul is developing a prophetic premise in these scrolls that has a direct bearing on this subject of the New Covenant that we wish to define in the clearest of terms."

"I picked that up as well, Peter," I responded. "Are you referring to Paul's discussion of the coming of the Day of the Lord in the Thessalonian letters and the portion near the middle of the letter to the Romans where he wrote that not all Israel are descendants of Israel and that a partial hardening has happened to Israel until the fullness of the Gentiles has come in?"

"Precisely the passages I am referring to," said Peter. "So let us sort this out and see if his premise is consistent with the teachings we have received.

"If you remember our Lord's discourse on the mount called Olivet just days prior to his crucifixion, he spoke to us about a coming judgment on Jerusalem in which there would be not one stone left upon another which would not be torn down. This, he predicted, would be seen by our generation, and he declared that some of us who were alive when he spoke this prophecy twenty-eight years ago would live to see its fulfillment."

"But there seems to be some confusion, Peter," I said, "for our Lord also spoke of a final judgment, where the dead will be raised, where the sheep will be divided from the goats, where all will stand before the judgment seat of Christ to give account for their deeds, and where every remnant of this old creation—all sin and death—will be put away, and all those who believe will live together with him, in his kingdom, on an earth and with a heaven that he has made new. Yet, from other things he said, I do not expect this judgment to come soon—perhaps not until long after our lifetimes. In many of his parables, he indicated that his leaving us would be for a long time—and he told us that no man would know the day or hour of his return. Do you believe these two coming judgments to be one and the same?"

"As you know," responded Peter, "our Lord chose to leave some things a mystery. If we had the answers to all of our questions, we would not need him, for he *is* the answer to all things. He allows us to see only what he wants to reveal to us and what we need to see; for everything else, faith in him is sufficient. But it seems that the Lord has shown something to Paul here to which we need to pay attention. Let me see if I can lay out the case before us.

"The prophets of old predicted that God would establish a new covenant with his people. And, as Paul quotes from Hosea, God would 'call those who were not my people, my people, and her who was not beloved, beloved. And it shall be that in place of where it was said to them'—meaning the Gentiles—'you are not my people, there they shall be called the sons of the living God.'

"But then Paul makes the delicate distinction between those who are Israel and those who are not—who are the people of the covenant, and who are not. First, he says that not all descendants of Israel *are* Israel—

making a distinction between a 'fleshly' Israel and a 'spiritual' Israel.

"Then he goes on to say how Elijah pleaded with God against Israel, that they had killed the prophets sent to them and torn down the altars of God, and that he was the only one left. But the divine response was that God had kept seven thousand for himself who had not bowed the knee to Baal. Paul then compares this to the remnant *present at this time*—of which Paul, you and me, and all others from among Israel who have believed in the Lord as the Messiah are part. We who have trusted in Christ from among the Jews are that remnant.

"He further goes on to say that his great desire is that he could somehow move to jealousy his fellow countrymen, who are seeing the Gentiles joyfully embrace the Messiah, so as to save some. Finally he says that once the fullness of the Gentiles comes in, *all* of Israel will be saved. I take that to mean that *all* Israel is 'the remnant' of the true, spiritual Israel."

"He is by no means saying that every Jew who is part of Israel by birth is destined for salvation," I said in agreement. "For as you yourself preached in the temple on the day five thousand Jews repented, the God of Abraham, Isaac, and Jacob glorified his servant, Jesus, the Prince of Life whom our people disowned in the presence of Pilate and put to death. You told them that unless they heeded him and repented, every soul would be utterly destroyed from among the people. There is no doubt that God loves the Jews, for he sent the Christ to them first, raising up his servant Jesus and sending him to bless them if they would but turn from their wicked ways. But not all will believe. As our brother Paul said, there will be only a remnant. And did not our Lord also say to those Pharisees and Jews whose hearts were hardened that they were not sons of Abraham, but sons of the devil? And did he not say that the kingdom of God would be taken away from them and given to a people producing the fruit of it? So what is the conclusion?"

"The conclusion is," said Peter, "as Paul has stated, that those who confess with their mouths Jesus as Lord, and believe in their hearts that God has raised him from the dead, will be saved. There is now *no* distinction between Jew and Greek, for the same is Lord of all, abounding in riches for all who call on him." Peter shook his head in wonder, no doubt recalling the day on the housetop in Caesarea when God had declared the Gentiles no longer unholy, but clean.

He continued, "This is also confirmed by what Paul wrote in the letter to the Galatians: 'For in Christ Jesus, neither circumcision nor uncircumcision means anything, but faith working through love.' And again, 'For neither is circumcision anything, nor uncircumcision, but a new creation.' In summary,

God is impartial. Both Jews and Greeks are all under sin, and as Paul quotes again from the prophets, 'There is none righteous, not even one,' and 'There is none who does good, there is not even one.' Faith, therefore, is the only means of salvation for both Jews and Greeks. It is by faith that the promise of salvation is guaranteed to all—not only to those who are of the law, but to those who are without the law, who share a similar faith to that of our father Abraham."

Peter was gaining speed, and he stood as he spoke—as though he were preaching to a crowd, like he so often did. "Therefore, the Jews are no longer God's covenant people. God's covenant is not with the people of Israel according to the flesh, but with spiritual Israel—which is now the real Israel of God, the church, consisting of both the remnant of Jews who believe and the Gentiles who put their faith in him. It would be a mistake to believe that two covenants still exist side by side today—one with the Jews and one with the church—for there is only one. It is the New Covenant, based on grace through faith, not on a biological bloodline."

I tried to interrupt with a question, but Peter would not be stopped.

"And furthermore," he said emphatically, slapping the open palm of his right hand on the table, "when the prophet Jeremiah unfolded the New Covenant he declared, 'Behold, days are coming, declares the Lord, when I will make a new covenant with the house of Israel and the house of Judah.' At first glance there is nothing said about this new covenant extending to the Gentiles. But we must look more closely. We must go all the way back to Joseph, one of the twelve sons of Jacob. As Pharaoh's top adviser, Joseph married an Egyptian woman named Asenath. She bore him two sons of mixed blood—half Egyptian and half from the line of Abraham's seed— Ephraim and Manasseh.

"When Jacob was old and about to die, he blessed his grandsons, Ephraim and Manasseh, saying, 'And may my name live on in them, and the names of my fathers Abraham and Isaac; and may they grow into a multitude in the midst of the earth.' And he crossed his hands, laying his right hand upon the head of the younger, Ephraim, and giving him the greater blessing. He said that the younger brother would be greater than the older and that his seed would become a multitude of nations."

I shook my head with a smile of bewilderment, but Peter wasn't finished. He charged on.

"After the reign of Solomon, Israel became a divided kingdom, the ten tribes of the northern kingdom ruled by the Ephraimite Jeraboam, and the two remaining tribes, Judah and Benjamin, ruled by Solomon's son

Rehoboam. Thus the northern kingdom became known as Israel, and the southern kingdom as Judah.

"Before Judah was taken into captivity by the Babylonians, it was the northern kingdom, Israel, that first declined into spiritual idolatry. Its people were attacked, taken from their homeland, and made slaves by the Assyrians. As time passed, these slaves were sold to other nations and eventually came to inhabit the entire known world. Even the prophet Hosea said that Ephraim had mixed himself with the nations.

"As the ten tribes were disbursed and scattered among the nations, and the bloodline of Abraham, Isaac, and Jacob continued to dilute—beginning with the marriage of Joseph to the Egyptian woman—today it is largely unrecognizable. We can see that Jeremiah's pronouncement of the New Covenant blessing to Israel and Judah was really a pronouncement of a covenant that God would make with all the peoples and nations of the world. Through the ten tribes of Israel, that covenant would be extended to the Gentiles, and through Judah, to the Jews. That is the beauty of God's plan—his unbiased and infinite love for the whole world! The New Covenant people of God—the church—is made up of all Jews and Gentiles who believe!"

Peter finished and sat back in his chair. The wisdom he had paraded before me could not be contested.

"I am sorry to have denied you your question, John," Peter said. "You know me and are gracious, for you know that sometimes I can become long-winded."

"What you said needs to be made clear," I responded. "But going back to Paul's writings, my question is, how do you see this partial hardening that has happened to Israel playing out until the fullness of the Gentiles comes?"

He nodded. "Do you remember how the Lord told us, concerning his coming judgment upon Israel and Jerusalem, that when we see Jerusalem surrounded by armies, we should recognize that her desolation is near? That those who are in Judea must flee to the mountains, and those who are in the midst of the city must leave, and those who are in the country must not enter the city because these would be the days of vengeance? That there would be great distress upon the land and wrath to this people, and that they would fall by the edge of the sword and be led captive into all the nations, and that Jerusalem would be trampled underfoot by the Gentiles until the times of the Gentiles were fulfilled?"

I nodded. I remembered Jesus's words well.

Peter continued, "It is becoming increasingly clear that we are destined for a head-on collision with Rome. There will be war between Rome and the Jews. The only question is when. When Rome attacks Jerusalem, we will see the fulfillment of these prophecies. But what must take place first?

"In his second letter to the Thessalonians, Paul speaks of an apostasy—a falling away, or a revolt—that must come before this judgment is to take place. We see this happening now and are watching it gain momentum. Just look around us, John! The Zealots are making more inroads among the masses of the Jews, inciting them to take up arms against Rome and revolt. Many are on the fence. But I can see the day coming when our countrymen totally arise to throw off the shackles of Rome, and because they did not receive Jesus the Messiah so as to be saved, God will send upon them a deluding influence, as Paul says, so that they will believe what is false in order that they all may be judged who did not believe the truth, but took pleasure in wickedness. This will lead to their destruction and to the destruction of Jerusalem and the temple, her festivals, her solemn assemblies, her burnt offerings, her peace offerings—everything that is a reminder of the Old Covenant will be judged and destroyed."

"If you will remember," I said, "Jesus also told the scribes and Pharisees to 'fill up, then, the measure of the guilt of your fathers' and that upon their generation would fall 'the guilt of all the righteous blood shed on the earth, from the blood of righteous Abel to the blood of Zechariah.' This reminds me of God's judgment upon those living in Canaan at the time Joshua led the people into the Promised Land. For we are told that the Amorites filled up the measure of their iniquity, and God used Israel to bring destruction upon them. For hundreds of years, God was longsuffering and patient, sending them warning after warning: the destruction of Sodom and Gomorrah, the judgments they had heard about in Egypt, the miracles of the Hebrews crossing the Red Sea and the Jordan, and the destruction of Jericho. But finally their iniquity was full, and judgment came upon that generation. That did not mean that in the future he would not again extend mercy to their posterity who survived. But for the generation that is alive at the time a nation's sin is filled up, judgment will come, for all sin must be punished. So it will be with Israel in this generation."

"I also find it interesting," continued Peter, tapping the table contemplatively, "that Paul wrote his letter to the Thessalonians nearly eight years ago, while Claudius was the emperor. As you remember, Claudius subscribed to Julius Caesar's cult of emperor worship. Four years ago Claudius was poisoned by Agrippina, his niece whom he had married, and her son, Nero, took the throne."

I shuddered. Peter hardly needed to remind me of the man—the monster—who sat on Rome's imperial throne.

"Could it be," Peter went on, "that Paul had some divine insight to see that it was Claudius who stood in the way of this man of lawlessness being revealed? Nero was only a boy of thirteen at the time of Paul's writing. And could it be that Paul was making a play on words when he implied that Claudius was the 'restrainer,' for in Latin, the word for *restraint* is *claudere?* Certainly all of the emperors live outside the law. Claudius recently executed his wife before marrying his niece. Collectively, they are all men of lawlessness—but could Nero become so evil as to merit that title alone?"

"He is already that evil," I muttered. "Reports of his infamy have already spread throughout the world."

"It is yet to be seen how Nero Caesar will be involved in a war with the Jews and the destruction of Jerusalem, but we can see this battle shaping up." Peter picked up the scroll to the Thessalonians and held it before me. "There is much more that we could discuss concerning this topic, but these prophecies must become a part of the record. A true prophet will only speak the things of God, or he should be stoned. These prophecies by Paul, if they come true—as I believe they will—will further serve to confirm the predictions Jesus made about the days of vengeance that will come and his coming in judgment on Jerusalem and the temple to bring to an end the age of God's exclusive relationship with people of the Jewish race. Our Lord's prophecies cannot fail, for he is the Prophet of whom Moses spoke when he said, 'The Lord your God will raise up for you a prophet like me from among you.'"

"I agree, Peter," I said. "But there is one thing in Paul's letter to the Thessalonians that is accurate but could also present confusion for some. Paul spent only four or five months raising up the church in Thessalonica—it is clear the church there had some questions that they sent to him in a letter. One of those questions was, what happens to those who die? Someone in their midst must have died, and they were grieving as do the Gentiles, who have no hope.

"Paul told them that if we believe that Jesus died and rose again, we who are alive and remain until the coming of the Lord would not precede those who have fallen asleep. For he will descend from heaven with a shout, with the voice of the archangel and with the trumpet of God, and the dead in Christ will rise first. Then we who are alive and remain will be caught up together with them in the clouds to meet the Lord in the air, and so we shall always be with the Lord.

"I am concerned that this coming—the final coming at the end of the world—could be confused with the Day of the Lord spoken of in connection with the destruction of Jerusalem. Those not familiar with the Old Covenant writings may not understand that the Day of the Lord is a term that does not necessarily refer to the end of the world. For instance, Isaiah spoke of the Day of the Lord when the Lord came in judgment to destroy Babylon. Obadiah and Zephaniah similarly spoke of the Day of the Lord in reference to the destruction of Jerusalem by Babylon. The term simply refers to any time that God directly intervenes to exercise judgment on human sin. Will readers become confused on this point?"

Peter pursed his lips. "Perhaps. But it seems the Thessalonians, in their initial letter, were not confused on the point—the 'Day of the Lord' Paul addresses here could not have referred to the end of the world and the dissolution of the present heavens and earth, because some thought it had already taken place. It seems they understand. The Lord will come again. And he will come in judgment of Jerusalem. What remains to be seen is if these two 'comings' are separate comings or if his coming to judge Jerusalem will also result in the end of the whole world as we know it."

"Either way," I said, "God has graciously granted the Jews a generation to repent, and during this time he has continued to call out for himself a remnant. But the day will come when his warnings, his pleadings, and his patience will cease. For he who said, 'Jerusalem, Jerusalem, who kills the prophets and stones those who are sent to her! How often I wanted to gather your children together the way a hen gathers her chicks under her wings, and you were unwilling' has also said, 'Behold, your house is being left to you desolate!' This will signal the final transition from the days of the Old Covenant to those of the New."

CHAPTER 7
SEVEN LETTERS & TWO BIOGRAPHIES INDUCTED AS HOLY WRIT

A.D. 59–60

Over the next three months, Peter and I continued to meet and pour over Paul's letters. But during that time, there were two other significant accomplishments in relation to our project.

James returned from his trip to the north with Matthew. While they were together, Matthew finished his version of the good news of the Christ. He wrote primarily for a Jewish audience, emphasizing that Jesus, indeed, was king. He included a genealogy of the Messiah, showing Jesus to be both the son of David and the son of Abraham.

Solomon, who was David's son, was but a foreshadowing of Christ, the true son of David whose throne would never end. Solomon built the physical temple, but Christ is building the real temple, a spiritual temple, which is his church, of which Solomon's temple was also only a picture.

In Genesis, God promised that all the nations of the earth would be blessed through Abraham's son Isaac. By tracing Christ to the son of Abraham, Matthew began laying out the case that Christ was not only the promised king, but the promised seed of Abraham as well, in whom all the nations of the earth would be blessed.

At the same time as Matthew was recording his biography of Jesus, Peter was working with John Mark. Together they finished their gospel account as well (though Mark would be credited as its author). We had decided that all of the writings should be translated into Greek, since that is the language read and understood by most people. Since only about ten percent of the population of the entire Roman Empire is literate, most all of the people will have these accounts read to them. So, in storytelling style, Peter and Mark selected stories and illustrations from the life of Christ, and in great detail portrayed him not only as a miracle worker and a teacher, but as God's Suffering Servant—the object of rejection, ridicule, humiliation, and ultimately, a shameful death. Besides his being the king, this too fulfilled part of his messianic identity according to the Old Testament Scriptures.

Matthew's biography for the Jews also emphasized the fulfillment of prophecy from the Old Covenant writings, even down to the smallest detail. Jesus was God's Son, who was called from Egypt. He was called a Nazarene. Matthew also included prophecy yet to be fulfilled when he wrote about Christ's predictions of his coming judgment and the coming end of the Old Covenant age. These things he learned from us, for only Peter, Andrew, my brother James, and I were present that day on the Mount of Olives when Jesus spoke to us about the destruction of Jerusalem and the temple.

Peter's influence is seen in Mark's account, for his audience favors both Jew and Gentile. It was Peter to whom our Lord gave the keys to the kingdom—to the Jew first, and then to the Gentile. On Pentecost, God used him to open the door for the Jews to enter into the kingdom and become part of the body of Christ. Then, in Caesarea in the home of Cornelius, the door was opened for the Gentiles. Peter's account, therefore, places more emphasis on Jesus's ministry among the Gentiles. For instance, it tells the story of when Jesus cast the demon out of the daughter of the woman from the Syrophoenician race, and it includes his description of the first Gentile evangelist, the demoniac from whom Jesus cast a legion of demons into a herd of swine. The man returned to his village, a whole person, and proclaimed the great things God had done for him among his people.

By this time, we now had one account of the life and teachings of our Lord primarily written for the Jews and another written for both Jews and Gentiles, and we hoped to soon have a third, written by Luke, that would be written mainly for a Gentile audience. In addition, we had agreed that Paul's letter to the Galatians, his letters to the Thessalonians, and his letter to the Romans should be included in the library as well. We marveled together at the Spirit's revelations to Paul. Since we had received the scrolls from our brother in prison, they had taught us and pushed us to a deeper understanding of many things.

"There is so much I would like to discuss with Paul about his writings—especially his letter to the Romans," Peter said as the two of us sat once again around his table. "It is brilliant—the work of a master lawyer, theologian, and apologist for the Christian faith. Indeed, he was set apart for the good news of God, which was promised beforehand through his prophets in the Holy Scriptures."

We dipped bread into oil together as Peter spoke of his favorite of Paul's scrolls. "In this marvelous letter, Paul flawlessly develops the major doctrines of the New Covenant—our justification, our sanctification, and even our glorification in Christ. But he is very clear that the good news is not a teaching, or a doctrine, or a concept. It is a *person*—the God-man, Jesus Christ.

"We can talk about being righteous before God, but what makes us righteous? We are justified and made righteous through faith. But what is our righteousness? It is Christ. Not only does God view us as if we had never sinned, but in his eyes, he sees us to be as righteous as his own holy Son, for Christ *is* our righteousness.

"Once we are saved, once we are justified, what then? We should not continue to live in sin, but we should live holy lives. But how can we live holy lives? Do we do so by exerting our own efforts, or by the strength of our own wills? As Paul discovered, and as you and I have learned, though he willed to do so, he could not live the Christian life! He was beside himself—as we have been. But what did he discover? He discovered that there is a law greater than the law of sin and death resident in his fallen flesh. And that is the law of the Spirit of life in Christ Jesus, implanted in us at our new birth, that sets us free and delivers us from the law of sin and death.

"The provision for holy living is in God's Spirit. Living by the life of Christ within us is our sanctification. As Paul said in the Corinthian letters that we are going to look at today, because God has put us in Christ, Christ 'became to us wisdom from God, and righteousness, and sanctification, and redemption.' What a glorious message we have! And what a spokesman for that message we have in our brother Paul!"

"I am convinced, Peter, that Paul must know that not only has he been called to be an apostle, but he has been called to participate in a prophetic role in the writing of sacred Scripture—just as you and I have. For read what he wrote in his first letter to the Corinthian church: 'If anyone thinks he is a prophet or spiritual, let him recognize that the things which I write to you are the Lord's commandment.' Paul was not shy, nor did he have a false humility. What God had given to him by revelation he boldly recorded, convinced that what he wrote could hold its own with any other piece of writing deemed to be inspired Scripture. He is an example to me as few other men have been."

I wiped my hands clean of crumbs and turned to the basket of scrolls. "But now, let us turn to these Corinthian letters. What is their uniqueness? What do they tell us that none of the other letters that we have reviewed, thus far, reveal to us?"

"To begin," said Peter, "these letters were written by Paul from Ephesus on his third missionary journey. According to Paul's notes, this first letter was written about three years ago to a church that was approximately five years old, planted on his second missionary expedition. The second letter was written at about the same time as his letter to the Romans, prior to his departure to come here to Jerusalem."

With the scrolls in his house, Peter had obviously taken advantage of his ability to go through them at his leisure. He already knew a great deal about the epistles before us, and he seemed eager to share.

"The church at Corinth is a church rich in doctrine, rich in gifts and teachings, but also rich with problems. At the time of his writing his first letter, it was not a spiritual church. They had problems of division among themselves, sin, suing one another, marriage problems; they were causing one another to stumble, and they were experiencing problems dealing with cultural issues like women's head coverings. They were making a mockery of the Lord's Table and boasting in their spiritual gifts, which were not being used to build up the body of Christ but rather for self-aggrandizement. They had problems with their doctrines, problems with giving, problems with submitting to one another, and problems expressing love to one another. And the list goes on."

"It sounds to me like a pretty normal church," I chuckled, scanning the scroll as Peter laid it out before us. "But in spite of all this, do you see how Paul addresses them? He begins his letter by calling them 'holy ones' and declaring that they have already been sanctified. He reminds them that they are 'in Christ.' Amazing, is it not, how Paul could maintain this perspective? For what is real is what the eyes of heaven see, not what the eyes of earth perceives."

"I am struck," replied Peter, "that with all the gifts, with all teachings, and with all the miracles which took place among them, Paul still saw these believers as babes in Christ. Just because people could speak in tongues, or prophesy, or even commit great acts of compassion, that did not mean they were spiritually mature. Though these manifestations of spiritual gifts are outward things that people can see, they do not guarantee that they are being employed to build up the body of Christ.

"But these two letters, together, contrast the carnal Christian with the spiritual Christian. For in his second letter, Paul shows the church what a spiritual man is. He does this because he writes to them about who *he* is. In the first epistle to the Corinthians, we see people who are saved but are living according to the flesh. In the second epistle, we see what it means to be saved but to live according to the Spirit. In this letter Paul exposes his heart in great detail, revealing his feelings, his afflictions, his questions, and even his doubts.

But overshadowing all this, Paul reveals to them his sufferings and what the cross has produced in his life. Out of suffering comes transformation. Out of transformation, the life of Christ is produced within us. And out of suffering comes ministry to others that truly builds up the body of Christ.

"It is not the gifts of the Spirit alone that God uses to build people up. In fact, it is the suffering in the lives of his servants that results in a true knowledge of Christ and gives people encouragement that they can pass on to others. For Paul said, 'Death works in us, but life in you.' This is truly the mark of a spiritual man."

"I am also struck by how clearly he distinguishes the ministry of the Old Covenant from that of the New," I told Peter. I pointed to a passage before us. "He writes that it is God who makes us adequate to be servants of a new covenant, not of the letter, but of the Spirit; for the letter kills, but the Spirit gives life. He even calls the law of commandments given to Moses 'the ministry of death,' for it cannot give life. But the ministry of the Spirit *does* give life, resulting in exceedingly more glory than the law. For Christ has sent his Spirit, and where the Spirit of the Lord is, there is liberty. So, what then, is our ministry? As Paul says, it is to behold, as a mirror, the glory of the Lord, and as we see him, as we abide in his presence, we are changed; the Lord himself transforms us from one degree of glory to another. It is the Lord who began the work in us by implanting himself within our spirits. He is the treasure who lives within these earthen vessels. And it is the Lord who does the work of transforming our souls so that we will be conformed to his very image. This he does through his Spirit, working in us as we spend time beholding him and yield to the work of the cross in our lives. And it will be the Lord who completes the work when we receive from him our glorified bodies. Praise be to God!"

"I am also impressed with one other thing I find in Paul's writings," said Peter. "And that is his view of women."

Intrigued, I sat back to listen. We had certainly seen something of our Lord's Spirit in Luke as he interacted with Mary and the other women. Perhaps he had learned from Paul in this regard.

"In the first Corinthian letter, Paul describes how the Lord gives gifts to the human race indiscriminately, having no regard for gender. Just like men, women are given teaching gifts and gifts of prophecy, just as the prophet Joel described when he prophesied that in these last days of the Old Covenant era, God would pour out his Spirit on all mankind, and our sons and daughters would prophesy, our young men would see visions and our old men would see dreams; even upon his bond slaves, both men and women, he would pour forth of his Spirit and they would prophesy.

"But we see also, in this letter, how some of the converts from the Jews who lived in Corinth still clung to their old thinking and old teachings originating from our oral laws and traditions. They believed that women should remain mute in the church, just as they do in the synagogues. You can tell this from the questions they raised in a prior letter to Paul that he is obviously responding to in this letter. For he quotes them where they said, 'The women are to keep silent in the churches; for they are not permitted to speak, but are to subject themselves, just as the law also says. If they desire to learn anything, let them ask their own husbands at home, for it is improper for a woman to speak in the church.'

"Surely this law they referred to was not the law of Moses, for nowhere in the law can we find such a statement. They referred, rather, to the oral body of law and traditions recorded in the Talmud—the traditions that Jesus frequently smashed before the eyes of the Jews in his words and deeds. For instance, I remember the time when he spit on the ground and made mud to put in the eyes of the blind man, thus restoring his sight. In our oral law it says, 'To heal a blind man on the Sabbath it is prohibited to inject wine into his eyes. It is also prohibited to make mud with spittle and smear it on his eyes.' Jesus continually opposed worthless traditions when they stood in the way of people seeing who he was.

"Similarly, only in the oral law are women silenced. Rabbis teach that women should know nothing but the use of their distaffs for spinning yarn. The Talmud also teaches that a woman's voice is prohibited from being heard because it is sexually provocative; that it is shameful for their voices to be heard among men; and that women are mentally inferior, cannot understand spiritual things, and therefore should be silenced."

I nodded—I knew the traditions well, and they had grieved me for some time. As a young man I had accepted them as right and proper, but by Jesus's own attitude, words, and deeds toward women (and children), he had shaken me up in this as in so many other things.

Peter went on, "Paul's adamant response to their assertions was to say, 'What! Nonsense! Was it from you, men, that the Word of God first went forth? Or has it come to you, men, only? If anyone thinks he is a prophet or spiritual, let him recognize that the things which I write to you are the Lord's commandments. But if anyone does not recognize this, he is not recognized. Therefore, my brothers and sisters, desire earnestly to prophesy, and do not forbid to speak in tongues. But all things must be done properly and in an orderly manner.'"

"Indeed, Paul has guts!" I laughed. "Everywhere we have evidence of men lording over women. Even in Herod's temple, which they have been working on now for nearly seventy years, there is a subtle, diminutive attitude toward women. The court of the women is fifteen steps lower than the court for the men. This was not so in the tabernacle in the wilderness, or in Solomon's temple. I wish that all men would be so bold as to encourage women to be liberated and release their gifts within the church."

"John, it is clear to me," said Peter, "that these two letters have their place, along with the others we have gone over, in the inspired volume we are seeking to assemble that will reveal the whole truth of the New Covenant. Both are unique. If we were to withhold either of them from being included, something would be lost. Truths would not be known. I believe what Paul has said, that what he has written are the Lord's commandments. I think our next step should be to make a trip to Caesarea and visit him in prison. We need to share with him where the Lord has brought us to this point."

CHAPTER 8
OPPORTUNITY MISSED

A.D. 60

The day I received news from Caesarea, we had gone as far as we could go on the assembly of documents for the New Testament. We intended to arrange a meeting with Paul, but things got busy for us in Jerusalem.

For one thing, within the prior year and a half, Porcius Festus had become procurator of Judea, succeeding Antonius Felix. Soon after his appointment, a dispute arose between the Jews and the Syrians inhabiting Caesarea. The Jews of the city felt that they were entitled to special privileges because Herod, a Jewish king, had founded the city. But an edict was issued by imperial Rome favoring the Syrians, which resulted in the Jews being reduced in status to second-class citizens. Jewish passions were inflamed. The decision embittered the Jews even more against Roman authority, and their feeling of being unfairly treated spread, even here to Jerusalem, and became the seeds that would eventually sprout in the outbreak of the war with Rome.

Not only that, but King Agrippa provoked the priests in Jerusalem by erecting a tower at his home near the temple from which he could watch the priests performing their sacrificial duties and monitor religious activities. The Jews responded by building a high wall to block his view. This further stoked the flames of antagonism against the governing authorities. On the political level, things were heating up.

We in the church continued to have our own problems with the unbelieving Jews. For instance, we were seeing more and more false prophets rise up, seeking to lead the people astray. And apostate Israel has surely been the greatest enemy of the church thus far, as we have seen not only here, but also in the Gentile world where the gospel is being spread. They have continually tried to manipulate the power of the pagan Roman Empire to put a stop to the growth of the church, just as they used their influence with Pilate in the crucifixion of our Lord.

But on top of these problems, there were two issues—related, but somewhat distinct—that I was grappling with as well. These were core issues that struck at the foundation of my personal belief structure. And they were brought more clearly into focus as a result of the discussions that Peter, James, and I had over Paul's letters.

For the previous several months, I had been allowing the content of those discussions to seep deep into my soul. They were constantly the source of my meditations. I sought the Lord for answers and for clarity, because there were great, practical ramifications to what God seemed to be revealing to me.

One conclusion I came to was that there were many true converts in Jerusalem—primarily those from among the scribes and Pharisees—who still carried an attitude of superiority toward the Gentile believers. The majority of Jews who have believed in Christ would now concur—at least in theory— that the Gentiles are fellow heirs of the promises of God and included in God's plan. But in their hearts, it is close to impossible for them to rid themselves of the idea that Christ came primarily for the Jews. They still view the Gentiles as merely an afterthought in God's redemption plan. Their attitude is that for the Gentiles to become partakers of the privileges afforded to those who are called by God and chosen, they should become Jewish proselytes. They interpret the Old Covenant Scriptures to say that Jews alone were selected to enter into a marriage covenant with the Almighty.

But our Jewish ancestors were granted this covenant status, not on the basis that they were superior to any other people, but through the merit of God's divine, unmerited favor alone. This attitude of superiority among our people simply cannot be extracted unless by divine intervention and revelation. Why can they not be thankful that this grace is extended to the Gentiles, as opposed to considering them second-class citizens in the kingdom? And as for the Gentiles, they should be thankful as well and not look down upon the Jews for this mercy that has been extended to them! They have now have been "grafted in" and are God's chosen people as well, just as Paul wrote in his letter to the Romans.

Now, as a result of what I was seeing all around me, I was beginning to believe that Paul had been entrusted with an even purer gospel than the one we preached among the Jews.

The second issue, though related, was even more hard-hitting: Had God now dissolved his marriage covenant with Israel? Were we merely in some transition period before this became more clear? Had he divorced Israel? Had he taken a new bride?

These issues troubled me. I still needed to process them more thoroughly.

And then on the practical side, there were the issues of how Jewish and Gentile believers could find common ground and express their unity one with another. For a Gentile, visiting a Judean church must seem like being in another world. Sabbaths are kept, foods that he is used to eating are considered unclean, the practice of circumcision is observed. Our prayers and practices model Jewish patterns, and the laws and rules we keep seem hardly distinguishable, for a Gentile, from Judaism itself.

For Jewish believers who visit Gentile churches, the shock is equally as great. How can they help but look with contempt on supposed followers of Christ who attend feasts in heathen temples with their pagan friends, eat foods that are unclean, have no regard for our traditions, and behave themselves with no sense of propriety in their meetings—exhibiting unbridled freedom? Why should they not believe that the Gentiles should just accept the rules and the customs of the Jerusalem church and accept the Jerusalem body as the final authority before which issues of disagreement must be decided?

How could these grave differences help but keep the two parties separate from one another, living in their own worlds? How could they ever find common ground in Christ?

The one closest to me, and the most likely person to talk with about these things, was Peter. But the one I really wanted to discuss them with was Paul.

I left my home that day determined to find Peter and press him to make some plans to journey with me to Caesarea to talk with Paul. But no sooner had I stepped out the door and closed it behind me than I saw someone walking in my direction. I recognized him. His name was Alexander. He was a brother from the church in Caesarea.

"Hello, John," he said, walking briskly toward me and greeting me with a smile, though his eyes were somber. "I just arrived in Jerusalem and was asked to deliver this letter to you. Something serious has happened with Paul. Luke said I should fill you in on the details at once."

I hastily took the letter from Alexander, unrolled it, and began to read.

> Dear John,
> Circumstances are changing very swiftly here in Caesarea. Upon Porcius Festus's arrival, he went immediately to Jerusalem to meet with the chief priests and leading men of the city. They requested that he bring Paul to Jerusalem to try him there, all the while planning to ambush and kill him on the way. But Festus insisted that the influential men among the Jews return to Caesarea with him and prosecute Paul there.
>
> When Festus returned along with the Jewish contingency, he summoned Paul and listened to the charges brought against him by the Jews, but which they could not prove. Finally, Festus asked Paul if he would be willing to go to Jerusalem and stand trial there.

Knowing that could mean imminent death, Paul glared at Festus and then at the others in the room and boldly proclaimed, *"Ad Caesarum pro voco"*—"I appeal my case to be heard by Caesar." This stunned Festus, but after consulting with his advisers, he answered Paul, "You have appealed to Caesar, to Caesar you shall go."

After several days, King Agrippa and his queen, Bernice, arrived in Caesarea. They were told of Paul and his appeal, and they requested to meet with him. Paul gave a strong defense, nearly persuading the king to become a Christian. But in the end, because he had appealed to Caesar, nothing more could be done.

I was told just today that an Adramyttian ship will be departing in three days, so by the time you receive this letter, we will be en route to Italy. Aristarchus and I will be accompanying Paul.

Where and when we will see each other again, I do not know. But this I do know. God has his purposes, and that which he has begun among us, he will complete.

Farewell, my friend. And please extend my greetings to Peter and James. Keep us in your prayers.

Luke

I was stunned. After all this time, the opportunity for us to meet with Paul in Caesarea had escaped us. My mind raced. When would we see him again? When would we be able to discuss his writings? To come to some agreement on what should be included in the New Testament writings? Or even to see what Luke had composed?

I stood and spoke with Alexander for a while longer. He informed me in more detail of the circumstances that had led to Paul's abrupt departure. Seeing that I was downcast, he concluded by trying to encourage me: "John, I can tell that this news comes as a great disappointment to you. But let this one thing encourage your heart. Before Paul was taken to Caesarea, when he was first taken into custody in Jerusalem and then allowed to present his case before the council, a great dissension broke out between the Pharisees and Sadducees, resulting in Paul's nearly being torn to pieces. The commander of the troops assigned to protect Paul ordered that he be taken away and returned to the barracks at the Roman Fortress of Antonia. But that night, the Lord himself appeared to Paul and stood by his side and said to him, 'Take courage; for as you have solemnly witnessed to my cause at Jerusalem, so you must witness at Rome also.' After three trials and two years of imprisonment,

Paul is finally headed for Rome. And the Lord even provided a free ticket. So John, be at peace. The Lord has plans for Paul in Rome, and we must accept this as the will of God."

Shaking my head while staring at the ground, I mumbled some form of acknowledgment to Alexander. Then, like a dark cloud, a heavy sadness engulfed me, as the uncertainty of completing our project quickly became my reality. I bade good-bye to Alexander and set out for Peter's home. The urgency to go to Caesarea to see Paul was no longer my concern, but what to do next?

CHAPTER 9

A SECOND CHANCE

A.D. 61

Over the next three months, Peter and I met intermittently to pray and discuss our options. At one of those meetings, he came up with an idea.

"I have been thinking, John," he said. "By now, Paul is probably somewhere in Rome under house arrest. Most likely he will be there for two years, because as a Roman citizen, he is obligated to wait that period of time from his appeal to Caesar before receiving a hearing."

I nodded—the two-year wait policy was intended to discourage everyone with a complaint from appealing to the emperor.

Peter finished, "So I think we should send an emissary to Paul, and I believe I know who that person should be."

"Who is that?" I asked.

"John Mark," Peter said.

I sat up straighter, startled. "John Mark? Why on earth John Mark? You know of his past history with Paul. At the best, they are not the closest of friends, and at the worst, I see them mixing like oil does with water."

"I am aware of that, John," responded Peter. "But that history is not all there is to this man. We both know he comes from a good home. He is Mary's son, Barnabas's nephew. For years Mary has opened her house to prayer meetings for the church. Notably, it was at a prayer meeting for me at her home, following the ruthless beheading of your brother James, that an angel of the Lord miraculously rescued me from my chains in prison. And even more than that, John Mark is my son in the faith."

"Yes," I responded, "but he is not Paul's. You know the story as well as I do: following Agabus's visit to Antioch and his prophecies concerning a coming famine in Judea, Paul and Barnabas and the church there took up a collection for the poor Jerusalem saints. Paul, Barnabas, and Titus delivered the gift, and then, upon their return, they took John Mark back to Antioch with them. Not long after they returned, the Holy Spirit commissioned Barnabas and Paul for their first missionary journey to the region of Galatia, and they decided to take Mark along with them as their baggage carrier and helper. But he did not last very long on that trip. He abandoned them."

"I know," said Peter. "He was not ready. But perhaps I know more of the story than you do. Following their brief sojourn on the island of Cyprus, the three set sail from Paphos to Pamphilia. Their destination was Antioch, Pisidia, but on the way they experienced a shipwreck. That terrified John Mark. And to get to Antioch, they would need to cross the Taurus Mountains, notorious for dangers from robbers and flash floods that cause rivers to overflow and sweep many a traveler away to his death. This was just too much for him. Plus, at this point, Paul was beginning to take the lead of the group, and that did not sit well with Mark, for he was keenly biased toward Barnabas because of their family relationship. So he informed the other two that he had decided to return home. I realize that this was a great disappointment and inexcusable to Paul—"

"And on Paul's second journey, the idea of John Mark accompanying Paul and Barnabas again became so contentious that Paul and Barnabas parted ways," I broke in. "Paul took Silas with him, and Barnabas headed off to Cyprus with John Mark. So, why, based on this past history, do you think John Mark is the one to go?"

"Because everyone deserves a second chance," Peter replied triumphantly.

"And that settles it?" I asked.

"You, as well as the angels, are my witness of how many second chances our Lord afforded me. I think this would be good for both John Mark and Paul, and it will prove the character of both men. Will John Mark be able to humble himself and ask Paul for forgiveness? Will Paul be able to forgive him? After all, Mark has worked closely with me on our account of the Lord's life, and he knows my heart. He has been drawn into this project as well. As such, I think he would be the perfect choice to send to Paul to show him what we have done."

"You make a good case, Peter," I responded. "But I think the first hurdle to determine whether or not this is God's will is to see how John Mark feels about this. Why don't we discuss this with him?"

We agreed to meet a few days later in the cave up on the Mount of Olives where the body of Jesus was placed, in the former tomb of Joseph of Arimathea—before he was raised from the dead. We frequently used it as a place to meet and to pray. Peter informed Mark that we wanted to meet with him, but he did not tell him the reason why.

The main room in the tomb was large enough to hold about a dozen people. Further inside was the space, carved out in the rock, where Jesus's body was laid. We all arrived at about the same time. Peter arranged three small wooden benches to face one another, and we sat down. First we prayed.

Peter looked up toward John Mark, his arms resting on his knees and his hands folded. Then he began.

"John Mark, we have asked you to come here today because we have a mission in mind which we would like you to consider." Then Peter laid out the whole plan.

At first, John Mark seemed reluctant to agree. "Brothers," he said, "you know my history with Paul. I have the greatest respect for him, for the calling of God upon his life and for all that he has suffered for the gospel's sake. But I have also contributed to that suffering, being the source of a great conflict between him and Barnabas and also greatly disappointing him when I abandoned him and Barnabas on their trip to Galatia. I feel humiliated over my conduct, and I have had to live with that for the past fourteen years. I do not think Paul would be thrilled if I were to show up to visit him in Rome."

John Mark hung his head, and my heart went out to him. Suddenly, I knew that Peter's suggestion had been absolutely right.

"Mark, I want to tell you something," I said. "It was fear that kept me putting off writing to Paul while he was in prison at the praetorium in Caesarea. I too am intimidated by Paul—by his great learning, and by his revelation, and by the way he has come to be among the most fruitful of apostles based solely on his knowledge of the resurrected Christ, not having walked with our Lord in the flesh as we did. But thank God that I confronted my fears. And look what has resulted! We are now well on our way to acquiring a written record of the New Covenant, and that with Paul's help. Confronting our fears can emancipate us and enable us to walk in the light, just as our Lord is light himself."

John Mark looked up, tears rolling down his cheeks.

"I have failed," he blurted out between sobs. "But I don't need to live the rest of my life with this condemnation hanging over my head. I want to be free from it, and above all, I would love to clear the air with Paul and be restored in fellowship with him once again. Whether he will accept me again, I do not know. But I am willing to take that risk. Besides, this work is too important to let differences between brothers stand in the way of its being completed. I am willing to go."

"Praise God!" Peter and I both exclaimed together.

We circled John Mark and wrapped our arms around him. Then we prayed for him, for wisdom and protection for his journey, for the right traveling companion to accompany him, and for what God would do when he reached Rome and met with Paul.

Peter finished his instructions with a smile. "You will take with you a copy of the biography that you and I wrote, as well as copies of Matthew's gospel, and James's letter. I suggest that you carry them with you in a waterproof satchel, in the event that you have the misfortune of another shipwreck along the way."

"Another shipwreck? No way!" scoffed John Mark. "I will face my fears with Paul, but I have nothing to gain by trying to overcome my fears of sailing on the open seas, or of shipwreck, or of the perpetual state of being seasick that I found myself in nearly the whole time we were on the water last time. I will go to Rome. But I will go by land!"

CHAPTER 10
THE DEATH OF JAMES

A.D. 62

John Mark chose as his traveling companion Jesus, also called Justus, a man slightly younger than Mark and of Jewish descent. Justus knew Greek and Latin, which would be helpful on the trip. He was a rising leader and a man of good standing in the church. They planned to leave in the early spring when the nights would not be so cold, for they knew they would sleep many a night under the stars on their long trek. But their departure would not come before the church would witness a tragic event.

The Roman governor, Festus, had just died in office. Nero appointed as his successor Lucceius Albinus, and King Agrippa named a new high priest, a Sadducee named Ananus ben Ananus. During the interim between Festus's death and the time Albinus arrived in Caesarea, Ananus hastily convened a session of the Sanhedrin and ordered James to appear.

James was highly regarded, even among the Jews, as a righteous man. He had earned a reputation as "James the Just." His influence was spreading rapidly among the religious Jews, and a number were coming to Christ. But Ananus wanted to see this stopped. This was his moment: void of the presence of any Roman authority, Ananus figured he could take revenge on some old enemies, and one of those enemies was James.

The Passover season was upon us, and thousands of pilgrims were arriving in Jerusalem. As James stood before the council, Ananus informed him that this sect following the Nazarene had gone too far and that James must publicly repudiate Jesus. He threatened him with dire consequences if he did not comply.

They then took James and led him up to the pinnacle of the temple. Below, a large crowd had gathered. Once again, Ananus charged James, "You must publicly repudiate Jesus and insist that the people no longer follow him and continue to be led astray."

Jewish law provides the death sentence by stoning for anyone convicted of leading the people astray—or they can also be thrown down from a great height and then stoned to death if they are still alive. So James, resigned to his fate, agreed to address the people. He looked down, eying the large crowd. All mouths were silent; all eyes riveted on him.

Knowing his hour had come, James seized this one last opportunity to bear witness to Christ in front of the thousands gathered. His words were bold and clear. Turning to his accusers, he cried out in a loud voice, "Why are you asking me concerning Jesus, the Son of Man? He sits in heaven at the right hand of the Great Power and is about to come upon the clouds of heaven!"

The crowd roared. A number of the saints from the church were mixed among the pilgrims and the Jewish residents of Jerusalem, and they began proclaiming at the top of their lungs, "Hosanna! Hosanna! Hosanna to the Son of David!"—the same accolades heard in Jerusalem some thirty years before when Jesus entered the city on the back of a donkey.

Seeing that their plan had failed miserably, one of Ananus's servants rushed at James and pushed him from the parapet. He fell a great distance, crashing to the temple floor.

The people gathered around him and found that he was still barely alive. His accusers quickly descended and began pelting him with the stones they had gathered for this purpose. Finally, one of them took a club and finished the job, beating him to death.

What Ananus had done was a flagrant violation of the law, as he had not gotten final approval for this from the Roman authority. A protest was sent to the new governor, and when King Agrippa heard it, he rapidly replaced Ananus with a new high priest named Jesus, the son of Damneus, after only three months of service.

But the deed was already done. And with it came consequences. Street fighting broke out between those who sided with Ananus and those who opposed him. More and more, believers felt unsafe and afraid in Jerusalem. It had not been this bad since the early days when Paul—then called Saul—oversaw the martyrdom of Stephen and hounded the church throughout Judea.

With the growing belief that war was coming with Rome and that the fulfillment of Jesus's prophecies might imminently be at hand, a steady stream of Jewish Christians had already begun to leave the city. James's death gave rise to another surge of believers fleeing.

When the time came for John Mark and Justus to depart, we held a prayer meeting to send them off. It was in the home of Mary, John Mark's mother. Following our prayer, Peter gave a farewell speech to the two disciples.

"We are sending you off, committing you into the mighty hands of the Great Shepherd of the sheep, who is able to protect you on your journey. But before you go, there is one last thing I want to give you to take along with you."

A stack of a half-dozen scrolls stood on a table near Peter. The stack consisted of an original letter, along with five copies. He reached for them with both hands, picked them up, and presented them to John Mark.

"This letter is one that our brother Silas and I have just finished composing. It is written to the scattered believers in Pontus, Galatia, Cappadocia, Asia, and Bithynia, territories that you will be traveling through on your way to Rome. Some of the churches you will find along the way, and where you will be receiving hospitality, know Silas and hold him in high esteem. He helped father some of them in the faith, along with Paul, on Paul's second missionary trip.

"They will be predominately Gentile churches. But the majority of the believers who have recently left Jerusalem, and continue to leave, are migrating north. By now, many have already arrived in the cities that you will be visiting and have become part of the Gentile assemblies there. This letter was written to encourage both Jew and Gentile believer alike, and to let them know that the trials they are experiencing are common to us all.

"For the Jew especially, since they have left the land of their forefathers, I wanted to remind them that they have a hope. And that hope is alive. It is Jesus Christ himself. They also have an inheritance. And that inheritance is also alive. And he is imperishable and undefiled and will not fade away, reserved in heaven for them. For they are protected by the power of God through faith for a salvation ready to be revealed in these last times. Unlike their fathers, who were promised the physical land as their inheritance, they have the promise of which that land was only a picture. We are now living under a New Covenant, and our inheritance is far greater. Our inheritance is the all-sufficient Christ. And his kingdom is not confined to the land of Israel but will cover the entire earth, as the waters cover the sea. So I wrote this, wanting them to look back with no regrets."

The saints nodded and murmured agreement as Peter continued. "And should they entertain any nostalgic thoughts about the temple, that too will soon be destroyed. For the end is near. The real and lasting temple is not one made of limestone blocks, but of stones that are alive. And we—they—are those stones, being built up together as a spiritual house for a holy priesthood, to offer up spiritual sacrifices acceptable to God through Jesus Christ.

"The letter contains many other practical words of advice, but it ends with an admonition for all to share in the sufferings of Christ. To the degree that they share in his sufferings, they should keep rejoicing, so that at the revelation of his glory, they may rejoice with exultation.

"I have also encouraged the elders in the churches that receive this letter to shepherd the flock of God among them not by lording it over them, but by being good examples. That will include being shepherds to the new believers from our midst whom they have already received and will soon be receiving. And for our people, my admonition to them is that they have submissive hearts and be willing to find their place in the body of Christ, respecting the leadership that God has already established and put in place.

"Finally, I wanted to send greetings from the whole church, so I ended my letter with these words: 'Through Silas, our faithful brother (for so I regard him), I have written to you briefly, exhorting and testifying that this is the true grace of God. Stand firm in it. She who is in Babylon . . .'" Peter paused for a moment and then looked up and scanned everyone in the room with a serious look in eye. With baited breath we all waited for his next words. Finally, he snickered and broke out in loud laughter. We immediately joined in his laughter, for we knew that his comparison of Jerusalem to Babylon was not only poignant, but accurate. Indeed, like Babylon of old, Jerusalem had become the capital of false religion and the persecutor of the one true faith.

Then he continued, "She who is in Babylon, chosen together with you, sends you greetings, and so does my son, Mark. Greet one another with a kiss of love. Peace be to all who are in Christ."

Many of us stayed late into the evening, saying our good-byes to John Mark and Justus. Finally, after the remaining brothers and sisters left and the candles and lamps were blown out, the two soon-to-be travelers went to bed. The following morning they joined three other families who had sold their possessions and taken with them only what they considered necessities, ready to head north to start a new life. Traveling together would be safer and help protect them from the brigands that roamed the countryside.

Two years would pass before we would see our brother, John Mark, again.

CHAPTER 11
THE ARRIVAL OF GOOD NEWS

A.D. 63

In the spring we received a letter that lifted our spirits. It was from John Mark. It was short, and it read,

> My dear brothers Peter and John,
>
> I send you greetings along with good news. It appears that our brother Paul will be released from house arrest soon. I am excited to report that God has richly blessed our time together and that the breach in our relationship has been healed completely and our relationship fully restored. Praise be to God!
>
> Paul was greatly encouraged by the letters you sent to him and has given me four more to bring to you. Dr. Luke sent two as well.
>
> Justus and I are preparing to return home in the next few days. I am sending this letter by way of a brother here in Rome who will be leaving by ship for Caesarea. He tried to persuade us to come with him, but I told him that we preferred to walk! We will be retracing the same route we took to get here and will be visiting some of the churches along the way. We hope to see you again not long after this letter arrives.
>
> Paul, along with the brothers and sisters from Rome, send their greetings.
>
> *John Mark*

Here in Jerusalem, the year and a half since we had last seen John Mark had been bleak. In the fall of the year that he and Justus departed for Rome, at the Feast of Tabernacles, a strange event occurred that caused another hemorrhage of believers (and nonbelieving Jews) to exit the city. A peasant man named Jesus, the son of Ananias, suddenly appeared and wandered the streets of Jerusalem proclaiming imminent doom. His prophetic words were powerful and bone-chilling, instilling fear in many hearts and precipitating another exodus.

There was also a growing feeling on the part of many of us original apostles of Christ that our time to leave was soon approaching as well. We had been meeting together for some time, praying about where each of us should go, for the Lord had told us that we would be his witnesses in Jerusalem, and in all Judea and Samaria, and even to the remotest parts of the earth. We sensed that the time was drawing near when we would be finally separated.

When John Mark and Justus at last arrived, we noticed a new confidence in Mark. It was as though he had been released from a heavy burden that he had carried, and he was more fully committed to the ministry. We knew that this had to do with him patching things up with Paul and the experience he had gained while in Rome, seeing what God was doing among the predominately Gentile churches.

Our reunion took place at Peter's home. Upon seeing us, John Mark rushed to embrace us—first Peter and then me—clinging to us and kissing us repeatedly on the cheeks.

"It is so good to see you again, brothers!" he said, barely able to contain himself. "I bring greetings to you from Paul and Luke and the church in Rome! Andronicus and Junia, as well as Rufus and his mother, also send you special greetings. And your letter, Peter, was happily received by every individual and every church that we had the chance to share it with along the way."

"Excellent," responded Peter, his eyes wide with delight to see John Mark again. "Sit down now and tell us, what news do you bring from Rome?"

"First, I will tell you about Paul," he began. "Once Paul arrived in Rome, Julius, the centurion guarding him, turned him over to Roman officials along with a very positive report. Since he was not a dangerous criminal, he was given the privilege of house arrest and was granted considerable freedom. He has been staying in the large, third-floor apartment of a rather poorly constructed, six-story *insula* built of timber and mud brick. Though constantly chained to the wrist of Roman guards who rotate every four hours, Paul entertains guests at will and teaches regularly and freely to both Jews and Greeks. Justus and I stayed at a similar insula, only on the fifth floor, which had no running water or sanitation but for which we paid cheaper rent. It was about a ten-minute walk away. Places like these are overcrowded firetraps. Two of the insulas in our neighborhood collapsed because of their poor construction, and a number of people were killed."

"What was it like for Paul to be constantly chained to a Roman soldier for nearly two years?" Peter asked with a furrowed brow. "He must not have had any privacy, whether awake or asleep. At least you had your freedom and could freely come and go!"

"Certainly it was a great inconvenience for him," John Mark replied, "but

I have never seen a man who could be so content living in heavenly realms in Christ even while in chains. Having known Christ for nearly thirty years, he could write in one of his letters to the Philippian church that he has learned the secret of being content regardless of his circumstances and that he can do all things through Christ, who strengthens him. He has an amazing, indomitable spirit, to which I bear witness. He was truly an inspiration, even to the Roman guards. So much so that several of them have come to Christ along with their families, and they are sharing their faith even in Nero's palace."

"Amazing," I marveled. "How do these Roman soldiers who are coming to Christ deal with the requirement of emperor worship and offering sacrifice to the emperor as a sign of loyalty? Do they still offer incense once a year to the emperor or to his image, as they are required to do?"

"Since Nero has been away, it has not come up with respect to these recent converts. As you know, under Herod, Caesar Augustus was persuaded to grant the Jews an exemption from emperor worship because he knew they would never acknowledge the divinity of a Roman emperor. To a large extent, the Romans still see Christians as some sect of Judaism. But it is becoming an issue for non-Jewish converts. For though Gentiles can freely worship their respective gods, they still must publicly acknowledge 'Caesar is Lord' and offer some pinch of incense and burn it upon an altar—or give some other form of sacrifice or pay money. Some Romans see a Christian exemption as nothing more than tax evasion, and they fear it might spread to other sects. So pressure is mounting on Gentile believers to show their loyalty to the emperor. It is not an easy position for them. Noncompliance can mean persecution, but compliance would be a clear act of idolatry."

"And what of Paul's trial?" Peter asked.

Mark made a face. "What an emperor to appeal to! Not long before Paul arrived in Rome, Nero murdered his own mother, Agrippina, and following that, spent about eighteen months flitting about in southern Italy. He was also preoccupied with his love affair with Poppaea while still married to Octavia, whom he later banished to Campania and then ordered to be beheaded.

"When he finally returned to Rome, there was a backlog of cases to be heard, including Paul's. But Paul's accusers had failed to arrive from Judea, most likely because of the insubstantial evidence they had to convict him, so it may be that Seneca, Nero's chief adviser, could try the case and he will be acquitted. But whether Paul stands before Nero or Seneca, we have confidence for a favorable outcome."

"In the letter we received just prior to your arrival, you also mentioned that Paul sent copies of more letters for us to see. Do you have them with you?" I asked.

Mark's face brightened. "Yes, John. Being given these letters alone was worth the trip!"

"Tell us, what did he give you?" demanded Peter.

Reaching into a large satchel, John Mark pulled out twelve separate scrolls.

"I have here three letters that Paul wrote to different churches—the churches in Ephesus, Colossae, and Philippi—a real treasure trove! Along with those, there is a personal letter to a slave owner named Philemon concerning his runaway slave, Onesimus, who found Paul in Rome and was led by him to Christ. And on top of all that, there are the two documents Luke sent: his account of the Lord's life and a history of the spread of the gospel from Jerusalem all the way to Rome. Paul sent one copy of each letter for both of you."

"I cannot wait to see what Luke has put together," I said.

"That may be true," Mark responded, "but wait until you read these prison letters written by Paul. They are unbelievably rich!"

He leaned back in his seat, beaming. "These letters were delivered by the hand of Tychicus and Onesimus to Colossae, Ephesians, Laodicea, and Hierapolis. The Philippian letter was delivered by Epaphroditus." His eyes sparkled. "But there is one other letter Paul and Luke asked me to deliver to the Hebrews who read your letter, Peter, and then to bring it here to Jerusalem for those who still remain. I have kept this letter to read together until after we have gone through the others."

"Very well," I said, overwhelmed by the riches John Mark had brought to us. "I suggest that Peter and I first spend time with Luke's gospel and his history, and then we all reconvene to discuss them. Following that, we can look at the other letters Paul sent, including the one you have been entrusted to deliver to the Hebrews."

"An excellent idea," agreed Peter. "Though we have known of Luke's writings for some time and have anxiously awaited their completion, John Mark has now really piqued my curiosity to read these other letters from Paul! We can meet two days from now to go over what Luke has written, but I am particularly anxious to read what new revelations may have stained these parchments from the ink dripping from the pen of our brother in chains."

CHAPTER 12
LUKE'S HISTORICAL ACCOUNT

A.D. 63

Once again we met in Peter's home. This time it was Peter, myself, and John Mark. The absence of James was palpable, and I swallowed a lump in my throat and quietly praised the Lord for taking our brother to be with him.

Sitting as usual around Peter's table, snacking on morsels of the day's bread and sipping from glasses half-filled with diluted wine, our conversation immediately turned to Luke's letters.

"I must confess," said Peter, "how much I loved these letters. They are both so personal. Luke addressed them directly to me, referring to me as *Theophilus,* the lover of God."

"But I thought they were written exclusively for me, for am I not Theophilus, the one who loves God?" I responded with a chuckle.

"You are both wrong. They were written to me! For I am Theophilus, the lover of God!" trumped John Mark as we all laughed with one another.

"Though Luke was not an eyewitness to the life and teachings of Christ, his investigation, down to the slightest detail, was done with impeccable accuracy," said Peter. "And I can see some subtleties in his account that would definitely appeal to a Gentile audience. For instance, Luke makes the point that one does not need to be an apostle to have the Lord appear to him— or her. The Lord—or angels, for that matter—appeared to Cleopas and the other disciple on the road to Emmaus, to the women—Mary Magdalene, Joanna, and Mary the mother of James, and the other women with them— and he can speak to any member of his body that he chooses to speak to, not just to reputed leaders. This was a lesson we certainly needed to learn! Direction does not always come from the top down. Jesus alone is the head of his church, which is his body here on earth, and he can appear to or speak through whomever he chooses."

"You have been reading ahead, Peter," quipped John Mark. "Did you pull that last phrase, 'Jesus being the head of his church, which is his body,' from something you read in Paul's latest letter to the Ephesians?"

Peter continued, with a smile, as if he never heard John Mark's comment.

"Luke also does an excellent job, as should all Scripture, of portraying the reality of events—even pointing out how God can work in spite of human weakness and failure. I recall telling him the story of when I denied the Lord. He included that story in his account. Our Lord said to me, 'Simon, Simon, behold, Satan has demanded to sift you like wheat; but I have prayed for you, that your faith may not fail; and you, when once you have turned again, strengthen your brothers.'

"But I said to him, 'Lord, I am ready to go both to prison and to death with you.'

"Then he said to me, 'Peter, the rooster will not crow today until you have denied three times that you know me.'

"The Lord needs to break us of self-confidence and pride. I learned a great lesson that day. That is, that there is one more powerful than me who wants to destroy me. That is Satan—Lucifer—the devil. All species have their own form of life. God is the possessor of the highest, most powerful life form in the universe. But Satan is strong, cunning, and possesses a life form himself—that of an archangel. That life was created, and though he fell and rebelled against God and cannot match the uncreated, divine Life of the Creator in strength or power, nonetheless, he can dominate fallen man. In our own strength, we are powerless to defeat him. There is only one way to overcome him and be victorious in this life. That is to learn to live by the victorious Life of Christ, which he has given to us and which is victorious over all."

"There are many other strong points Luke makes," I added. "His emphasis on God's boundless capacity to forgive, as in the stories of the prodigal son and the criminal crucified with Christ on the cross, whom he promised would be with him that day in paradise. And he places great stress on the Lord's heart to seek and to save that which is lost—the shepherd leaving the ninety-nine to search for the one lost sheep; the widow seeking for the one lost coin and rejoicing when she finds it. Indeed, whereas Matthew portrays Jesus as King, and you and I, Mark, as the Suffering Servant, Luke highlights him as the Savior of the World.

"Tell me, Peter: in our frequent discussions about the New Covenant and its relationship to the Old Covenant, is there anything new that you gleaned from Luke's biographical work?"

"One very small point caught my attention," said Peter. "It was in regard to Jesus's teaching concerning the fig tree."

Unsure as to the specific detail Peter was referring to, I nodded and waited to hear his thoughts.

"Following his triumphal entry into Jerusalem, Jesus saw a fig tree which was full of leaves but no fruit. He cursed that fig tree, and as even Mark and

I noted in our gospel account, it withered from its roots. This was an object lesson for the nation of Israel, its leaders, and its rulers. National Israel had the outward appearance of religion, as represented by the leaves, but was void of the fruit of righteousness. When the roots die, a tree cannot come back to life. The lesson we learned is that national Israel had become like that fig tree. It was barren. Jesus even said, 'No longer shall there ever be any fruit from you.'

"But Luke reminds us of another parable Jesus used concerning the fig tree that is in neither of the other two accounts. We read from Luke that Jesus said, 'A man had a fig tree which had been planted in his vineyard, and he came looking for fruit on it and did not find any. And he said to the vineyard-keeper, 'Behold, for three years I have come looking for fruit on this fig tree without finding any. Cut it down! Why does it even use up the ground? And he answered and said to him, "Let it alone, sir, for this year too, until I dig around it and put in fertilizer; and if it bears fruit, fine. But if not, cut it down."'

"By this time, Jesus was in the third year of his ministry and had found no fruit on the tree of national Israel. His verdict was: cut it down. It is dead. The roots are dead. It will never again come back to life.

"The same conclusions are found in the parable of the wicked vinedressers who rejected the prophets God sent, and when he finally sent his own son, they killed him too. When Jesus told that parable to the chief priests and the scribes, he asked what should be done to these men. They responded that he should 'bring those wretches to a wretched end, and rent out the vineyard to other vine-growers who will pay him the proceeds at the proper seasons.' Jesus then said to them, 'Therefore I say to you the kingdom of God will be taken from you and given to a people producing the fruit of it.' And they knew that he was speaking about them.

"It is clear from these and many other teachings that Jesus spoke concerning national Israel that their time of being treated as a favored people was over. In Jesus's view, national Israel was dead—withered at the roots and deserving only to be cut down. It was just taking up space in the land. We must praise God, however, that there continues to be a small remnant of Jews who believe, and that our Lord continues to extend a covenant relationship with them, as individuals, as he now does with all the tribes and tongues of the earth.

"Another distinctive of Luke's biography," Peter continued, "was in Jesus's genealogy. Writing primarily for the Jews, Matthew emphasized Jesus's roots as being traced back to the father of the Jewish race, Abraham, though he does include in that bloodline three Gentiles, all of whom are women: Rahab, the Canaanite and prostitute who hid the spies that Joshua sent out; Tamar, also a Canaanite; and Ruth, the Moabite. There is even some speculation that Bathsheba, also listed in Matthew's genealogy and the favorite wife of King David, was also a Gentile—either because she had Gentile blood flowing in her veins, or because she was formerly married to Uriah, the Hittite. This further proves that the promised 'seed of the woman' who would crush Satan's head would not come through an untainted bloodline stemming from Abraham, but that even Gentiles would be included in that line.

"But Luke, writing primarily for a Gentile audience, goes back even further than Abraham. He traces Jesus's genealogy all the way back to Adam, the father of the human race. The Holy Spirit is showing here that Jesus was the Son of God and the Son of Man, which was the title he most often used to refer to himself, and that this was a gospel intended for all of the inhabitants of the earth."

"One thing I noticed," said Mark, "was that Luke gave more attention to the birth of Christ than any of the other gospels. I especially like what he quoted the angel as saying to the shepherds: 'Do not be afraid; for behold, I bring you good news of great joy which will be for all the people; for today in the city of David there has been born for you a Savior, who is Christ the Lord.'

"The angel promised that there would be great joy for all people. Because I just finished reading Paul's letter to the Philippians again last night, for probably the twentieth time, I noticed that the great theme of that letter is that we can have joy even in the midst of severe trials; or, as in Paul's case, even while being in prison."

"I must correct you," I told John Mark. "Having joy in all of our circumstances is not the theme of that letter."

"Are you telling us that you also had time to sneak a preview of that letter, even while our assignment was to be prepared to discuss Luke's writings today?" asked Peter with a grin.

"If the truth be known, yes, Peter. I have been staying up late into the night, absorbed with all of Paul's letters." I replied.

"I will confess that I have done the same," replied Peter. "John Mark brought such a feast for us with these gifts from Rome! How could we help but taste from each of the delicacies? But do not let me interrupt. Tell us what you thought to be the theme of Paul's letter to the Philippians."

"It may be a fine distinction, but it is a great distinction," I answered. "The theme of Philippians is not joy. The theme of Philippians, as Paul stated, is 'For me to live *is* Christ.' The word *joy* or some derivative of it stands out in this letter, true. But it is used less than twenty times. The word *Christ,* however, is used more than seventy times. The theme of Philippians is knowing Christ as our Life. As we know him and are found in him, we will have joy. This is consistent with what Paul wrote to the Galatians, that one of the fruits of abiding in the Spirit is joy.

"It is clear that Paul's singular obsession is knowing Christ. He counts all things as loss in view of the surpassing value of knowing him."

Fumbling with the Philippian scroll and rolling it out before them, I found the exact quote I was looking for. Pointing to it with my index finger, I read each word aloud. "That I may know him and the power of his resurrection and the fellowship of his sufferings, being conformed to his death; in order that I may attain to the resurrection from the dead. Not that I have already obtained it or have already become mature, but I press on so that I may lay hold of that for which also I was laid hold of by Christ Jesus.' What beautiful words! Jesus Christ laid hold of us so that we could know him. Paul's quest is to know Christ and to be found in him. Fullness of joy comes from knowing him."

Peter stepped in. "Brothers, there is no question that Luke's biography of our Lord's life is an inspired work. And without spending more time on it, his history of the church is also accurate and should be included, as it is written, in what we are in the process of putting together. Luke's biography begins in Jerusalem, the center of the Jewish world, and his history ends in Rome, the center of the Gentile world."

I nodded but added, "I see the theme of Luke's history of the first thirty years of the church as not really the history of the acts of the apostles—rather, it is the continued history of the acts of The Apostle. He begins his account to the God-lover, Theophilus, by stating that his biography was about all that Jesus began to do and teach. His history picks up where Jesus left off, after his resurrection and ascension, where he continues to do and teach, but now he is doing so through his Spirit, through the agency of his body. Luke's biography is the story of Christ in the flesh. His history is the continued story of Christ, now in the Spirit. With these two pieces, we are one step closer to completing our task."

As Peter and Mark voiced their agreement, I took a deep breath. "As a result of our discussion today, I am getting clearer on some things. I have just decided, and announce to you now, that I too intend to write an account of our Lord's life."

To their surprised response, I continued. "There are many other things which Jesus did and taught other than what has been recorded by Matthew, Luke, and the two of you." I chuckled. "If they were written in detail, I suppose that even the world itself could not contain the books that could be written. But after having read all three accounts, I am still not at rest. There is yet much that remains unsaid. I must write the last volume and complete the gospel story. Though Matthew emphasizes that Jesus is indeed King, Mark, that he is the Suffering Servant, and Luke, that he is the Son of Man and Savior of all mankind, I feel that one last account must be written that displays Jesus as none other than God himself, come in the flesh to live among us.

"In the Old Covenant it is written of God, 'No man can see me and live!' But that glory that was once hidden and behind the veil became flesh, and our eyes beheld him. And he was full of grace, and full of reality. Matthew traced Jesus's lineage to Abraham, and Luke to Adam, but his lineage goes back even further than that, for he existed with God and was God—before time, space, these heavens, or this earth even came into being. In him was Life—the divine, eternal, uncreated Life of God—and when he came to earth, that was the Life that this man, Jesus, lived by. Now he has given that same Life to us, as a gift of pure grace through the impartation of his Spirit. That has been the plan in the heart of God for all eternity—to multiply his Life in people of every tribe and tongue and nation. I plan to write about this Life, for it was intended for every kind of person ever created. This will be my contribution to the message of the New Covenant!"

CHAPTER 13
THE PRISON LETTERS

A.D. 63

"John Mark, you were there in Rome when Paul wrote these three letters to the churches, and the one to the slave owner in Colossae named Philemon. Do you know the background that led to their being written?" I asked.

"One common thread in all the letters is that they were each preceded by a visit from someone from out of town. The rented apartment where Paul lives is more like an inn than a normal apartment. Visitors are coming and going all the time.

"He wrote the Ephesian letter following a visit from Tychicus, who came to bring Paul a report on the condition of the church in Ephesus. Epaphroditus, who started the churches both in Colossae and Laodicea, sailed to Rome to get Paul's advice on a situation developing in those two churches. The letter to the Colossians was written in response to that situation. He came from Philippi but got terribly sick along the way. The church there had sent him with a gift to help Paul pay his rent and cover his living expenses. Besides being a very encouraging epistle and addressing some issues between two of the sisters there, that letter basically started out as a thank-you for their love gift.

"Finally, Paul's letter to Philemon, his wife, Apphia, and their son, Archippus, in Colossae, was in response to another visitor who came to Paul while he was in chains—Onesimus. Onesimus was one of Philemon's slaves. He stole some money from his master and then ran away. He happened to board the same ship as Epaphroditus, bound for Rome. While journeying together, Epaphroditus convinced Onesimus that he should visit Paul to get some counsel. Onesimus knew Paul to be a good and fair man because he had met him in Ephesus while with Philemon, for Philemon frequently visited there for business. Paul had led Philemon to the Lord on one of those trips, and Philemon spoke often, and with gratitude, of Paul.

"When Onesimus came to Paul, Paul ended up leading him to the Lord as well. Onesimus was in serious trouble for stealing money and running away, but while in Rome with us, he became very useful to Paul. Paul wrote the letter to Philemon hoping to persuade him to forgive his runaway slave and set him free. Paul even promised to pay back, with his own funds, the money Onesimus had stolen."

Peter cut in, "I saw from what I read that Paul had never before even visited the church in Colossae. He had just heard of them from Epaphroditus. What do you know about the church there?"

"I know that there are two meetings there—one in the home of a sister named Nympha, and the other in Philemon's home. Epaphroditus bragged on the love they have for one another, how they are a growing church, and how, though they were only three to four years old at the time, they were stable and engaged in good works."

"But apparently there were some problems," said Peter.

"Yes," responded John Mark. "It had to do with the Knowers."

"The Knowers?" inquired Peter, as he wrinkled his brow. "Who are they?"

"They are called *Gnostics* in Greek. They were those who came to the church and were well received, but then subtly began exerting their influence on others. At first, it was hardly detected that their gospel had an emphasis to it that was not taught them by Epaphroditus, who learned his gospel from Paul. They taught that God was holy, but that everything in this material universe is evil. This even led them to deny the very humanity of Jesus, claiming that his body was not even real and that he did not really suffer. Since God was so far removed from man, in order to get closer to God, they teach there are things we should not touch, taste, or handle. To be spiritual, we must repudiate all material things and detach ourselves from the physical world."

"This sounds spiritual," I said, "and very . . . Greek. But as we already know, this is just another man-contrived system of works that will never justify people in the sight of God!"

"But even more insidious," John Mark said, "is that they teach that only a few of them really know the truth. That is why they refer to themselves as the Knowers. They claim to have exclusive insights and revelations of God. According to them, the only way for people to become closer to God is to become part of their group."

"We know," I said, "that these errors in doctrine and teaching that are creeping into the churches are not good. These 'Knowers' are only making an appeal to people's pride to be part of some exclusive group. But I can see God using these errors as a canvas for the masterpiece that Paul has so brilliantly painted through the inspiration of the Holy Spirit, to make known the antidote for this problem."

"And what is that?" Mark asked.

"The antidote for this, or any problem, is to see Christ and to see him as God, as the One and Only—preeminent in all things. Christ has no peers. He stands alone. He is the head of the church. He is the spiritual reality of all things. We have been raised with him, and all believers are already in union with him. Their only lack is that of revelation. They do not see it. But all of Christ has been given to us as our inheritance. There is nothing we can do to earn one drop more of him. Abstaining from certain foods will gain us no more credit in God's eyes. Refusing to touch something that was touched by someone who is considered unclean does not make us more pious or bring us closer to God. The only difference between Paul and the least of the believers is that God has opened his eyes to see that we have already been brought into union with Christ. Once they see, It should be the norm for every Christian to live in that reality."

"These prison letters," said Peter, "especially the Ephesian and Colossian letters, are, to me, among the highest peaks in the mountain range of God's written revelation to man. I have never read anything to compare with them.

"In Colossians we see Christ as the Creator, the one for whom, by whom, and through whom all things were created. He is the firstborn, who has received the double blessing and inherited all things. Whereas these Knowers try to convince people that everything in the physical universe is evil, Paul correctly reveals that God made Christ preeminent in all of creation. The entire creation is laced with pictures or shadows of him, and with eyes to see, we can learn from the creation about his nature, his character, and the principles inherent in his being.

"He existed before the creation and lives in the unseen realm. But the seen realm, this creation, reflects different aspects of him so that we can know more about him. The food we eat—the fruit, the grain, the bread, even the meat—that God has given us to enjoy is not the ultimate expression of real food, but a shadow of real food cast from the unseen realm into the seen. Real food existed before the first man became aware of his appetite in Eden's garden or God spoke this world into existence. Real food dwells in the unseen realm. Real food is Christ! Even the water we drink is not the ultimate expression of real water. Real water is alive—in the heavens—and that real water, too, is Christ. He refreshes and quenches the thirst in our spirits as we drink of him!

"Even the Jewish feasts and celebrations were pictures and shadows of Christ. The Sabbath was inaugurated through the law to teach us that Christ is our Sabbath and our real rest. Who would want to accept the miserable imitation that these Knowers are passing off for spirituality once they see the magnificence of Christ and what we have received in him?"

"I see two complementary truths in these two letters, which form a complete whole," I said. "The Colossian letter speaks of Christ as the source of all things, the headwaters of the life of the church and its all-governing head. The Ephesian letter emphasizes his unsearchable riches and that we are his body here on the earth, being fitted and framed together, by the supply of divine Life to each member, to be his dwelling place.

"As Paul so clearly articulates here, more so than in any other of his letters, this was the long-kept secret, the mystery that God kept hidden for ages. The unseen would become seen. The God in unseen realms would have a body in the visible realm, over which he is the invisible head. The unfathomable riches of Christ, who knows neither time nor boundary, are now manifest in time and in space, for all creation, including the angels, to see—*through the church!* And that mystery includes the Gentiles, who are now fellow heirs with those of Abraham's race, fellow members of the body, and fellow partakers of the promise, which is the Holy Spirit—the unseen God, in Christ, dwelling in us."

"These two letters are so rich," Peter said, in a voice of admiration directed, as it were, to both God and us. "I especially like how they begin, for this is so instructive: they both begin with prayers. And notice the content of Paul's prayers! Because we have been blessed with every spiritual blessing in the heavenly places in Christ, and because it is God's purpose to head up everything, both in the heavens and on the earth, in Christ, he prays for the Ephesians that God would give them a spirit of wisdom and revelation in the knowledge of him. He prays that the eyes of their hearts would be opened to see the glorious riches of their inheritance in one another, and that they would be strengthened with power in their inner man so that Christ would be alive in their hearts.

"For the Colossians, he prays that they would be filled with the knowledge of his will in all spiritual wisdom and understanding, walk in a manner worthy of the Lord, please him in all respects, bear fruit in every good work, increase in the knowledge of God, be strengthened with power, and have thankful hearts.

"Clearly, we are wealthy beyond imagination with all the blessings that God has bestowed upon us in Christ. He is ours. As Paul prays, all we need is the eyes to see what we have already been given!"

"I am reminded of the land that we Jews were given as our inheritance," I interjected, "but which is also only a picture of the wealth of our inheritance in Christ. Remember that the Lord instructed the people that he had given them the land and encouraged them to possess it, but that they would take it as their own 'little by little.' Christ is so rich, so unfathomable, that we could never possess all of him at once. It will take eternity for us to plumb, with all his saints, his heights and depths, length and breadth, and to know the love of God, which surpasses understanding. Every believer has access to the same treasury. As you say, our great need is just to see more! That is probably an example of the most spiritual prayer any Christian could pray: 'God, show us more of Christ.'"

"I also find it comforting to think that there are no 'great' Christians," replied Peter. "Paul, here, describes himself as 'the least of all saints,' and in others of his letters that we have read, as 'the least of the apostles' and a 'nobody.' I do not believe that Paul was feigning humility when he wrote these words. I believe he sincerely meant them. For indeed, I know of no man who was so full of religious pride—and justifiably so, as we read of his pedigree in the Philippian letter where he writes, 'If anyone else has a mind to put confidence in the flesh, I far more: circumcised the eighth day, of the nation of Israel, of the tribe of Benjamin, a Hebrew of Hebrews, as to the Law, a Pharisee, as to zeal, a persecutor of the church, as to the righteousness which is in the Law, found blameless!'

"Can you imagine anyone saying that—'As to the Law, found blameless'? Truly Paul saw himself as perhaps the most religious man our nation has ever produced—though diluted with pride over his self-righteousness, which resulted in him becoming a blasphemer; a murderer of men, women, and children; and a persecutor of the church. Surely the self-righteous are much further away from being able to receive the grace of God than the outright sinner! For at least the sinner is aware of his or her shortcomings and more open to receiving the forgiveness that Christ offers.

"Though many despise Paul, many others hold him in high esteem. But Paul's own life bears witness to the fact that God's gracious gift of giving him eyes to see who Christ was led to his salvation. If God could do that for a man so deceived by his own self-righteousness, he could do it for anybody. That should offer hope to any Christian. We are all nobodies—empty cisterns—apart from the grace and revelation of God. No wonder Paul wants to deflect attention away from himself and point others to the unfathomable riches that are in Christ! No wonder he prays for them that the eyes of their hearts be opened just as God graciously opened his!"

"I have one more thing I must point out about this Philippian letter," I added. My words were measured and given in a more solemn tone than the others had been speaking.

"There is something else in this letter that arrested me. It reminds me of why I was fearful of writing to Paul in the first place while he was yet in prison in Caesarea, sending him the letter that precipitated this whole quest to assemble a New Covenant body of writings. We can all attest to Paul's fearlessness in declaring the truth. That is undisputed. No one can take on imperial Rome by flatly defying emperor worship as he has done, boldly proclaiming that Jesus is the only Lord and that to him every knee shall bow, both in heaven and on earth and under the earth. But if that were not enough, look at how he then turns to pick a fight with the Judaizers, the Jews, and the nation of Israel, as well! He writes, 'Beware of the dogs, beware of evil workers, beware of the false circumcision, for *we* are the true circumcision, who worship in the Spirit of God and glory in Christ Jesus and put no confidence in the flesh.'

"Can you imagine turning the tables on the Jews and calling *them* dogs? This is a derogatory label that we Jews have always reserved for Gentiles, likening them to a pack of mangy, flea-bitten, savage animals that roam the streets untamed, foraging through garbage piles for food, snipping and barking at people to make them afraid. And on top of that he calls this same group 'the false circumcision,' claiming the true circumcision to be people like we read about in Luke's history who were present at the beginning of the Philippian church—a formerly demon-possessed slave girl, a Jewish businesswoman and her household, a Roman jailer and his Gentile brood, plus two other women who are mentioned in this letter, whom we can call 'Sweetie' and 'Lucky' based on the translation of their names. This unlikely crowd, plus Paul, and others like them who have believed from among the Gentiles, he calls the *true* circumcision! You can almost hear him shouting, 'The Jews are no longer the people of the covenant. *WE, the called-out ones—the remnant from among the Jews and the Gentiles who put their faith in Christ—WE are now the covenant people of God!*' If that would not make any Jew angrier than a guard dog trying to protect his bone from a stranger, I don't know what would! But there is still more!

"Following that, Paul lists his pedigree, which includes being circumcised and from the nation of Israel, and then says, 'I count all those things to be loss in the view of the surpassing value of knowing Christ, for whom I have suffered the loss of all things and count them as excrement'—something to be scraped from the bottom of one's sandals with a stick and cast away, should he have the misfortune of stepping in it.

"Paul could not possibly have used baser or more forceful words. Yet they are true! As frankly and forthrightly as it can be said, *no background—*

whether Jew or Gentile—can come even remotely close to benefiting a person when it comes to attaining the righteousness that can satisfy God. That righteousness comes from Christ alone, eliminating any thought that, apart from Christ and the grace of God, there is any special or favored people outside of the household of faith, consisting of those who believe in him."

A somber hush filled the room as Peter and John Mark lingered long upon my words.

Finally Peter broke the silence. "I believe that it is plain to us all that these letters and the revelation they contain must be included in the body of writings that we are assembling. In the Colossian letter we see the theme of Christ as the head, and in the Ephesian letter, we see the church as his body. In the Philippian letter we see that the Life that is in the head is the Life that flows through the body, for to live *is* Christ. All else is to be counted as loss. The only question that remains for me is, what shall we do with this short letter to Philemon? Do either of you have any thoughts?"

"Though this letter is brief, and written specifically to one man and his family, I see something of great value in it," responded Peter. "It has to do with the issue of spiritual authority."

"Go on," I said, intrigued.

"This letter gives us a wonderful insight into a man who has been given authority by God to build up the church. In it we see the heart of a father, expressed in loving persuasion, to one of his spiritual sons in the Lord. Savor these words as I read from Paul's letter aloud:

"'I thank my God always, making mention of you in my prayers, because I hear of your love, and of the faith which you have toward the Lord Jesus and toward all the saints; and I pray that the fellowship of your faith may become effective through the knowledge of every good thing which is in you for Christ's sake. For I have come to have much joy and comfort in your love, because the hearts of the saints have been refreshed through you, brother. Therefore, though I have enough confidence in Christ to order you to do that which is proper, yet for love's sake I rather appeal to you—since I am such a person as Paul, the aged, and now also a prisoner of Christ Jesus—I appeal to you for my child Onesimus, whom I have begotten in my imprisonment, who formerly was useless to you, but now is useful both to you and to me. I have sent him back to you in person, that is, sending my very heart, whom I wished to keep with me, so that on your behalf he might minister to me in my imprisonment for the gospel; but without your consent I did not want to do anything, so that your goodness would not be, in effect, by compulsion, but of your own free will.'"

Peter let the scroll drop to the table. For a long moment he looked each of us in the eyes. "Do we get the sense here that Paul is anxious to exercise his spiritual authority? After all, Philemon owed Paul his life, for Paul led him to Christ. But rather than ordering Philemon to do a particular thing in regard to Onesimus, Paul reasons with him. He persuades him. He lovingly builds a case, giving Philemon a choice to do what is right. This shows that Paul understands what spiritual authority is and how it is to be used. His example, his words, will be of great value to all who find themselves in places where God has put them in leadership. We must never think that leadership entitles us to order people around. For did not Christ teach us that, 'The kings of the Gentiles lord it over them; and those who have authority over them are called benefactors. But it is not this way with you, but the one who is greatest among you must become like the youngest, and the leader like the servant'?"

"I wholeheartedly agree with Peter," John Mark added hastily. "I watched Paul and how he lovingly worked with Onesimus, fathering him, instructing him, and discipling him, to the point that Onesimus was even willing to return to Philemon, knowing the consequences he might face. But he became convinced that it was the right thing to do. It seems that God laid on Paul's heart afresh that we are nobodies outside of the grace of God and that none of us deserves the high standing we have received in him. And, seeing the change in Onesimus's life that came from his believing in Jesus and being offered a second chance, I think, had a direct bearing on what God was doing in Paul's heart when he extended a second chance to me. I cherish this letter and believe it has a life-changing message."

"Very well, then," I concluded. "Including, as I think we should, the letter that Peter sent with John Mark and Justus to the saints scattered abroad, Luke's two letters, and these four prison letters, the total number of books and letters in our collection has now expanded to sixteen. And I have determined to write a gospel of my own. We must not be in a rush to complete this task, for God has been faithful to provide the material, thus far, as he sees fit. We do not know yet how much more he would have us include. But I believe that we can trust him and be confident that the same promise he gave to the Philippians will be true for us in this work: that 'he who began a good work in you will perfect it until the day of Christ Jesus.'"

CHAPTER 14
HEROD'S TEMPLE AND THE DIVIDING WALL

A.D. 63

The next day we received word from Rome that Paul had been released from house arrest. We were told that he was on the move again, possibly to leave for Spain to preach the gospel or to visit Philippi or Colossae, as he had promised to do in his most recent letters. We did not know. My heart was cheered to hear of his release, but more questions immediately filled my mind as to how, if, or when we would ever again meet with Paul to complete this task that God had called us all to. But there was much happening in Jerusalem and Judea to keep us occupied.

The exodus of believers and other Jews to various parts of the empire was accelerating. We bade good-bye to some of our dearest friends, coworkers, and fellow apostles as one by one people were realizing that it was time to leave and they must choose a direction in which to go. With each farewell there were floods of tears, mingled with joy, as we recalled what God had done among us in the years we had been together. We laughed, we cried, and we prayed for one another. And, when we said our last good-byes, knowing that this might be the final time we might ever lay eyes on one another again, in this life, we needed to be almost pried from our final embraces as we kissed one another and each one's families.

This time, the apostles were not exempt from the exodus. Philip and his family boarded a ship from Caesarea heading south to Carthage, North Africa. Matthew and Thomas felt called to head east, in the direction of Persia. Simon the Zealot and Thaddeus boarded a vessel heading west toward Spain, as did our brother Silas, who we later heard was preaching the gospel on the Island of Rhodes. Peter and I had been talking about going north to Asia, specifically to Ephesus. From there, we would trust the Lord for direction as to where he wanted each of us to go. It was not a question of *if* we would leave, only of when.

A long time had passed since Peter, John Mark, or I had visited the temple. So the following morning, we all decided to go up early and have one last look at this place that was like blood in the veins of every Jew. It was part of us—part of our history. From our youth we had visited this place every year during the times of the great festivals. Jesus had done many pivotal things here, and it was from the temple pinnacle that James had been thrown down. And by now, Peter and I had lived the latter halves of our lives in this city and in the shadow of the temple every waking day. It evoked a spectrum of feelings each time we set foot inside.

The three of us climbed the three-story stone staircase along with other worshipers and entered the temple. We passed through the two large gates in the southern wall surrounding the temple complex directly into the court of the Gentiles . We all experienced an eerie feeling, almost like the calm one senses before a great storm. We looked around, one last time, at this magnificent structure that summons the religious instincts of every man, woman, and child who has ever seen or longed to see it.

Nothing much had changed in the court of the Gentiles since the last time Jesus was here, when he overturned the tables of the moneychangers thirty-three years ago. The bazaar, the currency changers, the vendors, the food, the sacrificial animals—it was all pretty much the same. When Christ was last here, it had been forty-six years since Herod had first begun construction on this refurbished temple. Now the final touches were being made. Lucceius Albinus, the Roman procurator, had recently announced that by the following year the entire project would be complete. Many of the thousands of workers employed on the project were bracing for sweeping layoffs that would only add to the unemployment problems that were already causing many to take leave of the city. In all, the rebuilt temple that Herod the Great had initiated took eighty years to finish.

Within the court of the Gentiles, we looked in the direction of the Holy Place at the soreg, a four-and-a-half-foot barrier made of decorative marble. It had thirteen ornamental columns and was embellished with trelliswork. Beyond it, at a significantly higher elevation and behind more walls, was the temple itself. Staring at the barrier brought to my mind what Paul had written to the Ephesians concerning the dividing wall that no Gentile was allowed to pass to approach the temple, upon threat of death. This was the same wall the Jews had falsely accused Paul of taking Gentiles beyond, which had led to his arrest.

We walked to within arm's reach of the wall and read the inscription upon it once again, written in both Latin and Greek: "No Gentile may enter within the railing around the sanctuary and within the enclosure. Whosoever should be caught will render himself liable to the death penalty which will inevitably follow."

"The Roman government took away capital punishment from the Jews, but left them the right to kill anyone who goes beyond that wall," Peter muttered.

Then we gazed up, beyond the wall, at the flight of fourteen steps that led up to the *chel,* a fifteen-foot-wide terrace surrounding the inner wall of the temple.

I turned to Peter and Mark and addressed them.

"Never has seeing this wall impacted me the way it is today—especially after having read Paul's letter to the Ephesians. The words he wrote, specifically for the Gentiles, I have committed to memory and are echoing in my head:

"'But now you, Gentiles, who were formerly separate from Christ, excluded from the commonwealth of Israel, and strangers to the covenants of promise, having no hope and without God in the world, now in Christ Jesus you, who were formerly far off, have been brought near by the blood of Christ. For he himself is our peace, who made both groups into one and broke down the barrier of the dividing wall by abolishing in his flesh the enmity, which is the law of commandments contained in ordinances, so that in himself he might make the two into one new man, thus establishing peace, and might reconcile them both in one body to God through the cross, by it having put to death the enmity.'"

"Yes," replied Peter. "Though the Zealots glory in this temple's completion in anticipation that it will prepare the way for the Messiah they mistakenly await, who they think will lead them to political victory and overthrow Rome, Paul writes as if the temple has already been destroyed. Once again, he is correct. For in spiritual realms, it has already been torn down. It is only a matter of time before we see that here in the physical realm."

"I am struck," I continued, "by how much depth there is to those few words that God has 'broken down the barrier of the dividing wall.' Let me share what I am thinking.

"First, this temple was built by Herod the Great. He was indisputably ambitious and arguably the greatest builder in Jewish history. But he was also a madman. He murdered his own family. He ordered all the babies less than two years old killed at the time of Jesus's birth. He was ruthlessly cruel, paranoid, and despised by the Jews. He was half-Jew and half-Idumaean—a distant descendant of Esau. Though the temple was his greatest building achievement, unlike Moses's tabernacle and Solomon's temple, where the measurements and design were God-given, this temple, more magnificent, probably, than any religious structure ever built, reflects the convoluted thought of this half-religious and half-pagan man.

"Going all the way back to the time following his appointment by Rome as king of the Jews, Herod was accompanied by Antony and Octavian to the temple of Jupiter, where he offered pagan sacrifices. Not only did he decree to have the temple in Jerusalem rebuilt, but he also commissioned the building of the huge temple dedicated to the Roman god-emperor, Augustus Caesar, in Caesarea, as well as other pagan temples. These were paid for by heavy taxes on the local Jews. He was a pathetic, confused man who had no true conviction or accurate knowledge of anything pertaining to God.

"But the building of this temple was not completely of his doing. He had help and input from the Jewish leaders as to the architectural design, or else they would not have permitted its building. But look at result! Look what they came up with!" I said, looking upward once more toward the Holy Place, the interior structure of the temple, with its corridors and columns.

Pointing my finger toward the wall before us, I said, "Take this wall of separation. It is made of beautiful marble. It is hand chiseled. But as beautiful as it appears, it may as well be a trench filled with vipers! That would more accurately portray the thought behind its construction, for if it were possible, our people would have built a wall of separation between Jew and Gentile that would have separated them as far as one end of the earth is from the other! Moses did not order that wall to be built; yet here it is. This additional wall was man's invention and was not after the original pattern that Moses saw *in God* and was instructed to build.

"Now, as we are here in the outer court, look at this dirt upon which we stand. Strictly speaking, the outer court is not part of the temple, for anyone may enter here, except menstruating women. Its dirt is not sacred. But consider the soil on other side of the wall. That is thought to be holy dirt!

"And beyond that there are fourteen steps leading up to the court of the women, where there is another wall. There the ground is even more holy, because any ritually cleansed Jew, man or woman, can enter there.

"But beyond that are another twelve steps, and another wall, leading to the court of Israel—male Israel, that is. There the ground is even holier still.

"And further and higher yet are another five steps, and another wall, leading to the court of the priests where the sacrifices are performed, and the stones upon which the Levitical priests walk. These stones are considered even more holy!

"All of this—the hierarchy, the subtlety, and the image it all projects—reinforces the height of false religion. The Gentiles are the farthest away from God. They are the dogs. Where their feet walk is unholy ground. A step up from the Gentiles are women. Fourteen steps, to be precise! And on higher ground yet are men, because they are closer to God. But the average person is still not holy enough, because higher on the rung, and closer to God, are the priests. And above the priests is the high priest, who alone can enter the holy ground of the Holiest of All.

"Does not all that this temple projects corrupt the minds of all the people, so that in fact they believe that this is the manner in which God views all humankind? The sin of it all! The utter blasphemy and stench that rises from this beautiful, so-called monument to God!"

At this point I was livid. My passion had grown as I spoke. Peter and John Mark were both wide-eyed. They had involuntarily become the audience for my fiery sermon, but they were hanging on every word. The inspiration of the words Paul had written to the Ephesians about God breaking down the dividing wall between Jew and Gentile was becoming clearer to me by the second!

Yes, God did want to destroy this temple of stone. *He must be at the limits of his patience,* I thought, *not to have come in judgment already. How anxious he must be to erase this last remaining vestige of the barriers and walls that stand between Gentile and Jew, man and woman, priest and pauper!*

Never had it been so clear to me: what Jesus did at the cross was to bring into existence a new creation in which there are no denigrating distinctions. In this new species—the invisible head in heaven joined with his visible body on earth—there is no one holier than another, no one of higher rank than another before God. What Jesus paid for by his precious blood was to make all of his people one by his Spirit and to replace the enmity, the barriers, and the divisions with the unity, peace, and love found only in him.

"I know exactly how Jesus felt that day in which he departed from the temple for the last time," I told my companions. "This edifice has been left desolate. Christ's desire for his people is that there be no more walls, no more steps, no more gates, no more courts, no more veils. Let us depart from this place and never enter it again. Let us cling only to, and let our affections be forever and only toward, the new temple in which the Spirit of God dwells, which is his body, his people. Come, Lord Jesus. Come swiftly, and let your judgment fall upon this place!"

CHAPTER 15
THE TREATISE TO THE HEBREWS

A.D. 63

We exited the temple before the sun had reached its height in the sky and hastened down the staircase at a brisk pace, bounding from one step to the next.

"I am not as nimble as I was thirty-three years ago, when we followed behind our Lord as he left this place for the final time," we could hear Peter mumbling between short gasps for air as he lagged behind John Mark and me.

When we reached the bottom, we reconvened and huddled together in a small circle. John Mark had a curious gleam in his eye. Then he spoke.

"I think the two of you should have the full experience of retracing the steps you took with the Lord, James, and Andrew so long ago when you left this place," he said. "We should ascend the Mount of Olives from here to the exact location where the Lord Jesus sat with the three of you overlooking Jerusalem, where you listened as he prophetically spoke of the destruction which was to come. Though he will not be here physically to speak with us, his Spirit is with us. And I have something with me that I think you will find nearly as stimulating and provocative as what you heard from him in those days."

With that, he reached inside his outer garment and produced a scroll that he had tucked away from view.

"Here is the letter that Paul wrote for the Hebrews," he said. "I suggest that we go up on the Mount of Olives and read it together."

"Wonderful!" Peter exclaimed.

We headed to the Bridge of the Red Heifer and made our way across, looking down, as we walked, at the Kidron Valley below. Ascending the hill, we reached a small stone retaining wall on which Jesus had sat and taught so many years ago. Sitting down, overlooking Jerusalem and the temple, John Mark pulled out the scroll. Letting him take the lead, Peter and I sat and listened as he began to read.

"God, after he spoke long ago to the fathers in the prophets in many portions and in many ways, in these last days has spoken to us in his Son, whom he appointed heir of all things, through whom also he made the world."

"Wait just a minute," I interrupted, raising my hand motioning him to stop. "This is not how we have become accustomed to Paul starting his letters. In his other writings he gives a greeting by introducing himself, typically as the Lord's apostle, so that people will know from whom the letter has come. This is not consistent with his writing style. Why is this so?"

"You are right," John Mark responded. "Though in form it is a letter, this is more than a letter. It is a treatise—a teaching for the Hebrews. As you know, many of the Hebrew believers are wary of Paul. If the first thing they were to read or hear in this letter was his name, it would prejudice them. Many would not continue with it at all. By remaining anonymous, he hopes they will read this letter without any bias that might veil the great revelations of Christ contained in it. Collaborating with Luke, who carefully translated this from Hebrew to Greek, Paul thought this to be the best approach to take.

"When we get to the end, however, you will see that it does bear Paul's signature good-will remarks, which he says in his second letter to the Thessalonians and will be found at the end of all of his letters—'The grace of our Lord Jesus Christ be with you all.' And I think you will readily bear witness, once you hear this read, that the opening word of the letter, 'God,' is no error. There can be no mistake that the author of this letter truly *is* God, and that the Hebrews should receive it as coming from God himself and not from any man."

Sitting in the shade of a large almond tree, John Mark continued to read as Peter and I sat spellbound by the brilliance of this letter. We sipped intermittently from a skin of water that Peter had brought along, and we interrupted Mark on numerous occasions to stop and discuss the rich content. Time passed quickly. Before we knew it, it was early evening by the time he had finished reading the last lines. Within the hour the sun would set, and it would be time to return to our homes. In the remaining time we had left, we attempted to summarize what we had just absorbed.

"Paul discusses things in this letter that we have read nowhere else by any of the apostles or in any of the writings that we have considered so far. It is incomparable, bountiful with quotes from passages of the Old Covenant Scriptures. There is so much here to contemplate; so much to digest!" I exclaimed.

"What stands out to me above all else," said Peter, "is Paul's keen awareness of the heart condition of many of our Hebrew brothers—believers in Christ and nonbelievers alike. As we know, the wave of Jewish nationalism that is sweeping Judea and the whole Jewish Diaspora, wherein anyone with Jewish blood is aligning himself or herself against Rome, is building at an alarming rate. Hebrew Christians are experiencing tremendous pressure to join the Zealot cause or be viewed as traitors. As a result, many are showing political solidarity by returning to the temple and the synagogues and by participating in the festivals and all the activities that affirm the Jewish temple worship system. A number have fallen away and are compromising, shrinking back from following Christ. Others are even forsaking Christ altogether and returning completely to Judaism."

Peter shook his head. As a leader in the church in Jerusalem, these events had grieved him for some time. But we could see that Paul's letter had brought him renewed hope and encouragement. "Paul's remedy for this apostasy is to show them how superior Christ is, in all respects, to everything pertaining to the Old Covenant system—the temple, the sacrifices, and the priesthood. As he points out, we are living in the last days before all of this will be brought to an end, shaken, destroyed, made to disappear, and made obsolete.

"He begins by putting their eyes on Christ—that he is the Creator and superior to the angels. The Jews believe that the law was delivered to Moses through the agency of angels and that Moses was the mediator of that covenant. Here Paul shows that Christ is the Son of God, that the angels are his ministers, are subject to him, and worship at his feet. He further shows that Christ is also far superior to Moses, just as the builder of a house is given more glory than the house that he builds, as the mediator of a better covenant.

"Christ also became a superior sacrifice for sin—far better and more effective than that of bulls and goats. The holy Son of God offered himself one time, and for all sins. He has established a new and superior priesthood to that instituted under the law through Aaron, in which he serves as high priest forever according to the order of Melchizedek. All of these things he has done, but the people see that the temple still stands, the sacrifices continue, and the corrupted and inferior priesthood remains. So many of the believing Jews have drifted, taking their eyes off of Christ and their heavenly calling and fixing them instead on things of this earth which are destined to perish."

Turning to John Mark, I asked him, "What is it that strikes you most about this letter?"

"I have had a chance to read it a number of times since Paul first gave it to me. Each time I see something I have never seen before. The main revelation of this letter is that our Lord Jesus is our high priest. Thirty times he is referred to as a priest, and sixteen times as our high priest. More than any other letter, this reveals not only what Jesus has done, but what he is currently doing in heaven as our high priest. He is our intercessor. He dwells in the unseen. He knows the spiritual forces of wickedness that are aligned against us. When we are in trouble or have a need, he is continually praying for us and interceding on our behalf before the Father.

"He is also our mediator—the mediator of the New Covenant—the only one qualified to resolve differences between two conflicting parties because he is intimately familiar both with a holy God and sinful man. And he is our guarantee. As our guarantee, he has assumed full legal responsibility for us living up to God's standard in the law. He lived under the law and was the only one to perfectly fulfill the requirements of the law in their entirety. And now we have been placed in him, so that in God's eyes, we have also completely fulfilled those requirements because he sees us 'in Christ.'"

"And one more thing," I added. "Since you are speaking in legal and binding terms, he is also in the heavens as our advocate—our lawyer— pleading our case continually before the Father. As sinners, we deserve to die. Satan is constantly accusing us before the Father, pointing out to him our sins and our shortcomings. But as our heavenly lawyer, Christ is continually reminding the Father that though it is true that we sin, yet on the cross he bore all of our sins and all of the punishment we deserve. I can almost hear the sound of his voice pleading our case with the Father, saying, 'All of your wrath and anger for John Mark's sins, for Peter's sins, and for John's sins, and for the sins of the whole world, were poured out on me. There is not one drop of anger or wrath remaining, because you were totally satisfied with my sacrifice on the cross on their behalf. I became sin for them so that they could become righteous before you, in me.'"

"Praise God!" responded Peter. "How we desperately need such a high priest, who can sympathize with our weaknesses! But there is much more here that Paul brings out involving Christ's being the mediator of the New Covenant that so vividly contrasts the weaknesses of the Old Covenant with the superior promises of the New.

"The tendency of all flesh is to think that there must be something we can do outwardly that will make us more acceptable, more pleasing to the Lord than we already are. But in fact, there is nothing we can do to make the Lord love us one drop more than he already does.

"For the Jews, that quest for acceptability means keeping all the requirements of the law. But as believers—whether Jew or Gentile—there are countless other laws or codes of conduct that we continually put ourselves under, hoping that by living up to these, we will improve our favor with God. Attending more meetings, longer prayer times, more fasting, more giving, more service, watching our diets more closely, not touching certain things—none of these things can earn a person more of the Lord's love.

"To live under the Old Covenant is to live under a two-sided, conditional covenant. If a person fulfills the requirements of the law, he will be blessed. But if he disobeys or fails, he comes under a curse, resulting in punishment—as the prophet Habakkuk and our brother Paul, in his Galatian letter, both point out. And in this letter to the Hebrews, Paul goes further to say that the law, with its sacrifices, can *never* make those who approach God perfect, and that it is *impossible* for the blood of bulls and goats to take away sins.

"Quoting from Jeremiah concerning the New Covenant, he rightly says that this is a covenant that God makes with every believer, that he will write his laws upon our hearts. The New Covenant is a unilateral agreement. It is one-sided. There are no conditions we are required to keep. There are no ifs. God does not promise to bless us 'if.' It is an unconditional covenant. There are only 'I wills.' Look at these magnificent promises! Look at these 'I wills' as explained through the prophet Jeremiah!

"'I will put my laws within them and on their heart I will write it.'

"'I will be their God and they shall be my people.'

"'I will forgive their iniquity, and their sin I will remember no more.'

"As the mediator of the New Covenant, Christ has taken the responsibility for its execution. He has promised to perform in us what we could never do. This should truly be good news to all who know their own weaknesses or who have ever tried living under the law! You brothers know how important it is to have a covenant without any ifs. Our flesh cannot cope with any ifs. This New Covenant is a covenant of pure grace."

John Mark chimed in, "So he is our intercessor when we are in trouble or have a need. He is our advocate when we sin. He is our mediator when things are going as they should. And he is our guarantee, accepting full responsibility for our satisfying God's righteous standards. What a high priest!"

"This letter to the Hebrew clarifies and defines the New Covenant more completely than anything I have ever read," Peter added. "Our time in the temple today only further confirms these things. Praise God that the Old Covenant has been made obsolete!

"As I reflect, I can see how these New Covenant principles have operated in my own life. I remember the day that Jesus was walking beside the Sea of Galilee and saw my brother Andrew and me casting a net into the sea. He said to us, 'Follow me, and I will make you fishers of men.' This promise he has fulfilled. He did it in me. I did become a fisher of men, but it was not of my doing.

"On another occasion, when I saw Jesus walking on the water, I said to him, 'Lord, if it is you, command me to come to you on the water.' He responded and said to me, 'Come.' I stepped out of the boat and began to walk upon the waves. He commanded, and then he enabled me. But then I became afraid and started to sink, so he stretched out his hand and took hold of me and said, 'You of little faith, why did you doubt?'

"And did he not say, 'I *will* build my church, and the gates of Hades will not overpower it'? And 'I *will* give you the keys of the kingdom of heaven'? Have we not seen these come to pass as well? Is this not Jesus, acting in the capacity of the mediator of this New Covenant, fulfilling all the 'I wills' that he has promised?"

"Indeed it is, Peter," I said. "All the promises of God, in him, are yes and amen!"

"Now, Brother John," Peter replied, "it is your turn. Speak. What in this letter did you see that was new?"

"Melchizedek!" I shouted emphatically. "Melchizedek! This was brilliant!" They looked at me as if I were almost mad, but I charged on. "A high priest who was honored by Abraham, who was a Gentile and not a Jew! This is absolutely brilliant! A different line of priesthood! This is a nugget of gold hidden within the Scriptures that even the most learned of the Pharisees would never have considered.

"The only legitimate priesthood that a Jew has ever known is that of the line of Aaron. And to be such a priest requires that one be a descendant from the tribe of Levi. Jesus, while walking on this earth, could never even have qualified as a priest because he was a descendant of the tribe of Judah. Have you ever before heard of such a thing? That now there is a new priesthood, and Jesus its high priest? And that he was the eternal model upon which the picture of Melchizedek was based, not the other way around, because Jesus existed even before Melchizedek? And that the ultimate, everlasting model for the priesthood was not someone traced back to Aaron or Abraham, but a Gentile? Such teaching will cause the mind of any Jew to explode, for never before has anything like this even been considered! But now, God has shed this light. This is part of the mystery that has for so long been hidden, but has now been revealed. Glory to God!"

"To my recollection," said Peter, "this Melchizedek was only mentioned in two places in the Scriptures, once in Genesis and once in the 110th Psalm, and that amounting to only four short lines. But here, Paul takes a good portion of this whole letter to expound upon the meaning of Melchizedek. And then he adds that 'there is much more to say.'

"The beautiful picture that emerges is that Christ is our Melchizedek, our High Priest forever, who has no beginning and no end, who is the King of Peace (represented by Melchizedek being the king of *Salem,* which means peace) and the King of Righteousness, represented by the very meaning of Melchizedek's name. This priesthood is not based on the weakness of genealogy, as are the Aaronic or Levitical priesthoods, nor on the corruption of being purchased or acquired on the basis of influence, as it is today. But what qualifies Christ to be such a high priest is the perfection of his character and the power of his indestructible life."

"And," I interrupted, "this Melchizedek blessed Abraham, who is considered the father of the Hebrew faith. And Abraham was lesser in rank than Melchizedek, for Abraham paid tithes to him."

"And," injected John Mark, "Melchizedek brought out bread and wine to bless Abraham. These are the symbols of the New Covenant—the body and the blood of Christ! So the picture here—embedded in the Old Covenant Scriptures—is that faith receives the New Covenant blessing from our everlasting high priest, and that faith does not distinguish between Jew and Gentile but is intended for all nations."

"Paul summarized the main point of the whole letter," Peter added, "by saying, 'Now this is the main point of the things we are saying: We have such a high priest, who is seated at the right hand of the throne of the Majesty in the heavens.' Praise God, that Jesus not only *is* such a high priest, but that we *have* him!"

"I may not understand it all," said John Mark, shaking his head, "but we are like kings in possession of untold wealth consisting of gold, silver, and valuable stones—we do not know how all of those precious stones were formed in the earth, but *we have them!* And by having them, we are rich and can enjoy them. So it is with our high priest. We may not understand all of his attributes, his power, or his infinite ways, but we have him, and we can enjoy all of his benefits."

"Brothers," I concluded, "Paul most certainly does go beyond the elementary teachings of the Christian faith, as he calls them: repentance from dead works, faith toward God, being baptized, understanding the gifts and workings of the Holy Spirit as represented by the laying on of hands, and our share in his resurrection and reward in the eternal judgment. He challenges us to leave these behind and press on to maturity and perfection. These teachings that we have been discussing are, indeed, for the mature.

"It is getting dark, so let us end this blessed time together before the night totally engulfs us by considering this one final thought: at the end of this letter, Paul uses the phrase 'the eternal covenant.' There is, indeed, a covenant that was established long before the covenant God made with Moses at Sinai. That was the covenant he made with Abraham, when he was instructed to cut in two the heifer, the female goat, and the ram, and to take them, along with the turtledove and the young pigeon, and place them before God. And it came to pass that when the sun went down, there appeared a smoking oven and a burning torch that passed between those pieces. With this, God established the covenant with Abraham.

"But even before that covenant, there was a covenant made in realms of blazing light and glory, in eternity past, between God the Father and God the Son. That covenant—that agreement—was based on the love that the Father had for the Son. He loved the Son so much that he wanted to give him a gift: sons and daughters, who would be made like him and be his bride, his life companion, to rule and reign with him throughout all eternity. But in order for this to happen, the Lamb of God had to be slain. This was in accord with the eternal plan of God. This eternal covenant and the New Covenant are one and the same. Only now it has been more clearly revealed. This is a covenant of pure, unmerited grace. It has always been, and forever it shall be."

CHAPTER 16

THE FIRE AND FAREWELL!

A.D. 64

The conditions in Jerusalem and Judea continued to worsen. Lawlessness in the land was on the increase. Following the death of James and the migration of tens of thousands of believers, a number of the apostles, and scores of our brethren who had been with us from the beginning, the church that remained was seeing a growth of insubordination, questioning, and even the challenging of apostolic authority. The ears of many began to be turned to the rebels who were calling to take up arms against Rome. At this point, only three of the original apostles remained in Judea—Peter, Jude (the half-brother of our Lord and the brother of James), and me.

After three years as governor, Albinus was recalled to Rome, and Gessius Florus took his place. The people despised Florus even more than they did Albinus. He was greedy and corrupt, a man known for turning a blind eye to justice in favor of bribery and extortion. He allowed outlaws and thugs to roam freely in exchange for a share of their spoils. Florus would be the last Roman procurator of Judea before the outbreak of the war.

Jesus ben Ananias continued to walk the streets with his message of "coming doom to Jerusalem," and the population in Jerusalem and Judea continued to dwindle. There were also strange, supernatural omens taking place, warnings that the God of Israel had left, or was leaving, this place.

For more than thirty years, the massive gates of the Holy Place, in front of which hung the four-foot-thick curtain that had been torn in two on the day Christ was crucified, have opened of their own accord as if by the blowing of the wind. The westernmost light of the menorah in the Holy Place, which is to remain continually lit, has mysteriously, over the same period of time, gone out every night. Word of this has spread, causing some Jews to believe these are signs indicating that God is no longer to be found in the temple.

We also received some very troubling news from outside of Judea. In late summer, ships containing travelers and a few refugees from Rome began to arrive in Caesarea announcing the horrible fact that the capital of the empire, Rome itself, had caught on fire. The fire raged for six days and seven nights, burning seventy percent of the city to the ground. Untold numbers of people were trapped inside the wooden tenement buildings, which became like funeral pyres, consuming men, women, and children alive. It has been said that as many as ten of the fourteen districts of Rome were destroyed or nearly destroyed. Our first thoughts, concerns, and prayers were for the believers we knew there, but we had no news about them.

Not long after we heard these initial reports, more news began dribbling in. It was rumored that Nero himself was culpable for instigating the fire! In an attempt to deflect the accusations, he had laid blame on the Christians and begun to arrest them. We had no idea at the time of the devastating persecution that was soon to befall believers in Rome as a result of this madman and his imperial crime.

On another front, encouraging news arrived. We were told that Paul, having left Rome nearly a year before the fire, had been in Crete with Titus, and that he was now making his way to Asia Minor, presumably to Ephesus. After hearing this, I became convinced that it was time for Peter's family and mine to leave.

I met once again with Peter and John Mark and announced my intentions to depart. I had already decided that Anatolia, and specifically Ephesus, would be my destination. This would be the most likely place to find out about Paul and his whereabouts. It was a strategic location—the land that bridges the Near East with Europe—and the place where Paul's work had taken root and spread throughout Asia Minor. My plan was to take a tour of the whole region, visiting the different churches, before deciding on a place in which to settle.

In discussing my plans with Peter and John Mark, Peter suggested that I take Mark with me and that we go on ahead. He would join us later. I would be taking Mary, who was getting up in age, with me. It would not be easy for her to travel, and she was fearful of spending several weeks at sea. My thought was to get to Ephesus as quickly as possible, find a family for her to stay with, and then begin a tour of the region and hope to meet up with Paul. A number of the remaining witnesses of our Lord's appearance after his resurrection, and several elders, would be traveling as a group with us.

Nearly all of the prophetic indicators of the Lord's soon return in judgment have been fulfilled. Matthew rightly recorded our Lord's words in his gospel account where Jesus said, "This gospel of the kingdom shall be preached in the whole world as a testimony to all the nations, and then the end will come." Our Lord's marvelous plan for all nations to hear this gospel was launched on the day of Pentecost, when there were devout men from every nation under heaven who heard the gospel in their own tongues— Parthians and Medes and Elamites, and residents of Mesopotamia, Judea, and Cappadocia, Pontus and Asia, Phrygia and Pamphylia, Egypt and the districts of Libya around Cyrene, and visitors from Rome, both Jews and proselytes, Cretans and Arabs. This was nothing less than a divine strategy—to bring people from all the nations of the world together in one place, have them hear the gospel, and then return them to their own lands so that the Word of God could multiply.

Paul also wrote to the Colossians that the Word of truth, the gospel, had come to them just as in all the world also it is constantly bearing fruit and increasing. And even to the young church in Thessalonica he wrote that the Word of the Lord had sounded forth from them, not only in Macedonia and Achaia, but also in every place their faith toward God had gone forth. So by now, every known nation has heard the message, and the end of this age could come at any time.

We have not yet seen Jerusalem surrounded by armies, or the abomination of desolation which was spoken of through Daniel the prophet standing in the Holy Place, and only one of us, so far, has been put to death. Our Lord indicated that there would be others of us to whom he spoke those words who would suffer and even die for our faith. And this we are prepared to do.

As the time drew near for me to leave this land in which I grew up, my emotions were frequently touched with periods of nostalgia. Memories would intermittently flood my mind—good memories of growing up in Galilee, casting nets upon the sea, and walking about this land which was promised to our ancestors and is filled with so much history and interaction between Jehovah and the Jewish people. And of course, there were all the memories of being with Jesus and all that has transpired since. All of this caused me over and over again to ask myself the question, what is my relationship to this land?

The average Jew is convinced, beyond doubt, that his ancestral connection with Abraham has granted him special privileges, including the everlasting inheritance of the land. For as we have all been taught from our youth, God spoke to Abraham, saying, "I will establish my covenant between me and you and your seed after you throughout their generations for an everlasting covenant, to be God to you and to your seed after you. I will give to you and to your seed after you, the land of your sojournings, all the land of Canaan, for an everlasting possession, and I will be their God."

And in the covenant God made with Moses at Sinai, the land was once again promised to the Jewish people. So based on two covenants, how could a Jew not believe that the land has been eternally given to us?

A more careful study, however, reveals that as part of the Old Covenant given through Moses, the Jews *were* given the land, but the gift was conditional. In Deuteronomy it says that if the people were not careful to observe all the words of the law, "It shall come about that as the Lord delighted over you to prosper you, and multiply you, so the Lord will delight over you to make you perish and destroy you; and you will be torn from the land where you are entering to possess it." And again, "I call heaven and earth to witness against you today, that I have set before you life and death, the blessing and the curse. So choose life in order that you may live, you and your descendants, by loving the Lord your God, by obeying his voice, and by holding fast to him; for this is your life and the length of your days, that you may live in the land which the Lord swore to your fathers, to Abraham, Isaac, and Jacob, to give them."

And again in Joshua, "It shall come about that just as all the good words which the Lord your God spoke to you have come upon you, so the Lord will bring upon you all the threats, until he has destroyed you from off this good land which the Lord your God has given you. When you transgress the covenant of the Lord your God, which he commanded you, and go and serve other gods and bow down to them, then the anger of the Lord will burn against you, and you will perish quickly from off the good land which he has given you."

And once more in Leviticus, "You are therefore to keep all my statues and all my ordinances and do them, so that the land to which I am bringing you to live will not spew you out"—as it did those who dwelt there before them, whose wickedness the Lord God abhorred.

From these and other passages from the Old Covenant, it is clear. The land was a gift. It was ours conditionally. We were but tenants. If we as a people were not obedient, God had every right to take the land from us and spew us out of his mouth. And that is exactly what he did when, after disobeying God, the northern kingdom lost their land nearly eight hundred years ago, and Judah lost the land a little less than six hundred years ago for the same reason. How much more have the Jews of today violated the terms of the covenant by rejecting the very landowner—the Lord himself!

But if we have failed as a people to qualify to possess the land based on the conditions of the Mosaic Covenant, I have had to ask myself, are we not still entitled to the land based on God's previous covenant with Abraham?

Neither is this true. For God's promise to Abraham was to him and to *his seed,* which is Christ.

He goes on to tell Abraham that the dominion of his seed will extend to include all the territories of his enemies. The promise was not a land with fixed borders. Its inhabitants would be as numerous as the stars of heaven and the sands of the sea. God's intention was to unite the ends of the earth by the same faith our father Abraham possessed, under the king of all the earth, Christ.

For the psalms speak of him, "I will surely give the nations for your inheritance, the very ends of the earth your possession." And again, "The heavens are yours, the earth also is yours; the world and all it contains. You have founded them." He has ownership rights over the whole earth, as well as over Israel. Every knee to him shall bow. All things were created by him and for him, and he is the lawful heir of all things. So he is free to give the land of our fathers to whomever he should choose, even to a godless Rome if that should be his will. This one tiny speck of land is no more consequential. The physical land of Israel has no more role to play in the fulfillment of the Abrahamic covenant since the advent of Christ. He has inherited the whole earth, and it will be full of the knowledge of the Lord as the waters cover the sea.

Even Abraham had his eyes fixed on his heavenly inheritance. He was given the land of promise and yet lived here as an alien—in tents, with Isaac and Jacob. He did not consider this his permanent dwelling place, for he was looking for something better: a heavenly city whose builder and architect is God.

And neither, I have come to see, was the promise to Abraham concerning the land an eternal covenant—one that is forever, in the sense of eternity—as many believe. The Hebrew term *olam* (eternal) used in this context means "of long duration" or "until the end of a period of time." In the book of Samuel, Hannah vowed that her son would continue to live in the house of the Lord *olam,* but that did not mean for eternity; rather, he would dwell there in an open-ended perpetuity. Neither was the *olam* covenant God made with Aaron concerning the priesthood a covenant that was without end, for it has become obsolete. And the covenant of circumcision, associated with God's covenant with Abraham, was also designated as an *olam* covenant. But now circumcision is of no value as a sign of being set apart to be numbered among God's chosen people.

So, savoring a lifetime of memories and experiences from this land, I began making my final preparations to leave. My memories would come with me, but I intended to continue to walk by faith in possession of the even greater inheritance that the land only pictured, which is Christ himself. Wherever the sole of my foot shall tread, I shall proclaim him as Lord. More than ever before, I am convinced that I will never look back to something less.

CHAPTER 17
THE NET-MENDING MINISTRY OF JOHN
A.D. 65

Approximately two months after departing from Jerusalem, my traveling party and I arrived in Ephesus. The city itself is a lovely seaport on the west coast of Asia Minor on the Aegean Sea, known for its enviable climate, mediocre wine (flavored sparingly with seawater), and excellent selection of fresh fish. It is a multicultural, political, economic, and religious center and the most important trading hub in Asia.

Entering the harbor, we viewed an army of laborers lining the shores and in small boats, part of a large-scale effort to remove the silt buildup caused by the flow of the Cayster River, which emptied into the harbor. Disembarking from the ship, we walked a mile or so east on the Arcadian Way from the harbor past the agora and stadium on the wide, beautiful marble main street in Ephesus.

Lining the street on both sides were columns with oil lamps used to light the street at night, an indication of the city's great wealth. About a mile north of the stadium, which had a capacity of approximately 25,000 people, and located along the Artemision Way, was the famous Temple of Artemis—one of the seven wonders of the world.

I stayed for about a month, getting somewhat familiar with the church there. It was not as I had anticipated since the time I first heard about it from Titus some eight years earlier. A large influx of Jews from Jerusalem and Judea had arrived over the past two years and were settling in, finding jobs, and contributing to the reshaping of the personality of the church. There were problems that I picked up on right away. But Timothy was here, fighting the good fight and dealing with them.

Some of the new arrivals were using their newfound platform to expound on points of the law and were not transitioning well to a predominantly Gentile environment or submitting to local leadership. In a letter that Timothy received from Paul, Paul instructed him to remain in Ephesus and to appoint elders, and he laid out for him an explanation of what an elder was. This was not primarily for Timothy's benefit, but for others who would read the letter. Timothy had been with Paul, or worked closely with him, for the better part of the past eighteen years. He had raised up churches with

Paul, seen Paul ordain elders, met the elders in Jerusalem, and had no need to be told what an elder was.

Paul had also given instruction to Timothy to give attention to the public reading of the Scripture. And then, in regard to elders, he quoted from Deuteronomy, "For the Scripture says, 'You shall not muzzle the ox while he is threshing,'" and from Luke's gospel, "The laborer is worthy of his wages"— recognizing the New Covenant documents of Luke on a level with the Old Covenant writings, which were considered sacred.

With the large incursion of Jewish believers finding safe haven in Ephesus and in other Gentile churches throughout the empire, Paul also made the tactical decision that it would be best for the churches to make sure that Gentiles who were in leadership and acting in the capacity of elders, but who had not formally been acknowledged as such, be firmly in place and recognized. This would minimize confusion and appease the Jewish mind, for Jews everywhere were always mindful of who the elders were, whereas function was more important than title in the Gentile culture, and those functioning as elders were often not publicly ordained. (I learned later that Paul had written a similar letter at about the same time to Titus, who was in Crete, where they were also experiencing a large influx of believers from Jerusalem and Judea.)

There were also some pagan issues and teachings stemming from the worship of the local fertility goddess, Artemis, that had crept into the church. They were readily apparent and concerned me deeply. Women who sought favor from Artemis offered prayers at the temple in their most fancy clothes and jewelry, with the most fashionable braided hair designs. This practice had recently become noticeable in the church assemblies. There were also some women here who took their cue from the all-female priests at the temple, who had a practice of dominating the men who came to worship. It is not befitting of either sex to try to dominate the other. This too was a local issue that needed to be addressed, but I, being a fresh arrival myself and not having had the time to build significant relationships with the believers here, thought it best to stay in the background and let Timothy deal with these issues.

While in Ephesus, I had the pleasure of meeting the renowned and dedicated coworkers of Paul whom I had heard so much about, Priscilla and Aquila. They had fled Rome just in time to avoid being among those who met terrible fates at the hands of Nero. They related to me a firsthand account of what had happened. It was almost too horrible to contemplate.

Nero had not only blamed the Christians as the culprits who set the city ablaze, but he began rounding them up, and without trials, sentencing them to death. Initially only a few were arrested, but then, under threat of torture, many began informing the authorities about others, and a great number were arrested. The depraved emperor made spectacles of them with the most cruel and inhumane punishments and tortures imaginable. I have never heard of one who could invent such evil or who possessed such a fiendish mind as this beast of a man, Nero.

Some of our dear brothers and sisters he had dipped in wax and then impaled upon trees to be lit on fire at his garden parties. Others were torn apart by wild dogs and made sport of in the coliseum, suffering all kinds of inhumane cruelties. Among those who were martyred were nearly all those listed in Paul's letter to the Romans, to whom he had addressed his greetings. Aristarchus, who had remained in Rome after Paul's release from house arrest, was also among the casualties.

Our Lord promised that the world would hate us because it first hated him. Fortunately, for the time being, the persecution was localized. It had not yet spread throughout the empire, though there was fear that it would. And Christians who were Roman citizens did not face the same sadistic deaths as Christians who were not, for by law, the Roman government could not torture Roman citizens. One consequence, however, was that emperor worship, as a test of fidelity to Rome, was becoming more and more of an issue—especially for believers.

Previous to this, Christianity had been looked upon as merely a small sect, indistinguishable from Judaism. But Nero's persecution changed all that. The legal protection the church had enjoyed for a generation because of its relation to Judaism has ended. Now the government officially recognizes the distinction between Christian and Jew. This notoriety has caused many to wonder what it is that followers of Christ actually believe. Rather than thwart the growth of the church, it has actually had the opposite effect. The church is growing in spite of persecution.

Very soon after we arrived, I found a lovely Jewish-Christian family whom Mary had known in Judea and with whom she could stay. Rather than becoming actively involved in the life of the church in Ephesus, my first priority was to begin a tour of the region to learn of the conditions in all of the churches. I departed Ephesus with a half-dozen of the elders from Jerusalem, and we struck out north on the main road that connects Ephesus to six other cities—Smyrna, Pergamum, Thyatira, Sardis, Philadelphia, and Laodicea. We also planned to visit Colossae and Hierapolis to the east.

Along the way, we met many dear brothers and sisters in Christ. I was the first among the original apostles whom most of them had ever met. Most all of them were very gracious, receptive, and eager to hear from us. But in some places, we found smaller gatherings of believers led by men of small stature who opposed us, who were eager to build their own kingdoms rather than to fellowship with us and serve in *the* kingdom.

Each city and each church had its own character and distinctions. Particularly impressive to me, but in a distasteful way, was the city of Pergamum. This was the center for emperor worship in Asia. Temples dedicated to the Roman emperor and pagan gods and goddesses abounded— temples to Athena, Dionysus, and Hera, among others. And in the upper part of the acropolis was a colossal altar to Zeus upon which animal sacrifices were continually offered. Shaped in the form of a throne, this had become known as "Satan's throne" to the local believers.

But more striking than any aspect of pagan culture, we also witnessed a number of difficulties facing the churches, ranging from slight to serious. Pressuring the believers from the outside were the emperor cult fanatics, as well as apostate Jews who claimed to be following in the footsteps of Abraham but who lied, for they rejected Christ. Both groups were a menace. We also found no shortage of false teachings and immorality, the "Knowers" Paul had addressed in his letters, problems coming from within the church and from without. Like tattered fishing nets that had been torn and ripped, most all of the churches were in need of some kind of mending, repair, and restoration.

After being gone for about three months, we returned to Ephesus. It was then that I secluded myself and began immediately to work on my gospel of our Lord's life. I received a good deal of editorial help and collaboration from those few among the five hundred witnesses and elders who were with me.

Here in Asia Minor we learned firsthand of many of the prevailing philosophies and heresies that were being propagated and which ran counter to the true teaching and understanding of who Christ is. Some were claiming that Christ was not God, that he was not the Son of God, and that he did not really come in the flesh. To address this mistaken perception head-on, in the very beginning of my biography of the Christ, rather than cite our Lord's origin in the form of a genealogy, I began with, "In the beginning was the Word, and the Word was with God, and the Word was God, and, in him was Life—the very Life of the eternal God." This Word had become flesh and dwelt among us, and he was the only begotten Son.

One thing I have come to believe, with conviction, is that people do not need to be fed more religion. They do not need to be preached at about what they should be doing for God, for in themselves, they are incapable of doing anything to please God. And they cannot be satisfied with empty philosophies. What people need to hear is that Christ, who died on the cross for their salvation, is now in Spirit, and that he came to this earth to give to all men and women who receive him the same eternal, uncreated, all-powerful, divine Life that he and the Father live by and have shared for all eternity. This is my message and the focus of my gospel. I feel compelled—duty bound—to write about this life: that Christ is the bread of life; the water of life; the light of life; the resurrection and the life; the source of life; the way, the truth, and the life; and that he came to give away that Life and give it in abundance. If people draw one conclusion from my letter, I want it to be that Christ *is Life* and that Life is for them. Though there were many signs Jesus performed in our presence which I did not write about, the specific stories I selected were chosen so that those who read may believe that Jesus is Christ, the Son of God, and that believing, they may have life in his name.

I completed this biography and then sent copies of it out to circulate among the churches.

Shortly afterward, I felt the need to write three follow-up epistles. The first I addressed to believers of all ages—to the babes in Christ, to the young men, and to the fathers. My gospel was written that people might *believe* and *have Life,* while my second letter was written so that they might *know* they had eternal Life.

We have met many who say they have knowledge of the truth. They *say* that they have fellowship with God, but they also believe that they can do whatever they want to do in their own bodies and it would not be sin. Such as these are only talkers. They do not *know* the truth. To have fellowship with God requires more than talk. It requires walking in the light, as he is in the light. Walking in the light is a result of living by the *Life.*

The eternal Life that was manifested to us in the person of Christ, whom we saw, touched, and handled, is what we proclaim to others that they might have fellowship with us. Fellowship is simply reporting and sharing with one another what we see, hear, and experience of this Christ, who is now living in us, in Spirit. We know the truth, because the truth abides in us. His anointing is within us. In this letter I wanted to encourage those who have received this Life to *know that they know* him. They must learn to trust in the anointing that dwells within them and to abstain from all forms of worldliness that choke off the love of God. Those who are chasing after the things of the world are not loving God, for the love of the Father is not in them.

My second and third epistles were short. They were written to two precious believers whom I love dearly, and whom I hoped to visit soon.

The second epistle was written to a precious sister—a chosen lady—who hosts the church that meets in her home. This sister is a widow. She is an exceptionally warm, hospitable, and loving person. Loving others is not her problem, for she would open her doors to anyone. But loving "in truth" is something I felt the need to write to her about. For love and truth are two sides of the same coin.

It is an important message in these days, for in addition to the sincere, traveling ministers who go from city to city and place to place visiting the churches, spending time, teaching, building up believers, and then moving on, there are also many deceivers who have gone out into the world. They have an anti-Christ message. Certainly we are to love everyone. But that does not mean that we open our doors to anyone who wants to join in our fellowship!

We are to walk in love and in truth. To go too far in our understanding of love is to open our doors to everyone—even those who come to us with a different gospel, and who introduce false and destructive teachings to the church. To such as these, we need to become walls, not doors. But to go too far in the opposite direction, to be overly zealous for what we think is the truth, can lead to being cold and judgmental. Our Lord Jesus is the perfect blend of love and truth. In this sister's case, she needed encouragement to stand strong on the side of truth and to refuse fellowship with the deceivers who were knocking on her door and seeking access to the flock of God. It was a matter for her of not knowing whom to fellowship with or whom to refuse fellowship with; whom to receive and whom not to receive.

The third epistle was to my beloved Gaius, my child in the faith. With Gaius, it was not a question of whom *not* to have fellowship with, but whom *to* have fellowship with. Gaius needed encouragement to open up his home, receive the traveling ministers who have gone out from us, and send them on their way with a love gift of some support or money in a manner worthy of God. These traveling ministers were not going to find support from the pagans, who hated Christ, but from believers who were in fellowship with our Lord.

Mending nets in my boat on the Sea of Galilee occupied a large part of my time as a younger man while I was engaged in the fishing business. Mending nets now is the focus of my work among the churches, for as I wrote to our chosen lady, I do not want to see anyone lose what has been accomplished, but receive a full reward.

CHAPTER 18
PETER'S ARRIVAL

A.D. 65

By the time Peter and I finally met up with one another again in Ephesus, more than a half-year had lapsed. Mary prepared an elaborate dinner to welcome Peter, and we invited Timothy and John Mark to join us in celebration of his arrival. He caught us all up on the latest news from Jerusalem—rebellion was still seething, and the Christians continued to leave at a rapid rate—and I informed him of my travels and what I had learned of the situation among the churches in Asia Minor.

"What are your plans now that you are here?" I asked him. "Has the Lord been speaking to you about what you should do next?"

"Yes," Peter replied. "I am quite clear. I am going to Rome."

Surprised, I said to him, "The situation for believers is still quite dicey there. You have obviously heard by now what has transpired since the fire?"

"Yes, I have," said Peter. "Though the situation there is still grim, I am not deterred. Here is what I learned on my journey since my departure from Jerusalem."

He reclined as he spoke, launching into a long account. "I sailed directly from Caesarea to Crete. There I learned that Paul had written to Titus, summoning him to Nicopolis to pass the last winter with him. From there, he and Titus and Luke were planning to go to Rome. Paul was exceedingly burdened about the slaughter of saints there that was instigated by the emperor. He felt compelled to go, to see who had survived and what was the condition of the church, and to encourage the brethren. He calculated the danger, but as you know, even with the warnings he received from prophetic voices along the way that chains would befall him when he was determined to come to Jerusalem, nothing could stop him then, and no power on earth will stop him now.

"From Crete I wrote Paul a letter. I told him that you and John Mark were in Ephesus and that I was en route to join you. From there I would travel to Rome to seek him out. I was also quite clear that I would be coming alone. I felt that the danger would be too great if you were to come along."

"You would be crazy to go to Rome," I reacted in anger. "And who are you to determine that I should stay behind? I have as much vested interest in meeting with Paul as do you!"

"We will have to trust God to protect me, John. And to protect us all," Peter responded. "I have had much time to think about this. I believe it is important that we split up to minimize the chance that we will all be found together and apprehended. There is too much at stake if we are to complete our task successfully."

"I have heard something recently that might have a bearing on the current situation in Rome," said Timothy. "In the early spring there was a conspiracy to assassinate Nero. It was discovered that Gaius Calpurnius Piso was behind it. They planned to kill Nero during the Ludi Ceriales circus games, but the plot was uncovered, resulting in nineteen executions and suicides, including that of Lucan, the poet, and Seneca, Nero's adviser. A state of emergency was declared, and troops are patrolling the city everywhere. It is quite possible that attention has been turned to seek out and destroy those in political circles who have treasonous intentions toward Nero, rather than the hapless Christians."

"Let us hope that is the case," said Peter.

"You have never been to Rome before," I said. "How do you plan on finding Paul?"

"I am not certain," replied Peter. "I was hoping that Timothy or Mark might have some suggestions for me."

"I have heard that Linus and his wife Claudia survived the initial round of persecution," said Timothy. "Linus is an elder in the church. I can tell you how to find him. There are others I can name as well. I will make sure that you have their addresses before you leave."

"Which brings up the question, when are you thinking of leaving?" asked John Mark.

"I would like to rest up for about a week, and then I will take my leave," answered Peter.

"You will be here only a week?" I said, wanting him to stay here with us longer. Half-jokingly I continued, "In such a short time, you will not even have time to enjoy the Roman baths here—one of the delights of Ephesus."

"Nero is having new baths built in Rome, with marble floors that are heated by fires below. They will eclipse anything we have here, if pleasure is what you seek," said Timothy. "But I am sure it is not baths that brought you here, nor the baths in Rome that will draw you away."

"John, you do have all the scrolls here that we have collected, do you not?" Peter asked.

"Yes, I do."

"Good," said Peter. "I will take one copy of each with me, and we will have to pray that nothing befalls me or happens to these writings along the way."

"I do not mean to weigh you down on your journey, but I have four more letters—one biography and three epistles that you must take with you as well."

"You have completed your biography?" Peter asked excitedly.

"Yes, I have, at long last."

"May I see it?"

"Not this evening," I said. "Our conversation's tone has been rather serious, and I would prefer that we go over this letter on the morrow, when our minds are fresh and we can focus our attention on the writings and them only."

"That sounds reasonable," said Peter.

"Why don't the four of you plan on going out to some nice spot overlooking the harbor tomorrow and having your discussion there?" Mary added. She had been silently listening in on our conversation. "I will go to the fish market early in the morning and purchase some fish and then pick up fresh bread on the way home. I will prepare a basket for you with the fish, the bread, some olive oil, and some fresh fruit, and you can spend the whole day together."

CHAPTER 19

JOHN'S MESSAGE AND THE FINAL GOOD-BYES

A.D. 65

Peter spent the night at my home and would stay with me until his departure. Timothy and John Mark came by in the morning, and we headed out together for a secluded spot overlooking the harbor. We found a long, low marble bench shaded by trees that had a pleasant view of the water, ships, and boats, and there we sat down.

Timothy and John Mark were already familiar with the biography I had written. Peter had read a copy I had given him the night before. I began with a lengthy introduction.

"Ever since we embarked on this endeavor to capture the message of the New Covenant, write it down, and leave it for our posterity and future generations, I have given much consideration as to what would be my unique contribution. What could I say in one letter or one message that would capture the heart of God and yet be different from what had already been said and written?

"Nearly forty years spent with the Lord, both in the flesh and in the Spirit—the culmination of a lifetime of following him—was my preparation for what I have penned. In perspective, it is amazing to me that all of that time and all those experiences could be reduced to just over one word for each day of those forty years.

"At the heart of the New Covenant is the fact that from eternity past, God wanted to extend the divine family. The relationship, the oneness, the love, the respect, the mutual adoration, the fellowship, and the *Life* shared between the Father and the Son—he wanted to multiply and expand to his creation. By participating in this divine Life with the Creator, all those who are called, chosen, and marked off in him from before the beginning of time will ultimately fulfill the divine mandate given to the first man and woman in Eden's garden as his corporate body—to bear the image of God and to rule the earth. Of this, we have only a foretaste now."

I mulled over my thoughts as I spoke, recalling the wording I had written in my gospel. As I wrote, the sense that the Holy Spirit was with me—

inspiring the very words—had been strong. "For God so loved the world, that he gave his only begotten Son, that whosoever believes in him shall not perish, but have eternal life. In this gospel I set out to show that this offer of 'whosoever' leaves no one out. And this agreement, or covenant, made in eternity past between the Father and the Son, was from the beginning for every man, woman, and child, an outpouring of God's unmerited favor."

The others were nodding their agreement. I continued, "Simply stated, our Lord was sent to earth with a divine commission to accomplish two things. The first was redemption. He came to be our Savior. We are like empty bottles that were created for a purpose, but before realizing that purpose—through the sin of the first man, Adam—we were dropped to the ground in the mud and became filthy. Our Lord's first job was to clean the bottles. This he accomplished on the cross as the spotless Lamb of God who takes away the sin of the world. Having canceled out our debt of sin and made us righteous, holy, and clean in his sight, he was then free to accomplish the next phase of his purpose. That was to fill these vessels with his life, by his Spirit.

"With eyes to see and with the illumination of the Holy Spirit, each illustration that I have selected to write about demonstrates that our Lord was *full of grace and truth.*' Every time we see or are touched by the grace of God or understand the truth of who he is, we are changed. Experiencing his grace and knowing him as truth—as the reality of all things—is transformational. These are the experiences that caused us—you, Peter, and me—to fall in love with him, to want to follow him, and to be made more like him. I wish to share those experiences with others. So, with that introduction, let us delve in.

"The first story I wrote about was the wedding at Cana of Galilee. As we know, our Jewish culture is very rigid, law oriented, and unforgiving. Our law requires that those who make mistakes must pay the consequences. Grace is a rare commodity. But consider also the subculture that Peter and I grew up in as fishermen. We were rough, earthy, independent, judgmental, and crude men. What did we learn when we saw the Master deal with the situation when the hosts ran out of wine for their guests at the wedding party?

"Not planning to have enough food or drink at a wedding party could have been most embarrassing. It could easily have resulted in a stigma that the parents, the bride, and the groom of this village would have had to bear indefinitely. It could have made them the brunt of jokes and scorn. But that day, our Lord treated the situation in a way that none would have expected. Wanting to see no embarrassment come to the hosts on this special day—embarrassment which they would have deserved because of their poor planning—Jesus turned six large jars full of ordinary water into the best wine anyone had ever tasted. The lesson here is that Jesus is full of grace for the undeserving (and we are all undeserving). The truth is that he came to turn ordinary water, which represents our ordinary lives, into wine—which represents joy for us, and joy to impart to a world that is desperate for it.

"The second story I chose was the story of Nicodemus. You know our basic attitude toward the Pharisees. Inwardly we despised their religiosity. And did we not all secretly cheer when John the Baptist pronounced that they were nothing more than a brood of vipers? Can you imagine, if we had been given the opportunity to say what we wanted to Nicodemus, what we would have said? No doubt the first thing on our minds would have been to rail against him—and all those religious leaders who paraded around in their costumes, prayed and fasted to be noticed by others, and sat at the chief spots in any gatherings, for their hypocrisy. Surely, Jesus did not hold back in his criticisms of them as a group.

"But even to this Pharisee—who represented the *most* religious men of his day—Jesus was full of grace and truth. Though Nicodemus had risen to the highest position of prominence among the Jews and was among the most knowledgeable in Jewish law and tradition, Jesus perceived that on the inside, Nicodemus was empty and coming to him because he still had the heart of a seeker, desiring truth.

"The lesson we learned that day was that the grace of God extends to even the most religious men. And the truth was, that even as it takes a birth for a new, human life to enter into this world, it requires a second birth in which one is born of the Spirit—where Life is imparted by God—in order for one to enter and to see the kingdom of God."

"Nicodemus was an excellent example, indeed, to illustrate this point," nodded Peter.

"If the grace of God can extend to the most religious," I continued, "to those who exert every effort to keep the law and earn their salvation, then what about those on the opposite end of the scale? How far does the grace of God reach to the obvious, out-and-out sinner? For that, the Holy Spirit led me to use the example of the Samaritan woman whom Jesus encountered at the well."

Peter laughed out loud, and I grinned back at him. That day had shaken up all our worlds and left us looking as ignorant of God's devices as we truly were! I explained to Timothy and John Mark, "That was a day Jesus seemed to break all the rules of proper conduct for a Jew. We had gone to town to purchase some food, for it was midday, and left Jesus alone at Jacob's well. When we returned, we found him alone, talking with a Samaritan woman.

We were shocked because this seemed like indecorous behavior, if not scandalous—especially for a rabbi—to be found alone with a woman. But she was not only a woman, she was a Samaritan woman, and Jews have no dealings with Samaritans. And furthermore, she was not only a Samaritan woman, but she was known to be a very sinful one, a woman with five previous husbands who was currently living with a man to whom she was not married. She was a woman beyond shame, callously indifferent to what anyone thought of her.

"But Jesus saw a broken woman inside, an empty shell of one who was created to bear God's image, with great needs and a deep hunger for something satisfying and real. She had been through so many relationships, thinking that in them she would find the happiness that she longed for. But time after time she came up empty. Disregarding social customs and barriers, Jesus let the living waters from his Spirit flow into her and satisfy her soul like nothing she had ever known before. To this woman, Jesus also revealed the truth of true worship: that true worship is not conducted in a temple or on a mountain, but takes place within the spirit of the one who has become the temple of the living God."

"I vividly remember our dear sister," Peter injected. "She came to our Lord with an empty bucket, but walked away with water that was alive. She came to him as one who was a miserable failure and rejected, but she left accepted. She came hopeless, but left with hope. She came as one with questions, but she left with answers for others. Is this not the universal experience of all who have a personal and genuine encounter with Christ? As you well say, every time we *see him,* we are changed."

"Because he is so full of grace, Jesus is able to meet people in any condition: the undeserving, the religious, the sinner. But his grace extends even beyond that. Time and time again we saw him meet the needs of the helpless.

"As an example, consider the invalid he healed at the pool of Bethesda, outside of the temple in Jerusalem. That man had been helpless for thirty-eight years. If Jesus were in the business of trying to recruit an army of able-bodied followers who were going to usher in his kingdom—like even we initially thought he would do—this man was certainly no likely candidate! He had nothing to offer. He was not an influential member of the community. He was no one of standing or position. He had few, if any, friends. He was a nobody in terms of society's measure."

Peter was nodding in agreement, recalling the day. I smiled at Timothy and Mark, who were riveted to the story. "But that was the whole point. Jesus saw value in him, not because of what he could offer Jesus, but because this man was his creation, his precious child, and for that reason alone he had value. The grace that Jesus poured out upon him was not dependent on what the man could give in return. If we could all clearly understand the grace of God, we would see that we are all like this man. We were not chosen because of how good we are or because of what we have to offer Jesus. Grace was extended to each of us solely on the basis of Christ's unconditional love. For in him are the headwaters of all grace and love.

"So by these and other examples, whether people came to him hungry, blind, dead—spiritually or physically, as in the case of Lazarus—we see that Christ was full of grace to meet their deepest needs and full of truth to teach them that he was the ultimate reality of bread, water, light, healing, knowledge, guidance, Life, whatever it was they needed."

"And, may I add, John," cut in Peter, "that I so appreciate the way you included my story in your story. For you recounted the time at the Last Supper when the Lord laid aside his garments, took a towel and girded himself, and began to wash our feet. I would have none of it! He was the master and I was *his* servant. But Jesus had to show me—and all of us—that if we do not first let him serve us, we will have nothing with which to serve others. Those who would lead are not greater than their master. He came as a servant of all. It took a work of grace and revelation to see what a leader— and who the Master—really is.

"I thank you also, my brother, for using me again as an example to show that in Christ is grace for those who have suffered the devastation of going through the cross. There was grace even for me, the one who denied him. On the other side of the cross, there was grace, hope, and commission for service after we all learned the painful lesson that the cross brought into our lives. This same cross is a tool in God's hand to produce in us humility and bring us to the end of ourselves. In the end, our Lord is not looking for heroes, the brave, the bold, or the confident who think they can do something great for God. Jesus is simply looking for those who love him."

"By each of these stories and examples," I continued, "we were shown time and again that our teacher committed seemingly random, unreasonable, unmerited, and inconceivable acts of grace and divine kindness. As we observed and experienced that grace, indeed, we were changed. This resulted in us loving him all the more. This is my gospel. This is my testimony. This is my story."

We sat in silence for a while as we all paused to reflect on the grace of God that had been shown to each of us.

Then John Mark commented.

"I have now read all four gospel accounts. And Peter and I have even been involved in writing one. But this one has a depth, John, which goes beyond any of the others. May I humbly say to you that I believe your gospel will be the one most read."

Our day ended. I again suggested that Peter take my biography to Rome, along with the three epistles I had written. He readily agreed.

For the rest of that week, Peter and I spent much time together praying, fasting, going on long walks, laughing, and recounting our years together. The night before he was to depart, we stayed up late, sitting alone together at my table. Between us was a cup filled with wine and a loaf of bread—broken—from which we partook slowly, savoring it with great joy in the light of a dimly lit lamp as we reflected on our Lord and the life we had spent together.

"Do you remember that time by the Sea of Galilee, after our Lord's resurrection, when he appeared to us and prepared breakfast?" Peter asked after pinching a morsel from the bread, tearing it off, and placing it in his mouth.

"I cannot forget," I replied. "It is recorded in my gospel."

"Jesus said something to me that day that I cannot help thinking about as I consider this trip to Rome. He told me that if I loved him, I would feed his sheep. Then he said that when I was young, I would dress myself and go wherever I wished, but when I got old I would have to stretch out my hands while someone else would dress me and take me where I did not want to go. I confide in you, John, that this is how I feel as I look ahead to this trip to Rome."

He gripped the cup and raised it to his lips, extracted a few drops, then placed it back on the table. Following him, in like manner I did the same.

"I do not want to go," he continued. "Why would I want to walk straight into the jaws of what could lead to my death? This very well could be where the road ends for me. But I want to be faithful to feed the Master's sheep. He fed us. He gave us bread—even the bread of life. Now we must be faithful to leave behind that bread for others. I believe that he is calling me to Rome, and I must follow."

"Were it not for your strong insistence," I said, "I would be going with you."

"It was you, John," Peter replied, "who was commissioned by the Lord as a son of thunder—a son of the voice of God. You must complete what the Lord has called you to do. After I meet with Paul, if I should return, I will bring the final copies of all that we have worked on with me. If it is God's will that my journey end in Rome, then I will trust in God that he will make a way to send you what we have completed.

"You remember our Lord's words concerning you, that if you should remain until he came, that was not my business. I must follow him, and you must follow him. He has a specific plan for each of us to fulfill. The judgment he spoke of coming to Jerusalem has not yet occurred, but it must be very, very near. There still may be something left unsaid that he wishes to speak to you concerning his coming and the end of all things pertaining to this present age."

Hot, wet tears rolled down my cheeks as I gazed into Peter's face for what I knew might be the last time.

"Good-bye, old friend," I said to him.

We clutched each other's shoulders from across the table, staring into one another's tear-filled eyes. Rising to our feet, we held on to one another tightly as I buried my head in Peter's chest.

I could feel his tears falling on my head and his chest convulsing as he, too, wept uncontrollably.

"It has been some journey," he finally managed to say.

"Give my love to Paul," I blubbered. "Encourage him to be strong, and if he is taken, to finish well. If this is our last good-bye, I will joyfully look forward to the day when we will be reunited again in realms of glory and rest together once again on the bosom of the Beloved. It will be like old times, but even better."

Peter regained his composure. The last words I remember him saying to me were, "And we will eat bread and drink wine together with him once again. And we will be young, as before, and our bodies will be new. But what I am looking forward to most of all is to look, once again, into his eyes, to see his smile, and to hear him laugh."

CHAPTER 20

PAUL'S SECOND LETTER TO TIMOTHY

A.D. 65

It had been a week—perhaps two—since Peter left for Rome when I heard the urgent sound of knocking on my door. I rose from my seat at the table where I was studying some portions from the psalms with John Mark and answered the door. It was Timothy and Tychicus.

For a man of close to forty years by now, Timothy was in fairly good shape—although he did have frequent bouts with stomach problems. He and Tychicus, who was slightly younger, were both panting heavily and had beads of perspiration on their foreheads. It looked as if they had raced together to my home from Timothy's, which was about a half-mile away.

"Come in, brothers," I said. "Can I offer you some water? You both look as if you could use something to drink."

"Yes, thank you," said Timothy as they entered through the door and came inside.

I fetched some water, poured out two cups, and placed the cups before them at the table.

"What brings you here this morning?"

"Tychicus arrived from Rome only last night. Paul sent him. He has a report and a letter that Paul sent to me," Timothy said, introducing Tychicus while still breathing heavily.

Producing the scroll, Tychicus unrolled it, smoothed it out, and set it before us on the table. From there, he picked up the conversation.

"Paul was not in Rome long before he was once again apprehended by the praetorian guard and placed under house arrest. He was a marked man, identified by Nero as one of the ringleaders involved in the burning of the city. Because of fear, few Christians are willing to see him or be associated with him. At his preliminary hearing, no one was even willing to stand up for him as a character witness. It was too dangerous. Only Luke has stood by his side.

"Nero is away, and fortunately Paul was not assigned to the *tullianum*, the underground cell of the ancient prison located at the foot of the Capitoline

Hill. That place was formerly a cistern, about twelve feet underground, and prisoners—usually famous prisoners, or enemies of the state—are lowered into its dark confines through a hole in the floor to await their execution. The stench, the squalor, and the misery of prisoners there is said to be unimaginable. Some are left to die there—and are even eaten by rats.

"Instead, in the sovereignty and mercy of God, two of the guards assigned to him are ones to whom he was chained in his former imprisonment while awaiting trial before Nero. They are believers and are allowing him some freedom to receive visitors, although they are taking every precaution to keep his whereabouts unknown. Luke is attending to his needs. Onesiphorus, who traveled specifically from Ephesus to Rome to see Paul, found him and was willing to brave the danger to visit him, for which, Paul wrote, he was very grateful. By the time I left, Peter had not yet arrived."

"This letter written to me has a different tone than the previous one our brother wrote to the Philippians while in chains," Timothy said, with concern in his face. "In that letter he was optimistic about his release, and it came to pass. In this letter, it sounds as if he knows that he has the sentence of death within him and that his time is short. He has asked me to attend to some things here in Ephesus and then come to him quickly, before winter sets in. He also gave me some additional instructions about the project."

"What might those be?" I asked, saddened by the news I just heard about Paul, but also eager to hear more.

"He asked me to bring Mark with me. He said he had use for him. Since Peter will be joining him, it makes sense for Paul to want Mark to be there as well, since he has been involved both with Peter and with Paul in writing and delivering some of the other letters that have been selected. He also gave me another assignment to do along the way."

"Continue," I insisted.

"He wants me to stop by the home of Carpus and pick up some outer covers used for binding manuscripts together, along with some scrolls and parchments that he left with him."

"Who is Carpus?" I asked.

"A believer who specializes in bookmaking. He lives north of here, on the way to Rome, in the port city of Troas, next to Pergamum. Pergamum is the center of the book trade in all of Asia."

"What else did his letter say?" I asked, begging for more information.

Noting my anxiety, Timothy hastily replied, "I suggest we read it together and then discuss it."

So we did.

Huddled around the letter before us, we read it together silently. When we finished, I turned to Timothy and asked, "What did you take away from this letter, Timothy?"

"The church here in Ephesus is only about eleven years old. It was only two years ago that Paul wrote the letter from his first imprisonment in Rome that was read by the Ephesians. In that letter he referred to the church as God's household, God's building, a holy temple in the Lord, the dwelling of God in the Spirit, the body of Christ, the very flesh of Christ—his wife, his bride; and the armor-bearer of God. Then, not long ago—after his release—I received a letter from him in which he referred to the church as the pillar and support of the truth. What does a pillar do? It holds something up. What is a support? It is that upon which something is built. It is the platform upon which something greater is displayed."

Timothy held up his hands. "A pillar exists solely to hold something else up. It does not exist for itself. A base is not what is seen. What is seen is that which is built upon the base. The only reason for the church to exist is to hold up, support, and display the magnificent Christ! If it fails at that, it has ceased to be the church.

"As many have testified, we are living in the last days. We are already seeing the rebellion, or the apostasy against Rome that Paul spoke of in his second letter to the Thessalonians, taking place before our very eyes. The church is under attack both from within—false doctrines, myths, legalism, worldly philosophies—and from without by outright persecution. If we are to be honest, when we look at the church today, are we seeing Christ lifted up, exalted, and on display? Is the church expressing the life of the living God that has been placed inside of her? No, I do not think we can say that this is the case. She has lost her way and gotten off track."

Timothy spoke with all the passion of a man who had been building and serving the church from his youth. In his voice, I could hear the wisdom and maturity that had led Paul to choose him so many years ago.

"Let me refer you to this portion of the letter," Timothy said, pointing his index finger at a section of the scroll. It read, "Now in a large house there are not only gold and silver vessels, but also vessels of wood and of earthenware, and some to honor and some to dishonor. Therefore, if anyone cleanses himself from these, he will be a vessel for honor, sanctified, useful to the Master, prepared for every good work. Now flee from youthful lusts and pursue righteousness, faith, love, and peace, with those who call on the Lord from a pure heart."

"Gold and silver are precious things that are fairly rare," he continued.

"Wood and earthenware, on the other hand, are common and abundant. In Scripture, gold and silver always speak to us of something of God. Wood and earthenware speak to us of something of man.

"I think Paul is right. The church here in Ephesus has become overtaken with the common and ordinary. It has become overtaken with human thoughts, human ideas, human ways, and human teachings. It is no longer the pillar and support for the truth it once was."

"In such a situation, what are we to do?" asked Mark.

"Paul gives us the answer. He admonished me—and for that matter, all of us—to cleanse ourselves from vessels of dishonor and 'pursue righteousness, faith, love, and peace with those who call on the Lord out of a pure heart.'

"In his earlier letter, Paul talked about elders and deacons—necessities for there to be order in the church. But here he does not even mention them. Instead, he is telling me that what I have heard from him in the presence of many witnesses, I am to entrust to faithful men who will be able to teach others as well. What he seems to be saying is that we should not be so interested or concerned with outward things—including those who have been given a position or title. 'Faithful men' are more important than people occupying positions in a dead church. It is the inward reality that God is interested in, for God weighs the hearts.

"What we are to remain focused upon is working with others who call on the Lord from a pure heart and pursuing the Lord with them. We need to be in one accord and find fellowship with those who have Christ as their center and who are pursuing the Life that is in him."

"Amen, and Amen!" said Mark. Turning to me, he asked, "And what did you think of this letter, John?"

I turned my gaze toward Timothy and placed both of my hands square on his shoulders. Staring intently into his eyes, I said, in a solemn voice so that he would grasp the gravity of my words, "It is clear to me, Timothy, that in this letter Paul is passing the torch of his ministry on to you. I have known you, at times, to be somewhat shy—content to be in the background. But your gifts and callings from the Lord are evident. You are an apostle, an evangelist, and a teacher. Paul is telling you that it is now your turn to step up and be strong, for his time is short. We all bear witness to this admonition. Be strong, Timothy, in the grace that is in the Lord Jesus Christ!"

"I confirm that as well, Timothy," added Tychicus. "You were Paul's child in the faith. God's hand has been upon you since your childhood—even from the faith that you observed in your grandmother, Lois, and your mother, Eunice. Truly, you have been Paul's handpicked apprentice. You know the sacred Scriptures and have followed Paul's teaching, conduct, purpose, faith, patience, love, perseverance, persecutions, and sufferings, as he makes mention in this letter. We confirm that which he has admonished you. Now is the time for you to pick up the work where Paul is leaving off."

With that, we gathered around Timothy, laid our hands upon him, and took turns praying over him—offering his life to the Lord for the work that God had left to do through him. We could feel his body convulsing beneath our hands, as he wept without restraint.

When we finished, Timothy stood tall, with tears in his eyes, seemingly strengthened by our prayers.

"Thank you, brothers," he said in a brave but trembling voice. "Humanly speaking, to accept and to step out into this calling is daunting. But through the grace and the life supplied by the Lord Jesus, all things are possible. For as Paul said, 'I can do all things through Christ who strengthens me.'"

John Mark, Tychicus, and I all nodded in agreement.

"What are your plans now, Timothy?" I asked.

"John Mark and I will put our affairs in order and prepare to leave for Rome before week's end. There are some 'faithful men' I must meet with first. That should take a few days. Tychicus, I believe you should remain here and assist John in any way you can to strengthen the church."

"I will be waiting and plan to be here when you return," I said. "In the meantime, Tychicus and I will not be shy about proclaiming the Word of God and the testimony of Jesus. Give my love to Peter, Paul, and Luke when you see them. May God be with you. You will all be in my prayers."

CHAPTER 21
A LETTER FROM JUDE

A.D. 65

Timothy and John Mark left Ephesus by foot, taking the road north to Troas. I walked with them partway beyond the city before bidding them farewell. My heart swelled with pride as I watched these two soldiers of Christ march off together into the epicenter of battle, into the lair of Nero himself, to champion a higher cause and play their part in accomplishing the will of God, even if it meant risking their own lives.

It was not long after their departure that I received a letter from my cousin Jude, the brother of James and half-brother of our Lord Jesus, written from Caesarea. Jude, like his brother James, was not a true convert until after our Lord's resurrection. To have a brother who claimed to be God must have been unnerving, and at times, all the siblings thought he had lost his senses!

I imbibed deeply from the encouragement I found in this letter, though on the surface it could appear to be quite negative or even to instill fear. Jude wrote in the spirit of an Old Testament prophets, or like John the Baptizer, with emotion, passion, and vivid description. In the majority of his letter he warned about the apostates, or rebels, who were infiltrating the churches and were the "hidden reefs in their love feasts." We were seeing this here in Asia, as well, so his letter was most appropriate to circulate among all of the churches.

As I prayed and meditated upon this letter, I thought to myself that this could very well be the last epistle that we included in our compilation of New Covenant teachings, for it contained a theme unique to any other letter we had selected thus far. That theme is the keeping power of God.

Against the backdrop of apostasy, Jude's letter teaches that we are being kept by God and for God and that we are being kept by the means of grace. He begins with an introduction to this theme: "To those who are the called, beloved in God the Father, and kept *for* Jesus Christ."

From before the foundations of the world, God the Father chose us, marking us off *in* Christ and *for* Christ. He loved the Son so much that he purposed to give him a gift—the greatest gift—a corporate body, the church, who would know him in all his fullness and be one with him for all eternity.

Individually, we were each called, and as our Lord taught on so many occasions, no one can snatch us out of the Father's hand—or out of *his* hand, for Christ and the Father are one.

In his priestly prayer to the Father before his crucifixion, he prayed, "I have manifested your name to those you gave me out of the world. They were yours, and you gave them to me." And again, "I ask on their behalf, I do not ask on behalf of the world, but of those whom you have given me; for they are yours; and all things that are mine are yours, and yours are mine." Then he asked the Father to keep us—keep us in his name, for, "While I was with them, I was keeping them in your name and I guarded them, and not one of them perished but the son of perdition, so that the Scripture would be fulfilled." This, I also wrote in my gospel.

We are not of this world, even as he was not of this world. Though one man sinned, and through him all sinned, God's plan will not be hindered. We were saved *by* Christ and are being kept *for* Christ. One day we will be presented *to* Christ, where we will forever be with him where he is and see his glory, which the Father has given him, just as he prayed.

But who are these apostates?

These people whom Jude was describing were never saved in the first place. But because of our own sinful natures, we can see in them some of the traits in our own lives and thoughts, and this can cause us to fear. For are we not all, at times, grumblers and faultfinders, and at times do we not also follow after our own lusts, speak arrogantly, or flatter people for the sake of gain? And if their fate is destruction, could not ours be as well?

But what Jude wrote, in describing these apostates and exposing their characteristics, is actually a means whereby we can be kept from their errors. By our knowing the characteristics of the ungodly, the Holy Spirit, working in us, can help save us and keep us from walking in their ways.

Jude describes these people as having "gone the way of Cain, and for pay they have rushed headlong into the error of Balaam, and perished in the rebellion of Korah." We can recognize these apostates by their self-confidence—thinking that their own good works are sufficient to please God, as Cain did in presenting to God an offering from the works of his hands. Cain did not recognize himself as a sinner in need of approaching God on the basis of a redeeming blood of sacrifice. Moreover, these apostates are those who cause divisions; they are worldly minded and devoid of the Spirit.

To be sure, we all fall from time to time. And as we look around at those in the church—even our leaders—we see that even they can fall as well. And this could be cause for great discouragement, for when we see the characteristics of the apostates in our own lives, and within the lives of those who have crept in unnoticed to the church, it can give rise to the thought, "Could we be next?"

Finally, Jude prescribes a way for us to strive against the spirit of error that has crept into the churches: he encourages us to build ourselves up in the faith, pray according to the will of God, walk in a way pleasing to him by keeping ourselves in the love of God, and have a heart for others. These are all means of grace by which we will be kept.

I think, once again, of my dear brother Peter. Peter actually denied the Lord, and denied him three times. As a result, he fell and continued to fall into the pit of despair until at last he fell upon the prayers of Jesus, who had prayed for him, "Simon, Simon, behold, Satan has demanded to sift you like wheat; but *I have prayed for you, that your faith may not fail;* and you, when once you have turned again, strengthen your brothers."

It was not a pretty picture to see Peter in his state of denial. But look at him today! If it depends on us, eventually, we will hopelessly fail. If God were to withdraw his keeping power—for even a moment—none of us would be kept. Thank God, that greater is he who is in us than he who is in the world! And thank God for his keeping power.

As Jude so eloquently wrote, under the inspiration of the Holy Spirit, in his glorious benediction, "Now to him *who is able to keep you from stumbling, and to make you stand* in the presence of his glory blameless with great joy, to the only God our Savior, through Jesus Christ our Lord, be glory, majesty, dominion and authority, *before all time and now and forever.* Amen!"

This is the pulse, the heartbeat, of the eternal covenant that we proclaim and of the faith that was once for all delivered to the saints.

As I reviewed this letter with the other eyewitnesses to our Lord's resurrection who were here in Ephesus, there was unanimous consent that this, too, should be included in the sacred texts.

CHAPTER 22
ONLY THREE RETURN

A.D. 66

It was still two months before spring would fully arrive. There had been no word from Timothy and John Mark. I had no idea of their fate, and in spite of my prayers and the knowledge that God was in control, I was still terribly anxious to hear what had been taking place in Rome. Had Peter arrived and found Paul? Had they been able to meet together? Had Timothy and John Mark arrived safely? What had transpired in their discussions? All this was weighing heavily upon me.

Then one evening at a meeting in the home of Priscilla and Aquila, the door burst open, and in came three road-weary travelers. Our brothers Timothy and John Mark had returned, and Luke was with them. The room erupted with shouts of praise as one by one, each of the saints greeted them with hugs, excitement, and holy kisses.

Our brothers sat down in the middle of the room, and the meeting became theirs as they spoke late into the night about what had transpired in Rome.

Timothy and John Mark had arrived before winter, as Paul had requested, and gone straight to the home of Linus and Claudia. They stayed there for two nights; got some much needed rest and refreshment, and were informed as to the condition of the church in Rome.

Nero's persecution had been devastating; the atrocities he had committed unspeakable. Those from the church who had survived the intensive first wave of persecution kept a very low profile. Meetings had been suspended, except for very small, informal gatherings of saints in individual homes for prayer and worship.

Once Peter found Paul, he began meeting with him daily. Besides Onesiphorus, Peter was the only one brave enough to seek Paul out—save Luke, who was allowed to be with him because he is a medical doctor. Two of Paul's guards, who were fellow believers, proved to be trustworthy and faithful men, and they took great risks themselves in safeguarding Peter's identity and ensuring that their times together would be private and go undetected by others in their ranks who had been among the persecutors and were not sympathetic to the Christian cause.

Timothy described how he and Mark were informed of Paul's whereabouts and sought him out. "When we arrived," Timothy said, "we knocked on the door, and it was opened only a crack by one of the praetorian guards, who asked us to identify ourselves. When Paul heard that it was us, he leapt to his feet and let out a loud praise to God, hoisting the other guard he was chained to, to his feet as well! The door was opened to us and we were let inside. There at the table with Paul were Peter and Luke—both with huge smiles on their faces. What a reunion it was, and what joy for all of us!

"Throughout our time with Peter, Paul, and Luke, it was obvious that God had knit these men's hearts together in the deepest of ways in a bond of love and affection for one another. The time we all spent in fellowship, worship, and sharing together took on the atmosphere of heaven itself. No doubt it was a height in spiritual fellowship among the saints that few ever experience in this lifetime."

When we asked of Peter and Paul's physical condition, John Mark was quick to say that Paul often appeared weary and was fighting to maintain his stamina. The years of mistreatment, scourgings, infections, sufferings, and beatings had taken their toll. But he was also, for the most part, spirited and attentive, wanting to make the most of every precious moment that God had given him to live, for he knew that at any time, there could come a knock on the door and he would be led out to his own execution.

The church in Ephesus was aware of the mission and the circumstances under which Timothy and John Mark had gone to Rome. They knew about the work that had been done, so far, on the accumulation of writings that were to become the New Testament Scriptures.

Finally, Timothy could contain himself no longer.

"Brothers and sisters, there is much more we have to tell you about our time in Rome. I know that you want to hear more about the circumstances of our brothers—how they were when we last saw them and how we escaped with our lives, but first, I must tell you an amazing story!

"You know that, in his last letter to me, Paul asked that I take John Mark with me to join him in Rome. He also asked that we stop by the home of Carpus to pick up the book casing, the scrolls, and the parchments. I had no idea what book casing he was referring to, but I was to learn all about it when we finally met with Paul.

"When Paul, Peter, Luke, Timothy, and I were together, Paul shared an idea with us that had come to him—an idea that is revolutionary. As a matter of fact, Carpus was working on it for Paul, and what we picked up and brought to the others from his house was but a prototype—an original design for how this New Testament we have been working on will eventually be published.

"Let me give you an example. When we all first saw the scroll that Dr. Luke composed to Theophilus, containing his gospel account and the story of the first thirty years of the church, the scroll itself was nearly thirty feet long! Imagine someone attempting to carry around all of these scrolls comprising the New Covenant writings at one time! How clumsy! How cumbersome that would be! So here is an example of what Paul and Carpus came up with."

Pulling a small leather binding from a satchel he had with him, Timothy held it up in his right hand for all of us to see. The binding had leaves inside attached to a spine. Carefully, he opened it up and showed us the pages.

There were the very same documents that Luke had addressed to Theophilus—and both could be contained in one relatively small volume that Timothy could hold in his hand!

"Astounding!" I nearly shouted.

"Here is what was done," said John Mark, eager to show us more as he snatched the book back from Timothy's hand.

"First, uniform pages of papyrus were created and written on both sides, to compact the document and save space. Next, you will see that each word is written in capital letters and there are no spaces between the words. The letters we are accumulating will be one continual, flowing text, and they will all eventually be combined into one document. As you can imagine from this sample, every line from each of the writings will flow neatly from the bottom of one page to the top of the next so that there are no interruptions. This will reduce the size of the document even more. And the added value of putting it together in this method will be that there will be no way for anyone to change, insert, or delete words in the document to alter the meaning or revise the order."

Astonished but captivated by the wonder of it, I asked John Mark what this style of binding was called—I had never seen anything like it before.

"It is something new in the book world, only in the earliest stages of development. It is called a codex," he said with a grin.

"Pure genius!" I exclaimed. "Brilliant! Revolutionary! A divinely inspired innovation for a time such as this! Oh, how good, how creative, how unsearchable is God in all his wisdom and ways!"

Samples were passed around the room for everyone to see. We all marveled at the genius behind such an invention and could only faintly imagine what impact this would have in the distribution of the Scriptures among the churches.

As the excitement died down, John Mark proclaimed another announcement.

"We brought something else with us," he said. "It is another letter—another letter to be included in the New Covenant writings. It is a letter from Peter—his last. I am sure that you are anxious to have it read, but first I must tell you the extraordinary circumstances under which it was written and how, amazingly, we were able to deliver it to you."

As he spoke, I was marveling at all of this, savoring with sweet delight the sovereignty of God.

"Over the course of the three months that we met together, we completed our work and were in total agreement as to the contents of our New Testament: Four gospels containing the biographies of our Lord's life—the ones written by Matthew, Luke, John, and me. The history portion, written by Luke. The letter by James, Paul's letter to the Galatian churches, his two to the churches in Thessalonica and two to the Corinthians, his letters to the Romans and the Hebrews, as well as the two letters he wrote to me, and one letter that he wrote to Titus, which he left a copy of with Carpus that we picked up along the way. In addition, there are the three epistles written by our brother John, and this letter I hold in my hands, along with the earlier letter written by Peter. A few minor edits were made for clarification, but the work has been finished."

"There will be another letter," I interrupted. "One I received recently from Jude that you have not seen."

"Praise God!" responded Mark.

"Before we read Peter's letter, I need to tell you the circumstances under which it was penned and how we managed to escape from Rome with it," Timothy carried on. He appeared a bit heavy, a bit apprehensive as he picked up the story.

"Peter's presence and identity in Rome were successfully guarded, but somehow it eventually leaked out and the Roman officials learned of it. They were even told by some informer that he had been meeting with Paul while Paul was under house arrest. Paul's guards heard about this and became afraid for their own lives. When Peter, Timothy, and I arrived one morning and gave our customary knock on the door, the guard on duty opened it only halfway. He was visibly shaken. He warned us that we must flee immediately, for an all-out manhunt had been ordered to find Peter and to bring him into custody. We barely even had time to say our good-byes to Paul. Things happened so quickly. Luke was there waiting for us and had all of his belongings packed. We gathered all the parchments and scrolls and the bindings that were hidden securely away in a back room and left in haste.

"We determined that the first place they would look for us would be in the homes of the believers there. We did not want to cause risk to their lives or put them in jeopardy. So we decided to hide in a place where we thought there would be little chance of anyone finding us. There is a Jewish cemetery located just outside the city, alongside the Appian Way. It is actually a series of underground tunnels, or catacombs, which are not frequented that often. We thought it would make a good place to hide.

"We stayed underground for six days, coming up only briefly for an hour or two at a time to find food and drink. The tunnels were lined with carved-out spaces where bodies, wrapped in linen shrouds, were placed. Since it was no longer safe for us to be in Rome, we determined that our time there was over, and we started making plans to return here to Ephesus.

"There were only occasional visitors in the tunnels. One man who came took note of us and viewed us suspiciously. Perhaps it was because we had our baggage with us and looked like we might be staying for a while. He came again on another day and appeared to be watching us, but then he left, and we never saw him again." A look in Timothy's eye betrayed his suspicion that this man had become an informant.

"It was in the tunnels, by candlelight, that Peter wrote his final letter.

"The day after we had last seen our observer, we heard some voices in the tunnels. They sounded like Roman soldiers. Peter knew that the hunt was primarily for him. He quickly pointed in one direction and said, 'Take the writings and be off that way! I will go in the opposite direction. If we can escape their detection, let us meet back here at nightfall!'

"We had no time to argue. Clutching the satchels filled with writings, we fled. The tunnels were dark. They were less than three feet wide and not high enough to stand erect. We scampered away, bent over, feeling our way along. We heard Peter give out a shout. We knew he must have been trying to divert the guards from following us.

"We huddled together for several hours, whispering, listening. When we felt it was safe, we returned to the place we had last seen Peter. He was gone. We cautiously made our way to the entrance of the catacombs and peered outside. No one could be seen. Then we returned inside.

"Night fell, and the morning came. There was no sign of Peter.

"We waited one more full day and night. Convinced that he had been taken, we collected our things and got on the road and began our journey back."

A hush had fallen on the room. There was a sense of heaviness and sadness.

Finally, I said to Mark, softly, "Go ahead and read the letter. Let us hear what Peter had to say."

"Forgive me, but this might be too difficult for me to read," said Mark, passing the letter to Luke. "Can you read it for us?" he asked.

Luke agreed, took the letter, and began reading.

I can scarcely remember a word that was read. My thoughts, my emotions—as those of the others in the room—were too overwhelmed with the sense of pending loss. No doubt, we would soon receive news of what had happened to the two apostles in Rome.

CHAPTER 23

THE LAST HOUR

A.D. 66

Over the next few days I met with John Mark, Timothy, and Luke. There were many things to discuss. We spent a considerable amount of time talking about Peter and Paul and going over Peter's letter. Surprisingly, when we compared Peter's letter to that of Jude, we found many similarities in content.

"Was there any discussion as to the order in which our New Testament should be put together?" I asked the others.

"Yes," responded Luke. "Putting the letters together in codex form and binding them together will limit how big a volume we can produce. We discussed that it would probably be best to put the gospels, and perhaps the history, together in one book, the writings of Paul in another, and the letters to the Jewish brethren in another."

"I suggest that we begin with Matthew's gospel, because it was written primarily for a Jewish audience," I said. "It would be an appropriate opening, for the gospel went first to the Jew, and then to the Gentiles."

"A point that we all agreed upon already in Rome," replied Luke.

"We will need to think about and seek guidance from the Holy Spirit in the arranging of the individual pieces. I believe that Jude's letter should be the last. Its message and closing benediction sound such a high note." I paused. As I reviewed the books and epistles we had gathered, it seemed to me that an empty place still remained—a gap I wanted to close.

"Still, I am not at rest about one thing. Jerusalem's destruction is imminent. No writings thus far have addressed it, save with prophetic reference to it—primarily by our Lord in his discourse from the Mount of Olives. I feel that there is more to be said about these last days—even this last hour—in which we live. There needs to be a capstone, a finality—the last chapter in this story has not yet been written. May the Lord speak to us and deliver that message for the whole church."

In our discussions I noted that perhaps the thing I was most happy to see in Peter's letter was his heart's desire to remind his readers about the common faith we all have received, even though he knew that the laying aside of his earthly dwelling was imminent, as the Lord had made clear to him. His desire to combat error and the false teachings that had entered the churches was clear. He alluded to the Scriptures we had been accumulating when he wrote, "And I will also be diligent that at any time after my departure you will be able to call these things to mind."

It was Peter and James and I who were eyewitnesses to the Lord's majesty when he was transfigured on the mountain and clothed in light. We were the only ones who saw this spectacle and heard the proclamation by the Father from on high. James had already gone to be with the Lord. Peter and I were the only ones left. With that in mind he wrote,

> For *we* did not follow cleverly devised tales when *we* made known to you the power and coming of our Lord Jesus Christ, but *we* were eyewitnesses of his majesty. For when he received honor and glory from God the Father, such an utterance as this was made to him by the Majestic Glory, "This is my beloved Son with whom I am well-pleased," *and we ourselves* heard this utterance made from heaven when we were with him on the holy mountain. So *we* have the prophetic word made more sure, to which you do well to pay attention as to a lamp shining in a dark place, until the day dawns and the morning star arises in your hearts. But know this first of all, that no prophecy of Scripture is a matter of one's own interpretation, for no prophecy was ever made by an act of human will, but men moved by the Holy Spirit spoke from God.

He also upheld Paul as an author of Scripture when he wrote,

> Just as also our beloved brother Paul, according to the wisdom given him, wrote to you, as also in all his letters, speaking in them of these things, in which are some things hard to understand, which the untaught and unstable distort, as they do also the *rest of Scriptures,* to their own destruction.

So Peter has laid the groundwork. The saints who read this letter will have had their hearts prepared for the totality of the message which is forthcoming—the fruit of our all of our labors.

As I sat with my brothers and we talked about the final letters that had been added, we noted a common theme found in all of them. That theme is the message of Life.

In Peter's first letter, he stated that husband and wife were "fellow heirs of the grace of life." In his last letter, he began by reminding his readers that they had received the same kind of faith as he had, and that even this faith was a gift, not something they could produce of themselves. He went on to say that that by God's divine power they had received everything pertaining to *life* and godliness, that they might become partakers of the divine nature.

In Paul's first letter to Timothy, he encouraged him to take hold of the *eternal life* in which he was called, and for believers to "take hold of that which is *life* indeed." He began his last letter to Timothy by writing, "Paul, an apostle of Christ Jesus by the will of God, according to the *promise of life* in Christ Jesus." Later in the letter we read that God has saved us and called us according to his own purpose, and that the Lord Jesus "abolished death and *brought life and immortality to light through the gospel,* for which he [Paul] was appointed a preacher and an apostle and a teacher."

And of course, even my own gospel and the epistles I have written were based on this theme. The purpose of God from all eternity has been to dispense this Life to those willing recipients who have been chosen and called for this very purpose—regardless of race or nationality, whether Jew, Gentile, or Samaritan. The contract on the basis of which this Life flows from the throne of God into the spirits of all of God's chosen people is the eternal covenant, or the New Covenant, which was enacted through the shedding of the blood of the precious Lamb of God.

While we were together, we also decided that duplicate copies of all the letters should be made—one to go to Carpus, one for John Mark, one for Timothy, and one for me. We agreed to recruit some scribes from among the brethren to begin making copies of Peter's last letter and some messengers to begin distributing it among the churches.

Over the next six weeks, we waited anxiously for any news on the fate of our two brothers. We braced for the worst. Then the blow finally came. A brother from the church in Rome arrived with the scantest of information. Within days of when Timothy and the others escaped, Paul had been condemned to death. Since he was a Roman citizen, he could not be executed within the city, nor could he be crucified. So he was taken approximately three miles outside of the city walls to a place called Aquae Salviae, which is along the Ostian Way, and beheaded with a sword. Shortly thereafter, Peter was hauled away to Nero's circus and crucified upside down.

The sense of loss I felt cannot be described. But I know that my beloved brothers were faithful—even to the end—and have received their reward and the crown of life that our Lord promised to those who love him.

Word also came from Rome that soldiers had been dispatched to Greece and were on their way to Asia to inform local authorities that Christians were to be considered enemies of the state and their leaders rounded up.

My own life and freedom were in danger now. But I was not deterred. I was determined to finish my course, as did Peter and Paul, regardless of the consequences. One day while preaching the gospel openly in the agora, a local official challenged me. He asked me specifically, before the crowd, if the Roman emperor was "Lord." I told him, respectfully, that he was not. He was a mere man. Jesus is the King of all kings, and to him every knee will bow. Every tongue will confess that *he* is Lord.

The official then threatened me and said that I would be hearing from the authorities. Word is now out in Ephesus as to who I am—the last remaining of the original apostles. With Paul and Peter gone, it is clear that the net will soon close in on me. I would not be surprised if they came for me at any time.

If I should be taken, so be it. But I cling to the clear witness inside of me that my time has not yet come. There is still work to be done that I, alone, will be able to complete. What the Lord said to Peter has become, for me, a promise: that I should remain until he comes. This has become an anchor to my soul. The questions that remain about his coming must be answered, and those answers will need to come soon.

PART III

THE MARRIAGE: THE FINAL REVELATION

(FORMERLY AN EVENING IN EPHESUS, WITH JOHN THE SON OF ZEBEDEE)

A Dramatic Commentary on the book of Revelation

INTRODUCTION

I became a Christian in the spring of 1967 while attending the University of California, Santa Barbara. During the first year of my Christian life, I was involved in a student-led campus ministry. Since we had no formal leader, each week a dedicated group of us would pile into a car and make the two-hour drive to Los Angeles to hear prominent Bible teachers from this well-known parachurch organization. We enjoyed wonderful fellowship. We found ourselves in the midst of a revival that started among young people in Southern California and spread throughout the rest of the country like wildfire in the late 1960s and early 70s. Many refer to this as "The Jesus Movement."

During those days, many speakers emphasized the importance of Bible prophecy. Our heads were filled with teaching on the most recent world events and how they related to the last days. We were taught that Jesus was coming back in our generation. We became enthralled with Bible prophecy.

Yet, though our heads were swelled with *knowledge* about the second coming of Christ, still, our spirits yearned for something deeper. I believe that subconsciously we thought if we could just unravel all the mysteries about *how and when* the Lord would come, that alone would usher him in! He was just waiting for us to figure it out.

Fortunately, however, the Lord didn't leave us there. Our quest to understand Bible prophecy gave way to something greater. That deep longing in our hearts began to be satisfied as our attention focused more on knowing Christ himself—not just knowing *about* him, but knowing him.

During those same years, the Lord also began to show us more about his ultimate purpose. The closing chapters of Revelation reveal that God's purpose throughout the ages has been to have a bride. It was the mystery hidden for ages that Paul describes in Ephesians. It became clear to me that more than any other thing, what the Lord was waiting for before his long-anticipated return was for his bride to make herself ready. Therefore, knowing him and being a part of building up his church superseded the craving I once had to have all the answers and see all the pieces of the 'last days puzzle' fit neatly together regarding his coming.

My interest in eschatology lay dormant for over two decades. Then, about sixteen years ago, the Lord led me to think about the subject again. Gary DeMar's book *Last Days Madness* sparked my interest in the topic and opened the door to a new perspective on end-time theology. I began digging into other volumes written about the book of Revelation, books that interpreted the work from a more historical perspective. I believed that any valid interpretation had to take into account how Christians living in the first century, *to whom it was written,* would have understood it. After much study, I compiled what I had learned into a series of messages that were delivered to a home fellowship group in Charlottesville, Virginia, in 1998. Those messages became the basis for this part of the trilogy.

I hope that as you read, the promise of blessing made by the apostle John to "all who read and those who hear the words of the prophecy" will be yours as you spend *An Evening in Ephesus.*

CONTENTS: THE MARRIAGE: THE FINAL REVELATION

PROLOGUE

A.D. 72

Three men walked briskly through the streets of Ephesus. They did not want to be late for the meeting.

One of the three would speak that night. He needed no introduction. Beneath his tunic, scars marred his back from the flogging he had received in Jerusalem at the hands of the high priest, Sadducees, and religious leaders more than three decades prior. He wore them with pride. He had been counted worthy to suffer for his Lord. He had arrived in Ephesus, unexpectedly, by boat one week earlier. It had been six years since he had last set foot in this place. This was where he was apprehended as a criminal and sent into exile to the Island of Patmos.

The three men passed the huge theater built into Mount Pion in the center of the city, which seated up to 25,000 people. They crossed the seventy-foot-wide marble street, lined with columns that led from the center of town down to the harbor. Passing through the agora and weaving their way through the shoppers who filled the busy marketplace, they took a right turn down a winding street that led to the large home of one of the wealthier merchants in the church.

The sound of joyful singing drew them inside the house. They reached the door and pushed it open without a knock.

Inside, smiling saints greeted them with laughter, shouts, warm embraces, and praises to the Lord. Slowly, the three made their way through the packed house into the large room where the church was gathered.

They joined in the singing and waved to some familiar faces as they found a place on the floor. After a few songs and short testimonies, there was a sense in the room that it was time to hear from the man from Galilee.

His heart raced. Memories of being in Ephesus—in this very house— meeting with the saints before his exile flooded his mind. He had been asked this night to explain an apocalyptic letter that he had written and that had circulated among the seven churches of Asia some years earlier. He stood up slowly and moved to the front of the room. Turning and facing his audience, he saw a sea of expectant faces. Most of the crowd sat shoulder to shoulder on the floor. Others leaned against the walls or stood in the doorway.

The aging apostle squinted as he slowly looked around the room. Finally, he cleared his throat and began.

CHAPTER 1
WE BEHELD HIS GLORY

Greetings, my dear brothers and sisters! It has been some years now since I walked the streets of your city and entered into the precious fellowship of the holy ones who reside in Ephesus. Truly, it is good to be with you tonight. I thank you for your warm welcome!

I have been told that we have many who are here for the first time, as well as a few visitors from out of town. I recognize some of you from the church in Philadelphia. Welcome.

For those of you who do not know me, allow me to introduce myself: I am John, the son of Zebedee.

I worked as a fisherman and grew up north of Jerusalem, around the Sea of Galilee. One day over forty years ago, my brother James and I were sitting in a boat with our father, mending fishing nets. When the Lord Jesus Christ called to us, we left our nets and followed him. I have been following him ever since.

That was the day Jesus began gathering his disciples. Just moments earlier, Jesus had called Simon Peter and his brother Andrew to follow him as well. Peter was casting his net when he heard the Lord's call. That turned out to be symbolic of his spiritual calling and the role he would play as probably the greatest evangelist and "fisher of men" I have ever known.

The same masterful hand at work in Peter's life has been at work in my own. Peter was called as he cast his net. I was called while mending mine. The primary role I have played through the years, and even to this day, has been to mend problem situations that have developed in the churches—a restoring ministry, you might call it—and to explain the significance of the extraordinary events that have taken place in this generation.

In recent years, we have seen the church pass through much tribulation. At first, it came from the hands of the Jews and religious leaders who crucified the Lord; later, it came from Rome itself.

For a great while, Christianity was thought of only as a sect of Judaism. But two things changed that. The first was a combination of the persecution of believers at the hand of Nero, the Jewish War with Rome, and the subsequent destruction of the temple in Jerusalem, which occurred only two years ago. Jews who had become followers of Christ did not support the Jewish Zealots' rebellion, and consequently were seen as being distinct. Secondly, as the gospel has spread throughout the whole known world, especially to the Gentiles, a clear demarcation between the Jewish religion and the church has become evident to all.

With the severe persecution the church has recently endured, the false gospels that have been spread, and the recent deaths of many notable leaders among us, now, more than ever, is the time for mending broken nets. My heart is burdened to encourage, strengthen, and restore the churches during this difficult time we have been passing through.

I am here to talk with you tonight about the letter containing the revelation that I wrote to you from Patmos. Because of your fortunate location, you were the first to receive it before it was carried further down the road that connects Ephesus with the other six cities to whom it was addressed—Smyrna, Pergamum, Thyatira, Sardis, Philadelphia, and Laodicea. I am aware that parts of the letter are difficult to understand, and we will not have time to discuss it all. But I will do my best to give you an overview of the important events I described.

Before getting into the letter itself, I think it would be appropriate to give you some background about my own life and share a few of my experiences with you.

First, I want to make it clear: do not think of me as some great apostle. Yes, I was one of the original twelve, but I must remind you that I was also one who, like Peter, abandoned the Lord and fled in the garden of Gethsemane on the night in which he was betrayed and arrested. I have nothing to boast about in my flesh. I am just your brother. Think of me as I think of myself: as the disciple whom Jesus loved. I hope each of you will come to see yourself in that light as well.

People ask me why our Lord chose twelve of us as apostles. It should come as no surprise that God has a purpose in everything he does. Under the Old Covenant, YHWH, the I Am, chose and then gathered the twelve tribes of Israel around himself. When Jesus came as Immanuel, God with us, he chose twelve to represent the beginning of a *new nation* under a *New Covenant*. We were to become the foundation of the *new Israel of God*.

No hierarchy existed among us. We were all brothers, and the women who followed the Lord were all our sisters. However, there were a few special times when Peter, James, and I were taken into the Lord's inner circle. Consequently, on occasion we witnessed significant events and heard things that the others were not privy to firsthand.

For example, I remember the day when Peter, James, and I accompanied

Jesus to the house of Jairus, a synagogue official whose twelve-year-old daughter lay dying. Hours before, Jairus had pleaded with Jesus to come heal her. As we approached Jairus's home, we heard loud wailing coming from inside. When we entered the house, mourning friends and relatives told us the young girl had died.

Jesus waited for no introduction. He stepped to the middle of the room and commanded everyone to be silent. "The little girl has not died, she is just asleep," he declared in a firm voice. Then, Jesus led Jairus and his wife, along with the three of us, into the room where the girl's lifeless body lay. He took her by the hand and commanded her, "Little girl, get up!"

We had never before seen anyone raised from the dead! Recalling the astonishment and joy on the faces of her father and mother still sends shivers up my spine. We could not stop talking about it with the other apostles. It was an event none of us would ever forget.

Then there was the time the Lord led the three of us up a high mountain. We saw him transfigured before our very eyes. He was lit up in glory! Elijah and Moses appeared, and we heard the voice of God boom from the cloud. For once, I had enough sense to do the only thing appropriate for such an auspicious moment—I fell on my face in worship. But not so with Peter. I remember lying facedown in fear in the dirt and hearing my dear brother blurting out something about building three tabernacles!

On one other occasion, the three of us, along with Andrew, shared a very important time with the Lord that has a bearing on what I plan to speak to you about tonight. We were with him on the Mount of Olives only a few days before his crucifixion. There, he bared his heart to us about his rejection by the Jews, and he spoke of a coming judgment. Matthew, John Mark, and Luke detailed this event in their gospel accounts concerning the life of our Lord. They heard the story from us. Here is what happened:

Jesus had just finished delivering a blistering message to the scribes and Pharisees, calling them hypocrites and pronouncing all kinds of woes on them. He accused them of being the sons of those who murdered the prophets. Then, pointing at them with his finger and looking them straight in the eyes, in strong, serious, measured words, he said:

"I am sending you prophets and wise men and scribes; some of them you will kill and crucify, and some of them you will scourge in your synagogues, and persecute from city to city, so that upon you may fall the guilt of all the righteous blood shed on earth, from the blood of righteous Abel to the blood of Zechariah, the son of Berechiah, whom you murdered between the temple and the altar. Truly I say to you, all these things [all of these woes] will come upon this generation."

An awkward silence fell upon us all as we looked at one another. No one knew what to say. We were awestruck by the Lord's boldness and harshness. We left the temple, a leave-taking that turned out to be quite symbolic for Jesus. He was through with Judaism. Then, a disciple whose name I will not mention, in what seemed almost like nervous and idle chatter over Jesus's pronouncements, took that opportunity to say one of the dumbest things I have ever heard in all my life. It went something like this: "Teacher, what do you think of this beautiful temple with all of its magnificent stones and buildings?"

Jesus turned on his heels. His eyes flashed like fire. In an angry voice he shot back, "Do you see these great buildings? Not one stone shall be left upon another which will not be torn down!" His face was filled with emotion.

He exited the temple through the East Gate in a fast—almost defiant—walk. We had to hurry along behind just to keep up with him. Crossing the bridge spanning the Kidron Valley, which connects the Temple Mount with the Descent of the Mount of Olives, he made his way up the mountain. We followed about a stone's throw behind. After walking for about fifteen minutes, he left the road and made his way to a rock overlooking the city. We watched him sit down, still breathing heavily from the climb and from the intensity of his exchange with the Jews. Cautiously, the four of us approached him. We were fearful. We sat down next to him without uttering a word. Finally, it was I who mustered the courage to ask him to explain his words and tell us when these events would take place.

By this time Jesus had calmed down. He reached for a few blades of grass, and plucking them from the ground, tossed them into the air. His mood seemed to shift from anger to sadness. Taking one long last look across the valley at the temple and Jerusalem, he turned his attention to us. We moved closer and listened intently as he shared with us some incredible and even frightening prophecies.

He began by speaking to us about the false, self-proclaimed messiahs who would come in his name, and about wars and rumors of wars, and of uprisings of nations against nations and kingdoms against kingdoms. These, he said, would only be birth pangs leading up to the day when the temple would be utterly destroyed and the whole Jewish sacrificial system of worship would be overturned. He was talking about a coming judgment against the scribes and Pharisees and the whole religious system that they represented, a system that had come to oppose him. Jesus was warning us that when we saw these signs take place, we would know the end of the Old Covenant era was near.

You must understand that his warning of wars was frightening and surprising to us. During the period before Jesus's crucifixion and resurrection, and for a time following, the Roman Empire had experienced great peace and stability, known as the *Pax Romana*. Peace reigned from Augustus to Nero. Because of the political calm, we were all able to move freely across the Mediterranean world. This made it easy for the gospel message to spread so quickly throughout the empire. Though there were the Zealots already present in Judea, the conditions for war and the disaster that Jesus foretold from the mountain did not, at that time, seem remotely possible.

But as you know, just before Nero's death in A.D. 68, wars and rebellions became numerous. Peace was disrupted. Almost overnight, the empire was tearing at the seams. There were wars and rumors of wars. Nations rose against nations and kingdoms against kingdoms. Many questioned whether the empire would survive or continue to unravel and ultimately dissolve in chaos.

The Jewish War in Judea, which broke out in the spring of A.D. 67, sparked the beginning of this turmoil. The outbreak of wars peaked in A.D. 69, after which Vespasian regained control. From the time of Nero's death to the consolidation of power under Vespasian, Rome experienced four different emperors in just over one year. These revolts and uprisings were signs that the time that Jesus had spoken of was finally coming to pass.

Our Lord gave us another sign that would help us understand the end was near. He said, "This gospel of the kingdom shall be preached in the whole world as a testimony to all nations, and then the end will come." The whole world, as we understand it, is the Roman Empire. The preaching of the gospel to all nations began on the day of Pentecost, when God assembled in Jerusalem both Jews and proselytes from every nation under heaven to hear the good news proclaimed. Then, when the first wave of persecution hit the church a few years later, the Jewish-Christian disciples scattered throughout the empire. Some fled to Judea, others to Samaria, but many returned to their own countries. The gospel of the kingdom continued to spread, and Jesus's prediction began to come true.

By the time Jerusalem fell in A.D. 70, our dear brothers Paul, Barnabas, and Silas, to name some of the more prominent ones, had completed their missionary endeavors. The message of Christ had gone to the Gentiles. A new generation of apostles, such as Timothy—whom you know well—Titus, Epaphroditus, and others, have been busy carrying on the work of establishing a witness to all nations. So, within one generation of the time Jesus spoke about these matters, we confidently could say that the gospel of the kingdom had reached "the whole world." This was another clear indication that the end was near.

That day on the Mount of Olives, Jesus described the events which would precede the terrible judgment that would come upon the house of Israel for rejecting, and ultimately crucifying, their Messiah. It was obvious to me that he spoke about something many of us would live to see in our lifetimes. As if to drive home the point that he had just made to the scribes and Pharisees at the foot of the mountain about an hour earlier, he repeated the same words again to us: *"This generation* will not pass away until all these things take place."

Years later, as I sat as a prisoner on the Island of Patmos, looking out over the Aegean Sea toward the continent of Asia Minor in the direction of the seven churches, I pondered these teachings of Jesus. I knew in my heart that the time for the fulfillment of his words must be very near. I saw the storm clouds gathering over Jerusalem. Jesus's coming in judgment was imminent.

As a nation, the Jews, with the exception of a remnant who believed and became part of the church, rejected and crucified God's Son. They chose a worldly king over a heavenly one. As I reflect back to that day when Jesus stood innocently before Pilate, burned into my memory is the scene outside the praetorium where the angered mob of chief priests and Jews went berserk. Pilate came out to them after questioning Jesus and asked if he should crucify their king. Their frenzied cries rang out to heaven: "Away with him! Away with him! Crucify him! We have no king but Caesar!"

God, in his mercy, gave our people a whole generation to consider what they had done and to repent. Some did. Peter brought in three thousand on the day of Pentecost. Judgment was stayed—for a while. But God's patience and long-suffering had finally reached their limits. Those days leading up to the destruction of Jerusalem were filled with tribulation, both in Jerusalem and, as you know, for Christians throughout the Roman Empire. For Jerusalem, it was the end. Never in the pages of Jewish history had there ever been, nor will there ever be, anything like it.

I did not mention these things that Jesus discussed with us in the first work I wrote from Ephesus just a few years ago, documenting our Lord's life and teachings, which has become widely circulated and known as my gospel. However, in the revelation that I was shown on Patmos, I was instructed to write down, in apocalyptic form, the fulfillment of the discourse recorded by Matthew, John Mark, and Luke, that we heard on the Mount of Olives that day.

With that introduction, I am almost ready to begin. But first, I must tell you one final story.

After our Lord's resurrection, at one of his appearings, he instructed us to go to Galilee and wait for him there. That is where it all began. That is where we gave up everything to follow him. It was as if he sent us back to Galilee to remind us of our initial commitment to him. Would we be willing to do it all over again? Before we would really be ready for service, he had to return us to the place of first love.

There, while I was in Galilee, a rumor started about me. I would like to take a moment to clear it up. The rumor began to spread that I was not going to die! I will tell you how that happened, because I think it has a bearing on why I was chosen to receive this revelation.

One day after Jesus's resurrection, he appeared to some of us at the Sea of Galilee. Peter had wanted to go fishing, so six of us joined him. We wound up spending a long, discouraging night in the boat. We had caught nothing. Suddenly, from on the shore as the day was just breaking, someone called out to us, "Have you caught any fish?"

"No," we yelled back.

Then this man shouted back to us, telling us to cast our net on the right side of the boat where we would find a great catch. Sure enough, we did. Then it struck me. "It is the Lord!"

Peter was so excited he could hardly contain himself. He threw on his clothes, jumped overboard, and swam like a madman for the shore. The rest of us wanted to follow him, but someone had to be responsible and stay with the boat, so we rowed back as swiftly as we could. Soon we joined the Lord and Peter around a crackling fire on the beach with our great catch. That ranks as one of my most memorable breakfasts ever—not because of the food we ate, but because of the fellowship. We sat there spellbound in the presence of the greatest fisherman this world has ever known. What a morning of rejoicing—to be with the risen Christ!

After our meal, Jesus singled out Peter. The Lord looked at him with a gaze that penetrated Peter's very soul. Then he asked Peter, "Simon, son of John, do you love me unconditionally?"

Peter was not the same boastful, swashbuckling man he had been a few years earlier. For that matter, he was not the same man from a few *weeks* earlier. He did not walk with the same swagger. A crucifixion had changed that. This Peter was a broken man who had seen all of his dreams, and all of his expectations of God and of himself, demolished by the cross.

Peter knew that he could not fake his true feelings anymore. Sorrowfully, and with tears, he responded, knowing that he had failed, knowing he did not love the Lord with a divine, unconditional love that would follow him into death as he had boasted before denying him three times. He choked out, "Lord, you know that I am fond of you."

Then Jesus asked him once more, and his response was the same.

Finally, the Lord asked of him a third time, "Are you fond of me?"

Peter broke down, weeping uncontrollably, saying, "Lord, you know all things. You know that I am fond of you."

That was one of Peter's finest hours.

But the story did not end there. Forty years later, as I look back to that conversation, I am awed once again by the omnipotent, all-knowing sovereignty of the Son of God. Surely Jesus did know all things—even what was to come in the future, down to the last detail, just as Peter had said.

The Lord continued speaking to Peter. He gave him instructions to feed his lambs and even hinted at how Peter would die. At that moment, my dear brother turned around and saw me standing there with my mouth gaping, riveted on very word. Peter then looked back to Jesus and asked him about my future. "Lord, and what about this man?"

Jesus said to him, "If I want him to remain until I come, what is that to you? You follow me!"

Many of the disciples interpreted what he said to Peter to mean that I would not die. But that is not at all what he meant.

Years later, by the time I had recorded the revelation, two great men of God had kept their appointments with their Lord. Peter was crucified upside down. The great apostle Paul was beheaded. All this took place at the hands of that red-bearded beast of a man, Nero, at the latter end of his reign—the same tyrant who had me banished to Patmos.

My brother James, of course, was killed long ago in the first Christian persecution. Now, I alone of the three "inner-circle apostles" remain. Clearly, Jesus's words were fulfilled, because I *did* remain until his coming. But that coming was not what many expected. Many thought he was referring to his second coming at the end of the world, when he will judge the living and the dead. Not so. Jesus was referring to a coming in judgment upon Jerusalem to fulfill what the prophets spoke of long ago. I had to remain in order to record these things for the churches and to provide the final revelation for the glorious New Covenant, of which we have been made partakers and ministers.

I notice that some of you here tonight are Hellenistic Jews. I see you have a copy of my letter containing the revelation spread out in front of you on the floor. I would like to ask all of you who can read to cluster around these brothers in one corner of the room. You can look over their shoulders and follow along as I go through the letter. And the rest of you, who are beyond reach of a scroll, just get comfortable, sit back, and enjoy the story.

CHAPTER 2
IT HELPS TO BE JEWISH

Many of you here are Gentiles—some former followers of the goddess Artemis, members of the magic cults, soldiers, slaves, and artisans. In fact, it is apparent that most of you come from a heathen background. Coming to Christ with no prior religious training in the way of the Jews can have its advantages, because there is often much they must unlearn once they become new creatures in Christ. In many ways, you are like a blank scroll upon which the Lord can inscribe anything he wants.

But growing up with the sacred Scriptures and the prophets of the Old Covenant has its advantages as well. Soaked in this rich heritage as we Jews are, there is no question that we have an easier time understanding some of the language used in the revelation I am presenting to you tonight. So much of the writing, as the Holy Spirit led, draws on images and events embedded in the writings of Moses, Daniel, Ezekiel, Jeremiah, Isaiah, Zechariah, Hosea, and others.

For example, look at the beginning of this letter where I wrote, "Behold, he is coming with the clouds, and every eye will see him, even those who pierced him; and all the tribes of the land"—referring to the land of Israel, not the whole earth—"will mourn over him." I would wager that some of you Gentiles probably thought that meant that Christ would literally come back to earth riding on a soft, pillowy cloud and the whole world would see him! I am sorry to disappoint you, but that is not going to happen! For the Jew, that imagery invokes the recollection of the God who came in the clouds on many occasions, rendering judgment against different nations, as in Isaiah where the prophet said, "Behold, the Lord is riding on a swift cloud, and is about to come to Egypt; the idols of Egypt will tremble at his presence and the heart of the Egyptians will melt within them."

I will share other examples like this with you later, for it is important that you understand the revelation in the context of all of Scripture.

"Those who pierced him" refers to those responsible for his crucifixion in Jerusalem, now a little more than forty years ago. They belonged to the generation Jesus promised would "not pass away until all of these things were fulfilled." All the tribes of the *land* clearly refer to the twelve tribes in the land of Israel.

Before getting any further into an explanation of my letter, I feel that I must tell you that, henceforth, my ministry will be an itinerant one. I am not here to settle down. Now that I have been released from my exile, there are many churches I need to visit, so I will not remain here to answer all of your questions. But if, after I am gone, any one of you still has any questions about the symbolism in this letter, go talk to some of our religiously educated Jewish brothers and sisters in Christ. They may be able to provide you with some further insights as to the apocalyptic language used in this letter.

If you do not understand everything in detail, do not worry. I have known many who have not completely understood this revelation but who still lead lives that are perfectly pleasing to God. Yet, there is a blessing for all those who read and hear the words of this prophecy and keep the things that are written in it. It is my prayer that this blessing will be yours tonight. So, let us begin.

CHAPTER 3

THE THINGS THAT MUST SHORTLY TAKE PLACE

From the outset of this letter, you should immediately sense that I believed the events I described would come to pass soon. I wrote that these were things that would "soon take place" and that "the time is near." I even recorded the Lord saying, "I am coming quickly." When I put pen to parchment on the Island of Patmos, I was certain the final judgment coming upon Jerusalem was, at the outside, less than four years away.

Because this is such an apocalyptic letter, I have found it interesting to hear that some who have read it have interpreted it in a very curious way. They have concluded that these events will not take place *quickly,* but rather, at some time far into the future. They quote something Peter said, that a day to the Lord is as a thousand years. Some dear brothers and sisters actually believe that much of this revelation is about events that may not take place for another thousand or two thousand years!

If any of you in this audience tonight fall into this camp, I would only ask you two simple questions: First, if *you* had been given the job of writing these things down, how else would you have communicated that these were events which would soon take place without using the precise words that I chose? What other words would *you* have used besides *quickly, shortly,* and *the time is near?*

The second question I have for you is this: If these events were not to happen soon, then what relevance or comfort would there have been in this letter for you and for our brothers and sisters in the other churches to whom it was written? Why would the Lord instruct me to address a letter to *you,* which was largely irrelevant to your situation or the day and age in which you live? It would be comparable to writing to someone in distress and telling him, "Be encouraged! Help is on the way. But it might take a thousand or two thousand years or more to get to you!" Remember that I am just a simple fisherman. When I wrote *quickly,* I meant *quickly!*

But of course, you know this. The idea that my revelation speaks of a far future date is a strange one and without support. I am sorry to have gotten sidetracked on that. Now, where was I? Ah, yes, back to the story.

As you know, I received this revelation during a time when Christians in

Rome were being dipped in oil and lit up as torches in the emperor's garden. Some were wrapped in skins and thrown to wild animals to be torn apart. And persecution was on its way to you here in Ephesus and to the other churches in Asia. Under these circumstances, I had to write this letter as a cryptograph in order to veil its meaning from the minds of those in worldly positions of authority, in case it fell into their hands. If I had been too explicit—if I had named the beast instead of giving him the number 666, for example—it would have resulted in even further persecution to the churches and more bloodshed for our brothers and sisters in Christ, to say nothing of what would have happened to me—though I am ready to die for my Lord if need be. There were martyrs enough without me putting more saints at risk.

CHAPTER 4

THE REVELATION OF JESUS CHRIST

Our Lord Jesus Christ was given a revelation by his Father.

It was given to him *first*. All that he spoke to us on the Mount of Olives nearly forty years prior to that day on Patmos when I received the same revelation were events he had already seen. He saw the wars that would come. He saw the nations that would rise against nations. He saw Jerusalem surrounded by armies. He saw the temple destroyed, with not one stone left upon another. And he saw the joy that was set before him—his glorious bride, for whom he was willing to lay down everything and even endure death on the tree.

This was *his* revelation.

I do not know when Jesus received it from his Father—whether it came to him gradually or all at once. But I do know that it consumed him, especially in those final days he was here on earth. This revelation—which was *his*—was the one I received on the Island of Patmos. And this is what I was instructed to share with the churches.

"I was in spirit on the Lord's Day and I heard . . ."

I praise the Lord that over these many years, I have learned something about what it means to be "in spirit." First, I saw how Jesus lived by the Spirit of God that was in him. He heard the Father's voice and saw what the Father was doing—*in his spirit.*

Certainly it was wonderful to know him according to the flesh when he walked among us. But since that day behind locked doors, after the resurrection, when Christ appeared to me and the other apostles and breathed on us and said, "Receive the Holy Spirit," we started to know him in a new and different way. We began to know him as he knew his Father—*in spirit.* He had come to live in us—in our spirits. That has been your experience as well. Now, it is from our spirits that he speaks, reveals, and illumines our understanding so we can know him and know his will.

In this revelation, the very first thing I saw in my spirit was the seven churches in Asia, with the Lord himself walking in their midst. He was clothed in his priestly robes, fearful in appearance but full of all wisdom and knowledge. He knew what each church needed. He could identify with their trials and tribulations, having walked this earth and gone through the fires of testing himself, emerging with "feet like burnished bronze, when it has been made to glow in a furnace."

"His eyes were like a flame of fire." Those were the same flashing eyes that I saw on the day Jesus made his final exit from the temple and spoke of the judgment to come. I saw him as the everlasting High Priest, standing in the heavens before the lampstands, which were the churches. The function of a lampstand is to hold up the light, just as the purpose of the churches is to hold up Christ. Our Lord was in their midst, trimming the wicks, cutting back what was old, and adding fresh, new oil, so that the light of their testimony could burn brighter.

"Out of his mouth came a sharp two-edged sword." He was speaking to the churches, praising and encouraging them for what they were doing well, but also reproving and disciplining them for where they were falling short.

The churches were the seven *golden* lampstands. Gold, in the Scriptures, represents the nature of God. The churches were divine in origin. To be an expression of the church requires that a corporate group of chosen ones live together by a Life that is divine. As the woman was taken from the man in the garden, so the churches have come out of Christ. They are bone of his bone. What was divine and of Christ would remain, but what originated from man and fallen flesh needed to be trimmed away.

It is quite significant to me that among the seven churches in the vision, Jerusalem, the place where the church was born, the only and then the most prominent church in the early days, was not listed. Shortly after I wrote down the revelation, the church in Jerusalem ceased to exist. Christ had moved on. He had left Judaism behind. His primary work now has been among the Gentiles.

CHAPTER 5

THROUGH THE DOOR AND TO THE THRONE

Tonight, I am not going to discuss the messages the Lord gave to each of the seven churches in Asia. You, my dear Ephesians, already know your own portion of the revelation well. I praise God that most of you have heeded the warnings given you by the Spirit to repent and return to your first love. Though outwardly you were serving and doing many things well, yet inwardly, many of you were experiencing a problem in relation to your hearts. You must always remember that service to the Lord should come as a response to spending time with the Lord, loving him, and then responding to what he is doing within you. What counts is not how much you can do for God, but how much God can do working in and through you. He is looking for lovers first, not slaves!

From the questions about this letter that others have raised, I think most people become confused with the events *following* what the Lord said to the seven churches. So that is what I will be discussing this evening. I would like for you to come with me to the point in the letter where I looked and saw a door open in heaven.

A voice called to me, "Come up here!" And immediately I was once again in spirit.

The first vision I had was of Christ in the midst of the churches. This next vision took me to the throne.

What these eyes beheld, in spiritual realms, defies words. Pen and ink cannot describe the reality of the spiritual world that I was allowed to see! This *was* the heavenly sanctuary that Moses saw, which became the pattern for the tabernacle. My eyes were fixed on the reality of what the mercy seat in the tabernacle only represented: the throne of God. And I saw the glory of the one who sits on that throne!

Human language cannot stretch far enough to describe what I saw. I saw him who dwells in unapproachable light! Brilliant, like the most brilliant jasper stone one could ever imagine! A diamond beyond any diamond. Enthroned above all creation, he is so transparently pure, clear, yet sparkling and blazing. The most perfect diamond that has ever been dug from any mine on this earth is, at best, a worthless shadow of this one who fills the heavens with his glory. He is pure, resplendent light, and in him is no darkness at all.

Clothed in this brilliant light, he appeared to me also as a sardius stone, blood-red in its hue, projecting royalty and power beyond compare.

The rainbow surrounding his throne was a reminder of the faithfulness of the covenant-keeping, Almighty One. Not only was the bow a remembrance of the promise that he made with Noah and every living creature on the earth that the earth would never again be destroyed by a flood, but it testified to his faithfulness to fulfill all the words of the covenants made with Abraham and Moses, spoken by the prophets and Jesus himself, pertaining to those things which would quickly come to pass.

As for the living creatures and the elders, you are probably curious as to who they were. I am sorry to disappoint you. They did not stop to introduce themselves! I was not the center of attention, nor were they. All I know is that they represented the whole of creation, both man and beast, and that all eyes, including theirs and mine, were riveted on the spectacle before us—the one sitting upon the throne.

The living creatures incessantly proclaimed, "Holy, holy, holy is the Lord God, the Almighty!" without pause, giving him honor, glory, and thanks. Indeed, there is none like him. He is truly distinct, separated, totally elevated above all creation, awe-inspiring in transcendence and perfection.

At the sound of the creatures' praise, the twenty-four elders who sat on their thrones fell to their knees in worship, casting their glorious crowns before him, giving him praise as the source of all honor, glory, and power.

Of this I can assure you: it is of no matter whether we are elders, the highest of creatures of God's creation, angels, or men—when that which is created beholds the Creator, there is only one response, and that is to worship.

May I stop here and admonish you, my dear brothers and sisters, once again? Love God. Become his worshipers. For never has there been on the mountain of Jerusalem, or on Mount Gerizim in Samaria, or in any heathen temple or terrestrial place, such worship as there is in heavenly places! So practice! Get ready! For one day, you all will join in that heavenly chorus. Learn to worship him now in your spirits and in reality—even if it is by faith. For the Father seeks such people to be his worshipers.

CHAPTER 6
THE CELESTIAL COURTROOM

On the other side of heaven's door, in that timeless, unseen dimension, was the mother of all courtrooms. Presiding over that courtroom was the Almighty. In his right hand was a scroll sealed with seven seals.

Court was in session. Through the revelation shown to me in spirit, I was given access to this spectacular scene—a witness, if you will, or a messenger—summoned to see and then to report back to earth the judgment that was being handed down. For a moment, near blinded, I gazed upon this one whose light was unapproachable—but I saw no one worthy to approach him, to take the scroll, and to execute the judgment. So I wept greatly.

Suddenly, one appeared. Instantly I recognized him! It was the Lord Jesus, the Lamb who had been slain, but who was now standing! Only he was worthy to take the scroll and to carry out the judgments that it contained.

You must forgive me if I depart, on occasion, from my description of the vision. At times, like now, I may feel compelled to share something with you that our Lord did or said while he was with us on earth to help clarify what I saw.

You may remember having been told about or reading the story of that Sabbath day in Jerusalem when the Lord healed the man who had been sick for thirty-eight years. This poor soul had been coming to the pool of Bethesda for years hoping to receive healing from its waters, but he never had the strength or opportunity to lift himself in. Jesus did what that religious pool could never do. Jesus said to the man, "Get up, pick up your pallet and walk."

Because of this miracle, the Jews sought to kill Jesus. To them, he had committed two crimes: First, he had healed a man on the Sabbath. Second, he had made himself out to be equal with God.

Following that incident, Jesus told the Jews that he was the one to whom all judgment was given.

"For just as the Father raises the dead and gives them life, even so the Son also gives life to whom he wishes. For not even the Father judges anyone, but he has given all judgment to the Son, so that all will honor the Son, even as they honor the Father."

Jesus then continued, "... and he gave me authority to execute judgment, because I am the Son of Man."

The Son took on flesh and blood and became a man. He was fully and perfectly human, yet fully and perfectly divine. Therefore judgment was given to him to judge all of mankind.

Now, back to the scene at the throne.

The scroll that was given to Christ in the heavenly vision was national Israel's divorce decree. Under the Old Covenant, God had taken Israel to be his wife. But because of her repeated unfaithfulness, harlotry, and idolatry—and because of the final act of putting the Son of his love to death—that special relationship was over. Jesus spoke of enacting a New Covenant with a new people who would be his followers and love him as a bride loves her husband. But before this New Covenant could fully be implemented, it was necessary that the judgments set forth for those who had violated the Old Covenant be carried out. The only one worthy to execute that judgment was the Son of Man himself. As is customary, a will or a divorce decree such as this must be opened in front of witnesses. The witnesses in this courtroom were the four living creatures, the twenty-four elders, myriads upon myriads of heavenly hosts, and me.

Prior to my banishment to Patmos, copies of the letters written by Matthew, John Mark, and Luke made their way to Asia and circulated among you. They each record the parable Jesus told about the landowner who planted a vineyard and then went on a long journey. At harvest time he sent his slaves to the vine-growers to receive his produce. The slaves were beaten, killed, and stoned. Again he sent another group of slaves, larger than the first, and the same thing happened to them. Finally, he sent his son, thinking they would respect him. But the wicked vine-growers seized him, threw him out of the vineyard, and killed him as well.

When Jesus asked the chief priests and the Pharisees what the owner would do to these vine-growers, they answered him, "He will bring those wretches to a wretched end, and will rent out the vineyard to other vine-growers."

Continuing, Jesus said, "Therefore I say to you the kingdom of God will be taken away from you and given to a people producing the fruit of it." The chief priests and Pharisees heard that parable and others like it, and they understood that he was speaking of them.

Following that teaching, Jesus addressed them with another parable about a king who wanted to give a wedding feast for his son. Those who were invited were not interested, and they seized, mistreated, and killed the messengers. Then he said, "But the king was enraged and he sent his armies and destroyed those murderers and set their city on fire."

My friends, Israel rejected her bridegroom. The resurrected Lamb of God, who was standing before the throne with the scroll in his hand, was about to break open the seals. When he did, all that he had spoken to Peter, James, Andrew, and me nearly forty years earlier would come to pass. Judgment was about to come on the vine-growers of Israel.

CHAPTER 7
A SHORT HISTORY LESSON

The plaintiffs in this heavenly courtroom scene were the martyrs. The chief martyr was the Lord himself. The accused was Jerusalem. Next, "I saw underneath the altar the souls of those who had been slain because of the word of God, and because of the testimony which they had maintained."

Before the temple was destroyed, when the Jewish priests used to place sacrifices upon the altar and kill them, the blood from the slain animals accumulated underneath the altar. In like fashion, under this heavenly altar, the blood of the martyrs had accumulated, "And they cried out to heaven with a loud voice saying, 'How long, O Lord, holy and true, will you refrain from judging and avenging our blood on those who dwell in the land?'"

The time for judgment had come! There was no turning back. About 650 years earlier, God had used foreign invaders, the Babylonians, to bring judgment on Jerusalem for her unfaithfulness. Now she was about to be judged and fall again. This time it would be at the hands of the Romans.

Before I continue, a short history lesson might be beneficial. Some of you might not be familiar with both Roman and Judean history.

Prior to 63 B.C., Jerusalem was part of the Hasmonean Kingdom. Then Pompey, head of the Roman army, captured the city. In 37 B.C. the Romans named Herod, a half-Jew, as king of the Jews. He governed Judea for thirty-six years. After taking control, Herod launched an ambitious building program. The crown jewel of his efforts was the reconstruction of the Jerusalem temple. Despite this, the Jews hated him. They viewed him as a despot. He had murdered his wife, children, relatives, and anyone he suspected of opposing him. Augustus said of him, "Better to be Herod's swine than his son!"

Though king of the Jews, Herod was far from faithful to the Jewish religion. Even though he rebuilt the temple, he also offered sacrifices at the pagan temple of Jupiter and commissioned the building of many other heathen temples. In addition, he was responsible for the slaughter of all the young children in Bethlehem after the visit by the Magi who came from the east to see Jesus. The Jews never forgave him for that despicable act.

Archelaus, Herod's eldest son, succeeded him and ruled from 1 B.C. to A.D. 6. He started his reign off on the wrong foot by ruthlessly crushing a revolt, slaughtering three thousand Jews in the temple court. One rebellion followed another, and finally Archelaus was deposed and banished. His younger brother, Herod Antipas, inherited his father's kingdom.

Determined to stabilize the region, Roman officials appointed a procurator, or governor, for Judea. This man reported directly to the emperor. You have all heard of Pontius Pilate. He was the procurator who sentenced Jesus to death.

Jerusalem came under more direct Roman control as Roman troops moved in to occupy the city. They were housed at the Roman garrison called the Fortress of Antonia that bordered the temple on the north.

Herod Antipas is best remembered among Christians as the king who was denounced by John the Baptist for marrying his brother's wife. That got John's head cut off. In A.D. 39, Agrippa I, also called Herod, replaced Antipas. Agrippa's attack on the church resulted in his sudden death at age fifty-four in A.D. 44. He was the one who put my brother James to death with a sword and who also imprisoned Peter. But the Lord struck him. He was eaten by worms and died. His son, also named Agrippa, then became king and was ruling at the time of the Jewish uprising against Rome. Beginning in Jerusalem, the revolt spread quickly throughout most of Judea and Galilee and then to Jews residing throughout the empire.

Jews frequently rioted against Roman rule. The Zealot party had been doing so since the days of Herod the Great. They despised Roman occupation and heavy taxation. Their slogan became, "No God but Yahweh, no tax but to the temple, no friend but the Zealot."

One by one, false "messiahs" arose from among the Zealots, claiming to bring liberation. They instigated riots. Most of them were arrested and crucified.

Jesus, too, was accused of treason and crucified. In the years following his death and resurrection, Roman rule became a harder yoke to bear, and rioting became more frequent. Finally, in A.D. 66, the Jews successfully revolted and seized control of Jerusalem.

Commissioned by the emperor Nero, Vespasian marched on Jerusalem with fifty thousand troops in order to retake the city. He arrived in the spring of A.D. 67. Ultimately, Vespasian's son Titus completed the campaign after a brutal five-month siege that ended in the late summer of A.D. 70.

The period of time between the beginning of the fighting and the destruction of the temple spanned forty-two months, or three-and-a-half years. This is significant, as you will see in a short while.

Now, let us return to the scroll and the breaking of the seals.

CHAPTER 8
THE BREAKING OF THE SEALS

The breaking of the first four seals released four horsemen. The first horseman was riding on a white horse with a bow in his hand and a crown on his head. This was the Lord Jesus, who was leading the battle. No arrow was in his bow. It had already been shot and found its mark. The victory has been won. His enemies have been defeated. The crown on his head indicated that his victory had already been secured.

"And another, a red horse, went out; and to him who sat on it was granted to take peace from the land; and that men should slay one another."

The red horse represents war and blood. Three-and-a-half years of war between the Jews and Rome produced over one million Jewish casualties. Thousands more were taken captive as slaves or sent to fight wild beasts in the amphitheaters of Caesarea and Antioch. Peace was taken from the land. The commencement of the Jewish War marked the official end of the Pax Romana.

"That men would slay one another" refers to the great civil war fought within Jerusalem itself, as three warring factions of Jews and religious zealots fought viciously—brutally butchering one another. John of Gischala led one faction, Simon bar Gioras another, and Eleazer, son of Simon, a third. Not only did the Jews have to contend with attacking Roman armies from outside the city, but at the same time, their own civil war raged even *within* its sacred walls.

The third seal was broken, and I saw a black horse. "And he who sat on it had a pair of scales in his hand. And I heard something like a voice in the center of the four living creatures saying, 'A quart of wheat for a denarius and three quarts of barley for a denarius.'"

The food supply became scarce as Jerusalem was surrounded. Titus built a siege wall around the city in order to starve out the inhabitants. On the heels of war came famine. A denarius was a whole day's wage, and it was only enough to buy bread for one person. The famine became so cruel that elderly people, women, and children lay dead in the streets from starvation. Jerusalem's inhabitants threw off all restraint. Children stole food from the mouths of their parents, and parents, likewise, from the mouths of their children. Within the city, people could no longer gather food, so many resorted to eating belts and shoes, searching the sewers, foraging through old cattle dunghills, and devouring anything they could find.

In the final days, Jews trapped inside the city even resorted to the most detestable and heinous practice of cannibalism. Desperate women ate their own babies. This fulfilled another curse recorded in Deuteronomy, which was a consequence for the peoples' breaking of the covenant:

"Then you shall eat the offspring of your own body, the flesh of your sons and of your daughters whom the Lord your God has given you, during the siege and the distress by which your enemy shall oppress you."

The fourth horse to ride through the land was ashen in appearance. This horse represents pestilence. Putrefying bodies covered the ground. Birds of prey feasted on the carnage. The smell of rotting human flesh engulfed the city. With the lack of adequate sanitation, disease was rampant.

Jews were being slaughtered everywhere, not only inside the city, but also in the countryside of Judea. Roman soldiers massacred them as they fled, forcing them into the Jordan River. Blood from the slaughter colored the waters red. The river carried these bloated bodies and dumped them into the Dead Sea. The water supply became polluted. Death, starvation, disease, and horror stalked the streets of the great city, swallowing up their victims.

Brothers and sisters, I see your heavy hearts as you bow your heads, contemplating the unfathomable grief of the catastrophe I have just described. I assure you, I share your grief.

CHAPTER 9

A JEWISH HISTORIAN

So far, I have given you my account of the destruction of Jerusalem as I saw it in the vision. But tonight, I would also like to share how one eyewitness described these same events.

Prior to my coming here to Ephesus, a kinsman visited me as he traveled through this region from the empire's capital. He had some scrolls given to him by an acquaintance, a Jewish historian who lives in Rome. He gave them to me because he wanted to lighten his load and knew that I would take good care of them. I brought them along tonight because I thought you might like to hear a firsthand account for yourselves.

I was told that the author plans to put these writings into a book about the history of the Jewish people. I have here some of the rough drafts. One day you might see them for yourselves, bound in leather, being sold by merchants at the agora.

The author is a man named Flavius Josephus. He is a controversial figure among the Jews. Many consider him a traitor.

Josephus visited Rome in A.D. 63, prior to the Jewish War. He was deeply impressed by the strength and glory he beheld in the capital city. He returned to Judea only to find his countrymen embroiled in the controversy against Rome, which he strongly opposed.

God had it that Josephus came to be employed by Titus, the son of Vespasian, during the final siege of Jerusalem. Josephus acted both as a translator for and negotiator with the Jewish rebels. Being on the scene and in the victor's camp, he had opportunity to document the events that took place. After the war, he retired to Rome where he is now compiling all his materials.

I am not sure why Josephus gave these manuscripts to our brother. But they are proving to be greatly valuable to me. It almost seems as if God placed Josephus on the scene in Jerusalem to document and bear witness to the fulfillment of what I saw in my vision.

Let me read you a brief portion that seems to fit at this point in our story.

In reference to the battle that raged from one end of Israel's borders to the other as the Roman troops made their way to Jerusalem, Josephus describes a scene at the Lake of Gennesareth, also known as the Sea of Galilee:

"As many of these were repulsed when they were getting ashore as were killed by the darts upon the lake; and the Romans leaped out of their vessels, and destroyed a great many more upon the land; one might then see the lake all bloody, and full of dead bodies, for not one of them escaped. And a terrible stink, and a very sad sight there was on the following days over that country; for as for the shores, they were full of shipwrecks, and dead bodies all swelled."[31]

He continues to describe the scene at the Lake Asphaltitis, where the Jordan River empties into the Dead Sea, as it is also known:

" ... because not only the whole of the country through which they had fled was filled with slaughter, and Jordan could not be passed over, by reason of the dead bodies that were in it, but because the lake Asphaltitis was also full of dead bodies, that were carried down into it by the river."[32]

I believe God will use Josephus's writings in future generations as a witness to confirm that what I am telling you is true. I will have more to share from his account of these events in a moment. But let us now return to the revelation.

Following the scene of the pestilence being released on the land, the fifth seal was broken. I saw the martyrs, whose prayers had reached the throne of heaven, crying out for justice against those in the land who had spilled their innocent blood.

As the sin and hardness of Israel increased leading up to the destruction of Jerusalem and the temple in A.D. 70, the persecuted church in Jerusalem began to pray for the Lord's judgment to come quickly. Those prayers originated in heaven and were poured out of the golden censer to earth by an angel who stood at the altar. When the church returned them to heaven, they found their answer. Before God works, he reveals his will to the prophets. Heaven and earth were now in harmony, and God was swift to act.

When the sixth seal was opened, I saw the sun turning black, the moon becoming like blood, and the stars falling from the sky. The whole Jewish political, civil, and religious framework came crashing down like a palace crumbling in an earthquake.

Once again I need to remind you, especially you Gentiles, of the poetic and figurative language used in our Hebrew writings. For those of you who can read, if you go back to the writings of Isaiah and the story of the Lord's judgment of Babylon, you will find the same kind of descriptive language used. Isaiah wrote about how the Lord stirred up the Medes to conquer the Babylonians and described it this way:

"For the stars of heaven and their constellations will not flash forth their light; the sun will be dark when it rises, and the moon will not shed its light."

In Isaiah's account, the heavenly lights that guided the Babylonians were extinguished. The sun, moon, and stars represented the kings, rulers, and authorities whose lights were darkened.

Daniel's writings also employed the same terms and style:

"Those who have insight will shine brightly like the brightness of the expanse of heaven and those who lead the many to righteousness, like the stars forever and ever."

In our day, Israel's rulers and spiritual leaders, who were intended to provide insight and lead many to righteousness, were in darkness. Their lights had gone out, so they were brought down.

Ezekiel also used similar imagery. But this time, it was in reference to God's judgment on Egypt:

"And when I extinguish you, I will cover the heavens, and darken their stars; I will cover the sun with a cloud, and the moon will not give its light. All the shining lights in the heavens I will darken over you and will set darkness on your land."

For those of you who are waiting for the sun literally to become black, for the moon to turn to blood, and for the stars to fall from the sky, wait no longer! That was symbolic language. Just as the four horses represented by the first four seals were symbolic, so the extinguishing of these heavenly lights was also symbolic. It meant there was no light left in Israel.

"Then the kings of the land and the great men and the commanders and the rich and the strong and every slave and free man hid themselves in the caves and among the rocks of the mountains."

This describes the last days of the siege against Jerusalem when defeat at the hands of the Romans was inevitable. Jews tried to escape by hiding themselves in caves and among the rocks and rubble, hoping the Roman soldiers would not find them and add their blood to that which already flowed in the streets.

Let the words of Josephus bear witness once again. In Jerusalem, he says, dead bodies "obstructed the very lanes" and "made the whole city run down with blood to such a degree indeed that the fire of many of the houses was quenched with these men's blood."[33]

"And they said to the mountains and to the rocks, 'Fall on us and hide us from the presence of him who sits on the throne, and from the wrath of the Lamb; for the great day of their wrath has come; and who is able to stand?'"

CHAPTER 10

SIGNED, SEALED AND DELIVERED: THE 144,000

In my vision, a brief interlude occurred between the breaking of the sixth and seventh seals. A strong angel cried out to the four angels to whom it was granted to harm the land and the sea:

"Do not harm the land or the sea or the trees until we have sealed the bond-servants of our God on their foreheads . . . And I heard the number of those who were sealed, one hundred and forty-four thousand sealed from every tribe of the sons of Israel."

Now, the question before us is: who were those 144,000?

Here is what I was shown about them:

"These are the ones who have come out of the great tribulation, and they have washed their robes and made them white in the blood of the Lamb. For this reason, they are before the throne of God; and they serve him day and night in his temple; and he who sits on the throne will spread his tabernacle over them. They will hunger no longer, nor thirst anymore; nor will the sun beat down on them, nor any heat; for the Lamb in the center of the throne will be their shepherd, and will guide them to springs of water of life; and God will wipe every tear from their eyes."

I want to go back to the scene of the destruction at Jerusalem. I have been talking about the plight of the Jews. But what happened to the church there? What became of those Jewish Christians who were the firstfruits to believe in Christ?

I was shown in the vision that the total destruction of the land was to be suspended until a remnant from every tribe of the believing sons of Israel was sealed.

This 144,000 was the remnant of Jews who had heard the gospel of the kingdom that we preached beginning on the day of Pentecost, and who recognized Jesus as their Messiah. Some of these same believers were those who, in the early days of the church in Jerusalem, sold their property to help take care of the needs of the saints when we lived with all things in common. Selling real estate in Jerusalem in those days was a prudent response to Jesus's warning about the coming destruction. Property values were about to plummet to zero! Though many fled Jerusalem prior to this, in the years leading up to the war with Rome, there were those who stayed until the end. God marked off this remnant and sealed them from the coming destruction. How he did that was nothing short of amazing!

Notice that these 144,000 were those who had come out of the *great tribulation*. In our nation's history, there has never been a tribulation so great, so concentrated, or so devastating as what the city of Jerusalem experienced in those three-and-a-half years at the hands of the Romans. Yet, while the Jews were facing their judgment, innocent Christians were still entrapped within the city. Not all of them would die a martyr's death. There was a plan for their rescue. And that plan was as miraculous as the day the Israelites escaped from the Egyptians and walked on dry land to pass through the Red Sea!

Our Lord had warned us years before from the Mount of Olives of what we were to do when we saw all these signs come to pass:

"But when you see Jerusalem surrounded by armies, then recognize that her desolation is near. Then those who are in Judea must flee to the mountains, and those who are in the midst of the city must leave, and those who are in the country must not enter the city; because these are days of vengeance, so that all things which are written will be fulfilled."

In addition to our Lord's warning, confirming prophecies came through various brothers and sisters in the church that Jerusalem's desolation was at hand. The Roman armies had surrounded the city. It was time to flee.

Yet, escape seemed impossible. The Romans attacked relentlessly. Then, for no apparent reason, Vespasian suddenly, but briefly, suspended the barrage on the city. Later, we discovered that he had been distracted by news of civil war breaking out in other parts of the empire following Nero's suicide. He returned to Rome, turning the command for the war with the Jews over to his son, Titus, and eventually became emperor, bringing some stability back to the empire.

Behind the scenes, though, it was the Lamb, seated on the throne in unseen realms, who had orchestrated this lull in the battle. During that window of opportunity, he led an exodus of Jewish believers out of the city to a safe haven called Pella, about sixty miles north of Jerusalem, on the other side of the Jordan River. There they found refuge. The 144,000 were safely sealed and had come out of the great tribulation!

Now, my dear brothers and sisters in Asia Minor, Jews and Gentiles alike: we know that our Lord promised us persecution and tribulation. But does this story not give you hope? Jesus Christ is enthroned in the heavens and rules over the kings of the earth. You are graven in the palm of his hands. If he was so concerned about our Judean brethren as to seal, protect, and deliver them from the wrath that was to come, do you not think that he is equally concerned about you?

CHAPTER 11
CURTAIN CALL FOR JERUSALEM

The final curtain fell on Jerusalem with the opening of the seventh seal. An angel took a golden censor "filled with the fire of the altar and threw it down to the land."

The Roman armies entered the city, slaughtered or took captive those who were left, plundered its gold and riches, razed the city, and then set it ablaze. At first, Titus opposed destroying the magnificent temple. But as his soldiers overran the temple area, God's purposes overruled the determinations of men. Titus's orders were ignored. They set the temple aflame. In the words of Josephus:

"But as for the legions that came running thither, neither any persuasions nor any threatenings could restrain their violence, but each one's own passion was his commander at this time; and as they were crowding into the temple together, many of them were trampled on by one another, while a great number fell among the ruins of the cloisters, which were still hot and smoking, and were destroyed in the same miserable way with those whom they had conquered: and when they were come near the holy house, they made as if they did not so much as hear Caesar's orders to the contrary; but they encouraged those that were before them to set it on fire . . . And thus it was the holy house burnt down, without Caesar's approbation."[34]

Orders were given to leave nothing standing, with the exception of three towers along with the western wall so that generations to come would see with what power Rome had demolished such a great city. As for the temple, Jesus's solemn prediction had come to pass: "Truly I say to you, not one stone here will be left upon another, which will not be torn down."

Little did the victorious Roman army know that their part in this drama was not to show to future generations the power of Rome! Rather, it was to show God's wrath toward those who forsook the covenant and committed the greatest crime that history has ever recorded.

CHAPTER 12
A BITTERSWEET VISION

Having been raised a Jew, I find it painful to talk about this tragedy in Jewish history. I have many fond memories of growing up as a boy around the Sea of Galilee. I enjoyed the holidays and the festivals. All my friends and relatives were Jewish.

And we revered the city of Jerusalem. It was the City of David. It was where Solomon built the temple. It was the place for the ark. It was where the tribes came up to worship the Lord.

For travelers approaching Jerusalem, the city was like no other. It stood as a city set on a hill. At night, its glow lit up the darkness for miles around.

From Mount Ebo, the place across the Jordan where Moses looked out over the Promised Land, one could view the rooftops of the city, and at its center, see the cream stones and gold of its magnificent temple. Josephus, our young historian, gave this eloquent description of Jerusalem: "When the morning sun burst upon the white marble of the Temple, Mount Moriah glittered like a hill of snow; and when its rays struck the golden roof of the sacred edifice, the whole mount gleamed and sparkled as if it were in flames."[35]

I remember the faces of certain of my countrymen in Jerusalem—those in the shops and marketplaces buying and selling. These were the very ones who were starved, raped, killed, and sold into slavery in the war with Rome. The thought of their fate brings pain and sadness to my heart.

I also remember the religious leaders, and I recall how Jesus warned us about the leaven of the Pharisees, who daily paraded around the city in their religious attire. They relished their place of prominence and performed their rituals in order to be noticed by men. They, too, were destroyed.

Our Lord came to his own, but his own did not receive him. As a result of that rejection, that great city, with all its memories, is no longer standing today.

I am getting a little ahead of myself in the letter. But the fate of Jerusalem and Israel was the bitterness in my stomach that I described when the angel gave me the little book, which was the revelation, and told me to eat it. The sweetness referred to the glories to follow.

"I took the little book out of the angel's hand and ate it and in my mouth it was as sweet as honey, and when I had eaten it, my stomach was made bitter."

There is much more to tell. I am sorry to say that the story gets worse before it gets better. Trust me, though, there is a glorious ending!

CHAPTER 13
MULTIFACETED SPECTACLE

When I stepped through the door into heavenly places, I entered a dimension that was not limited by time and space. I was in a heavenly, timeless realm, viewing things that were about to *quickly* take place on earth.

Being earthbound, we think linearly: one, two, three, four; this happened, then that. But as you attempt to determine the sequence of events in this revelation, linear thinking does not apply.

The best way I can describe the order in which events occurred is to compare it to watching a multifaceted theatrical performance in your grand amphitheater. Imagine observing several acts taking place simultaneously, with one act sometimes spilling over to another. Imagine also that you had arrived at the play just as it was about to start, and someone told you to hurry and take your seat because it was about to start *quickly*.

Now, apply that same perspective to the revelation I am describing to you. I have just finished talking about the meaning of the scroll and the seven seals that were broken. Following that in the letter comes the seven trumpets; then the two witnesses; a woman who was with child, clothed with the sun, with the moon under her feet and a crown of twelve stars on her head; and then a beast coming up out of the sea. To our natural way of thinking, one thing happened, followed by the next, and then the next. The reality is, much of this was going on *here on earth,* simultaneously! I was watching one play, so to speak, but trying to describe what was going on in several acts or scenes that were taking place at the same time. What is important for you to remember is what I wrote in the first sentence of the letter. These were things that must *shortly* take place.

CHAPTER 14

THE TRUMPETS

The first trumpet brought "hail and fire, mixed with blood, and they were thrown to the land; and a third of the land was burned up, and a third of the trees were burned up, and all the green grass was burned up."

This described what happened as a result of the Roman scorched-earth decimation of Judea as they set fire to trees, fields, and vegetation. Again, our historian, Josephus, vividly describes the scene:

"The countryside, like the city, was a pitiful sight, for where once there had been a multitude of trees and parks, there was now an utter wilderness stripped bare of timber; and no stranger who had seen the old Judea and the glorious suburbs of her capital, and now beheld utter desolation, could refrain from tears or suppress a groan at so terrible a change. The war had blotted out every trace of beauty, and no one who had known it in the past and came upon it suddenly would have recognized the place."[36]

I have told you of the breaking of the seals. The seals breaking and the trumpets sounding were taking place simultaneously. The second, third, and fourth trumpets merely announced what was released on earth as the seals were broken and give more detail about happenings I have already discussed.

With the fifth trumpet I saw "a star from heaven which had fallen to earth; and the key of the bottomless pit was given to him. He opened the bottomless pit; and smoke went up out of the pit, like the smoke of a great furnace . . . then out of the smoke came locusts upon the land, and power was given them, as the scorpions."

And the angels were told that they should only hurt those "who do not have the seal of God on their foreheads."

These locusts were given power "to torment." Their faces were like "the faces of men and they had hair like the hair of women, and their teeth were like the teeth of lions."

It should be clear to you that the forces I described were demonic. The locusts that were given power were the demons of hell that were released into the land by the prince of demons. Within Jerusalem, the inhabitants had as much to fear from the demonic activity of those days, which manifested itself in murdering, butchering, rape, sodomy, and lawlessness, as they did from the Romans. Josephus again describes the depravity he witnessed, especially among the Zealots:

"With their insatiable hunger for loot, [the Zealots] ransacked the houses of the wealthy, murdered men and violated women for sport; they drank their spoils with blood, and from mere satiety they shamelessly gave themselves up to effeminate practices, plaiting their hair and putting on women's clothes, drenching themselves with perfumes and painting their eyelids to make themselves attractive. They copied not merely the dress, but also the passions of women, devising in the excess of licentiousness unlawful pleasures in which they wallowed as in a brothel. Thus they entirely polluted the city with their foul practices. Yet though they wore women's faces, their hands were murderous. They would approach with mincing steps, then suddenly become fighting men, and whipping out their swords from under their dyed cloaks, they would run through every passerby."[37]

Hell was in session in Jerusalem. Demonic spirits tormented those who had not repented and turned to Christ. The only ones exempt from this demonic activity were the remnant—the 144,000 whom God had sealed. His hand mercifully protected them as it protected those few in the wicked cities of Sodom and Gomorrah just before their utter annihilation.

CHAPTER 15

THE MYSTERY OF GOD

A sixth angel sounded, and "four angels who are bound at the great river Euphrates" were released. "And the number of their armies were two myriads of myriads."

As in times past when foreign invaders crossed over the Euphrates to make war with apostate Israel, I saw a horde of mounted Roman reinforcements—the tenth legion—cross the Euphrates and enter the battle. Their number seemed beyond human comprehension. But in the spiritual realm I saw an invisible force of two hundred million demons riding with them. Killing, burning, and devastation followed in their wake as they headed for Jerusalem.

During these days, the official announcement came from heaven: "The mystery of God is finished."

With the fall of Jerusalem, all shadows and types from the old sacrificial system of worship were destroyed. Not one reminder of the old system was left standing. The days of pictures were over. The altar from which our forefathers offered sacrifices was only a picture pointing to the cross. With Christ's death, there was no need for a physical altar any longer.

The sacrifices and burnt offerings that the priests continually offered up were also all pictures of Christ. There was no longer any need for thousands of animals to be slaughtered each year to remind us that without the shedding of blood, there is no remission of sins. Christ had shed his blood, and his sacrifice has once and for all cleansed us from our sins.

The temple, made up of limestone blocks that were built together and inhabited by the Spirit of God, was only a picture of the *real* temple of God. The church, which is his body made up of living stones, and Christ indwelling us, have made the old temple obsolete.

What is that mystery of God?

The mystery referred to here is exactly what our brother Paul described in the letter he wrote to you some years ago. It is the mystery "which in other generations was not made known to the sons of men, as it has now been revealed to his holy apostles and prophets in spirit; to be specific, that the Gentiles are fellow heirs and fellow members of the body, and fellow partakers of the promise in Christ Jesus through the gospel."

The body of Christ recognizes neither Jew nor Greek, slave nor free, male nor female. In Christ, we are all one.

In my vision, the angel announced the end to the days of pictures and types when God worked through only one earthly nation. The mystery is now in full view. Our Lord Jesus has been established now as the head of a new, holy nation, which he and his Father had purposed would be brought into existence in time, and in space, from all eternity. That holy nation is the church, comprised of both Gentiles and a remnant of believing Jews. With the destruction of Jerusalem, the Old Covenant has become completely obsolete, and a New Covenant, with the new people of God, established.

CHAPTER 16
FORTY-TWO MONTHS OF DESTRUCTION

I mentioned to you earlier that some hold to a future fulfillment of this prophecy. You, who received this letter while I was still on Patmos, do not need to be told that I wrote it *before* the temple in Jerusalem was destroyed. Yet, you know as well as I that our letters travel far! Somewhere out in the future, if you or your posterity should ever encounter those who doubt a pre–Jewish War date for its writing, you need only point out to them that I was told to "*measure the temple* of God, and the altar, and those who worship in it and leave out the court which is outside the temple, and do not measure it, for it has been given to the nations; and they will tread underfoot the holy city for forty-two months."

In my vision, the temple was still standing. Anyone who looks to some later date in history for these prophesies to be fulfilled would also do well to consider that I wrote that Jerusalem was soon to be trampled underfoot by Roman soldiers for a period of forty-two months. In his gospel account written years ago, Doctor Luke recorded Jesus as saying:

"When you see Jerusalem surrounded by armies, then recognize that her desolation is near . . . Woe to those who are pregnant and to those who are nursing babes in those days; for there will be great distress upon the land, and wrath to this people, and they will fall by the edge of the sword, and will be led captive into all the nations; and Jerusalem will be *trampled underfoot by the Gentiles* until the times of the Gentiles be fulfilled." In the Jewish War, all happened just as Jesus said.

CHAPTER 17
MY TWO WITNESSES

"And I will grant authority to my two witnesses, and they will prophesy for twelve hundred and sixty days, clothed in sackcloth."

I have often been asked about these two witnesses. Are they real people, or are they just symbolic?

Some mistakenly think that I was referring to Peter and James, believing them to be in Jerusalem just before the destruction of the temple. But we know that Peter had been martyred in Rome, and James died earlier. So clearly, they were not the two witnesses.

As in so much of the revelation, what I saw and wrote was symbolic. Do you remember that I described these two witnesses as being clothed in sackcloth? Sackcloth is something associated with the Old Covenant, not the new. It was worn as a sign of mourning for the dead or at times of national or personal disaster. Not to belabor the point, but I knew Peter, and I knew James, well. Though they knew this destruction was coming, a description of two witnesses wearing sackcloth would hardly have fit them at all! They never walked the streets of Jerusalem dressed in clothing made of dark, coarse goat's hair. Especially Peter. It certainly was not his style!

These witnesses had "power to shut up the sky . . . and they have power over the waters to turn them into blood and to strike the earth with every plague, as often as they desire."

Now, I have a question for you Old Covenant scholars. Which two figures come to mind when you think of "shutting up the sky" and "turning waters to blood"?

Ah, thank you for your enthusiastic response! Quite so, of course—Elijah and Moses.

Elijah was the one who shut up the sky, causing a great drought in Israel. Moses was the one who turned the waters of the Nile to blood.

Moses and Elijah were the same men I saw bear witness to Christ on the Mount of Transfiguration over forty years ago. The witnesses I wrote about in the revelation are symbolic. They represent the law and the prophets.

The witnesses prophesied for 1260 days, which is equal to forty-two months or three-and-a-half years. When they finished their testimony, the beast that came up out of the abyss (more on him later) overcame them and killed them. This took place in the great city, Jerusalem.

"And their dead bodies will lie in the street of the great city which mystically is called Sodom and Egypt, where also their Lord was crucified."

The law and the prophets warned again and again what would befall Jerusalem if she abandoned the covenant and rejected the Messiah. The Jews were given ample opportunity to repent, but instead, they suppressed the voice of conscience and the warnings from their own sacred Scriptures and murdered the testimony of these two witnesses.

The people of the land threw off all restraint and rejoiced over the death of these witnesses. After all, they had served as constant reminders of how far the people had fallen. After three-and-a-half days, "The breath of life from God came into them," they came back to life, and a loud voice from heaven called to them, "Come up here!" They went up into heaven—a sign that God had totally abandoned national Israel and those living in Jerusalem at the time and removed his witness from them. The time for their judgment had arrived.

All that the law and prophets pointed to was fulfilled in Christ. Under the New Covenant, the Lord said, "I will put my law within them, and on their heart I will write it; and I will be their God, and they shall be my people." No longer are the external law and the prophets of the Old Covenant to be our guides in fulfilling the righteous requirements of God. Now, the Lord himself fulfills those requirements as the mediator of the New Covenant from heaven, by his all-powerful Spirit who lives in us.

My eyes followed those witnesses into the heavens, where I heard another loud chorus of praise: "The kingdom of the world has become the kingdom of our Lord and his Christ, and he will reign forever and ever." His laws are no longer written on tablets of stones, but on the tablets of human hearts, where he has purposed from eternity to rule and reign.

"And the twenty-four elders who sat on their thrones before God, fell on their faces and worshiped God saying, 'We give you thanks, O Lord God, the Almighty, who is and who was, because you have taken your great power and have begun to reign.'"

CHAPTER 18

THE WOMAN WITH CHILD

"A great sign appeared in heaven; a woman clothed with the sun, and the moon under her feet, and on her head a crown of twelve stars; and she was with child; and she cried out, being in labor and in pain to give birth . . . And the dragon stood before the woman who was about to give birth, so that when she gave birth he might devour her child. And she gave birth to a son, a male child, who is to rule all the nations with a rod of iron; and her child was caught up to God and to his throne."

Who was this woman?

The symbolism used to describe her would remind any Jew of the story of Joseph and his dreams from the book of Genesis. He dreamed that the sun and the moon and eleven stars would one day all bow down to him. When he related the dream to his father, Jacob, and his brothers, Jacob rebuked him and said to him, "What is this dream that you have had? Shall I and your mother and your brothers actually come to bow ourselves down before you to the ground?"

The sun, then, represents Jacob; the moon, Rachel; and the stars, Jacob's brothers. The woman in the vision represents all of faithful Israel. They were those Jews who for centuries endured "labor and pain" while waiting for the promised Seed spoken of in Genesis, who would crush the serpent's head. This Seed, of course, is Jesus, the Messiah.

The son born to the woman would "rule all the nations with a rod of iron." You will find the same prophecy concerning Christ in the second psalm, where the Father addresses the Son and says to him, "You are my Son . . . ask of me, and I will surely give the nations as your inheritance, and the very ends of the earth as your possession. You shall rule them with a rod of iron."

The story pictured in this vision should be familiar to all of you. Satan desperately wanted to devour this child because he knew this was the promised Seed who would usher in his demise. Herod the Great became a tool of Satan in his attempt to kill the Christ child. Herod ordered all the male children in Bethlehem and its environs to be killed, but an angel of the Lord appeared to Joseph, telling him to take the child and his mother and flee to Egypt.

Satan was unsuccessful in thwarting God's plan. Jesus died on the cross as our Savior and Redeemer and then was raised from the dead and "caught up to God, and to his throne." As the invisible head of the church, his body, Christ now rules from heaven. And he will continue to reign until he has put all things under his feet.

Next, I saw the woman flee into the wilderness, "where she had a place prepared by God." This occurred when the faithful Jewish-Christian remnant escaped into the wilderness to Pella, just before Jerusalem's destruction.

And the devil pursued the woman, spewing water "like a river out of his mouth after the woman, so that he might cause her to be swept away with the flood." Satan was locked in mortal combat with the woman. He was not unaware of God's eternal purpose for man to bear God's image and rule over the earth—even over the creeping things. For in Genesis it says, "Let us make man in our image, according to our likeness; and let them rule over the fish of the sea and over the birds of the sky and over the cattle and over all the earth, and over every creeping thing that creeps on the earth."

That purpose had a corporate dimension. Let *them* rule.

God secured *one* man who bore his image and ruled with his authority on the earth: Jesus Christ. But he wanted a whole *race!* A "*them*"! Christ was the firstborn among *many* brethren. He is the head, joined to the body of the corporate man—the church. God destined the church from before the world began to bear the image of Christ, to rule with his authority, and ultimately to defeat God's enemy, Satan, the serpent of old.

In desperation, Satan directed all of his fury toward the woman. But our Lord safely guided her out of Jerusalem and into the wilderness. "But the land helped the woman, and the land opened its mouth and drank up the river which the dragon poured out of his mouth."

On the one hand, the holocaust in Jerusalem was God's judgment on the nation that crucified the Messiah. At the same time, it was the climax of the fury that Satan unleashed on the church in an attempt to destroy her. The land absorbed that fury and drank up the river that came from his mouth. God used Satan to fulfill his purpose, while the woman was transported on eagle's wings to safety.

"And they overcame him because of the blood of the Lamb and because of the word of their testimony, and they did not love their life even when faced with death."

The devil "was enraged with the woman, and went off to make war with the rest of her children."

It should come as no surprise to you who that offspring was. The devil was unsuccessful in eliminating the Jewish church, which was born in Jerusalem. So next, he went after the Gentile church, which had rapidly been spreading to the nations. This "war with her children" is the persecution against the church that began in Rome with Nero and quickly spread to you.

I would wager that you never knew how furious you make the devil!

And I will also wager that you do not fully realize how *terrified* he is of *you*.

CHAPTER 19

THE BEAST

He was born into this world on December 15, A.D. 37, as Lucius Domitius Ahenobarbus in the court of his uncle, the emperor Caligula. His father was a vile man and died when Lucius was quite young. Lucius grew up under the tutoring of Greek teachers, from whom he developed a love for music, poetry, and sports.

His mother was an ambitious and scheming woman named Agrippina, sister of Caligula. After Caligula's death, Claudius took the throne to become head of the Roman Empire. Following the death of Claudius's wife, Agrippina arranged for Lucius to be married to his daughter. Shortly after that, Agrippina married Claudius (her own uncle!) and secured the adoption of Lucius as the emperor's son.

Five years later, Agrippina fed Claudius a bowl of poisoned mushrooms, and he died. So, at the tender age of seventeen, her son was enthroned as the ruler of the most powerful kingdom on earth. You know him by his adopted name: Nero Caesar.

In every way, the word "beast" fits this man.

As you do not need to be told, Nero's perversity and foul character were well known throughout the empire. He was a homosexual and sodomist. He actually castrated and then married a young boy named Sporus and tried to make a woman out of him. That gave rise to the widely circulated statement that people "wished that Nero's father had such a wife as Sporus!" For amusement, he invented a game in which he dressed himself in the skins of wild animals and then released himself from a cage in front of naked men and women who were bound to stakes. The vulgar deeds that befell these victims are too shameful to speak about in public.

He had his first wife, Octavia, murdered. Her head was sent to his mistress Poppaea, whom he then married. While Poppaea was pregnant, he kicked her to death in a fit of rage. When he was twenty-two, he became aggravated by his mother's meddlings and had her killed. At the moment of her death, she bared her stomach and invited the murderers to stab her where the ungrateful Nero had come from.

Along with these perversities, history will record that it was Nero Caesar who was the first imperial power ever to declare war on the church. It came about in this way:

Nero was not pleased with the architectural shortcomings of the palaces and buildings of Rome. He had ambitious plans to rebuild the city and name it after himself—Neropolis. An evil plot began to hatch in his mind, but Nero needed a scapegoat for what he was about to do. The Christians in Rome refused to worship the emperor. They were the perfect ones to blame for what was about to happen.

From what we know, we can safely say that Nero himself was behind the fire that broke out in the Circus Maximus on July 18, A.D. 64. It burned for nine days and destroyed two-thirds of the city. The Christians were falsely accused and rounded up en masse. A vicious and violent persecution followed.

You have heard stories of how some of our brothers and sisters were wrapped in animal skins and thrown to dogs to be devoured. Others were dipped in pitch, then fastened to crosses and made into human torches at Nero's garden parties. It is all true.

Nero played his fiddle while Rome burned and innocent martyrs spilled their blood. He became Satan's vessel to unleash widespread persecution against the church.

In the vision, I saw a beast coming up out of the sea. From where I stood on Patmos, or from Ephesus or Jerusalem, for that matter, to look westward toward the sea is to look in the direction of Rome.

"And the beast which I saw was like a leopard, and his feet were like those of a bear, and his mouth like the mouth of a lion. And the dragon gave him his power and his throne and great authority."

CHAPTER 20
AND THEY WORSHIPED THE BEAST

The cult of emperor worship was born with Julius Caesar. Many of you walked by the temple of Quirinius on your way to the meeting tonight. As you know, it houses a statue of Julius with the inscription, "To the invincible god." You are all familiar with the line of Caesars following him: Augustus, Tiberius, Caligula, and Claudius, all of whom blasphemously equated themselves with deity and had statues and temples erected to themselves.

But it was Nero, along with Caligula, who took emperor worship to another level. Nero demanded to be worshiped as God while he was still alive.

Here in Ephesus, the emperor cult referred to Nero as "Almighty God and Savior." Truly, he was given power for a short time. But even his power could not stand up for long against the King of kings and the Lord of lords.

Nero's persecution of Christians began in November of A.D. 64. In 67, Nero left Rome for Greece. He was gone for a little more than a year, performing at Greek festivals as a musician and actor. The Greeks deified him as Zeus. They even erected a statue to him in the temple of Apollo.

The reign of terror against the church continued even while he was away from Rome, caught up in his vain theatrical pursuits. However, the harsh persecution he initiated was short-lived. Civil war was breaking out throughout the empire. Nero returned from Greece in A.D. 68, only to find enemies plotting his overthrow. On June 9, A.D. 68, at the age of thirty-one, Nero committed suicide by running a dagger through his own throat.

And "they worshiped the dragon because he gave his authority to the beast, and they worshiped the beast, saying, 'Who is like the beast, and who is able to wage war with him?' There was given to him a mouth speaking arrogant words and blasphemies, and authority to act for forty-two months was given to him."

With Nero's death, the persecution of Christians subsided. Rome's attention was turned to its civil wars. The church had survived. This siege upon the church lasted for precisely forty-two months—just as the word of the Lord had said.

The time period during which Rome was persecuting Christians overlapped with the time the Jews were at war with Rome. This was the hour of testing I was instructed to write about to the church in Philadelphia that was "about to come upon the whole world."

I hope that when this letter came to you and you read it for the first time, you took comfort in the fact that though this persecution would be severe, it would not last for long.

CHAPTER 21

DEADLY HEAD WOUND HEALED

The beast I saw in the revelation had a corporate, as well as an individual, aspect. It referred not only to Nero, but also to the government of Rome itself.

It had ten horns and seven heads. The ten horns were the ten Roman provinces: Italy, Achaia, Asia, Syria, Egypt, Africa, Germany, Spain, Gaul, and Britain.

The seven heads were seven hills. Rome is known throughout the world as the city with seven hills. So, in part, the beast represents the Roman Empire. The individual aspect that is also present is seen in the seven heads, which are also said to be seven kings. "Five have fallen, one is, the other has not yet come; and when he comes, he must remain a little while."

The five kings that had fallen when I saw the revelation were Julius Caesar (who began his reign in 49 B.C.), Augustus Caesar (31 B.C.–A.D. 14), Tiberius Caesar (A.D. 14–37), Caligula, or Gaius Caesar (A.D. 37–41), and Claudius (A.D. 41–54). The one reigning during my banishment to Patmos was Nero Caesar. He reigned from A.D. 54–68. The one to come was Galba, who had the shortest reign of them all. He was only in power for six months.

And I saw one of the heads of the beast "as if it had been slain, and his fatal wound was healed. And the whole earth was amazed and followed after the beast."

By the time of Nero's death, the whole empire was writhing in turmoil. With insurrections, civil wars, and nations rising against nations, it looked as if the empire had been struck a deathblow. Astonishingly, though, it recovered.

Vespasian returned to Rome from Judea, leaving his son Titus in charge of the campaign against Jerusalem. This seasoned war veteran miraculously unified the empire. Nero was dead, but the empire revived.

So the beast's corporate identity was the kingdom represented by the Roman Empire. Its individual identity was embodied in the seven heads. All the evil of Satan was personified in the head of the beast that was alive during the time I composed this revelation—Nero Caesar.

When speaking with our Lord during his temptation in the wilderness,

Satan offered Jesus all the kingdoms of the world if Jesus would only fall down and worship him. No doubt the Roman Empire was one of those kingdoms.

But thanks be to our Lord for his response! "It is written, you shall worship the Lord your God, and serve him only."

CHAPTER 22

666

In the revelation, I did not plainly disclose the name of the beast—Nero—because I needed to communicate in veiled terms. However, I did leave clues as to his identity. I address this now because with the passing of time, I have heard some strange theories as to the meaning of these clues.

As you know, in our languages, letters of the alphabet carry dual meanings, serving both as letters and as numbers.

We have all seen the witty riddles and letters written by young lovers who do not want to expose their identities. They have become very popular in our day. These messages are written in code, using numbers to represent words.

Many of you know our tent-maker friends, Aquila and Priscilla, who lived among you. It would not surprise me if Aquila wrote one of these coded verses for his lovely Priscilla during their courtship. It might have read something like this: "Aquila is madly in love with 481!" The number 481 would have been a code for Priscilla's name, a code only the two of them knew for sure, but others would have to figure out.

By using the numerical value for each letter in Nero's name, I made it easy for you and all the Christians throughout the empire to see that he was the beast.

"Here is wisdom. Let him who has understanding calculate the number of the beast, for the number is that of a man; and his number is six hundred and sixty six."

In the Hebrew alphabet, the name Nero Caesar is spelled:
NRWN QSR
The Hebrew value of those letters:

N = 50
R = 200
W = 6
N = 50
Q = 100
S = 60
R = 200

The total equals: 666.

CHAPTER 23

THE MARK OF THE BEAST

"And he causes all, the small and the great, and the rich and the poor, and the free men and the slaves, to be given a mark on their right hand or on their forehead."

To explain the mark of the beast, I would like to go back to the letters in the revelation addressed to the seven churches. Let us begin by looking at the word of the Lord to the church in Philadelphia:

"He who overcomes, I will make him a pillar in the temple of my God, and he will not go out from it anymore; and I will write on him the name of my God, and the name of the city of my God, the new Jerusalem, which comes down out of heaven from my God, and my new name."

We have some brothers and sisters here tonight from the church in Philadelphia. I would like to ask all of you a question. Have you ever met anyone or heard of anyone from the church in Philadelphia who had some kind of visible tattoo mysteriously written on his or her forehead with the name of God and with the name of the city of God, New Jerusalem?

You haven't? Well, I am not surprised!

Do you also remember the 144,000, who were "the firstfruits to God and to the Lamb" from among our Judean brethren? I also described them as having "his name and the name of his Father written on their foreheads."

I can tell you for certain that in all my days in the church in Jerusalem, and from everyone I have talked to who was part of the great exodus of Jewish believers from Jerusalem to Pella, no one has ever seen any believers in Christ walking around with the names of the Father and the Son stamped on their foreheads either!

Our God is one who writes with invisible ink!

I have read our brother Paul's letters to the church in Corinth. In one of them he said that *they* were a letter, known and read by all men. He called them a "letter of Christ . . . written not with ink, but with the Spirit of the living God, not on tablets of stone, but on tablets of human hearts."

Since no one has come forward to witness that God literally wrote on the foreheads of those who were his own, why should anyone expect those who followed the beast to have his mark literally branded on their foreheads?

The interpretation of the mark of the beast is simple. It is symbolic, and it speaks of ownership. Those who received the mark on their right hand or on their foreheads were those whose deeds and thoughts were swayed by the beast. In the same way, those who had the Lord's name written on their foreheads were those who were single-minded in their devotion to him.

"And he provides that no one will be able to buy or to sell, except the one who has the mark."

Those who aligned themselves with the beast wanted nothing to do with the Christians. During Nero's fierce persecution, many nonbelievers avoided the Christians because they did not want to be mistaken for one of them and suffer their fate. This made it difficult for followers of Christ even to buy and sell in the marketplace—as many of you experienced, firsthand, yourselves.

CHAPTER 24

THE SECOND BEAST

"Then I saw another beast coming up out of the land . . . he exercises all the authority of the first beast in his presence. And he makes the land and those who dwell in it to worship the first beast . . . he performs great signs . . . and he deceives those who dwell on the land."

Who was this second beast? Later in the revelation, I wrote that this beast was "the false prophet."

The Lord Jesus solemnly warned us on the Mount of Olives that many false prophets would arise and mislead many. He also said, "Then if anyone says to you, 'Behold, here is the Christ,' or 'There he is,' do not believe him. For false Christs and false prophets will arise and will show great signs and wonders, so as to mislead, if possible, even the elect. Behold, I have told you in advance. So if they say to you, 'Behold, he is in the wilderness,' do not go out, or, 'Behold, he is in the inner rooms,' do not believe them."

Our Lord's words once again proved true. Josephus recorded that during this time period, "the country was full of robbers, magicians, false prophets, false Messiahs, and impostors, who deluded the people with promises of great events."[38]

All of this occurred during the generation that Jesus promised would not pass away until all these things took place.

The second beast came up out of the land of Israel. It had "two horns like a lamb, and he spoke as a dragon." A lamb is a religious symbol. This beast had a religious appearance but spoke with the deception of the dragon. The first beast had ten horns, indicating that this second beast was subservient to the first and not as powerful.

As I have said before, and have even been inspired to put into writing in one of my epistles, this whole world lies in the power of the Evil One. If anyone loves the world, or the things in the world, the love of the Father is not in him.

We Christians are called to battle. The battle between Jesus and Satan has already been won. Jesus defeated Satan at the cross and rendered him powerless. But he has enlisted the church, his body, to do the cleanup work. So now the fight is between Satan and the church. Satan will use any weapon at his disposal to war against us. He will draw from the political world—

Nero, for example—or from the religious world, as in the case of the false prophet that was raised up out of the land of Israel. He will also use the *kosmos,* this world system, along with the lust of the flesh, the lust of the eyes, and the boastful pride of life, in an attempt to entice us and lure us away from the Lord. We need to be familiar with all his strategies.

Satan's kingdom is an intricate web spread out all over this earth. He enlists governments, man-made religions and religious systems, philosophies and education, entertainment, and anything else he can use to keep us from the knowledge of Christ and from being one with him in his purpose.

In the last days before the temple was destroyed, false messiahs and false prophets arose from the religious establishment in Jerusalem. Satan used the old wineskin of the Jewish religion and its leaders in an attempt to mislead people and turn them away from Christ. These false prophets were even given power from Satan to perform great signs, so as to deceive many.

Do you remember the story that our brother Luke recorded in his chronicle about the early days of the church, about the man from Samaria named Simon who was known to all as "the Great Power of God"? I knew this fellow. He was one of many deceivers and magicians who managed to gain a large following through such deception.

When the gospel went to Samaria, the church in Jerusalem sent Peter and me to attest to the fact that the Lord Jesus also had come to the Samaritans. We laid our hands on them and prayed that they too might receive the Holy Spirit.

This Simon of Samaria saw the work the Lord was doing through us and wanted the same power we had. He even offered to buy the gift of God from us for money!

Peter sternly rebuked him, perceiving that he was "poisoned by bitterness and in the bondage of iniquity," and that "his heart was not right before God." He was an example of the many false prophets our Lord had warned us about.

You had firsthand experience with another one of these deceivers who came "up from out of the land." Some of you probably remember the seven sons of Sceva, the Jewish chief priest, who traveled all the way up here to Ephesus. These misguided Jewish exorcists, like many others, even tried to use the Lord's name to cast out demons.

One time while Sceva's band was performing their craft in the house of an Ephesian man, the evil spirit in the man answered them and said, "I recognize Jesus, and I know about Paul, but who are you?" The evil spirit then empowered the man to overcome and beat the stuffing out of all seven of Sceva's sons. They bolted out of his house naked and wounded, and they never returned!

As a result, the fear of God fell on Ephesus, and many people came to Christ—including even some of you who are in this room tonight.

These are just two examples of the false messiahs and prophets that our Lord warned us about. Deceptive, religious impostors, employed by Satan as his mouthpieces, comprised the second beast I described.

Satan, working through the world's political and religious systems (Pilate and the Jewish religious leaders) had our Lord crucified. It should come as no surprise that persecution can come from either political or religious sources once they have come under the influence of the Evil One.

CHAPTER 25

THE LAMB STANDING ON MOUNT ZION

Following my vision of the beast coming up out of the sea and the second beast coming up out of the land, the scene shifted back to the heavenly Mount Zion. I looked again, and "Behold, the Lamb was standing on Mount Zion, and with him one hundred and forty-four thousand, having his name and the name of his Father written on their foreheads." These were the ones who were called the "first fruits to God and to the Lamb."

In his letter, James, our Lord's earthly brother and son of Mary and Joseph, addressed a message to the Christians of the twelve tribes in the dispersion. In that letter, he referred to those Jewish believers as the "first fruits among his creatures." The 144,000 I saw here were the same faithful Jews who had converted to Christ who were mentioned earlier. They worshiped the Lord and kept themselves pure.

Then I heard an angel triumphantly proclaim, "Fallen, fallen is Babylon the great," and another angel announce, "If anyone worships the beast and his image, and receives a mark on his forehead or on his hand, he also will drink of the wine of the wrath of God."

Often, when a condemned man is crucified or put to death, he is offered a drink of sour wine. Likewise, Babylon and all who had aligned themselves with the beast were sentenced to judgment and would be made to drink from the wine of his wrath.

I will have more to say about Babylon in a moment. But let me first emphasize that, ultimately, there are only two cups from which one can drink: the cup of blessing or the cup of wrath. Every person will raise one or the other of these cups to his lips. By the grace of God, those of us who believe will enjoy the cup of blessing because our Lord drank the cup of wrath for us.

CHAPTER 26
THE LORD'S VINE

In the days of the Old Covenant, the prophet Isaiah proclaimed, "The vineyard of the Lord of Hosts is the house of Israel."

The next thing I saw in the vision was the Son of Man sitting on a white cloud, "having a golden crown on his head, and a sharp sickle in his hand." And a loud voice cried out, "Put in your sickle and reap, for the hour to reap has come, because the harvest of the land is ripe. Then he who sat on the cloud swung his sickle over the land; and the land was reaped."

If you have been following me so far, you will know who it was who got reaped. It was the firstfruits! The Lord took those who were his from the vine of Israel—the 144,000—in the first swing of the sickle.

Then, a second time, the sharp sickle struck. With one swift stroke, it cut cleanly through the trunk of the vine itself. The vine of national Israel was cut down and thrown into the great winepress of the wrath of God.

"So the angel swung his sickle to the land, and gathered the vine of the land, and threw it into the great wine press of the wrath of God. And the wine press was trodden outside the city, and blood came out from the wine press, up to the horses' bridles, for a distance of sixteen hundred stadia."

Sixteen hundred stadia are about the length of the land of Israel. Blood flowed from one end of the land to the other and did not cease to flow until Jerusalem was utterly and completely destroyed in A.D. 70.

Jesus foresaw the destruction of this vine. Just before the evening he gave his farewell discourse to us apostles, Jesus sent Peter and me from where we were staying on the Mount of Olives into Jerusalem to prepare the Passover meal. He told us to look for a man carrying water who would lead us to the place where we would observe this ancient celebration.

Upon entering the city, we spotted a man dressed in a white habit, carrying water. Normally this was a woman's job, but we recognized that he was from the Essene community. Among other things, the Essenes practiced celibacy; therefore, there were no women among them to perform this task. He led us to their monastery, located in the upper part of the city, and showed us to the guest room. That is where we took the Last Supper with our Lord together.

Peter and I were unaware at the time we prepared that little lamb to eat that we were about to gain a whole new appreciation for the Passover. Within hours, we would witness the most dramatic event in human history—the Lamb of God shedding his own blood.

Jesus had much to say to us that night in his parting words before going to the cross. But one thing he made a point of sharing about was the Vine of God. He did not speak to us about Israel. He spoke about himself. He announced to us that he was the *true* Vine. We are the branches. National Israel has been disqualified. As we abide in him and draw our life from him, the Father is glorified, and we will bear much fruit.

CHAPTER 27

ARMAGEDDON

The staging area for the final siege upon Jerusalem was in the north, inland from the vicinity of Caesarea, at a place called Armageddon. The word *Armageddon* comes from the Hebrew *Har Megiddo,* which means mountain of Megiddo. It is located close to Nazareth, the city where our Lord grew up.

From atop the hill in Nazareth, known as the Mount of the Precipice, the hometown crowd nearly succeeded in hurling Jesus to his death after he spoke against them in their synagogue. Their anger was kindled because they could not accept the fact that Jesus cited two Gentiles from the Old Testament as heroes of the faith. The two were Zarephath, the widow from Sidon to whom Elijah was sent in the days of famine, and Naaman, the leper from Syria whom he cleansed. At the heart of their rejection, they could not accept that God's grace was available to every nation! Can we not pause and learn a lesson here? This dangerous precipice of exclusivity can lurk in the depths of every human heart, and it must be rejected.

Standing on that hill, one can see Mount Carmel, the Gilboa Mountains, Mount Tabor, the Jordan Valley, and directly below, the spacious plains of Megiddo. Jesus looked out at that plain many a time, knowing full well what would one day take place there. It was there that all the troops were gathered together in the place known as Armageddon."

Historically, many battles have been fought on the plains of Megiddo. This was where Deborah and Barak defeated Sisera, the captain of the army of Jabin, the king of Canaan, who had oppressed the Israelites for twenty years. It was also the site where Josiah, king of Judah, met his death and Pharaoh Neco defeated his army.

But in the vision I saw, no battle was fought there. It was simply the designated place where the Roman armies would meet, strategize, and regroup before their final assault on Jerusalem.

Even Josephus, an eyewitness to these events, recorded how Titus, the Roman general and son of Vespasian, led the fifteenth legion of troops out of Alexandria, Egypt, where they were stationed, north along the shores of the Mediterranean Sea—skirting Jerusalem—to meet up with other troops from Rome, Syria, and beyond the Euphrates. From the hill of

Megiddo Titus could look out and survey this vast army, consisting of four legions along with all of their auxiliaries and cavalry units, numbering in the vicinity of eighty thousand men. Once they were all assembled and battle plans drawn, they marched together for what would be the last battle against Jerusalem.

CHAPTER 28

THE WOMAN CAUGHT IN ADULTERY

So far, I have been speaking about the Lord's judgment and the fall of Jerusalem. At this point, I want to tell you another story that will provide a stunning contrast to what you will hear next. It is a story that made such a deep impression on me that I recorded it in my gospel.

One day, a crowd was gathered in the temple area among the porticos in the court of the Gentiles to hear Jesus teach. The scribes and Pharisees disrupted the gathering by dragging a woman caught in adultery in front of Jesus and all the people. They asked him, "Teacher, this woman has been caught in adultery, in the very act. Now in the law Moses commanded us to stone such women; what then do you say?"

Of course, they were saying this to test him, hoping that he might say something they could use to accuse him.

They persisted in trying to extract a response, but Jesus merely stooped down and began writing with his finger on the ground. Finally, he straightened up and said to them, "He who is without sin among you, let him be the first to throw a stone at her."

You may be curious to know what he wrote. I will tell you. He wrote the names of her accusers! This fulfilled an ancient prophecy made by Jeremiah where he said, "O Lord, the hope of Israel, all who forsake you will be put to shame. Those who turn away from you will be written in the dust because they have forsaken the Lord, the spring of living water."

It was only the day before, on the last day—the great day of the Feast of Tabernacles—that Jesus had stood in the temple and cried out, saying, "If anyone is thirsty, let him come to me and drink. He who believes in me, as the Scripture said, 'From his innermost being will flow rivers of living water.'"

In the high drama of the moment, none of us could have guessed what would happen next. His answer stunned them. His accusers knew this Scripture and, beginning with the older ones, each one dropped his stone, turned, and walked quietly out of the temple area.

The woman buried her face in her hands. She wept and trembled. Guilt, embarrassment, and shame were written all over her face as she slowly looked up at Jesus. Streams of tears ran down her cheeks as she struggled to hold her head up and look into the eyes of the Master.

Jesus said to her, "Woman, where are they? Did no one condemn you?"

She replied that no one had.

Then Jesus said, "I do not condemn you, either. Go. From now on sin no more."

The way Jesus dealt with that woman left all of us speechless. We saw mercy triumph over justice. She who deserved to be condemned received a pardon.

Why do I bring up this story? Because of the contrast between her and another adulterous woman I watched Jesus deal with. The second woman was the one I saw in my vision. This adulterous woman was Jerusalem. She was to be the Lord's wife, but she had played the harlot time and time again. Unlike the woman in the temple whom Jesus pardoned, this adulteress had no contrition of heart, no remorse, no sense of humility, no shame. Her brazen heart was hardened beyond the point of repentance.

When Jesus looked at her, he knew that for years she had consciously rejected him and closed her heart to receiving his mercy. The forty years since his crucifixion had been time enough for her to repent. Now, nothing could stand in the way of judgment.

There was only one who was capable of righteously judging this harlot: the one who was without sin, whom she had crucified. Since stoning was the prescribed form of capital punishment for such offenses, Jesus himself picked up the first stone. Taking one last, lingering look, he cocked his arm behind his head, then hurled the first stone full force at the woman.

This is what it looked like in the vision:

"Huge hailstones, about one hundred pounds each, came down from heaven upon men; and men blasphemed God because of the plague of the hail, because its plague was extremely severe."

While Titus and the Roman armies surrounded Jerusalem during the final five months of battle, the inhabitants were implored, time and time again, to surrender. But they would not. Titus responded by using a weapon called the *ballista,* a huge slingshot-like contraption, to launch these seventy-five to one-hundred-pound stones over a quarter of a mile into the city. These immense white stones rained into the city like hailstones.

Josephus, who saw it firsthand, recorded it like this:

"The engines [the ballistas], that all the legions had ready prepared for them, were admirably contrived; but still more extraordinary ones belonged to the tenth legion; those that threw darts and those that threw stones were more forcible and larger than the rest, by which they not only repelled the excursions of the Jews, but drove those away that were upon the walls also. Now the stones that were cast, *were of weight one talent,* and were carried two furlongs and further. The blow they gave was no way to be sustained, not only by those that stood first in the way, but by those that were beyond them for a great space. As for the Jews, they at first watched the coming of the stone, for it was of a white color, and could therefore not only be perceived by the great noise it made, but could be seen also before it came, by its brightness."[39]

Not only was the rain of hailstones deadly and destructive, but this stubborn adulteress continued to blaspheme God right up until the end.

Josephus continues:

"The watchmen that sat upon the towers gave them [the people] notice when the engine was let go, and the stone came from it, and cried out aloud, in their own country language, *'Here comes the Son!'*"[40]

What mockery! The Jewish watchmen knew full well what these stones raining upon the city meant. Not only had Jesus warned them, but for forty years the Christians had continued to echo Peter's warnings from the day of Pentecost: "Be saved from this perverse generation!" In their delirium, like drunken madmen, while God's vengeance was being unleashed in all its fury, the remaining Jews in Jerusalem went down cursing and blaspheming the Son of God to the very last breath.

CHAPTER 29

"FALLEN, FALLEN IS BABYLON THE GREAT"

On four separate occasions in the revelation, I recorded that I was "caught up in spirit." The first time it was to see the vision of Christ walking in the midst of the churches. The second was to see the one sitting on the throne. The third time was when I was taken to the wilderness to see the fall of the great harlot. And the final time was to see the bride, the wife of the Lamb.

All four of these visions are significant and reveal a different aspect of the Lord and his purpose. As Christians, we grow in our knowledge of the Christ by having him revealed to us in spirit. These four visions the Lord showed me and instructed me to write down were things that are important for believers in all the churches to see.

First, we need to see that Jesus lives and walks among the churches. We were each, individually, called by the Lord. But we also were called to be a part of his body. To fully realize the Lord's purpose in our lives, we need to be built together, by *his* Life, into a body—a temple—with other Christians, where Christ can make his home among us.

Second, we need to see that he is on the throne. He is in control. He rules this world. Nothing is outside of his sovereignty. I have committed to memory an eloquent passage from a letter our brother Paul wrote on this theme to the believers in Rome. It goes like this:

"For I am convinced that neither death, nor life, nor angels, nor principalities, nor things present, nor things to come, nor powers, nor height, nor depth, nor any other created thing, will be able to separate us from the love of God, which is in Christ Jesus our Lord."

Sometimes we experience various trials that are perplexing and discouraging, and sometimes they even cause us to question our Lord's love and sovereignty. Yet, we should not be surprised by these trials. They come upon us for our testing, that we might be refined as pure gold is refined by fire. Behind all the trials we are allowed to experience is the sovereign hand of a loving God. His transforming work in our lives comes through both inward revelation and outward trials. We need to have this revelation.

In our pursuit of the Lord, we need to practice turning to our spirits over and over again to make contact with the one who sits on the throne. Turning to the Lord and spending time in his presence renews our minds. Then we must abide in him, where he is, far above all rule and authority and power and dominion.

Next, it is important to see that Babylon has fallen. She and all of her offspring have already been judged. We must steer clear of false religion and, as I wrote specifically to you here in Ephesus in this letter, we need to hold fast to our first love. Put another way, it is essential that we maintain a simple and pure devotion to Christ.

And finally, we need to see the bride of Christ—his ultimate purpose and final dwelling place.

Now, who is this "Babylon"? Who is this one called, "The Mother of Harlots"?

To explain, I would like to go all the way back to the story found in Genesis of the Tower of Babel. We will find some lessons and imagery there that will help us. In the book of beginnings, Moses recorded that as men moved eastward:

". . . They found a plain in the land of Shinar and settled there. They said to each other, 'Come, let us make bricks and burn them thoroughly.' And they used brick for stone, and they used tar for mortar. Then they said, 'Come, let us build for ourselves a city, and a tower whose top will reach into heaven, and let us make for ourselves a name, otherwise we will be scattered abroad over the face of the whole earth.'"

The Lord came down and judged these people, confused their languages, and scattered them all over the earth.

One of the main lessons we learn from the Tower of Babel is that man gets into trouble when he tries to build something *for* God. *God* is the builder. When God builds, he builds with stone. But man builds with brick—something that comes from his own hand. The Tower of Babel represents man's attempt to build something for God through human effort. They desired to become famous and make a name for themselves. They also wanted a place that would provide security—but a security apart from God.

This stands in stark contrast to the environment in the garden of Eden before the fall, where the man and the woman were created to find their significance and security in the presence of God alone.

The Babylon I described in the revelation possesses the same characteristics that we see in the builders of the ancient Tower of Babel: pride, self-reliance, self-effort to reach God, unity apart from God, and rebellion.

Historically, Babylon was also the kingdom the Lord used to judge and persecute Israel when she had fallen away from following God.

Nebuchadnezzar had Jerusalem destroyed and took the Jews captive to Babylon. So Babylon also represents a place where God's people are held captive.

Put all this together, and the picture should become clear for you.

"And he carried me away in the Spirit into a wilderness; and I saw a woman sitting on a scarlet beast, full of blasphemous names, having seven heads and ten horns. The woman was clothed in purple and scarlet, and adorned with gold and precious stones and pearls, having in her hand a gold cup full of abominations and of the unclean things of her immorality, and on her forehead a name was written, a mystery, 'BABYLON THE GREAT, THE MOTHER OF HARLOTS AND OF THE ABOMINATIONS OF THE LAND.'"

This harlot was sitting on the first beast, which is Rome. She was not Rome, because she sat *on* the beast, which represented the worldly Roman Empire. She was separate and distinct, but supported by the beast. The rulers in Jerusalem had abandoned their dependence on God and depended instead on their alliance with Rome to maintain their status, wealth, and positions of power.

Actually, it was Satan, the prince of this world, working through the beast, who propped up this woman. She had become proud and self-reliant. She had abandoned true worship of the one and only God for a man-made religion. She found security in her own traditions, not in the presence of God. She had crucified Jesus and persecuted his followers and his prophets. She was reeling, "drunk with the blood of the saints, and with the blood of the witnesses of Jesus."

She was clothed "in purple and scarlet, and adorned with gold and precious stones and pearls." Purple and scarlet were the colors of the woven garments made for the high priests, as commanded by Moses. Blue was also one of the colors used in the high priest's attire, but I saw no blue in this woman's clothing. Blue represents the heavens, and this harlot had nothing heavenly about her.

She was decorated with gold, precious stones, and pearls. These were her trophies—spoils from her war against the Lamb, the prophets, and all the saints.

"And in her was found the blood of prophets and of saints and of all who have been slain on the land. . .The woman whom you saw is the great city, which reigns over the kings of the land."

In my writing, I called her "the *great* city," in contrast to the *holy* city, which could only characterize the true City of God. Earlier in this letter when I described the two witnesses, I referred to "the great city" and identified it as

Jerusalem. It was "the great city which mystically is called Sodom and Egypt, where their Lord was crucified."

Isaiah had lamented years earlier, "How the faithful city has become a harlot, she who was full of justice! Righteousness once lodged in her, but now murderers."

By A.D. 70, Jerusalem had become as morally corrupt as Sodom, as enslaved to the world as were the people of God in Egypt, and as captive to man-made religion as those who were carried off to Babylon. The great city that I saw in the vision, where the Lord was crucified, was none other than Jerusalem. *She* was the harlot! *She* was the mysterious "Babylon the Great."

CHAPTER 30

WEEPING AND MOURNING OVER HER

The great harlot, whose hour of judgment had come, sat on many waters. These waters are "peoples and multitudes and nations and tongues."

Jerusalem's influence reached throughout the empire to people of different nations and languages. Jewish synagogues are in every major city. Jewish pilgrims make their way back to Jerusalem each year for the special feasts and holidays. Dr. Luke's list of visitors in Jerusalem on the day of Pentecost, when the church was born, included Parthians, Medes, Elamites, residents of Mesopotamia, Judea, Cappadocia, Pontus, Asia, Phrygia, Pamphylia, Egypt, Libya, Cyrene, and Rome.

Jerusalem had become an important commercial city and trade center for all of Israel. With her downfall, "the merchants of the land weep and mourn over her, because no one buys their cargoes any more... And the kings of the land, who committed acts of immorality and lived sensuously with her, will weep and lament over her when they see the smoke of her burning, standing at a distance because of the fear of her torment, saying 'Woe, woe, the great city, Babylon, the strong city! For in one hour your judgment has come.

"And every shipmaster and every passenger and sailor, and as many as make their living by the sea, stood at a distance, and were crying out as they saw the smoke of her burning, saying 'What city is like the great city?' And they threw dust on their heads and were crying out, weeping and mourning, saying, 'Woe, woe, the great city, in which all who had ships at sea became rich by her wealth, for in one hour she has been laid waste!

"Fallen, fallen is Babylon the great!"

Finally, the blood of the martyrs, the prophets, and the saints had been avenged.

"Rejoice over her, O heaven, and you saints and apostles and prophets, because God has pronounced judgment for you against her . . . After these things I heard as it were, a loud voice of a great multitude in heaven, saying, 'Hallelujah! Salvation and glory and power belong to our God; because his judgments are true and righteous, for he has judged the great harlot who was corrupting the land with her immorality, and he has avenged the blood of his bond-servants on her.'"

CHAPTER 31
GREETINGS FROM BABYLON

Shortly after the church in Jerusalem was born, the Jewish leaders attempted to stop the church's growth by threatening and beating some of its leaders, myself included. Then, beginning with Stephen's death, a man named Saul (with whom you are quite familiar, though by another name!) led a great persecution against the church. I was still living in Jerusalem with the other apostles. By this time, it was clear to all of us that Jerusalem had become a "Babylon."

When Peter wrote his epistle of encouragement to the Jewish Christians who had fled Jerusalem and were scattered as aliens throughout Pontus, Galatia, Cappadocia, Asia, and Bithynia, he ended his letter by sending greetings from the church "in Babylon."

This is what he wrote: "Through Silvanus, our faithful brother (for so I regard him), I have written to you briefly, exhorting and testifying that this is the true grace of God. Stand firm in it! She who is in Babylon, chosen together with you, sends you greetings, and so does my son, Mark."

Some of you know of Silas—or Silvanus, as he is also called. He was the brother from the church in Jerusalem whom we sent up to Antioch when we first heard the gospel had gone to the Gentiles. Silas also accompanied Paul on his second missionary journey. But his home was in the "great city," Jerusalem, where he was living at the time Peter wrote his letter.

John Mark you also know. He was also a Jerusalem resident. He was the son of Mary, whose home was one of the many the church used as a place to meet and pray. We gathered there regularly. On the day the angel let Peter out of prison, he came straight to Mary's house because he knew he would find us there gathered together for prayer.

Young John Mark received the Lord through Peter's preaching, and accompanied Paul and Barnabas on their first missionary trip until the going got too tough. He'd had enough after a shipwreck on the Mediterranean and some other hardships, so he returned home to Jerusalem. Paul was none too happy about it. But later, he and Paul reconciled, and he became a great help to Paul and Peter in the compiling of the letters that became the Scriptures of the New Covenant.

With John Mark at his side, Peter dictated his letter to Silas. They all sent greetings to the dispersed saints from the church "in Babylon." Clearly, Peter was in Jerusalem while writing his letter.

So not only in the revelation, but elsewhere in the thinking of the church of the time, Jerusalem was called "Babylon the Great, The Mother of Harlots." She will not be the last to commit spiritual adultery. Nor will she be the last to persecute the people of God. Others will follow. However, they will only be the unholy offspring of apostate Jerusalem, who is the mother of them all.

CHAPTER 32

THE MARRIAGE SUPPER OF THE LAMB

Following the fall of Babylon, I heard one loud, united, booming voice come from a great multitude in heaven. Deafening, thunderous peals of praise erupted in a fourfold *"Hallelujah!"* to the one seated on the throne.

The first praises were in celebration of the judgment of the harlot; the last chorus was to celebrate that Christ reigned and that his bride had made herself ready.

What I saw next made me feel as if I were being swept along in a joyous wedding procession. It was the first time I caught a glimpse of the bride. I only saw her from a distance. She was beautifully arrayed in her clean and bright wedding garments of righteousness.

Then an angel said to me, "Write, 'Blessed are those who are invited to the marriage supper of the Lamb.'" He added, "These are true words of God."

I have attended many weddings in my lifetime. The most memorable was the one in Cana of Galilee, where the Lord performed his first miracle by turning the water into wine. Such joy abounded at that wedding! But like all earthly weddings, that was only a shadow of the heavenly union of Christ and his bride.

As at the celebration in Cana, singing, merrymaking, and dancing usually follow a wedding procession. The wedding party, along with family and guests, ends up at the house of the groom for a time of feasting and celebration.

At this heavenly marriage feast, however, I saw the redeemed enjoying Christ himself as the *real* marriage supper! *He* is the food, and *he* is the wine. Enjoying him as the spiritual reality of that which is represented by the earthly symbols of bread and wine *is* the marriage supper to which all who believe are invited. Each time we partake, we are renewing our wedding vows and affirming our relationship to him as part of his loving bride.

In speaking of the New Covenant and offering us the bread and the wine, Jesus said, "This is my body, which is given for you." In the book of Genesis, where we find the first picture of this bridegroom-bride relationship—which has been, eternally, Christ's purpose for the church—we see the man and the woman forsaking father and mother and clinging to one another, becoming one in body and soul (the man giving his body to his wife, and she to him). In offering the bread, Jesus in essence was saying, "I am giving myself to you as a husband gives himself to his wife. That complete oneness is the kind of oneness I desire to have with you."

As joyous as the marriage supper was to behold, it was only part of the celebration leading up to the ultimate union when the bride and bridegroom become one for all eternity. The marriage supper is only a foretaste of the bliss that all saints will experience when they see Christ face to face, and he becomes our All, and in all!

CHAPTER 33

A GLIMPSE INTO THE HEART OF GOD

All that has been explained so far took place within a few years after I received the revelation on the Island of Patmos. Jesus correctly predicted that all these events would come upon the very generation that rejected him. The fate of the Jews and Jerusalem has been most tragic.

However, that is not where the story ends. As this letter circulated among the churches, I was confident that God wanted to bring hope and encouragement to all the saints who endured this great tribulation period that came upon the world between A.D. 66–70.

When the Lord Jesus spoke to us that day from the Mount of Olives, the revelation that God had given him caused him to see far beyond the destruction of Jerusalem and the persecution that would beset the church at the hands of Nero. What he saw gave him hope. We could see it in his eyes. His hope became the joy that made him willing to endure the cross. It was anchored in something he saw in the far distant future. That revelation is what the church needed to see during her hour of crisis.

To grasp what it was our Lord saw, let us step back for a moment and get a bird's-eye view of the eternal purpose of God from its inception to completion.

Our Lord Jesus is a *lover*. He has been a lover for all eternity. But until he created this earthly ball, surrounded it with the galaxies, created man out of the red dirt, and breathed into him the breath of life, he was alone. There was no one (outside the Godhead) on whom he could pour out that divine love which had been bound up in him since eternity past.

The first man, Adam, soon discovered something that God had always known: it is not good to be alone. So God caused a deep sleep to fall upon Adam, took a rib from his side, and built a woman. Adam had his bride. The two blissfully became one. Adam was made complete. But God was still alone.

On that joyful day of union in the garden, when the first man and woman became one, our Lord began to reveal the secret behind all of his creation. Adam was a picture of our Lord Jesus Christ. In order for Eve to be produced, it was necessary for Adam to be put to sleep. Similarly, in order for the church to be produced, it was necessary for Christ to die. This mystery, which has been hidden for ages, is the very purpose and passion that compelled God to create. God's eternal desire could only be satisfied by having a bride of his own, someone with whom he could become one. Someone he could love. Someone who would be his life partner and rule and reign with him for all eternity.

God has been building that glorious bride throughout the ages. One day, she will be complete.

Now, what stands between us and God fully realizing that purpose? It is a day called the *Last Day*. Next in the revelation, I saw what the Lord knew would take place between now and *that* day.

CHAPTER 34

SATAN CHAINED, THE SAINTS REIGN

Babylon is fallen! The New Jerusalem, the bride, has replaced Old Jerusalem, the harlot. No doubt you are wondering how all of this works out.

In my visions, I saw Babylon destroyed, and the beast and the false prophet and all of their followers thrown into the lake of fire. But what about Satan?

Moments later in the vision, I saw Satan judged, erased, eliminated, and cast into the lake of fire that burns forever and ever. In the timeless, heavenly realms, though we may not fully see that reality now on earth, that too has already happened!

But how do we get there from here?

"Then I saw an angel coming down from heaven, holding the key of the abyss and a great chain in his hand. And he laid hold of the dragon, the serpent of old, who is the devil and Satan, and bound him for a thousand years, and he threw him into the abyss, and shut it and sealed it over him, so that he would not deceive the nations any longer, until the thousand years were completed; after these things he must be released for a short time."

There will be a period of time, "a thousand years," in which Satan's activity on this earth will be limited. Like a prisoner fastened to a chain who has only a small area in which to roam, he can only go so far.

In the psalms, the Father promised to give our Lord Jesus Christ the nations as his inheritance and the very ends of the earth as his possession. With Christ's victory on the cross, the strong man, Satan, has been bound. His power, authority, and right to rule have been stripped away.

The King of kings and Lord of lords, the one who sits on a white horse and who is called "Faithful and True," will continue to ride forward victoriously through the corridors of time, followed by the armies of heaven. He will be converting the nations, calling out a people for himself from every kindred, tribe, tongue, and nation and building them into his bride.

"From his mouth comes a sharp sword, so that with it he may strike the nations, and he will rule [or shepherd] them with a rod of iron."

During this thousand-year period—let us give it a name, the Church Age—the gospel will go forth until the Lord's kingdom spreads throughout the earth. If you ask me, "Is this thousand years literal?" I would reply by asking you, "Is there a literal key to the abyss, and is the great chain in the angel's hand something to be taken literally as well?" I think not.

The thousand years is no more literal than the Lord owning the cattle on a thousand hills. Does this mean that he does not own the cattle on hill number one thousand and one? The thousand years is a way of saying that Satan's ability to deceive the nations will be limited until this long period of time—the length of which no one knows—has elapsed. Then, Satan will be released for a short period, just before the final judgment.

CHAPTER 35

THE WHITE THRONE JUDGMENT

While he was on earth, I heard the Lord Jesus speak often about "the Last Day." He frequently said things like, "This is the will of him who sent me, that of all that he has given me I lose nothing, but raise it up on the last day. For this is the will of my Father, that everyone who beholds the Son and believes in him will have eternal life, and I myself will raise him up on the last day."

He also spoke of the final judgment, saying, "An hour is coming in which all who are in the tombs will hear his voice [the voice of the Son of Man], and will come forth; those who did good to a resurrection of life, those who committed the evil deeds to a resurrection of judgment."

Matthew, the tax collector who compiled many of the Lord's teachings and sayings, recorded the parable of the wheat and the tares. The Lord was careful to instruct his slaves not to gather up the tares, "For while you are gathering up the tares, you may uproot the wheat with them. Allow both to grow together until the harvest; and in the time of the harvest I will say to the reapers, 'First gather up the tares and bind them in bundles to burn them up; but gather the wheat into my barn.'"

When we asked the Lord to explain this parable to us, he told us that he was the one who sows the good seed. The field was the world. The good seed were the sons of the kingdom, and the tares were the sons of the Evil One. These were to grow up together until the harvest, which would come at the consummation, or the end of the age.

So here is what you need to know: There *will* be a day of judgment for all who have breathed air on this planet, and that will be at the end of the age, on *the Last Day.* You do not have to worry about being left behind! You are not going to miss it. When it comes, we will all be there.

And I heard a voice saying, "Blessed and holy is the one who has a part in the first resurrection; over these the second death has no power, but they will be priests of God and of Christ and will reign with him for a thousand years."

The first resurrection, which we have a part in, was Christ's resurrection. We were *in* him when he conquered death. Practically speaking, as it has worked itself out in our experience, that was the resurrection of our spirits.

We were made alive together with him—joined to the Lord, his Spirit to our spirits. Now, together we are "one spirit" with him.

The second resurrection will be that of our bodies on "the Last Day." That will be the day of our glorification, to which we all look forward. On that day we will receive resurrected, glorified bodies. I am sure that you older ones, whose joints creak when you stand up, can appreciate much more than our younger brothers and sisters how wonderful this will be!

A brief skirmish will mark the end of the "thousand years" in which Satan is released from his prison to make war against the saints. Fire will come down from heaven and devour Satan and his armies. Finally, time will catch up with eternity, and the devil will be thrown into the lake of fire, followed by Death and Hades and anyone whose name is not found written in the Lamb's Book of Life.

Peter described it this way:

"But the day of the Lord will come like a thief, in which the heavens will pass away with a roar and the elements will be destroyed with intense heat, and the earth and its works will be burned up . . . but according to his promise we are looking for new heavens and a new earth, in which righteousness dwells."

The Last Day was rightly named. Beyond that, time will be no more.

CHAPTER 36

THE NEW JERUSALEM

"Then I saw a new heaven and a new earth; for the first heaven and the first earth passed away, and there is no longer any sea. And I saw the holy city, New Jerusalem, coming down out of heaven from God, made ready as a bride adorned for her husband."

There she was: the bride of Christ, the lady of God—Mrs. God! She was breathtakingly beautiful. A new home had been prepared for her: a new heaven and a new earth. It is a place without sin, death, mourning, crying, or pain. All things have become new.

In one sense, she is yet to come. In another sense, she has been in the making throughout the ages. Christ has been building his church. She is and will be unfolding on the pages of time throughout the generations. Time will indeed evaporate into eternity, the invisible will be married to the visible, and God will forever dwell among his people. *All* whom the Son has received from the Father will be assembled together: Christ and the church, inseparably one!

Many years ago I was witness to the most ghastly scene imaginable to human eyes—the wounded body of the Lamb of God hanging from a bloodstained tree between two criminals. I watched as he agonized. Nails ran through his hands and feet; his side was pierced. And I heard his anguished cry, "It is finished!"

Now this same one, not from the cross but from the throne, in all of his majestic splendor, declared once again, "It is done. I am the Alpha and Omega, the beginning and the end."

This was the fourth time I was caught up in spirit. From a great and high mountain I saw the holy city, New Jerusalem, the wife of the Lamb. This is what she looked like to me:

She was without spot or wrinkle. She has no trace of sin. She has no wrinkles, indicating that there is nothing old about her. She is brilliantly robed in the glory of God. Just like the one on the throne, her appearance is like that of a sparkling diamond. She is young, new, and alive. Her beauty is beyond compare. And, dear brothers and sisters, you are a part of that bride! This is how glorious you look through the eyes of your Lord!

This bride-city, the dwelling place of God, had a great and high wall with twelve gates, inscribed with the names of the twelve tribes of the sons of Israel. This signifies that through Israel, a way was made for the entire world to enter into the City of God. And the wall of the city was twelve foundation stones, and on them were the names of the twelve apostles of the Lamb.

I must stop here and humbly comment that in this vision of the heavenly Jerusalem, I saw myself and the brothers with whom I have been built together, as the foundation stones upon which the whole city was built. But why were we made the foundation? Was it because we were so gifted? Because we were so special? No.

We are the foundation, for we were Jesus's original followers during his earthly ministry and witnesses of the resurrection. But there is another factor, equally as important but overlooked by many. That is: I do not know if there have ever been twelve men this side of eternity who loved one another as we loved one another. I hope that I am wrong, and that others have walked in this way—but I have not seen it. The love that the Lord gave us for one another did not come naturally, however. It was hard won. It came with a price.

How did he bring it about? How was it that some fishermen, a rich tax collector, some Galilean peasants, a doubter, and a Zealot, to highlight a few, were so tightly knit together as one? What was our Lord's recipe for building that love into us? I will sum it all up in this statement: we shared *his* Life together.

Yes, we heard him teach as no one had ever taught. But it was more than just hearing the teaching. We eagerly drank from the wisdom that rolled off his lips. We watched him in different situations. We saw him heal and perform miracles. At the end of each day together, we sat around a campfire or stayed up late in someone's home, talking for hours with him and about him. Yet, it was even more than all of this.

Part of that building between us came as our masks came off and we were exposed to one another for who we really were. We learned to repent. We learned from his example to wash each other's feet. And then there was the cross. Scattering and abandoning him during his darkest hour showed us all what kind of fabric we were really made of.

Still, the Lord saw in us material that he could use for his building. All I can say is, "Worthy is the Lamb!"

From dust to stones, and from stones to precious stones: that was the work of the stonemason from Nazareth. That is our testimony.

It took fiery trials and intense pressure to transform lumps of clay like us into precious stones. That is how diamonds are made, you know! We each paid our dues in the quarry of God. He never gave up working on us—chipping away at our rough edges until we were made smooth and could fit and function together as one.

We also needed to experience a resurrection and ascension in order for the Lord to mold us together in such a way that we could be the foundation of this building.

You have all heard stories of the day of Pentecost when three thousand were saved. It is true that Peter preached a powerful message that day. But when he stepped out to address that crowd, there was a wall of men standing shoulder to shoulder beside him. Peter was just the spokesman. Living for three-and-a-half years in the presence of Christ and being gradually knit together produced a unity such as the world had never seen. This unity was the foundation upon which the Lord would build his church.

And this same unity is the work he wants to produce in your lives as well!

As I looked from the high mountain, the city appeared to me as a cube—the same shape as the Holy of Holies that housed the presence of God in the earthly temple made of stones. I recorded its dimensions: 1,500 miles in length, width, and height. That is the same distance as from here to Spain! And as tall! And as wide! The walls of the city, however, were only as high as the length of a stadium field, so that the glory of the city could radiate through eternal realms with no obstruction. Huge gates remained open in the middle of each wall. Each was a colossal pearl, reminding us that it is through much tribulation that we enter the kingdom of God.

I anticipate that some of you want to know if these measurements are literal. Will there really be a city that long, that tall, and that high, made up of all the redeemed, with us apostles occupying the ground floor? I will answer that question before you ask. These measurements and dimensions were given to convey to our human understanding and finite minds how magnificent and holy this city is. And it must be so, because it contains such a great God!

The streets were of pure gold, and the walls transparent gold. This depicts our fellowship with God, which will be as priceless and transparent as the most costly gold. There will be no alloy to corrupt our knowing him as he really is.

To enhance her beauty, this city-bride was adorned with every kind of precious stone. There is such variety in the City of God! Each stone that makes up that city is a unique creation and perfectly displays the beauty and uniqueness that God intended before the beginning of time.

And "I saw no temple in it, for the Lord God, the Almighty, and the

Lamb, are its temple. And the city has no need of the sun or of the moon to shine upon it, for the glory of God has illumined it, and its lamp is the Lamb."

Christ, the menorah of God, will forever be the heavenly lampstand lifting up the eternal God, who is the source of all light. It was this Christ whom Moses saw when he stepped outside of time and was given his vision from Mount Sinai. The lampstand, which was made to illumine the Holy Place of the earthly tabernacle, only represented the one who fills the heavens with light.

Finally, my eyes beheld the very center of the city. There, I saw a "river of the water of life, clear as crystal, coming from the throne of God and of the Lamb." The river wound through the middle of the city, and on either side of it was the Tree of Life. Those who make their abode in the city can eat and drink freely from the fountainhead of divine Life.

Way back at the beginning of time in Eden's garden, when Adam and Eve first drew breath in an environment of sinless perfection, it was all there: a man and a woman, a tree, a river, the gold, the pearls, and the precious stones. All the building materials for God's eternal plan were in place. But now, we finally see this glorious building in its magnificent completion—a spotless and pure bride, the wife of the Lamb.

His promises forever will stand. He will be our God and we will be his people. His laws will be written in our hearts. And there will be no trace of sin. The "I wills" of God—the New Covenant—or more accurately, the Eternal Covenant, in all of its fullness will be ours to enjoy for ages without end!

May the grace of the Lord Jesus be with you all. Amen!"

EPILOGUE

It has been my pleasure to be with you this evening. I hope that your hearts have been encouraged.

I would like to conclude by answering a question that is on the minds of many in regard to the destruction that took place in Jerusalem just a few short years ago. There is talk and hope even now among the Jews that one day, maybe far off in the future, the temple will be rebuilt again and offerings resumed. They cite from the Scriptures the vision of the prophet Ezekiel of a glorious temple that they say has yet to find its fulfillment.

In response to this, I will borrow the words of our dear brother Stephen, who was martyred for Christ's sake, which he spoke just moments before he was seized, driven from Jerusalem, and stoned to death: "The Most High does not dwell in houses made by human hands."

In Ezekiel's vision, the prophet saw a magnificent temple, filled with the glory of God, where God dwelt with his people. A river flowed by way of the altar from the house, becoming deeper and wider as it flowed.

You will find much symbolism here, but let me get right to the point and make it very clear. When Jesus came, *he* was the *real* tabernacle of God. *He* was filled with the glory of God. *He* was Immanuel, God with us. He said, "If anyone is thirsty, let him come to me and drink." He ended the debate with the woman at the well about where to worship—neither in Jerusalem, nor on Mount Gerizim, the sacred mountain of the Samaritans. From that time forth, *true* worshipers would worship *in spirit* and *in reality*.

Jesus is the reality behind *all* the pictures and shadows of the Old Covenant. When he hung on the cross in fulfillment of all that the altar foreshadowed, his side was pierced, and blood and water flowed out. The blood was for our cleansing; the water represented the Spirit.

The Spirit, which began to flow on the day of Pentecost—and is still flowing—is the river that flows from the throne of the heavenly city, New Jerusalem. The temple that Ezekiel saw will not find its future fulfillment in a building made with human hands. The vision of the heavenly temple that Ezekiel saw was *Christ!* From God's perspective, the days of pictures are over! There will never be need of a future temple made with hands, because the *reality* has arrived.

Any future attempt by the Jews to rebuild the temple and once again offer sacrifices will not be a fulfillment of prophecy, but only another display of ignorance and disobedience. So, if you ever hear talk of such things, pay no attention to them.

And now, it is getting late, and it is time for us to go home. If I do not see you after tonight, be assured that we will meet again. Next time, it may even be in Jerusalem—the New Jerusalem—before the throne of grace. There, we will enjoy the fullness of the blessings afforded us by the New Covenant and we will forever fill our cups together and joyfully drink from the living water that proceeds from the throne of God and of the Lamb!

APPENDICES

APPENDIX A:

THE LORD'S SUPPER: THE CELEBRATION OF THE NEW COVENANT

When people think of the New Testament, they typically think of the collection of writings consisting of the four gospels, the book of Acts, the various epistles written to churches and Christian workers, and then the finale—the book of Revelation. This body of writings, combined with the Old Testament to total sixty-six books, makes up the entire Bible.

However, the New Testament is more than a collection of books and letters glued and stitched together between a leather jacket along with the writings of the Old Testament. The words *testament* and *covenant* are interchangeable. Therefore, to properly think of the New Testament (or the New Covenant), we should understand it as the present, eternal, relational reality between God and his people.

To amplify this point, the word *testament* can also be thought of as a will. When a person's last will and testament is executed after that person has died, the covenant or contract takes effect, and the inheritance is received by those named in the will. As the author of the book of Hebrews wrote:

"For where a covenant is, there must of necessity be the death of the one who made it. For a covenant is valid only when men are dead, for it is never in force while the one who made it lives."

In ancient times, the shedding of blood ratified covenants. The agreement between two parties was made, and then an animal was slain, signifying that if either party failed to meet its obligations in the contract, a similar vengeance or retribution as in the slaying of that animal should be taken out upon them.

With the death of Christ, we received our inheritance as spelled out in the New Covenant. To celebrate that covenant, our Lord initiated for us the Lord's Supper.

Since its inauguration, believers throughout the centuries have participated in celebrating the Lord's Supper. For some, it has been just that—a celebration. But this has not been the case for the vast majority of those who have lifted the cup to their lips and shared in the breaking of the bread over the past two millenniums. For most, it has become an event not marked by joy, but rather by something less satisfying, less fulfilling, and not in keeping with the teaching of the New Covenant. The Lord's Supper as it is most commonly practiced today has become a solemn, superstitious, fearful event that causes the Lord's people to engage in morbid, soul-searching introspection rather than to look joyfully and thankfully into the face of the glorious one who, for the joy before him, paid such a price on their behalf.

Sadly, for most of the believing community, the true meaning of the Lord's Supper has been virtually lost, and its practice has become so misconfigured so as to render it unrecognizable in comparison to the way in which it was practiced in the first century. Draping it in layers of institutionalism, superstition, and religious attitudes borrowed from pagan religion, the enemy has done a magnificent job of robbing the Christian church of our true inheritance in understanding and celebrating the elevated, sacred, and mysterious significance of this simple transaction that governs our relationship with our Creator and Redeemer.

In framing the significance and meaning of Lord's Supper, it is important that we look at it within the overarching theme of the whole Bible. We must ask ourselves, what does this simple but profound sacrament mean in light of God's plan for all eternity, and how does it relate to the New Covenant— the present, eternal, relational reality that governs our relationship with the Father and with his Son, the Lord Jesus Christ?

THE BIBLE IS A LOVE STORY
When we step back from the Scriptures and look at the Bible in its entirety, a simple conclusion emerges. The Bible is a love story. Its bridal theme is central—the love of Christ for his bride.

Take, for example, the stories of these Bible couples:

- Adam and Eve
- Isaac and Rebekah
- Boaz and Ruth
- Esther and the King
- Hosea and Gomer
- Solomon and the Shulamite
- God and Israel (even in the Old Testament, Israel is referred to as God's bride)

"Bridal Theology" is a term sometimes used to describe looking at the Scriptures through the lens of its romantic theme.

Down through the ages, there have been believers (considered by some to be Christian mystics) who have tapped into this revelation of God and written about it—people like:

- Origen of Alexandria—third century
- Saint Ambrose and Saint Gregory of Nyssa—fourth century
- Bernard of Clairvaux and William of Saint Thierry—twelfth century
- Saint Teresa of Avila and Saint John of the Cross—sixteenth century
- Madame Guyon—sixteenth–seventeenth century

And many times it resulted in persecution.

If the theme of the Bible is indeed a romance, and if Christ is our Bridegroom and we are his bride, then the Lord's Supper must somehow fit into this theme.

THE LORD'S SUPPER: A WEDDING CELEBRATION

In celebrating the Lord's Supper, we are celebrating our union with our Bridegroom, the King of all kings and Lover of our souls.

From eternity past, long before the world was created, before time, matter, or anything physical had ever been created, God had a plan. It was his purpose—his eternal purpose. That purpose was to have a bride for his Son.

The Father loved his Son so much that he wanted to give him a gift: a bride whom he could love, and who would love him in return, who would be his life companion and rule and reign with him for all eternity.

We see the picture, or foreshadowing of that purpose in Genesis chapters 1 and 2, where God created Adam, then put him to sleep. He took a rib from his side to fashion (build) Eve, and the two became one flesh, husband and wife.

With the passage of thousands of years, and when the fullness of time had come, we see the reality of that picture finally fulfilled. Christ came to earth, died on the tree (slept for three days), then rose again. By his Spirit, he has been fashioning (building) his church ever since.

In Revelation 21 and 22, we see God's plan complete: a new heaven and a new earth with the bride (the church—the New Jerusalem) descending out of heaven to become eternally one with Christ (her Bridegroom).

CHRIST AS THE BRIDEGROOM IN THE GOSPELS

Even in the gospels, if we have eyes to see, we can see Christ coming as the Bridegroom. John the Baptizer identified him as such when he said, "He who has the bride is the bridegroom, but the friend of the bridegroom, who stands and hears him, rejoices greatly because of the bridegroom's voice. So this joy of mine has been made full." (John 3:29)

When Christ came out of the water at his baptism, a voice from heaven proclaimed, "This is my beloved Son, in whom I am well-pleased." (Matthew 3:17) A more accurate rendering is found in *Young's Literal Translation of the Bible,* which reads, "This is my Son—the Beloved, in whom I did delight," calling attention to Christ being the fulfillment of King Solomon in the Song of Songs, who was referred to as "The Beloved." In this love song portraying the king and his Shulamite bride, the king pictures Christ, and the Shulamite the church.

In John 4, in the story of the Samaritan woman, we see Christ as the fulfillment of Jacob, who came seeking his bride and found her at the well (Genesis 29, John 4:5–39). The woman in John 4 was a Samaritan—a half-breed, half-Jew, half-Gentile—another picture of the bride that Christ purchased with his own blood.

We see a hint of Christ as the Bridegroom in the first miracle he performed at the wedding in Cana of Galilee in John 2, verses 1–11. When the wine ran out, Jesus's mother said to him, "They have no wine," to which Jesus replied, "Woman, what does that have to do with us? My hour has not yet come." What hour was he referring to? The hour of his wedding! The hour of his wedding had not yet come.

In the passage in Luke in which the Lord initiates the Lord's Supper with his disciples, it says, *"When the hour had come,* he reclined at the table and the apostles with him . . . and when he had taken a cup [of wine] and given thanks, he said, 'Take this and share it among yourselves.'" (Luke 22:14-17)

When our Lord took the Lord's Supper with his disciples, the hour of his wedding had finally come!

ANCIENT JEWISH WEDDING CUSTOMS

We can better begin to understand the significance of the Lord's Supper when we take into account ancient Jewish wedding customs that were observed at the time of Christ. Let's start with the engagement.

In Jewish culture, when a young man and woman became engaged, it was customary for the bridegroom's father to choose the bride for his son. A meeting took place under the supervision of the father of the groom and the father of the bride, and a meal was prepared.

THE NEW COVENANT IS A WEDDING COVENANT

We can see the apostle Paul's spiritual understanding of this concept and of this relationship of Christ as our Bridegroom and God the Father choosing a bride for his Son. We can almost imagine him taking the place of the father of the bride when he wrote to the Corinthians, "For I am jealous for you with a godly jealousy; for I betrothed you to one husband, so that to Christ I might present you as a pure virgin." (2 Corinthians 11:2)

Following the meal, the bridegroom proposed marriage by offering a written contract to the woman called the *ketuba*. This was a legally binding document spelling out in detail the promises and obligations the bridegroom would perform for his bride.

The bride, on the other hand, was not obligated to make *any* promises to her husband. But she had the right of refusal.

The legally binding contract the Lord Jesus offered at the Lord's Supper was the New Covenant. Comparing that to the woman's right of refusal, we see the role of free will in our entrance into this marriage covenant.

"And in the same way the cup, after they had eaten, saying 'This cup which is poured out for you is the new covenant in my blood.'" (1 Corinthians 11:25)

Unlike the Old Covenant, which had conditions ("I will bless you *if* you do this," or "I will curse you *if* you do that") the New Covenant is a *unilateral covenant*. It is one-sided. It consists only of "I wills."

Jeremiah 31:31–34 spells out the terms of the New Covenant.

"'Behold, the days are coming,' declares the Lord, 'when I will make a new covenant with the house of Israel and the house of Judah.'"

- "I will put my law within them and on their heart I will write it."
- "I will be their God, and they shall be my people."
- "I will forgive their iniquity, and their sin I will remember no more."

Once the disciples partook of the cup, in the eyes of God, they had accepted the Bridegroom's proposal. They were legally wed to Christ! When we partake of the cup of wine, we are proclaiming that Christ is our Bridegroom and we are the bride of Christ. We are his body. We are inseparably one with him. By drinking, the contract has been ratified, and we are legally, once and for all, forever his.

In addition to the contract, the bridegroom offered a price that he was willing to pay for his bride.

Adam gave up bone in order to have his bride. Christ paid the highest price of all. He gave his very life.

"Unless a grain of wheat falls into the earth and dies, it remains alone; but if it dies, it bears much fruit." (John 12:24)

After offering the bride the ketuba (the contract) and declaring the price, the bridegroom would pour wine into a cup. He would drink half and then offer the cup to his prospective bride. If she refused to drink, there would be no wedding. But if she did take the cup and drink, this instantly sealed the marriage! From the moment the wine touched her lips, she became a legally married woman (even though the wedding had not yet been consummated).

The groom would then present the bride with a gift as a tangible reminder that it would not be long before their wedding day and the consummation of their marriage would come. Jesus has given us his Holy Spirit, the reminder that we are betrothed to Christ and that when we finally see him face to face, the complete oneness and marriage relationship that we are longing for will come (Ephesians 1:13–14).

Once the marriage was agreed upon, the bridegroom would go away to prepare a home for them to live in. Usually, he would go to his father's home and "add on" by preparing a place for him and his bride to live. Jesus said, "In my Father's house are many dwelling places; if it were not so, I would have told you, for I go to prepare a place for you. If I go and prepare a place for you, I will come again and receive you to myself; that where I am, there you may be also." (John 14:2-3)

Before parting, the bridegroom made a promise to the bride that he would not drink of the fruit of the vine again until he had finished building their home. Following the Last Supper, Jesus said, "I will not drink of the fruit of the vine from now on until the kingdom of God comes." (Luke 22:18)

The bride, on the other hand, would then spend her time preparing to be the bridegroom's wife.

"'Let us rejoice and be glad and give the glory to him, for the marriage of the Lamb has come and his bride has made herself ready.' It was given to her to clothe herself in fine linen, bright and clean; for the fine linen is the righteous acts of the saints. Then he [the angel] said to me, 'Write, Blessed are those who are invited to the marriage supper of the Lamb.'" (Revelation 19:7-9)

So in the context of the wedding (the wedding supper), the tradition of celebrating with wine not only brought joy to the festivity, but also commemorated that the promise that the complete union between the couple was soon to be fulfilled.

When the bride has made herself ready, Christ, our Bridegroom, will come for his bride. There will be great feasting, and the marriage will be consummated. We will live together—forever in union with him—as husband and wife. This is the consummation when Christ will be All and in all.

So the cup represents a marriage covenant—signifying that we have been married to Christ and are partakers of the New Covenant—of the "I wills" of God.

THE LIFE IS IN THE BLOOD

"Is not the cup of blessing which we bless a sharing in the blood of Christ?" (1 Corinthians 10:16)

The Bible teaches, "the life of all flesh is in the blood." (Leviticus 17:11) To share in the blood of Christ is to share in the Life of Christ. In order for Christ to have a bride, he needed to have a partner who shared the same *Life* that he lived by. On earth, Christ lived by the divine, uncreated Life that he had shared with his Father for all eternity, before the world was ever created. When he rose from the dead and breathed his Spirit into his disciples, it was that *Life* that he breathed into them.

When we take the cup, we celebrate our marriage, our oneness with him. It is our testimony that we have been given the same divine, uncreated, eternal Life that our Bridegroom in heaven lives by. It is a celebration that we, as sons of men, can live by a higher Life—by the very Life of the eternal God! Jesus said, "I came that you might have *life* [Greek: *zoe,* meaning *divine life]* and have it in abundantly!" (John 10:10)

THE BREAD

"For I received from the Lord that which I also delivered to you, that the Lord Jesus in the night in which He was betrayed took bread; and when he had given thanks, He broke it and said, 'This is My body which is given for you; do this in remembrance of Me.'" (1 Corinthians 11:23-24)

In Genesis, the man said, "This is now bone of my bones, and flesh of my flesh. She shall be called Woman, because she was taken out of Man. For this reason a man shall leave his father and his mother, and be joined to his wife [give his body and soul to his wife], and they shall become one flesh." (Genesis 2: 23-24)

Just like Adam became "one flesh" with Eve, Christ became "one spirit" with his bride.

"But the one who joins himself to the Lord is one spirit with him." (1 Corinthians 6:17)

Christ's giving us the bread represents his giving us his body and becoming one with us. By sharing in the bread, we are testifying that we not only have his life living in us and belong to him, but that we all, together, share that same life and belong to one another. By partaking of the bread, we are affirming and celebrating our oneness and eternal union with Christ and with one another. By partaking of the cup, we affirm, are reminded of, and celebrate our wedding vows with the Lord, as spelled out in the New Covenant.

Each time we partake of the wine and the bread, we are also reminded of the simple but eternal principle found in God himself: Without the crushing of the grapes, there could be no wine. Without the dying of the wheat, there could be no bread. In order for us to receive the life of God and become the bride of Christ, Christ needed to die.

OLD TESTAMENT PICTURES FORESHADOWING
THE LORD'S SUPPER: MELCHIZEDEK

"And Melchizedek, king of Salem, brought out bread and wine [to Abraham]; now he was a priest of God Most High. He blessed him and said, 'Blessed be Abram of God Most High, possessor of heaven and earth; and blessed be God Most High, who has delivered your enemies into your hand.' He [Abraham] gave him a tenth of all." (Genesis 14:18-20)

"You [Christ] are a priest forever according to the order of Melchizedek." (Hebrews 7:17)

Melchizedek did not exist before Jesus; Jesus existed before Melchizedek ("Before Abraham was born, *I am*"). Melchizedek's name meant "King of Righteousness." He was also king of Salem, which is "King of Peace" (see Hebrews 7:2).

This Old Testament picture tells us that Christ, our heavenly Bridegroom, who is our righteousness and peace, would come to the people of faith (represented by Abraham, the father of faith), offering them bread and wine, the symbols of the New Covenant.

THE ELEMENTS WITHIN THE HOLY PLACE

In the Holy Place in the tabernacle in the wilderness was the table with the bread of the presence (twelve loaves, one for each of the twelve tribes of Israel) and wine. We are told in Exodus that on that table were the holy dishes, along with pans, jars, and bowls with which to pour drink offerings. These articles were made of pure gold (see Exodus 25:29–30). The drink offering consisted of strong wine (see Exodus 29:38–41, Numbers 28:7). The wine was to be pure in the sense that it was not to be watered down. It was to be potent and of full strength.

Besides the bread and the wine on the table, there was also frankincense.

"Then you shall take fine four and bake twelve cakes with it; two-tenths of an ephah shall be in each cake. You shall set them in two rows, six to a row, on the pure gold table before the Lord. You shall put pure frankincense on each row that it may be a memorial portion for the bread, even an offering by fire to the Lord."

Frankincense was one of the ingredients in the exclusive formula for incense to be burned before the Lord as a sweet-smelling aroma. These substances—the bread, wine, and frankincense—were only available to the priests. There in the Holy Place was where the priests could enjoy intimate communion and fellowship with God. This picture should remind us that it is only as we take up our place as ministering priests to the Lord that we enjoy the intimacy of communion and fellowship with him, as represented by the bread and the wine.

The frankincense (representing resurrection, a sweet-smelling fragrance rising to God) adds to the mystery of this picture. It was not until the resurrection of Christ that we could truly celebrate, with joy, his life and our oneness with him.

THE OLD TESTAMENT TABERNACLE: ONLY A PICTURE

The tabernacle that Moses constructed in the wilderness was only a pattern or replica of something (someone!) that God revealed to him in the heavens. The writer of Hebrews, when speaking of the priests, said that they served a "copy or a shadow of heavenly things, just as Moses was warned by God when he was about to erect the tabernacle: for, 'See,' he says, 'that you make all things according to the pattern which was shown you on the mountain.'"

Christ is the reality—the "pattern" after which the Old Testament tabernacle was made!

"And the Word became flesh and dwelt [tabernacled] among us, and we saw his glory, glory as of the only begotten from the Father, full of grace and truth."

"And I heard a loud voice from the throne, saying, 'Behold, the tabernacle of God [Christ] is among men.'"

In Christ there has always been the eternal reality of the New Covenant as represented by the wine and the bread pictured in the Holy Place in the tabernacle in the wilderness: *The "I wills" of God and the Life of God are in him, and through him, made available to man!*

THE DAILY SACRIFICES: ANOTHER PICTURE

We also see grain and wine in connection with the daily sacrifices. Burnt offerings were sacrificed day and night. Accompanying the burnt offering was a grain and a drink offering. It often goes unnoticed, but we can see here that bread and wine were offered along with the burnt offering.

"Now this is what you shall offer on the altar: two one year old lambs each day, continuously. The one lamb you shall offer in the morning and the other lamb you shall offer at twilight; and there shall be one-tenth of an ephah of fine flour mixed with one-fourth of a hin of beaten oil, and one-fourth of a hin of wine for a drink offering with one lamb. The other lamb you shall offer at twilight and shall offer with it the same grain offering and the same drink offering as in the morning, for a soothing aroma, an offering by fire to the Lord."

A "hin" of wine was approximately a gallon and a half, or about twenty-two liters. A quarter of a hin (5.5 liters) is about the same amount of blood an adult man would have in his body. What an appropriate picture we find in the Scriptures portraying Jesus's blood poured out for us!

Christ is the reality of the burnt offering. His life was wholly and totally consumed, continually offered to God, night and day, as a sweet-smelling aroma to God. The grain and the drink offerings (bread and wine) accompanying the burnt offering were reminders that the life Christ lived and the price he paid could not be separated from the blessings of the New Covenant which he secured for his beloved bride.

Under the law, drink offerings were not to be offered alone but in connection with the offerings of "soothing aroma" to the Lord, namely the burnt, meal, and peace offerings. They were never to be offered with the sin or trespass offerings. There was something about the drink offering of wine in the Old Testament that brought joy to God. There was joy for God in the burnt offering (Christ's life of total obedience), his sinless life (the meal offering), and his being our peace and reconciliation to God (the peace offering). But there was no joy for God in Christ's suffering when he became sin upon the cross (sin offering) and was the recipient of the wrath of God for each and every one of our sins (the trespass offering). This explains the absence of any drink offering accompanying the sin and trespass offerings.

THE PASSOVER CELEBRATION AND THE FEAST OF UNLEAVENED BREAD

Many people use the picture of the Passover celebration as a foreshadowing of the Lord's Supper. Lamb, unleavened bread, bitter herbs, and wine are prominent in that celebration. But interestingly, in the account of the Passover and Feast of Unleavened Bread recorded in Exodus 12, three of these elements were mentioned—but not the fourth. Wine is not mentioned. History tells us that wine only became part of the Passover celebration sometime following the captives' return from Babylon. But it is never mentioned in the Old Testament as part of the Passover celebration.

Why is this? Could it be that the symbols of the New Covenant—the bread *and the wine*—were only fully realized after the finished work of Christ on the cross, when the New Covenant was initiated and the Old Covenant was made obsolete?

SUMMARY OF CHRIST IN THE OLD TESTAMENT PICTURES
It is Christ who is:

- Our high priest after the order of Melchizedek
- The I Am, who existed in eternity long before Abraham or the Levitical priesthood ever came into existence
- The reality of the Old Testament tabernacle (and temple) and the bread and wine contained therein
- The reality of the Old Testament sacrifices that were accompanied by the symbols of the New Covenant (bread and wine)

PRACTICAL APPLICATIONS FOR CELEBRATING THE LORD'S SUPPER
For the early Christians, the Lord's Supper was part of a festive meal. The first "Lord's Supper" was a full meal the Lord ate together with his disciples (actually a Passover Feast). It was *not* the "Lord's appetizer" or the "Lord's snack" consisting of a small, thin wafer and a thimbleful of wine or grape juice. It was a "supper," a banquet, or a festive meal, and in the early church it was known as an "agape feast." It was equivalent to what we would call a potluck today.

"*While they were eating,* he took some bread and after a blessing he broke it and gave it to them, and said, 'Take it, this is my body.' And when he had taken a cup and given thanks, he gave it to them, and they all drank from it. And he said to them, 'This is my blood of the covenant, which is poured out for many.'" (Mark 14:22-24)

Twenty years later, when the church in Corinth was coming together to celebrate the Lord's Supper, they were taking a meal together.

"So then, my brothers and sisters, when you come together *to eat* . . ." (I Corinthians 11:33)

Though the Lord's Supper was celebrated as a full meal, the focal element or showcase of that meal was "the cup and the bread."

"Is not the cup of blessing which we bless a sharing in the blood of Christ? Is not the bread which we break a sharing in the body of Christ? Since there is one bread, we who are many are one body; for we all partake of the one bread." (1 Corinthians 10:16-17)

Dining with others, as they did in the book of Acts where they broke bread together, was associated with fellowship, gladness of heart, and praising God.

"They were continually devoting themselves to the apostles' teaching and to fellowship, to the breaking of bread and to prayer." (Acts 2:42)

"Day by day continuing with one mind in the temple, and breaking bread from house to house, they were taking their meals together with gladness and sincerity of heart, praising God and having favor with all the people. And the Lord was adding to their number day by day those who were being saved." (Acts 2:46-47)

By way of contrast, what is the basic mood or atmosphere in most churches today when the Lord's Supper is taken? Is it one of celebration, joy, and gladness of heart—such as the atmosphere at a wedding? Or could it be better described as the atmosphere one would expect at a funeral—silence, sobriety, introspection, and seriousness?

The Lord's Supper was celebrated in homes, not in cathedrals; in smaller, dinner-sized groups, not in large formal gatherings.

"Day by day continuing with one mind in the temple, and breaking bread from house to house."

DO THIS IN REMEMBRANCE OF ME

When we partake of the Lord's Supper, we remember the Lord of the New Covenant together.

"I will put my law within them and on their heart I will write it."

When we gather for the Lord's Supper, we remember the things the Lord has done *in us* that we were unable to do ourselves. For example, when the Lord enables us to forgive someone who has offended us, when we were unable to forgive them ourselves, that's Lord's Supper material to bring to the meal and share with others!

"I will be their God, and they shall be my people."

When we gather for the Lord's Supper, we remember how he has been our God. For example, we remember his leading (he is our shepherd, our guide). When the Lord puts someone in our path with whom we end up sharing the gospel, that's Lord's Supper material to bring to the meal and share with others!

We can share about his deliverance (he is our deliverer). For example, when the Lord delivers us from some sin or some harmful circumstance, heals us, enlightens our minds to see where we may have been living in darkness, and then enables us to live in the light, that's

Lord's Supper material to bring to the meal and share with others!

We can share about his feeding (he is our spiritual food and spiritual drink). For example, when he shows us something in the Word that strengthens us or puts a song in our hearts to encourage us, that is spiritual food and spiritual drink; that's Lord's Supper material to bring to the meal and share with others!

We can share about his peace (he is our peace; he is our rest). For example, when we have a difficult decision to make, and after we pray about it the Lord gives us peace and we know the direction we must go, that's Lord's Supper material to bring to the meal and share with others!

The same thing is true of knowing his victory (he is our victory), his goodness (he is our goodness), his mercy and grace (he is mercy and grace), his love (he is love), his life (he is our life), his wisdom (he is wisdom), the fellowship we have with other believers (he is our fellowship), and the benefits of being in his house (he is the source of all spiritual blessings). Knowing him in all of these ways (and more), that's Lord's Supper material to bring to the meal and share with others!

"I will forgive their iniquity, and their sin I will remember no more."

When we gather for the Lord's Supper, we also remember his forgiveness. He has forgiven us for all of our sins—past, present, and future. God poured out all of his wrath for sin on his Son. His wrath is totally satisfied. There is not one drop left to pour out on us. Our sins and lawless deeds he remembers no more. When he sees us, he sees us in Christ as righteous, totally forgiven, holy, blameless, without spot or wrinkle, and beautiful. Thankfulness for his forgiveness and for his love, for his dying on the cross for us, that's Lord's Supper material that we can bring to the meal and share with others!

THE LORD'S SUPPER: THE LOVE FEAST

Referred to in 1 Corinthians 11:33 and Jude 12, the Lord's Supper was known as a love feast. It was a meal at which believers from every ethnicity, background, and social and economic status came together to share a common meal, demonstrate their oneness in Christ, and remember the Lord. It was a time to re-member or re-constitute the body of Christ under its spiritual head and king, the Lord Jesus. The physical feast was meant to be a picture of the spiritual feast that is ours to enjoy in the person of the Lord Jesus. It is a time for *all* to share and partake of physical food and for *all* to share with one another the spiritual food (Christ) by which we all have been nourished, for mutual benefit and encouragement.

PROBLEMS CONCERNING THE PRACTICE OF THE LORD'S SUPPER IN THE NEW TESTAMENT: 1 CORINTHIANS 11:17–34

"But in giving this instruction, I do not praise you, because you come together not for the better but for the worse."

Eating in an Unworthy Manner:

First Corinthians 11:27 presents a difficult passage for many Christians: "Therefore whoever eats the bread or drinks the cup of the Lord in an unworthy manner, shall be guilty of the body and the blood of the Lord."

When we look at the context of this verse, we find that a problem had developed in the way the Corinthian believers were taking the Lord's Supper. There were a few in the church who were wealthy and who brought food and wine to the banquet, and others who were not so wealthy who brought what they could. Then there were the slaves and the unemployed, who could bring nothing. The slaves, who often had to work late, would finally arrive to find that all the food had been eaten and all the wine had been drunk.

The picture that they were all one in Christ and all had become partakers of the same spiritual food had broken down. Some of the early guests could not control themselves and wait for the others. They were gluttons. They ate all the food, leaving nothing for latecomers. They drank more than their portion of wine, and some got drunk, some got sick, and others passed out ("fell asleep").

Eating in an Unworthy Manner Resulting in Judgment:

"But a person must examine himself, and in so doing he is to eat of the bread and drink of the cup. For he who eats and drinks, eats and drinks judgment to himself if he does not judge the body rightly."

The judgment here is judgment from the body, not judgment resulting in loss of salvation.

"So then, my brothers and sisters, when you come together to eat, wait for one another. If anyone is hungry, let him eat at home so that you will not come together for judgment."

In Roman society, the rich didn't like eating with the poor. The wealthier Christians in Corinth were judging the poor with evil motives. They did not see them as equal members in the body of Christ, so they did not wait for them.

When people came in late and all the food was gone and people were drunk, the latecomers judged those who had not waited for them as being selfish and indulgent, gluttons and drunkards. This, too, brought disunity in the body. This was not what the Lord's Supper was intended to represent. It was intended to portray a corporate sharing and partaking of the life of the Lord, not every person for himself.

Examining Yourselves:

"But a person must examine himself, and in so doing he is to eat of the bread and drink of the cup."

Examining oneself does not mean to become pious and introspective, trying to think of every sin you might have ever committed and confessing it so as to become worthy to partake of the Lord's Supper. We could *never* become worthy by anything we do. But Christ has *made* us worthy by his death on the cross, once for all.

"Examine yourself" was an admonition to make sure that the believers in Corinth were thinking of others and not taking more than their share of food or drink so as to incur judgment by the rest of the body, resulting in impaired relationships, broken fellowship, and disunity in the body of Christ. Many places today where only a small thimble-full of wine and a small wafer are offered as the substance for the Lord's Supper, this admonition would not even apply!

The way the Lord's Supper is practiced today has become perverted. The common belief that people must examine themselves, reflect upon their sins, and confess every possible sin before they partake of the Lord's Supper in order to avoid judgment and damnation creates an atmosphere of fear and gloom which negates Christ's finished work on the cross.

Is there "now no condemnation for those who are in Christ Jesus," or if we fail to confess every single sin and partake of the Lord's Supper in an "unworthy manner" will we be incurring his wrath and condemnation? Which is it?

Earlier in 1 Corinthians, Paul wrote to them that:

- They had been sanctified
- They were saints (holy ones)
- They were not lacking in any gift
- Christ would confirm them to the end, blameless
- They were in Christ, who became to them wisdom from God,
- righteousness, sanctification, and redemption
- They were a temple of God, and the Spirit of God dwelt in them
- The temple of God is holy (which they were)
- They were filled, rich, kings

- They were washed, sanctified, and justified
- They were joined (married) to the Lord, and were one spirit with him

In Corinth, the problem was a case of rich/poor prejudice. In some places, there may be prejudice based on skin color, ethnicity, nationality, or place in the cultural caste system. Regardless, these kinds of divisions are wrong. If we have impaired relationships with our brothers and sisters, we are to seek reconciliation so that we can truly celebrate our unity in Christ, just as our Lord taught, "Therefore if you are presenting your offering at the altar, and there remember that your brother has something against you, leave your offering there before the altar and go first be reconciled to your brother, and then come and present your offering." (Matthew 5:24)

Some may protest and say that there is grave danger of judgment from the Lord if we take the Lord's Supper in an "unworthy manner." I would respond by saying, yes, if people persist in disregarding the Lord's voice, ignoring his warnings, and hardening their hearts toward him and members of his body, we should expect that he will exercise some form of discipline or judgment. But it would be a redemptive judgment with a view of restoration—not of eternal damnation.

The cup that we drink is, indeed, the cup of the New Covenant, in which we can celebrate that our sins and lawless deeds he will remember no more (see Hebrews 10:7)! Therefore, we can approach the Lord's Supper with an attitude of celebration, not of fear.

The cup we drink as we celebrate the Lord's Supper is to be a Cup of Joy!

FREEDOM TO CELEBRATE

The celebration of the Lord's Supper as a communal Christian banquet in the first century was *never* a sacred ritual performed by a sacred person in a sacred building. Nowhere in the New Testament does it say that the Lord's Supper must be administered by a pastor, a clergyman, or a priest or conducted inside a building with a cross on top of it. And where on earth did we ever get the notion that the bread and the wine, taken as a meal along with other believers in someone's home, is out of date and has been superseded by a superior model of partaking of a small, tasteless wafer and a thimble-sized portion of grape juice while sitting on a hard bench in a warehouse-sized room full of people, most of whom you don't know?

The message of the Lord's Supper is revolutionary! It was as revolutionary then as it is today.

It is interesting to note that three primary questions fueled the fires of a revolution in the 1960s in America known as the Jesus Movement. Young people were questioning America's involvement in the Vietnam War, "hippies" were dropping out of society and displaying their distinctions by growing their hair long, wearing "holey jeans" and flowers in their hair, and smoking pot. Traditional morality and marriage were being questioned. Traditional values were being questioned, like the necessity for completing college and getting a "good job."

Within the church, too, people started to question. This was an era when many people—especially young people—dropped out of the traditional church because they didn't find it relevant. They just couldn't relate. This resulted in number of alternatives for traditional church being born, such as Christian communes, coffeehouses, and numerous parachurch organizations. As was the chant in secular society, so became the chant within the organized church: "Power to the people!"

Within both evangelical and charismatic circles, Christian leaders whom the majority of young people in that generation were looking to were focusing on three main questions:

1. Where in the New Testament does it say that you have to be an ordained pastor, clergyman, or priest with a seminary education, in order to preside over the Lord's Supper?
2. Where in the New Testament does it say that you have to be an ordained pastor, clergyman, or priest with a seminary education, in order to baptize someone?
3. And where does it say that this has to happen inside a church building?

SUMMARY
"Therefore let us celebrate the feast . . . with the unleavened bread of sincerity and truth." (1 Corinthians 5:8)

The Lord's Supper Is a Celebration of Our Oneness with Christ
"The sons of this age marry and are given in marriage, but those who are considered worthy to attain to that age and the resurrection from the dead, neither marry nor are given in marriage." (Luke 20:34-35)

We are the bride of Christ! The reason there will be no marriage in the age to come is because we will be married to Christ! This is true whether we've realized it or not. When we said "yes" and accepted him as our Lord and Savior, that relationship began! He is our Bridegroom. We will be one with him to enjoy him, to be to him a life companion, and to rule and reign with him for all eternity.

THE MYSTERIES OF GOD

The New Testament is filled with mysteries! Mark wrote of the mystery of the kingdom. John wrote of the mystery of the seven stars and the seven golden lampstands and the mystery of Babylon the Great in the book of Revelation. But it is Paul's writings most of all that are full of mysteries.

Paul wrote of:

- The mystery of the partial hardening of Israel until the fullness of the Gentiles has come
- The mystery of the resurrection
- The mystery of God's will—the summing up of all things in Christ
- The mystery hidden from the ages that the Gentiles were fellow heirs with the Jews, of the same body, and partakers of the same promises in Christ
- The mystery that through the church the manifold wisdom of God would be made known to the principalities and powers in heavenly places according to God's eternal purpose
- The mystery of the gospel
- The mystery of Christ in you, the hope of glory
- The mystery of lawlessness
- The mystery of the faith
- The mystery of godliness

The Mega-Mystery

But there is one other mystery that Paul wrote about. He called it the "great mystery," or in the Greek, the *mega*-mystery. It was the granddaddy of all mysteries, the whopper! This also is revealed in the letter to the Ephesians.

Think about how we use the word *mega* today. The mega-rich—people who are not just rich, but fabulously rich. Mega-churches—not just small churches, but churches with membership in the thousands.

Paul wrote of many mysteries, but this mystery, he calls the mega-mystery!

What is this mystery? It is the mystery that the husband-wife relationship is a picture to us that we are the bride of Christ—the wife of the Lamb!

In the passage where Paul wrote of the marriage relationship between man and woman and husbands loving their wives as Christ loved the church and gave himself for her, he concluded with a quote from Genesis and then identified the mystery of all mysteries.

"For this reason a man shall leave his father and mother and be joined to his wife, and the two shall become one flesh."

Then he dropped the bomb: "This mystery is great [Greek: *mega*] but I am speaking with reference to Christ and the church." (Ephesians 5:31-32)

This mega-mystery was foretold in the Old Testament:

"'And it will come about in that day,' declares the Lord, 'That you will call me Ishi [my husband] and will no longer call me Baali [my master, or my Baal] . . . I will betroth you to me forever; Yes, I will betroth you to me in righteousness and in justice.'" (Hosea 2:16, 19)

THIS MEGA-MYSTERY IS THAT TO THE LORD ALONE WE HAVE BEEN ETERNALLY BONDED IN A ONENESS FAR GREATER THAN THE EARTHLY PICTURE OF MARRIAGE COULD BUT FAINTLY PORTRAY. THIS IS THE MYSTERY WE CELEBRATE EVERY TIME WE TAKE THE LORD'S SUPPER!

BIBLIOGRAPHY

PART I

Cohen, Abraham. *Everyman's Talmud: The Major Teachings of the Rabbinic Sages.* New York: Schocken Books, 1975.

Danby, Herbert. *The Mishnah.* Oxford: Oxford University Press, 1933.

Edersheim, Alfred. *The Life and Times of Jesus the Messiah.* Peabody, MA: Hendrickson Publishers, 1993.

—*The Temple, Its Ministry and Services.* Peabody, MA: Hendrickson Publishers, 1994.

Edwards, Gene Edwards. *Acts in First-Person.* Sargent, GA: Seedsowers, 1996.

—*Revolution.* Sargent, GA: Seedsowers, 1975.

—*The Story of My Life as told by Jesus Christ.* Sargent, GA: Seedsowers, 1999.

Gentry, Kenneth. *He Shall Have Dominion.* Tyler, TX: Institute for Christian Economics, 1992.

Holwerda, David E. *Jesus & Israel One Covenant or Two?* Grand Rapids: W.B. Eerdmans, 1995.

Josephus, Flavius. *The Complete Works of Josephus.* Grand Rapids: Kregel Publications, 1981.

Jukes, Andrew. *The Law of the Offerings, The Five Tabernacle Offerings and Their Spiritual Significance.* Grand Rapids: Kregel Publications, 1994.

Kaung, Stephen. *The Life of Our Lord Jesus.* Richmond, VA: Christian Tape Ministry, 1997.

—*Worship.* Richmond, VA: Christian Tape Ministry, 1998.

Kilpatrick, Martha. *Adoration.* Sargent, GA: Seedsowers, 1999.

Lawrence, John W. *The Six Trials of Jesus.* Grand Rapids: Kregel Publications, 1996.

Levy, David M. *The Tabernacle, Shadows of the Messiah.* Grand Rapids: Kregel Publications, 2003.

Maier, Paul L. *In the Fullness of Time.* Grand Rapids: Kregel Publications, 1991.

—*Pontius Pilate.* Grand Rapids: Kregel Publications, 1968.

Martin, Ernest Martin. *Restoring the Original Bible.* Portland, OR: Associates for Scriptural Knowledge, 1994.

—*Secrets of Golgotha*. Portland, OR: Associates for Scriptural Knowledge, 1996.

—*The Temples that Jerusalem Forgot*. Portland, OR: Associates for Scriptural Knowledge, 2000.

McDonough, Mary E. *God's Plan of Redemption*. Shoals, IN: Old Paths Tract Society, (year not listed).

Nee, Watchman. *Not I But Christ*. New York: Christian Fellowship Publishers, 1974.

Page, Charles R. II. *Jesus & the Land*. Nashville: Abingdon Press, 1995.

Smith, William. *Smith's Bible Dictionary*. Uhrichsville, OH: Barbour Publishing, Inc. 2012.

Soltau, Henry W. *The Holy Vessels and Furniture of the Tabernacle*. Grand Rapids: Kregel Publications, 1971.

—*The Tabernacle, The Priesthood, and the Offerings*. Grand Rapids: Kregel Publications, 1972.

Strobel, Lee. *The Case for Christ*. Grand Rapids: Zondervan, 1998.

Wampler, Dee. *The Trial of Christ*. Enumclaw, WA: WinePress Publishing, 2006

Warnock, George H. The Feast of Tabernacles. Cranbrook, BC: George H. Warnock, 1986.

PART II

Allen, David L. *Lukan Authorship of Hebrews*. Nashville: B&H Publishing Group, 2010.

Allen, Roland. *Missionary Methods: St. Paul's or Ours?* London: World Dominion Press, 1956.

Austin-Sparks, T. *The On-High Calling*. Jacksonville, FL: Seedsowers Publishing, 2002.

Bruce, F.F. *Israel & the Nations: The History of Israel from the Exodus to the Fall of the Second Temple*. Downers Grove, IL: InterVarsity Press, 1997.

--*The Books and the Parchments* London: Pickering & Inglis, 1950.

Burge, Gary M. *Whose Land? Whose Promise? What Christians Are Not Being Told about Israel and the Palestinians*. Cleveland: The Pilgrim Press, 2003.

Comfort, Philip. *The Origin of the Bible*. Wheaton, IL: Tyndale House, 2003.

—*Early Manuscripts & Modern Translations of the New Testament*. Grand Rapids: Baker Books, 1996.

Edwards, Gene. *Christian Woman . . . Set Free*. Jacksonville, FL: Seedsowers Publishing, 2005.

—*The Gaius Diary.* Wheaton, IL: Tyndale House, 2002.

—*Revolutionary Bible Study.* Jacksonville, FL: Seedsowers Publishing, 2009.

Holwerda, David E. *Jesus & Israel One Covenant or Two?* Grand Rapids: W.B. Eerdmans, 2000.

Jewish Encyclopedia. New York: Funk and Wagnalls, 1906.

Josephus, Flavius. *The Complete Works of Josephus.* Grand Rapids: Kregel Publications, 1981.

Kaung, Stephen. *Seeing Christ in the New Testament, Volume 2, 4.* Richmond, VA: Christian Tape Ministry, 2004.

Martin, Ernest. *Restoring the Original Bible.* Portland, OR: Associates for Scriptural Knowledge, 1994.

—*Secrets of Golgotha.* Portland, OR: Associates for Scriptural Knowledge, 1996.

Miller, Ed. *Book of Hebrews, Book of Philippians,* Audio. Posted 2004. Bible Study Ministries, Inc. Tape ministry. www.biblestudiesministriesinc.org. Newport, Rhode Island. Posted 2004.

Murphy-O'Connor, Jerome. *St. Paul's Ephesus: Texts and Archaeology,* Collegeville, MN; Liturgical Press. 2008

Sachar, Abram Leon. *History of the Jews.* New York: Alfred A. Knopf, 1972.

Schatz, Cheryl. *Women in Ministry: Silenced or Set Free?* Nelson, BC: MM Outreach, 2006.

Stark, Rodney. *The Rise of Christianity.* New York: HarperSanFrancisco, 1997.

Urquhart, John. *The Bible, Its Structure and Purpose.* New York, NY: Gospel Publishing House, 1904.

Viola, Frank. *The Untold Story of the New Testament Church.* Shippenburg, PA: Destiny Image Publishers, 2004.

Zens, John. What's with Paul and Women? Omaha, NE: Ecclesia Press, 2010

PART III

Bass, Ralph E. Jr. *Back to the Future: A Study in the Book of Revelation.* Living Hope Press, 2004.

Chapman, Colin. *Whose Promised Land? The Continuing Crisis Over Israel and Palestine.* Grand Rapids, MI: Baker Books, 2003.

Chilton, David. *Days of Vengeance: An Exposition of the Book of Revelation.* Fort Worth, TX: Dominion Press, 1987.

DeMar, Gary. *Last Days Madness: Obsession of the Modern Church*. Powder Springs, GA: American Vision Press, 1999.

Gentry, Kenneth L. Jr. *Before Jerusalem Fell*. Powder Springs, GA: American Vision Press, 1998.

—*He Shall Have Dominion*. Tyler, Texas: Institute for Christian Economics, 1992.

—*The Book of Revelation Made Easy*. Powder Springs, GA.; American Vision Press, 2008

Gregg, Stephen. *Revelation: Four Views: A Parallel Commentary*. Nashville, TN: Thomas Nelson, 1997.

Gundry, Stanley N. and Marvin C. Pate. *Four Views on the Book of Revelation*. Grand Rapids, MI: Zondervan, 1998.

Josephus, Flavius. *The Complete Works of Josephus*. Grand Rapids, MI: Kregel Publications, 1981.

Leithard, Peter J. *The Promise of His Appearing*. Moscow, ID: Cannon Press, 2004.

Mathison, Keith A. *When Shall These Things Be?* Phillipsburg, NJ: P & R Publishing, 2004.

Sproul, R.C. The Last Days According to Jesus. Grand Rapids, MI: Baker Books, 1998.

APPENDIX A:

Amaral, Joe, *Understanding Jesus,* New York, NY: Faith Words, a division of Hachette Book Group, Inc., 2011.

Davidson, Mark, *Becoming the Beloved,* White Oaks, TX: Shulamite Ministries Publishing, 2010.

George, Bob, *Baptism and the Lord's Supper, a Visual Aid to Spiritual Truth,* [Audio Cassettes], Dallas, TX: People to People.

Witherington III, Ben, *Making a Meal of It,* Waco, TX; Baylor University Press, 2007.

SCRIPTURE INDEX

Galatians 2:20-21

CHAPTER 4
Galatians 2:20
Colossians 1:27
Matthew 23:27
James 1:2
Matthew 5:21-22
Matthew 5:28
Psalm 141:3

CHAPTER 5
John 19:26-27
Isaiah 9:6-7
Luke 1:42-44
Luke 1:46-48

CHAPTER 6
Hosea 1:10/Romans
　9:25-26
Romans 10: 9-11
Galatians 5:6
Galatians 6:15
Romans 3:10-12
Jeremiah 31:31
Genesis 48:16
Matthew 23:32
Matthew 23:35
Deuteronomy 18:15
1 Thessalonians 4:14-17
Matthew 23:37-38

CHAPTER 7
1 Corinthians 1:30
1 Corinthians 14:37
2 Corinthians 4:12
2 Corinthians 3:7
1 Corinthians 14:34-35
1 Corinthians 14:36-40

CHAPTER 8
Romans 11:17

Acts 25:12
Acts 23:11
Chapter 10
1 Peter 1:3-5
1 Peter 2:4-5
1 Peter 5:12-14

CHAPTER 11
Philippians 4:13

CHAPTER 12
Luke 22:31-34
Matthew 21:19
Luke 13:6-9
Matthew 21:41-43
Luke 2:10-11
Philippians 1:21
Philippians 3:10-13
John 221:25
Exodus 33:20

CHAPTER 13
Ephesians 1:3, 17, 18
Colossians 1: 9, 10
Philippians 2:10-11
Philippians 3:2-9
Philemon 1:4-14
Luke 22:25-26
Philippians 1:6

CHAPTER 14
Ephesians 2:11-16

CHAPTER 15
Hebrews 1:1
2 Thessalonians 3:18
Jeremiah 31:33-34
Matthew 4:19
Matthew 14:28-31
Matthew 16:18-19
2 Corinthians 1:20
Hebrews 5:11

Hebrews 8:1
Genesis 15: 9-18

CHAPTER 16
Matthew 24:14
Acts 2:9-11
Colossians 1: 5-6
1 Thessalonians 5:8
Genesis 17:7-8
Deuteronomy 28:63
Deuteronomy 30:19-20
Joshua 23:15-16
Leviticus 20:22
Psalm 2:8
Psalm 89:11

CHAPTER 17
1 Timothy 5:18
John 1:1, 4
Chapter 19
John 3:16
John 1:14
John 21: 15-18

CHAPTER 20
Ephesians 2:19-22
Ephesians 1:23
1 Timothy 3: 15
2 Timothy 2: 2-22
Philippians 4:13

CHAPTER 21
Jude 1:12
Jude 1:1
John 17:6
John 17:9-10
John 17:12
Jude 1:11
Luke 22:31-32
Jude 1:24-25

CHAPTER 23

2 Corinthians 3:2–3
Revelation 22:21

CHAPTER 24
Revelation 13:11–14
Matthew 24:23–26
Revelation 13:11
1 John 2: 15-16
Acts 8:10
Acts 8:23
Acts 8:21
Acts 9:15

CHAPTER 25
Revelation 14:1
Revelation 14:4
James 1:18
Revelation 14:8–10

CHAPTER 26
Isaiah 5:7
Revelation 14:14-16
Revelation 14:19–20

CHAPTER 27
Revelation 16:16

CHAPTER 28
John 8:4–5
John 8:7
Jeremiah 17:13
John 7:37– 38
John 8:10-11
Revelation 16:21
Acts 2:40

CHAPTER 29
Romans 8:38–39
Revelation 17:5
Genesis 11:2–4
Revelation 17:3–6
Revelation 18:24

Revelation 17:18
Revelation 11:8
Isaiah 1:21

CHAPTER 30
Revelation 17:15
Revelation 18:11
Revelation 18:9
Revelation 18:17–20
Revelation 18:2
Revelation 19:1–2

CHAPTER 31
1 Peter 5:12–13
Revelation 17:15

CHAPTER 32
Revelation 19:9
Luke 22:19

CHAPTER 34
Revelation 20:1–3
Revelation 19:11
Revelation 19:15

CHAPTER 35
John 6:39–40
John 5:28–29
Matthew 13:29–30
Revelation 20:6
2 Peter 3:10, 13

CHAPTER 36
Revelation 21:1–2
John 19:30
Revelation 21:6
Revelation 21:22-23
Revelation 22:1
Revelation 22:8
Epilogue
Acts 7:48
John 7:37

APPENDIX A
Hebrews 9:16–17
John 3:29
Matthew 3:17
John 2:3-4
Luke 22:14–20
2 Corinthians 11:2
Luke 22:20
Jeremiah 31:34
John 12:24
John 14:2–3
Luke 22:18
Revelation 19:7–9
1 Corinthians 10:16
Leviticus 17:14
John 10:10
Luke 22:19
Genesis 2:23–24
1 Corinthians 6:17
Genesis 14:18–20
Psalm 110: 4, Hebrews 7–17
John 8:58
Leviticus 24:5–7
Isaiah 28:16, Amplified Bible
Matthew 21:42, quoting from Psalm 118:22
Exodus 29:38–41
Numbers 15:1–13
Leviticus 10:9
Hebrews 8:5
John 1:14
Revelation 21:3
Mark 14:22–24
1 Corinthians 11:33
1 Corinthians 10:16–17
Acts 2:42

ENDNOTES

1. There is a strong possibility that Jesus and his disciples took the Last Supper together in the guest room of an Essene monastery located in Jerusalem.

   And he sent two of his disciples, and said to them, "Go into the city, and a man will meet you carrying a pitcher of water; follow him. Wherever he enters, say to the owner of the house, 'The Teacher says, "Where is my guest room in which I may eat the Passover with my disciples?"' And he himself will show you a large upper room furnished and ready; and prepare for us there." (Mark 14:13–15)

   In those days, the job of fetching and carrying water was something reserved for women, girls, and young boys, not for men. However, here we see Jesus instructing his disciples to look for a man carrying water, who would lead them to the place where they were to prepare the Passover meal. Most likely this was an Essene. The Essenes lived in communities, practiced celibacy, pursued virtuous living, and were known for their hospitality.

2. Estimates of the population of Jerusalem during the time of Christ vary. Paul Maier estimates it to be 50,000, while historian Will Durant pegs it at about 100,000, and Old Testament scholar Alfred Edersheim places the number closer to between 200,000 and 250,000. I have chosen to use 100,000, but the truth may lie somewhere between that and Edersheim's higher figure. We do get a clue from the book of Revelation, though, as to the population about a decade after May, AD 58, when I chose to place this narrative. There is strong evidence to suggest that the apostle John wrote the book of Revelation somewhere around AD 66 or 67, just prior to the fall of Jerusalem (see Part III, "The Marriage: The Final Revelation"). John begins Revelation by stating that the things he is describing "must shortly take place" (Revelation 1:1). Revelation 11:13, which describes the fall of Jerusalem, says, "And in that hour there was a great earthquake, and a tenth of the city fell; and seven thousand people were killed in the earthquake." Seven thousand is a tenth of seventy thousand, which was the population of Jerusalem at the time of the destruction.

   Why so dramatic a downsizing? We know that in the few years prior to the Roman invasion in AD 66, a mass exodus of people left the city. This was due not only to the anticipation of an inevitable conflict, but also to the fact that citizens of Jerusalem were aware of Jesus's solemn prophecy made nearly forty years earlier upon the Mount of Olives. In the Olivet Discourse, Jesus predicted the destruction of Jerusalem, saying that no stone of the temple would be left upon another. He also said that this would take place within a generation (a biblical generation is forty years). He made that prediction just prior to his crucifixion in AD 30, and in AD 70—forty years later—Jerusalem was completely destroyed. So, in AD 58 there may well have been 100,000 people or more living in Jerusalem, considering that the exodus in the following years caused the population to dwindle to seventy thousand by the time full-scale war with Rome had broken out.

3. "The causeway for the [Red] Heifer was built by the High Priests at their own charges." *Mishnah,* Shekalim 4:2.

"They made a causeway from the Temple Mount to the Mount of Olives, an arched way built over an arched way, with an arch directly above each pier [of the arch below], for fear of any grave in the depths below. By it the priest that was to burn the Heifer, and the Heifer, and all that aided him went forth to the Mount of Olives." *Mishnah,* Parah 4:2.

4. "And they brought it to Jesus, and they threw their garments on the colt and put Jesus on it. And as he was going, they were spreading their garments in the road. And as he was now approaching, near *the descent of the Mount of Olives,* the whole multitude of the disciples began to praise God joyfully with a loud voice for all the miracles which they had seen." Luke 19:35–37, emphasis mine.

5. (Footnote 1) The amount of riches David contributed to build the temple of God can be found in two passages in 1 Chronicles: "Now behold, with great pains I have prepared for the house of the LORD **100,000 talents** of gold and **1,000,000 talents** of silver, and bronze and iron beyond weight, for they are in great quantity; also timber and stone I have prepared, and you may add to them" (1 Chronicles 24:14). And 1 Chronicles 29:3–4 says, "Moreover, in my delight in the house of my God, the treasure I have of gold and silver, I give to the house o for my God, over and above all that I have already provided for the holy temple, namely **3,000 talents** of gold, of the gold of Ophir, and **7,000 talents** of refined silver . . ."

The weight of a talent (depending on the source one relies on) can range between 50 and 130 pounds. An average of 75 pounds was used in this calculation. The equivalent value in today's dollars for 100,000 talents of gold and 1,000,000 talents of silver (using the average price per troy ounce of gold in 2011, $1500 per ounce, and the average price of silver at $35 per ounce) would be more than $202 billion dollars ($164 billion in gold, and $38 billion in silver). In addition to the amount contributed from the spoils of war, there was the amount contributed from David's own personal treasury of 3,000 talents of gold (close to $5 billion dollars) and 700,000 talents of silver (nearly $27 billion), coming to almost $32 billion from David's own personal wealth. This brings the total amount of money that David contributed for the building of the temple (in today's dollars) to $234 billion dollars.

But there is still more! There was also the bronze and iron, beyond weight, and the timber and stones. And besides that, there was the contribution that David inspired the people to give:

"After giving all this, King David then said to the entire assembly, 'Who then is willing to consecrate himself this day to the Lord?'" (1 Chronicles 29:5). The people had seen David's heart. They had seen him give all. And what was their response?

Then the rulers of the fathers' households, and the princes of the tribes of Israel, and the commanders of thousands and of hundreds, with the overseers over the king's work, offered willingly; and for the service for the house of God they gave 5,000 talents and 10,000 darics of gold, and 10,000 talents of silver, and 18,000 talents of brass, and 100,000 talents of iron. Whoever possessed precious stones gave them to the treasury of the house of the Lord, in care of Jehiel the Gershonite. Then the people rejoiced because they had offered so willingly, for they made their offering to the Lord with a whole heart; and King David also rejoiced greatly. (1 Chronicles 29:6–9)

So the actual amount of money (in today's dollars) that it took to build the temple was significantly higher than $234 billion dollars. Regardless of the precise amount, even in King David's day, a vast fortune went in to building the house of God!

6. "And the Word became flesh and dwelt [tabernacled] among us, and we beheld his glory, the glory as of the only begotten of the Father, full of grace and truth." John 1:14

"Then I, John, saw the holy city, New Jerusalem, coming down out of heaven from God, prepared as a bride adorned for her husband. And I heard a loud voice from heaven saying, 'Behold, the tabernacle of God is with men, and he will dwell with them, and they shall be his people. God himself will be with them and be their God.'" Revelation 21:2–3

"Now this is the main point of the things we are saying: We have such a high priest, who has taken his seat at the right hand of the throne of the Majesty in the heavens, a minister in the sanctuary and in the true tabernacle, which the Lord pitched, not man. For every high priest is appointed to offer both gifts and sacrifices; so it is necessary that this high priest also have something to offer. Now if he were on earth, he would not be a priest at all, since there are those who offer the gifts according to the Law; who serve a copy and shadow of the heavenly things, just as Moses was warned by God when he was about to erect the tabernacle; for, 'See,' he says, 'that you make all things according to the pattern which was shown you on the mountain." Hebrews 8:1–5

7. Josephus describes the large curtain this way:

"But before these doors there was a veil of equal largeness with the doors. It was a Babylonian curtain, embroidered with blue and fine linen, and scarlet, and purple, and of a contexture that was truly wonderful. Nor was this mixture of colours without its mystical interpretation, but was a kind of image of the universe; for by the scarlet, there seemed to be enigmatically signified fire, by the fine flax the earth, by the blue the air, and by the purple the sea; two of them having their colours this foundation of this resemblance;

but the fine flax and the purple have their own origin for that foundation, the earth producing the one, and the sea the other. This curtain had also embroidered upon it all that was mystical in the heavens, excepting that of the [twelve] signs, representing living creatures." Josephus, (Wars V.V.4)

Luke 23:44–47, Matthew 27:50–51, and Mark 15:37–39 record that at Jesus's death darkness was over the land, there was a great earthquake, rocks split open, and the curtain of the Holy Place was torn in two from top to bottom. In Luke's version it says that the centurion, having seen these things occur, gave glory to God. "These things" included the tearing of the curtain. Therefore, the centurion saw the large, 82' x 24' curtain covering the entrance to the Holy Place (dimensions come from a reference in Josephus, War, V.210–214) torn in two. Apparently the earthquake caused the huge marble lintel from which the curtain hung to split, resulting in the curtain being torn in two from top to bottom. This could only be seen if the centurion was standing up on the Mount of Olives and looking back toward the temple, bolstering the case that Christ was crucified on the Mount of Olives, not at the site of the current tourist location in Jerusalem where the Church of the Holy Sepulcher stands.

This case has other points in its favor. For one thing, the Church of the Holy Sepulcher is located almost directly behind (to the west) of the entrance to the Holy Place, where the curtain hung. There is no possible way that the tearing of the curtain could have been seen from that location. In addition, that location would be inside what was considered to be the camp of Israel at the time of Jesus. The book of Hebrews clearly states that Jesus was crucified outside the camp (Hebrews 13:12–13). Finally, those who have ever been to the Church of the Holy Sepulcher, as I have, know that the spiritual darkness and religious depravity there is incredible. Not only is this supposed to be the location of Golgotha and the location of the tomb of Joseph of Arimathea, but it is also purported to be the very location of the tomb of Adam and the place at which his skull was found! Ernest Martin, in *Secrets of Golgotha,* does an excellent job using historical evidence to debunk these myths, although common sense and a small dose of intellectual honesty alone are sufficient to discredit these long-standing traditions.

8. Jerusalem, the temple, and the priesthood—all pictures:

Jerusalem: In Galatians chapter 4, Paul writes of the allegory of Abraham's two sons—one coming through the bondwoman (Hagar) and one through the free woman (Sarah). In verse 25 he says that Hagar corresponds to the present (earthly) Jerusalem and that she was in slavery with her children, "but the Jerusalem above is free; she is our mother" (v. 26). Our identity, as Christians, is with the Jerusalem above, not with the Jerusalem of this earth.

"And I saw the holy city, new Jerusalem, coming down out of heaven from God, made ready as a bride adorned for her husband." (Revelation 21:2)

The Temple: "Do you not know that you are a temple of God and that the Spirit of God dwells in you? If any man destroys the temple of God, God will destroy him, for the temple of God is holy, and that is what you are." (1 Corinthians 3:16–17)

"The Holy Spirit is signifying this, that the way into the Holy Place has not yet been disclosed while the first tabernacle is still standing, which is a symbol for the present time." (Hebrews 9:8–9)

"Now if he were on earth, he would not be a priest at all, since there are those who offer the gifts according to the Law; who serve a copy and shadow of heavenly things, just as Moses was warned by God when he was about to erect the tabernacle; for 'See,' he says, 'that you make all things according to the pattern which was shown you on the mountain.'" (Hebrews 8:4–5)

The Priesthood: "But you [believers in Christ] are a chosen race, a royal priesthood." (1 Peter 2:9)

"And he has made us a kingdom, priests to his God and Father." (Revelation 1:6)

The book of Hebrews was written sometime in the decade prior to AD 70—before the destruction of Jerusalem, the temple, the priesthood, and the whole Jewish sacrificial system. At the time of the letter, there was a great wave of Jewish patriotism against Rome, both in Palestine and throughout the empire. Zealots were calling for revolt. Any Jew not participating in the festivals and temple or synagogue worship was viewed as a traitor and came under great pressure to return to Judaism to show political solidarity.

But the letter to the Hebrews was a clear call to leave Judaism—to give up the pictures. In his great love for the Hebrew Christians, God inspired this message to be written to them because he knew what was about to take place and did not want them clinging to a system that would soon be destroyed.

Their problem was that they were looking at the things they could see—the breathtaking temple and the beautiful pomp, costumes, and ceremonies of the priests that dated back 1,500 years. The traditions of beautiful buildings and religious ceremonies are hard to give up in any age—even our own—because they have their allure. But we have been called to fix our eyes on the things that are not seen. We are to look to a living Christ and to leave the pictures behind.

9. According to Exodus 19:1, the Israelites arrived in the wilderness of Sinai in the third month after leaving Egypt. Numbers 10:11 says that on the twentieth day of the second month in the second year, they departed Sinai. Assuming they arrived in Sinai on the first day of the third month, they were probably camped in the Sinai wilderness around eleven months and nineteen days.

10. Did Nicodemus also oppose the conviction of Christ by the Sanhedrin?

Paul Maier, in his book *In the Fullness of Time,* speculates that the vote of the

Sanhedrin was probably 69 to 2, with Joseph of Arimathea and Nicodemus abstaining (page 144). There is nothing in the biblical record that states that Nicodemus registered his formal protest at the vote, but it does say that he brought spices after Jesus was crucified and assisted Joseph in preparing his body for burial. So he definitely was a follower of Christ, although at that particular point, he may have been more of a secret one.

11. "The Talmud testifies: Forty years before the destruction of the Temple [that would have been in AD 30], the Sanhedrin was banished [from the Chamber of Hewn Stone] and sat in the trading-station [on the Temple Mount]." (Shab. 15a). *Everyman's Talmud, The Major Teachings of the Rabbinic Sages*, Abraham Cohen.

   Forty years before the destruction of the temple would have put the year of the Sanhedrin's moving to the Trading Center as the same year in which Christ was crucified. A rational explanation for the esteemed council's moving from that beautiful chamber to something less suitable would most likely be that the Chamber of Hewn Stone was severely damaged in the earthquake that was also responsible for the large curtain over the Holy Place tearing in two and the lintel above it splitting.

12. In his book *Pontius Pilate,* Paul Maier arrived at this conclusion about Pilate's death:

   "(Many) would invent the most terrifying, and certainly imaginative, punishments for him: torture, exile, insanity, compulsive hand-washing, suicide, drowning, decapitation, being swallowed by the earth, and even that ancient punishment for parricide—being sewn up in an ox-skin with a cock, a viper, and a monkey, and pitched into a river. Medieval legends would add the familiar stories of his restless corpse, accompanied by squads of demons, disrupting localities from Vienne in France to Mt. Pilatus in Switzerland, causing storms, earthquake, and other havoc.

   "On the basis of the earliest sources, however, it is clear that nothing of the sort ever happened to Pilate, let alone his corpse" (page 349).

   He goes on to say that the Greek Orthodox Church, which recognizes October 27 as Saint Procula's Day, has canonized Procula. In his notes he also states, "According to a very early tradition, Pilate's wife became a Christian. See Origen, *Commentarii in Matthaeum,* 121–22 (ed. Migne, XIII, 918). According to Dee Wampler, *The Trial of Christ,* Procula was the granddaughter of Augustus Caesar.

13. Beth Chaduda was the place in the wilderness where the scapegoat was led to die. See Ernest Martin's article, "The Lake of Fire: Where is it located?" Feb. 1, 1981, on the ASK website: www.askelm.com.

14. There is no dispute that the Bible teaches Christ's death came by way of crucifixion. However, an interesting statement coming from the crowd as Christ stood before Pilate,

along with some other evidence, gives rise to the speculation that Christ may have suffered even more agony than the crucifixion inflicted.

"The Jews answered [Pilate], 'We have a law, and by that law he ought to die because he made himself out to be the Son of God.'" (John 19:7)

The questions to be addressed here are: What was the crime Jesus was accused of? And what was the Jewish punishment for such a crime?

The Sanhedrin accused Jesus of blasphemy—a crime meriting capital punishment. Leviticus 24:16 is very clear in stating the manner in which death should be inflicted: "Moreover, the one who blasphemes the name of the Lord shall surely be put to death; all the congregation shall certainly stone him."

Though the Bible never mentions that Jesus was also stoned while hanging on the cross, that does not negate the possibility that it happened.

In his book *Pontius Pilate,* Paul Maier writes, "The Great Sanhedrin published the following notice for arrest and punishment. A court crier had to announce publicly or post such an official handbill in the major towns of Judea some forty days prior to a trial.

"WANTED FOR ARREST

"Yeshu Hannosri or Jesus the Nazarene

"He shall be stoned because he has practiced sorcery and enticed Israel to apostasy. Anyone who can say anything in his favor let him come forward and plead on his behalf. Anyone who knows where he is, let him declare it to the Great Sanhedrin in Jerusalem" (page 191).

On several occasions when Jesus claimed or inferred that he was God's Son and one with deity, the Jews sought to stone him for blasphemy. This happened in his hometown of Nazareth, but he escaped. It happened again at the temple when he was teaching (John 8:59), and another time at the Feast of the Dedication that took place at Jerusalem (John 10:31–33):

"The Jews picked up stones again to stone him. Jesus answered them, 'I showed you many good works from the Father; for which of them are you stoning me?' The Jews answered him, 'For a good work we do not stone you, but for blasphemy; and because you, being a man, make yourself out to be God.'"

Isaiah's prophecy, seven hundred years before the crucifixion, said of the Suffering Servant that "his appearance was marred more than any man and his form more than the sons of men," and that he was "like one from whom men turned their face" (Isaiah 52:14 and 53:3).

We are not told whether a stoning happened or not. But given the rage and loss of control of the frenzied mob and the Jewish leaders, it is easy to imagine that some among the crowd vented their indignation by picking up those sharp-edged flint rocks that to this day lie on the ground on the Mount of Olives and pelted Jesus with them, compounding his agony.

To have his appearance "marred more than any man" would not have been the result of the nails driven into his wrists and feet. Nor was it because of the lashes he received. Though his flesh was severely bloodied and torn as a result of those lashes, they were inflicted only on the front and back of his torso and legs. Most likely, it was not because of the crown of thorns pressed into his head by the mocking Roman guards. And, conceivably, it did not come from the slapping and beating he received. To be rendered unrecognizable could very well have been the result of rocks hitting him in the face. This could also have been a contributing factor as to why he died prior to the other two criminals crucified with him (who were not stoned because they were not accused as blasphemers).

What has been mentioned here is only speculation, and not conclusive. I think it would be a mistake to insist that this, indeed, did happen. But if it did, it can only magnify our deep sense of awe at Christ's worthiness for what he was willing to suffer to pay the price to redeem you and me.

For a further development of this topic, see the chapter in Ernest Martin's book *The Secrets of Golgotha*, "The Surprising Cause of Jesus' Death."

15. "In the basement/courtyard of the Sisters of Zion Convent, as well as in surrounding chapels, pieces of the game board of 'King's Game' have been preserved. Jesus was probably the victim of this cruel game, which was popular among soldiers stationed in Palestine in the first century. In this game a condemned prisoner would be used as the game piece, being moved around a game board etched into the stone pavement. A roll of the dice determined the movements.

"The 'King's Game' apparently helped to boost the morale of soldiers posted in Judea, which was considered the worst assignment in the Roman army. By throwing dice, the soldiers would choose a burlesque 'king'; following additional throws of the dice, the 'king' would be mocked and abused verbally and physically.

"The resemblance between this game and the mockery of Jesus by the soldiers reported in the Gospel (Matthew 27:27–31; Mark 15:16–20) is striking." (Charles R. Page II, *Jesus and the Land,* pages 149–151)

16. *The Camp:* Joshua 3:4: "However, there shall be between you and [the ark of the covenant] a distance of about 2,000 cubits by measure."

"But Rabban Gamaliel the Elder ordained that they might walk within two thousand cubits in any direction. And not these, only, but a midwife that comes to help a delivery, or any that comes to rescue from a burning house or ravaging troops, or from a river-flood or a fallen house; they, too, are deemed to be people of the city and may move within two thousand cubits in any direction." (*Mishnah*, Danby. Rosh ha-Shanah 2:5)

17. "You shall also take the bull for the sin offering; and it shall be burned in the appointed

place [numbering place, or in Hebrew, *miphkad*] of the house, outside the sanctuary." (Ezekiel 43:21)

"For the bodies of those animals whose blood is brought into the Holy Place by the high priest as an offering for sin, are burned outside the camp. Therefore Jesus also, that he might sanctify the people through his own blood, suffered outside the gate. Hence, let us go out to him outside the camp, bearing his reproach." (Hebrews 13:11–13)

18. For a description of the red heifer sacrifice, see Numbers 19, verses 1–10.

19. "All the walls there were high, save only the eastern wall, because the [High] Priest that burns the [Red] Heifer and stands on the top of the Mount of Olives should be able to look directly into the entrance of the Sanctuary when the blood is sprinkled." *Mishnah,* Danby. Middoth 2:4

20. "There can actually be no doubt that the 'clean place' for burning the sin offerings on the Day of Atonement as well as performing the Red Heifer sacrifice was located directly east of the Temple. It was a permanent site called the Beth ha-Deshen (the House of the Ashes) where also the 'ashes are poured out' from the animals consumed on the Altar of Burnt Offering in the Temple (Leviticus 4:12)." Ernest Martin, *Secrets of Golgotha,* page 24.

21. Bethphage was the second official meeting place of the Sanhedrin. See Ernest Martin's *Secrets of Golgotha,* chapter 12, "The Sanhedrin and the Mount of Olives."

"There were three courts in Jerusalem, (one in the Chamber of Hewn Stone), one on the Temple mount [at Bethphage], and one in the Chel." (*Everyman's Talmud, The Major Teachings of the Rabbinic Sages,* Abraham Cohen, page 299).

Also see Sanhedrin 14a, b; Sotah 44b; 45a, 47a, *Babylonian Talmud.*

22. Friday, April 5, AD 30.

23. Most people's image of the cross on which Christ was crucified is shaped just like the kind many people wear as jewelry around their necks. Furthermore, when they think of the scene at Golgotha, they picture three separate wooden crosses, with Christ occupying the middle one and the two criminals impaled on their own crosses equidistant from where our Lord hung. Most art, pictures in books, and hillside reminders of three empty crosses reinforce this notion. But the Bible clearly teaches something different. The Bible teaches that Christ was crucified on a tree.

"Now in the place where he was crucified there was a garden" (John 19:41). "Garden" here has the connotation of an orchard, or a place of trees.

"The God of our fathers raised up Jesus, whom you had put to death by hanging him on a tree." Acts 5:30

"We are witnesses of all things which he did both in the land of the Jews and in Jerusalem. They also put him to death by hanging him on a tree." Acts 10:39

"And he himself bore our sins in his body on the tree, so that we might die to sin and live to righteousness, for by his wounds you were healed." 1 Peter 2:24

"When they had carried out all that was written concerning him, they took him down from the tree and laid him in a tomb." Acts 13:29

"Christ redeemed us from the curse of the Law, having become a curse for us—for it is written, 'Cursed is everyone who hangs on a tree.'" Galatians 3:13

In many translations this word for "tree"—the Greek *stauros*—is rendered "cross."

Ernest Martin, in *Secrets of Golgotha* (pages 295–296), points out that in the first century, stauros had "at least three different meanings in the New Testament alone (which the KJV simply translates 'cross'). Note that the board plank that supported the arms of Jesus (called the patibulum in Latin) was called a stauros (Luke 23:26). But it had a further meaning. The actual pole or the tree trunk on which the patibulum was nailed was also called a stauros (John 19:19). And the complex together (both patibulum and the bough of the tree were reckoned as a single executionary device) was called a stauros (John 19:25)."

He then cites the Scripture from John 19:31–33:

"'The Jews therefore, because it was the preparation, that the bodies [note the plural, BODIES] should not remain on the STAUROS [singular] on the Sabbath day (for that day was an high day), besought Pilate that their legs might be broken, and that they might be taken away. Then came the soldiers, and brake the legs of the first, and of the other crucified with him. But when they came to Jesus, and saw that he was dead already, they brake not his legs.'

"These verses tell us very much. They show us that there were three men crucified ON ONE STAUROS."

24. What did Christ take with him to the cross?
- Our sins: Hebrews 9:28
- Our sin nature, our old man (old self): Romans 6:6–7
- The flesh: Galatians 5:24
- The law: Ephesians 2:13–16
- The world: Galatians 6:14
- Decrees/accusations against us: Colossians 2:14
- Rulers, principalities, and authorities: Colossians 2:15
- Satan: Hebrews 2:14
- You and me: Galatians 2:20
- Death: 1 Corinthians 15:26, 54–57

25. What did Christ take with him from the grave?
   - You and me: Colossians 3:1–4, Ephesians 2:4–7

26. "But now Christ has been raised from the dead, the first fruits of those who are asleep." (1 Corinthians 15:20)

   "But each in his own order: Christ the first fruits, after that those who are Christ's at his coming." (1 Corinthians 15:23)

27. Sunday, April 7, AD 30.

28. *They Ate and Drank with God:* "Then Moses went up with Aaron, Nadab and Abihu, and seventy of the elders of Israel, and they saw the God of Israel, and under his feet there appeared to be a pavement of sapphire, as clear as the sky itself. Yet he did not stretch out his hand against the nobles of the sons of Israel; and they saw God, and they ate and drank." (Exodus 24:9–12)

29. May 30, AD 30.

30. F.F. Bruce, *The Books and the Parchments* (London: Pickering & Inglis, 1950), 111

31. John Urquhart, *The Bible, Its Structure and Purpose* (New York: Gospel Publishing House, 1904), 37.

32. Josephus, *Wars,* Book 3, 10:9

33. Josephus, *Wars,* Book 4, 4:6

34. Josephus, *Wars,* Book 6: 8:5

35. Josephus, *Wars,* Book 6: 4:6,7

36. Josephus, *Wars,* Book 5: 4,6

37. Josephus, *Wars,* Book 6, 1:1

38. Josephus, *Wars,* Book 4, 9:10

39. Josephus, *Wars,* Book 20: 8: 5-6

40. Josephus, *Wars,* Book 5, 6:3

41. Josephus, *Wars,* Book 5, 6:3

HIS DESIRE IS FOR ME
A 30-Day Devotional and Commentary on the Song of Songs

Blending fiction, commentary, and 30-days of devotions, *His Desire Is for Me* provides daily, bite-sized portions of the Song of Songs for you to savor, meditate upon, and enjoy. It reveals the different stages believe go through on the road to spiritual maturity in their love for the Lord, from an initial love, to an increasing love, and finally unfolding into a mature love. Read it, and you will come to believe, with conviction, that His desire is truly for you!

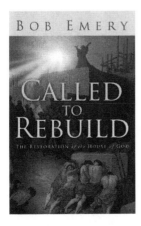

CALLED TO REBUILD
The Restoration of the House of God

A commentary on Ezra and Nehemiah, along with the other "remnant books" of the Old Testament – Haggai, Zechariah, and Malachi. *Called to Rebuild* examines these precious books and draws application for those who would be the spiritual descendants of that remnant in this generation. This book is for those who have a heart to rebuild and see the church become all that God intended for it to be.